P9-AOV-644

145-180

HUMAN RELATIONS IN INDUSTRY

HUMAN

RELATIONS

IN INDUSTRY

BURLEIGH B. GARDNER, Ph.D.
Executive Director of Social Research,
Inc.

DAVID G. MOORE, Ph.D.
Assistant Professor of Sociology and
Business Administration, Industrial Re-
lations Center, University of Chicago

THIRD EDITION   1955

RICHARD D. IRWIN, INC.
HOMEWOOD, ILLINOIS

PREFACE

TEN years have passed since the original publication of *Human Relations in Industry*. At that time, the application of the social sciences to the problems of management, organization, and industrial relations was new and undeveloped. To be sure, considerable research had been conducted by Harvard University's Graduate School of Business Administration and by the University of Chicago's Committee on Human Relations in Industry. Moreover, a few major industries, like Western Electric and Sears, Roebuck and Co., had shown a great deal of interest in utilizing some of the research findings and concepts of the social sciences. Beyond this, however, knowledge of what could be understood and accomplished in industrial organizations through the systematic analysis of human relations was relatively slight.

During the past decade, however, there has been a growing interest in the human processes and problems of organization. Many industries and unions have made extensive use of the social sciences in building more effective organizations and developing more satisfying relations among employees. Human relations ideas have gained a certain currency, and it is no longer unusual to hear executives discussing problems of organization and administration in human relations terms. A number of companies and unions have "opened their doors" to social science research, very much as Sears did during the forties and Western Electric in the preceding decades. The opening of these doors has not been easy, since most ongoing organizations like to keep their human affairs private, very much as a family likes to keep its personal problems to itself. This research has been made possible by the growing understanding by business and union leadership of the significance of the human aspects of organization and by the increasing skills of researchers in the field in establishing effective relationships.

Academic interest in extending social science research in the industrial field has also grown over the past decade. This interest is evidenced by the increasing body of literature and research reports in the field and by the establishment of human relations research centers throughout the country. Among these centers are the Industrial Relations Center at the University of Chicago, the Yale Labor-Management Center, the New York State School of Industrial Relations at

Cornell, the Institute of Labor and Industrial Relations at the University of Illinois, and the Survey Research Center at Michigan. In addition, a great deal of research has been conducted by sociologists and others in a number of universities.

During the same period, we have also witnessed great changes in the industrial scene. The period of mass unionization of employees in industry has ended. At the same time, the preoccupation with labor-management relations so common between 1935 and 1945 has diminished. Instead, we have seen an increasing interest in organization and patterns of effective administration. Of great concern in industry has been the problem of size and decentralization and delegation of authority to avoid the bureaucracy, inertia, and inefficiencies typical of large organizations. There has been a considerable interest, too, in the question of executive manpower. Many companies have faced the problem of management succession, discovering too late that second-level executives were trained only for second-level responsibilities and were not competent to cope with the problems of top management. Developing effective middle-management and first-level supervision capable of dealing with the complex problems of employee co-ordination and motivation in getting the work out has been a perennial problem in industry. As a consequence, there has been a veritable deluge of programs during the past ten years for assessing executive needs, evaluating performance, and developing managerial effectiveness at all levels.

There has been a widespread concern, also, with communications. Management has become keenly aware of the troubles arising out of a lack of common understanding and point of view between management and workers or between levels of management and supervision. Here, again, we have seen a welter of programs, some adapted from advertising and public relations, some utilizing the sophisticated insights of group dynamics, semantics, and social psychology, and some representing simply "man-to-man," "straight-talk," which somehow never seems so "straight" when it reaches the work level.

We have no doubt that there will be other concentrations of interests in industry during the coming decade. Yet, these changes in interests only emphasize the continued significance and value of an understanding of the basic principles of human relations in industry. While conditions and emphases change, the basic elements of human relations remain. People at all levels still go on acting and reacting in the same old ways. For this reason, the current revision includes much of what has been said in previous editions. However, an effort has been made to focus greater attention on the dynamics of business and the underlying forces which shape management's strategies, policies, and decisions with reference to the organization structure and patterns of administration. An industrial or business organization is a human phenomenon, too, reflecting the needs, interests, and patterns of behavior of people. We have also attempted to present certain basic concepts derived from the general social sciences regarding human behavior in order to make explicit to the student in the industrial field the conceptual framework used in the analysis of human relations in industry. Our aim has been to present these concepts in a heuristic rather than systematic way. Other changes include the reorganization of material in a more orderly fashion. In addition, a more complete bibliography has been included, as an aid to the student in developing further reading in the field.

BURLEIGH B. GARDNER
DAVID G. MOORE

December, 1954

TABLE OF CONTENTS

1. THE DYNAMICS OF BUSINESS

THERE is a tendency to regard business organization as having two sides to its character, the "business" side and the "human" side. The so-called "human" side, interestingly enough, is generally reserved for employees. Moreover, the term "human relations" is often regarded as synonymous with "employee relations." As a result, we find business management continuously being admonished not to forget the "human side" of business in pursuing its economic and administrative interests.

While this kind of preaching has had salutary effects on management and most certainly has helped to "right the wrongs" of a business world which often seems carried away by its rampant, consuming drive for efficiency and profits, it misses the important fact that what management does is very human too. Management's concern with the problems of business and the patterns of behavior which it develops in the pursuit of its economic interests are just as human as the reactions exhibited by employees within the organization. We cannot, therefore, say that there is a clear-cut distinction between the human behavior which develops among employees and the human behavior which develops at the management level. There is nothing fundamentally different in the way people behave whether they are "top dogs" or "under dogs," managers or employees, stockholders or customers. Their emotions, problems of adjustment, needs and interests, and patterns of behavior are all human in origin and subject to the same scientific scrutiny and analysis.

In this chapter we shall direct our attention to the dynamics of management and organization and seek to understand the principal factors influencing the decisions of management and the processes of organization. We shall analyze the basic business drives which develop at the management level and shall show how these become compelling forces which limit perspectives and divert attention from employee relations. We shall review the common patterns of administration and organization which emerge out of management's business interests. We shall, in short, describe the underlying factors which shape the industrial environment and ultimately influence the human relations which develop within it.

1

BUSINESS OBJECTIVES AND STRATEGIES

If we examine the objectives of any business, they appear at first blush to be simple and uncomplicated. Sears, Roebuck and Company, for example, sells goods direct to the consuming public; United Air Lines provides air transportation; Corn Products Refining Company grinds corn; and each company performs these functions at a profit. The picture appears complete enough; yet it lacks something! It is too dead, too static! There is no explanation of the dynamic aspects of business enterprise, of the drive, motivation, and compulsion which characterize men in business.

Our description assumes that each company more or less passively occupies a particular technological or economic position in our society. It in no way describes the manner in which this position has been secured by the business enterprise in question, nor does it even suggest the struggle and effort which goes into the maintenance and development of this position once secured. The fact remains that a business enterprise is not just an organization fulfilling certain technological or economic functions. It is a far more active force than this. Indeed, it is largely a dynamic expression and embodiment of the efforts of a group of men to secure, consolidate, and extend a profitable position in the business community.

We all know, at least abstractly, that any business, to survive and prosper, must maintain a set of relations with various elements in the socioeconomic environment. These elements are, for the most part, described in terms of certain socioeconomic roles, such as investors, customers, vendors, management, labor, etc. Each of these groups supply one or another of the essential "ingredients" of business enterprise. Investors supply money; vendors supply materials, machines, tools, and products; customers supply buying power; labor supplies skill and work effort; etc. Each will provide the necessary "ingredients" which are in his power to give if he is "induced" to do so.

The major questions in every businessman's mind are: "How can the other party be 'induced' to part with his money, materials, machines, tools, goods, labor, ideas, or services?" and "How can a 'gain' be secured in these transactions?" Finding answers to these questions is intriguing but difficult because the socioeconomic environment with which the businessman must deal is complex, frequently unpredictable, and constantly changing. It is apparent that the businessman cannot have complete information about the world around him. Therefore, his answers often are simply good guesses, based at best on an analysis of probabilities and at worst on pure hunches. The test of his guesswork lies in what happens in the future.

In spite of the difficulties, the socioeconomic environment can be manipulated and controlled in various ways. However, you have to find the right formula or strategy[1] and play it to the limit. Indeed, it is frequently in the determination, single-mindedness, and purposefulness of the player that we find the difference between success or failure in business. A businessman can, if he is imaginative and aggressive, envision and act on a business situation not yet perceived by others. He can, if he is persuasive, change the perception of others regarding a particular business situation. Within certain legal and ethical limits, he can utilize every political, psychological, social, technological, and economic device in the books to achieve an advantageous position.

Our description is by no means complete. However, we can begin to sense the dynamic aspects of business enterprise. It is essentially a game of strategy in which the participants seek the right formula for dealing with the various elements of the socioeconomic environment. It is a purposeful, goal-directed game where every move should fit into the over-all strategic objectives of the business. It is an undertaking where the stakes are high, where control is possible, and yet where there is sufficient unpredictability to provide an element of chance. This is the kind of situation, it will be recognized, that excites people, motivates them, puts them on the edge of their chairs. It absorbs interest and attention, concentrates energies, and creates an almost consuming interest. As one businessman said, "Never get involved with the stock market. It's like a drug addiction." While most businessmen are not as keyed up as our description would indicate, nevertheless, something like this underlies the compelling drives and interests of business management. Under these circumstances, it is understandable why problems of human relations in industry sometimes appear outside the world of reality to management.

DEVELOPMENT OF BUSINESS ORGANIZATION

Thus far, we have been discussing business activity in its purely commercial and entrepreneurial sense without reference to business

---

[1] John Von Neumann and Oskar Morgenstern, *Theory of Games and Economic Behavior* (Princeton: Princeton University Press, 1944).

organization. Our purpose has been to understand the mainsprings to action in the business world because they have a direct and powerful influence on the needs and interests of management, the decisions it makes, and the kind of organization it develops.

Few businesses begin with a full-blown organization. An organization, after all, is an expensive apparatus. Unless a business activity exists to support it, even a small organization, with its machinery costs, material and power costs, and especially payroll costs, is impossible. Most business organizations tend to evolve and develop through more or less well-defined stages. The first stage is the creation of the business activity itself. Businesses come into existence in a variety of ways. However, the process is largely the same. Someone or some small group of individuals possesses, develops, or stumbles on potential assets or resources which, when combined with certain other assets, provide the conditions favorable to the development of a business. A potential asset can be almost anything—money, real estate, talent, skill, class position, personality, and invention, or what have you. The act of combining is the crucial element of a creative strategy; a single asset is valuable only in combination.

The strategy in this initial stage, then, is twofold: envisioning an advantageous situation and doing something about it. An advantageous combination might be something as mundane and unoriginal as putting Aunt Mabel's bequest and Junior's interest in tinkering with other people's automobiles together with an empty lot on a busy corner and opening a gas station. Or it may be as imaginative and unique as combining, in the manner of Henry Ford, mechanical ingenuity, a buggy, a gasoline engine, and new ideas of mass production to create an automobile industry.

The creative strategy of a business is frequently undeveloped and unbalanced in its initial form. It tends to emphasize the special interests, talents, possessions, behavior, and general orientation of the founding father. If the business is to survive in a competitive and changing world, the original strategy and business activity developing therefrom must be consolidated.

Most businesses tend to go through a rather rapid evolution in which all of the necessary economic relationships which the business must maintain are secured and developed. Thus, the new business which starts off, let us say, with a new product quickly develops a sales strategy, a system for financing its needs, a way of securing necessary materials and equipment in the right quantities and at the right time, and a method of handling all of the other relationships typical of a modern business. If the first stage of a business requires a promoter, the next stage requires a businessman or consolidator. This is the stage when the business develops "sound business practices."

As the business grows and problems of getting the work done increase, a new stage is reached—that of organization. The excess work and new functions created by the consolidation of the business must be accomplished through people and/or machines. At first the organization may develop in a haphazard fashion; an employee or machine is introduced here and there to handle a specific activity or function. However, at some point in the growth of the business, a strategy of organization emerges. Thus, the organization itself becomes a strategic device for insuring an advantageous position in the socioeconomic environment. This is the stage of the manager or administrator.

A mature, established business organization develops, over a period of years, a set of strategies for dealing with all of the important elements of the socioeconomic environment. Certain strategies have to do with the way the organization fits into the chain of economic and technological events which mold and process the materials of the earth and distribute the product of these efforts to the customer. A business or industrial organization must maintain and develop its relations with those socioeconomic groups which precede it in the economic chain —that is, its sources of money, machines, tools, and materials—and those which follow it—that is, its customers. These strategies have to do with the economic metabolism of the organization, its intake and output. They also define the particular technological or commercial activity of the organization—what it does for a living, so-to-speak. For want of a better designation, we can refer to these strategies as the *external economic strategies* of the organization.

Other strategies concern the relations which the organization maintains with the broader community, including the general public, government bodies, organized charities, schools, etc. Here we view the organization as a social entity having certain rights and privileges, duties, and obligations. These strategies we call *external social strategies*.

Finally, there are strategies which have to do with the way in which the organization does its job; the way in which employees are motivated, co-ordinated, and controlled; the technology and use of machines and tools; the division of labor; hierarchy of authority; etc.

These are the strategies of management with which we are primarily concerned in this book. We call them the *internal organizational strategies.*

The strategies which develop in a company for dealing with its external and internal relations are many and varied but reasonably consistent. Indeed, it is surprising to observe the manner in which new strategies are built on the old. In a way, a business tends to develop like an individual, that is, developing new patterns of adjustment which are consistent with its past experiences and previous modes of behavior. Most companies appear to develop a kind of business "character" or "personality" which differentiates them from other companies.

For example, one of the national airlines operates on the basic belief that success in this business depends upon maintaining quality service which attracts first-class customers. The management of this company believes that cheap air transportation means a sloppy and unsafe service which ultimately will weigh against the competitive advantage of air speed. This basic view of management influences many other aspects of the business.

First, the major emphasis of the company is on passenger service. Stewardesses are very well trained. The food, of which the company is very proud, is excellent and prepared by Swiss chefs. Second, the company is never first, but always a close second, in introducing new equipment. It prefers to let its competitors try out new equipment and iron out the "bugs" which might exist. Third, it regards "coach" or "air tourist" service as unsafe, particularly when passengers are crammed into planes with narrow aisles and poor opportunities for escape if the planes should catch fire. Moreover, it feels that coach service does not attract new passengers but merely takes customers away from the first-class flights. Fourth, it regards too much competition as ruinous and tending to down-grade the kind of passenger service which should be provided. Fifth, it sees the primary use of air transportation in long flights. Sixth, it has developed an organization which emphasizes specialization of functions. In this respect, it sacrifices co-ordination in order to achieve perfection in the specific functions performed. Seventh, it has one of the finest maintenance bases in the airlines industry. In these and other ways, this company has made a consistent effort to develop a "quality" service, aimed at attracting first-class customers.

Another example of consistent character development is a large merchandising organization which acts on the principle that people, if given the "right" opportunity, will respond in the "right" way without coercion or manipulation. This fundamental idea emerges in a variety of ways in this company. In dealing with its customers, it follows a "low pressure" merchandising pattern. It believes that customers will buy if given an opportunity to purchase good quality merchandise at the lowest possible cost. It attempts to educate its customers through careful labeling of the merchandise. It has developed techniques of buying and selling which have materially reduced the cost of distribution. It has a definite policy of customer satisfaction. There is little or no hedging on this policy because of the belief that most customers are fundamentally honest.

Internally, this company is operated on a highly decentralized plan with delegation of authority to the lowest possible levels. Employees are given maximum freedom on the job. Supervision is exercised with a minimum of overt authority. There is an active policy of promotion from within. The company has a long-standing profit-sharing plan through which it distributes a large share of the profits to employees. At present, approximately one-third of the company is owned by its employees.

It is apparent from the examples given that the strategies of management imply certain assumptions about the probable behavior of customers, employees, stockholders, and other groups participating in the enterprise. In the case of the airline, it is assumed that it is primarily the "higher class" customer who travels by air. The "higher class" customer likes good food, service, and attention. He must be weaned away from first-class rail travel by guarantees of safety and assurances of speed as well as comfort. In the case of the merchandising organization, it is assumed, as we already indicated, that people, if given the "right" opportunity, will respond in the "right" way without coercion or manipulation. The assumptions about human behavior underlying the strategies of the management of any company reflect a variety of influences. Often they are shaped at least in part by the needs, interests, personalities, and ideologies of top management. In the examples given, there is some evidence of a "class" versus "mass" ideology reflected in the thinking of the two management groups. It is possible to point to a number of companies where the personality and emotional needs of a dominant management figure have molded the strategies of the entire organization.

The strategies of a company are also determined, in many cases, by imitation of the successful actions of others. Large, successful companies serve as models for smaller enterprises. If Sears, Roebuck and Company has a policy of decentralization, then other companies adopt this administrative pattern simply because it appears to have been successfully utilized in Sears. Management groups like to keep in "style" and follow the fad of the moment as much as any other human group. Indeed, the itinerant management consultant often acts as a communiction link from one company to the next, carrying the news about the latest trends in administrative styles.

It is apparent, without pursuing the subject further, that the strategies of an organization are influenced and shaped in the same way as any other human behavior. The influences operating range from purely emotional factors, through social factors, to rational, scientific efforts to analyze and understand human behavior. More and more, business management is attempting to develop its key strategies on the basis of a thorough understanding of the social and economic world in which the business exists. There is a growing recognition of the importance of a broad knowledge of human nature and human behavior in various settings and relationships. It is no longer possible to operate a well-established, successful company which is fulfilling all of its social and economic responsibilities with limited and ill-conceived notions about society and the human beings within it. Chester Barnard, formerly president of New Jersey Bell Telephone Company, has said:

A need of the executive of the future is for broad interests and wide imagination and understanding. Whether or not narrowness of interest has limited present-day executives in their contribution to the general society which impinges on all their immediate activities and has also thereby restricted the performance of their direct duties is a matter of opinion. At any rate, nothing can be done about them now. However, there is a narrow-mindedness associated with the concentration heretofore deemed indispensable. In the future it would seriously limit the capacity of men to serve effectively both in the major and in the intermediate executive positions of large and small organizations. The emphasis I am placing here is upon the so-called humanities and also upon science as a part of general education. It is an emphasis that applies not merely to instruction in the schools but also to pursuits after graduation. I hope it needs no argument that persons occupying positions of leadership in the community need an understanding of what goes on in the world and of the nature of the interests served by and underlying its activities.[2]

---

[2] Chester I. Barnard, *Organization and Management* (Cambridge, Mass.: Harvard University Press, 1948), p. 195.

COMMON PATTERNS OF ORGANIZATION AND ADMINISTRATION IN BUSINESS

We have indicated previously that we shall be concerned in this book with the internal organizational strategies of management. We are primarily interested in the ways in which employees adjust and react to the patterns of organization and administration which management develops in order to perform the necessary functions of the business enterprise. The behavior of employees and their problems of adjustment represent only part of the important elements of business enterprise. We could, for example, be concerned with the human aspects of company-customer relations or company-stockholder relations or company-community relations.

From a strictly business standpoint, management views organization as one useful technique for securing and maintaining a profitable position in the business community. Organized work effort has three rather obvious strategic advantages. First, it is possible to accomplish tasks through organization which would be impossible otherwise. Second, organization permits a saving in time and money through the development of efficient ways of getting the job done. Finally, organization makes it possible for management to exercise some degree of control over the business. For the most part, the common patterns of organization and administration which have emerged in the industrial and business world are a direct outgrowth of management efforts to foster and develop these three strategic advantages of organization.

Management is continuously asking the questions: What is the best way of getting the job done? How can it be done as efficiently as possible? How can the organization be stabilized and controlled? Because organization is regarded as a means to an end, there is a tendency for management to view it logically, and even coldly, as something to be manipulated and changed in order to meet the more important strategic aims of the business. There is a tendency to look for the right "system," the most logical and rational organization of work effort and managerial control.

DIVISION OF LABOR

One of the key ideas in management's search for the right "system" of work is division of labor. In its elemental forms, division of labor is as old as human society itself. It begins, in a sense, with the natural biological division of labor between man and woman. This sexually based specialization is extended to work tasks in the family and larger community. The men do the hunting, while the women stay at home taking care of the children and tending the garden. From the standpoint of efficient organization of work tasks, the advantages of division of labor, even in a primitive society, are many. First, such division permits a higher degree of specialization and proficiency than would otherwise be the case. Second, it makes possible the assignment of duties and responsibilities in terms of the strength, skill, and maturity of the individuals involved. Third, it allows the simultaneous performance of different tasks. The man can be hunting and the children tending the garden, while the wife is cooking the dinner.

It is only in modern industrial society, however, that we find division of labor being used consciously and aggressively to achieve greater productivity and efficiency. The idea of division of labor is hardly a profound one. Yet, it underlies the development of machines as well as the intricate organization of men and work in the modern factory. It can be an absorbing, even fascinating, notion when conceived on the grand scale of modern industry. Note, for example, the opening statement of Adam Smith in his *Wealth of Nations:* "The greatest improvement in the productive powers of labour, and the greater part of the skill, dexterity, and judgment with which it is anywhere directed or applied, seem to have been the effect of the division of labor."[3] The idea of division of labor involving the co-ordination of work tasks and intricate combinations of power, machines, and men in the production of goods has had a persistent fascination right down to the present day.

Job Specialization

There are several important aspects of division of labor which should be discussed. One of these is *job specialization.* Job specialization is based on the notion that the employee who concentrates his energies and attention on one task is able to achieve a higher degree of skill and proficiency than if he scatters his efforts among several activities. Furthermore, he does not lose time moving from one job to the next. Moreover, it is easier to train him and takes less time. In addition, job specialization facilitates better administrative control

---

[3] Adam Smith, *An Inquiry into the Nature and Causes of the Wealth of Nations,* ed. by James E. Thorold Rogers (Oxford at the Clarendon Press, 1869), p. 5.

over work activities. Finally, wages and salaries can be more accurately adjusted to the level of work performed and to the skill and proficiency involved. For all these reasons, job specialization is one of the key ideas which influences management's thinking about the organization of work.

Jobs can be specialized in two dimensions—namely, by function and level of skill. There are two major sets of functions and two more or less subsidiary sets of functions performed by the typical business organization. The major functions, for want of better names, we can designate the "external" and "internal" functions of the organization. The subsidiary functions, which are auxiliary to the major functions

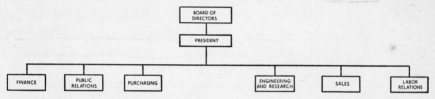

FIGURE 1.—"External" Functions of Typical Manufacturing Company

and designed to aid and support them, might be called the "administrative control" functions and the "centralized service" activities. The specialization of jobs by function generally follows this fourfold classification. The so-called "external" functions of the organization have to do with the external relations which any business must develop and maintain if it is to survive in the socioeconomic world. These include relations with customers, stockholders, unions, sources of supply, governmental agencies, and the general community. Most mature business organizations of any size have developed specific departments specializing in each one of these external relations, such as the sales department, labor relations department, purchasing department, research department, legal department, finance department, and public relations department (see Fig. 1).

The "internal" functions of the organization have to do with the internal processes through which it produces salable goods, services, or ideas. The internal processes vary with the kind of business to a much greater extent than the external relations, which tend to be similar although variously developed from one company to the next. For example, in a manufacturing business the internal processes are very elaborate because of the great variety of methods of fabrication. The typical retail store, on the other hand, has a very simple technology. The processing of goods is at a minimum, consisting of little more than removing merchandise from boxes, marking and ticketing it, cleaning it up if this is needed, and transporting it to the sales floor, warehouse, or stockroom. The actual internal functions which develop in a business organization depend upon what it produces and the technology employed in producing it. However, it is common practice to break down the internal functions in terms of the steps in the technological process. Thus, in the typical factory, we can determine the stages of production from the receipt of the raw material to the shipment of the final product simply by reviewing the names of the individual departments (see Fig. 2).

The auxiliary functions including the "administrative control" activities and the "centralized service" activities can be lumped to-

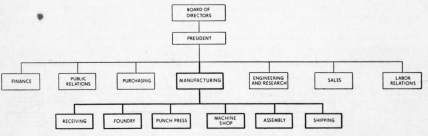

FIGURE 2.—"Internal" Functions of Typical Manufacturing Company

gether for our purposes here. In most organizations, certain functions are separated out of the main-line activities either to achieve greater administrative control or to gain savings in personnel, machinery, tools, and materials, or both. For example, the accounting department is primarily a control activity, although to some extent it also performs a centralized service for the main-line departments. By the same token, the maintenance department is primarily a service activity, and yet it often maintains certain kinds of administrative control over the use of machinery, hand tools, and parts by the production departments. Whatever the specific management purpose of the auxiliary departments, there are a great variety of functions which develop in the typical business organization and which cluster around the main-line activities, giving advice, performing needed services, seeking information, and applying rules and policies. Typical auxiliary activities in manufacturing are: accounting, maintenance, industrial engineering, the employment office, parts and stores, warehousing, etc. (see Fig. 3).

Another dimension in which job specialization can take place is in terms of the level of skill involved. It is obvious that real savings in payroll costs can be achieved if the less skilled portions of jobs can be separated out and performed by lower-skilled and lower-paid employees. The deskilling of complex jobs has been accomplished on a grand scale in modern industry. Indeed, the modern factory might well be regarded as a system for performing complex production tasks with relatively unskilled, low-cost employees. The deskilling of jobs has largely been achieved by the breaking-down of jobs into their simplest possible components and the reduction of work to a set of elemental motions. This transformation of complex jobs into simple work tasks also underlies the development of production machinery.

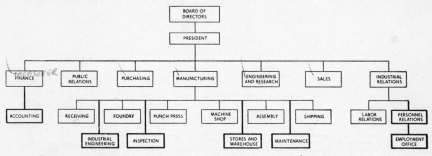

FIGURE 3.—"Auxiliary" Functions of Typical Manufacturing Company

Thus, the skills of the work are in a sense taken out of the man and put into the system of production and the production machine. The model guiding those who would ultimately reduce production to standardized work atoms is the completely automatic factory in which units of productive energy can be integrated in a variety of ways through electronic controls.

It is apparent that the deskilling of work can best take place in production activities and manufacturing. However, we find application of the same idea to selling and other more or less intangible activities, such as research. Here, however, the application is more difficult and its advantage is less clear. In retail selling, a distinction is made between the salesperson who actually "sells" the customer and the salesclerk who simply "waits on" him. Furthermore, stock work is sometimes performed by specialized, lower-skilled personnel in order to maximize selling time for the salesperson. In many stores, there has been a strong trend in recent years toward rationalized, "Piggly Wiggly" systems of selling in which employees simply maintain displays, keep the merchandise in stock, and perform cashiering functions. In the same way, research laboratories employ technicians to perform routine functions in order to save the time and energies of more highly trained scientists.

With the reduction of work to its simplest possible components and the introduction of repetitive, lower-skilled tasks, a fundamental division of labor tends to evolve between those who work within the system, performing routine functions and tending machines, and those who conceive the systems of production and develop the production machines through which the total job is accomplished. This clear separation between those who presumably "do" the work from those who plan and "think" about the work is one of the important aspects of modern industrial organization.

Co-ordination of Work Tasks

It is apparent that job specialization implies a need for the co-ordination of work tasks. Much of management's time and effort is devoted to the often "sticky" problem of co-ordinating the efforts of specialized men and machines. In fact, this is the key problem of administration. In co-ordinating the work, the strategic aim of management is the elimination of "stand around" time for employees, machines, raw materials, work in process, and finished goods. Perfection in co-ordination is achieved when raw materials can move uninterrupted through the various technological processes, meet simultaneously at an appointed place for final assembly, and proceed directly without warehousing to the customer. Perfect unity of this kind, however, is extremely difficult to secure because each organization, with the possible exceptions of large horizontal industrial empires, controls only a narrow segment of the total economy. Even within the organization, perfect co-ordination is a will-o'-the-wisp which management at the various levels fervently and hopefully chases and often fails to capture.

The co-ordination of work tasks in the factory, where it is most important, requires an intimate knowledge of the productive capacities of men and machines and of the flow of work and lead-time needed for the various pieces which go into the final assembly. The work flow might be likened to a river with various tributaries of different lengths leading into it. However, unlike a river system, the work flow stops if any of the tributaries become clogged and run dry. It can be seen that the co-ordination of work in the modern factory involves an immense complexity of detail and is difficult of achievement even on paper, let alone in actual practice. To meet these problems, many organizations develop a production planning department whose function it is to co-ordinate production in each department and to determine what should be produced at what time and in what quantities.

Organizations are frequently set up with little or no built-in flexibility, as though perfect co-ordination were the rule rather than the exception. Human error, machine breakdowns, shortage of materials, variations in materials, shortage of help, and other organizational "gremlins" all combine to create modern industrial management's major administrative headache. Since middle management and first-level supervision are primarily responsible for internal co-ordination, this group is most affected by the lack of flexibility in organization and finds itself continuously in the position of trying to meet a myriad of what appears to be impossible demands. Where perfection is expected and anything short of this decried, it is understandable why middle management and supervision face a punishing and often frustrating situation in many industries.

Standardized Production

Job specialization and the co-ordination of work tasks in the factory also require standardized production units and interchangeable parts. The pieces which go into the final assembly must, within very narrow tolerances, be the same. The pieces must fit together; nuts must fit bolts; holes must be aligned. The well-nigh universal micrometer and other measuring instruments in the modern factory attest to the extreme importance of precision in production. Without precision, the breaking-down of jobs into specialized work tasks would be impossible.

PATTERNS OF AUTHORITY IN BUSINESS

Thus far, we have been discussing common patterns of organization and administration growing out of management's efforts to develop the "right system" of work. Other common patterns emerge from management's attempt to co-ordinate and control the human aspects of organization. One of the principal techniques of control is through the authority hierarchy or chain of command. Most organizations develop from the top down, beginning, as we have indicated, with an individual or small group of men who conceive and develop a business activity which ultimately expands into an organized effort involving many persons. The organization in the business sense is an apparatus for securing and maintaining a commercial enterprise and, as such, is controlled in terms of the strategic aims of the enterprise. Business organizations, as a consequence, are essentially authoritarian, developing elaborate chains of command to insure that over-all goals are achieved.

The chain of command develops out of management's needs to fix responsibility for activities performed in the organization. The chain of command represents a system of accountability and a technique for simplifying administrative control. For each set of activities, someone is placed "in charge." At the lowest levels the person in charge is responsible for very specific functions, generally involving tangible work effort. As we move up the line of authority, middle management and higher levels of management are responsible for broader and broader aspects of the organization. At the highest levels, management is concerned both with the external relations of the business and the internal processes.

The chain of command is essentially a social device for achieving a unity of purpose and effort amidst the natural diversity of interests and aims which characterize human beings. It serves as a technique for linking together the external concerns of the enterprise with its internal processes. It is the principal system by which orders and directions move downward in the organization and information about problems at the work level move upward. More than this, however, it is a technique for achieving social control and motivation among employees.

Control through a hierarchy of authority appears to be a natural human pattern as old as the father-son relation or chief-tribal member relation. Hierarchical patterns are found in every human society. While in modern society superior-subordinate relationships always involve a degree of tension, nevertheless it is surprising to find the willingness with which humans "knuckle down" in a hierarchical system. If it were otherwise, the chain of command simply would not work at all.

The fixing of responsibility in an industrial organization is guided by several principles. Of first importance is what appears logical from the standpoint of the functions performed by the organization. For practically every identifiable function, someone is placed in charge and held accountable. When the specific function involves several levels of skill, we find a hierarchy of authority and responsibility developing with certain persons being responsible for getting the work out, while others spend more time integrating the specific activity with other activities in the organization and planning and adjusting the activity to the needs of the business and organization in general.

A second factor influencing the fixing of responsibility is the prevailing notions of span of control in the organization, that is, notions concerning the number of subordinates which one man can or should control. Where close control in an organization is needed, such as in a factory, there is a tendency to try to solve the problems of communication, co-ordination, and control by adding new layers of supervision. As a consequence, we find organizations of this type developing very steep hierarchies of authority and many layers of supervision between management and employees. There appears to be a point at which the addition of new levels of supervision creates more problems than it solves, but this varies from one organization to the next, and there are no hard and fast rules. Some students of administration, such as Graicunas, have attempted to determine how many subordinates one supervisor can control on the basis of mathematical analyses of the number of relationships involved.[4] With five or more subordinates, the number of relationships that can occur among employees and between employees and supervision becomes astronomical.

A third factor influencing the fixing of responsibility in an organization is based on notions regarding the relations which ought to exist between the superior and his subordinates. The greater the responsibility accorded rank-and-file employees, the less supervision is required. In highly decentralized organizations, the layers of supervision are few in number. In such companies, greater reliance is placed on employees, and management is characterized by its confidence in the ability of well-trained employees to solve problems at the work level without constant administrative intervention. However, most management groups, especially in organizations where the system of work is intricate and works efficiently only with perfect timing and co-ordination, find it reassuring to maintain tight supervisory control.

Whatever principles of control operate in a given organization, the

[4] See: V. A. Graicunas, "Relationship in Organization," *Papers on the Science of Administration*, Luther Gulick and L. Urwick (eds.) (New York: Columbia University Institute of Public Administration, 1937).

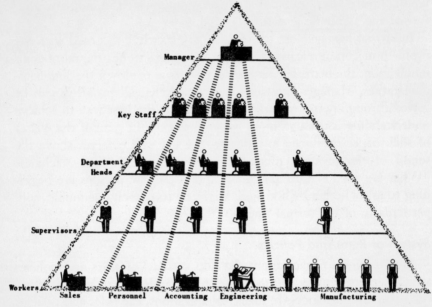

FIGURE 4.—Authority Hierarchy in Typical Manufacturing Company

supervisory hierarchy develops in characteristic pyramidal units with responsibilities fixed in terms of function and level (see Fig. 4).

System of Communication

In any on-going social endeavor, communication obviously is necessary. Men are bound together in society through communication—verbal, written, or symbolic. Indeed, the system of communication in society might be likened to the nervous system of the physical organism. However, unlike the nervous system, communication among men is not automatic. There are all kinds of interferences which act as barriers to understanding. In a closely knit work team like the modern factory, communication is of crucial importance. As a consequence, we find the typical industrial organization to be a tangled, weedy morass of communications, whether verbal, written, or otherwise.

The principal channel of communication, as we have already indicated, is the line of authority. However, most industrial organizations have developed auxiliary techniques for getting orders and information down the line, up the line, and across the line. In this regard, management is primarily concerned with the formal aspects of communication—that is, "official" communication. However, as we shall learn later, much of what is communicated in industry is informal and symbolic in nature.

Industrial management seems to be constantly concerned with the problem of communication. The pattern seems to be: the more communication, the better! This is especially true of down-the-line communication. Management seems convinced that all problems can be solved through better understanding and that the best way to achieve understanding is through more communication. In spite of the welter of slick paper produced in industry, the cry still emerges above the sound of the printing presses, mimeographs, and ditto machines: "What we need is more communication!" A few persons are beginning to ask whether or not there might be too much communication, particularly of the formal variety.

System of Rules and Policies

Most business organizations develop systems of rules and policies which serve as guides to the behavior of employees in various situations and circumstances. In many organizations, the rules and policies are developed in an almost legal way and are set forth in operations manuals, personnel policy manuals, and statements of general policy which can be consulted by those most concerned with the application of the rules. In other organizations, the system of rules and policies is much less developed than this.

The nature of authority exercised in an organization can be studied and analyzed through its system of rules and policies. Sometimes rules are applied in a willy-nilly, capricious fashion without regard for precedent. It is more usual, however, in modern industry to find a more consistent application. Rules can vary all the way from suggestions concerning what one ought to do to stringent definitions of behavior. When the rules are especially stringent and carefully defined and applied consistently without too much regard for specific circumstances, we think of the organization as "bureaucratic" and involving a great deal of "red tape." In some cases the application of rules becomes more important than accomplishing the job. Indeed, all mature business organizations face the danger of losing their flexibility and adaptability because of the tendency to accept and apply the system of rules even when they are not appropriate.

Wage and Salary System

One of the key devices utilized by management in securing control in the organization is the wage and salary system. For the great majority of our citizens the only source of sustenance, material satisfaction, and social position is the pay check. Money, therefore, constitutes a powerful motivation to work. An organization with money can attract employees.

The pay check can be used in two ways. For the mass of employees, it is primarily used as a means of buying labor. From a strictly business standpoint, labor is a commodity to be purchased like machinery and raw materials. It is simply one of the expenses of the business. Most business organizations have developed elaborate systems for determining a "fair" wage both within the company and within the broader community. One of the important functions of the union is negotiating wages in terms of the "value" of labor. The pay check can also be used as a device for motivating employees. At the lower levels, many organizations have set up incentive plans in order to induce employees to produce more on the job. Commission methods of pay are used in sales organizations. So-called "merit rating" is utilized extensively on white-collar and supervisory jobs. Some organizations have developed profit-sharing plans. At higher levels, executives are rewarded through bonuses, stock options, and profit sharing. A great deal of management effort has been devoted to the problem of motivating and controlling employees through the pay check and various benefit programs.

Other Systems of Rewards

The mature business organization makes use of a variety of techniques for motivating employees other than the pay check. Since these techniques run the gamut of psychological and social devices, we shall discuss only a few of the more common of them here. Position in the organization can serve as a powerful source of motivation for some employees. Any hierarchical organization is characterized by status levels, with the higher levels enjoying greater prestige and recognition than the lower. Management can exercise considerable control over employees by dispensing prestige rewards and providing opportunities for advancement.

Employees find considerable motivation in the job itself. The development of job skill and a sense of craftsmanship can serve as a source of stimulation and satisfaction. In some companies this sense of craftsmanship is deliberately fostered by management through personal recognition of various groups of employees and their contribution to the over-all accomplishments of the organization. At present also, there is a trend toward job enlargement aimed at creating greater satisfaction and sense of craftsmanship on the job.

There has been a strong trend in recent years to motivate employees through institutional factors. Most business organizations develop certain institutional qualities—just like any on-going concern in our society, such as, the church, the school, or the fraternal order. Some companies have made conscious and aggressive use of these institutional characteristics to develop greater employee loyalty and support. In a number of instances, this has taken the form of "selling" the company and its economic system to employees through elaborate training and film programs.

The utilization of psychological and social techniques of employee motivation in industry has been typically sporadic and often poorly conceived. They are usually applied like a palliative without any real integration with the main stem of managerial activities. Without such integration, they are at best a soothing balm which has only a temporary effect on the organization, and at worst a medicine man's elixir. There is a tendency for some management groups to jump from one fad to the next, looking for that miraculous tonic which will infuse employees with vigor and vitality. The care and treatment of "sick" organizations obviously must be more basic than this.

ORGANIZATION CHANGE

Brief mention should be made of change as an important characteristic of modern business organization. In spite of the relative stability of any on-going institution, business generally is subjected to considerable change compared with other institutions in our society. Change occurs because of fluctuations in business conditions, market trends, new technological methods, labor turnover, executive turnover, and often simply because change is fostered for the sake of change itself. In short, business is dynamic. It expands and contracts, creates new products, develops new systems for producing the products, changes job activities, shifts employees about, and adjusts its rules and policies. Sometimes management appears to be demonstrating its ability to manage simply by changing things. This is especially true of "new" management.

The most dramatic changes in organization occur when there is a shift in managerial power. Most business organizations are characterized by internal politics, which are more or less intense and built primarily around various strategic notions about how best to run the organization. Most organizations contain a number of "strategic camps." These camps often become rallying points for employees of particular interests and ambitions. Covert or open struggles for power ensue, the results of which determine the particular strategic orientations which will determine major company policy.

Because most employees in industrial organizations—even in key positions—are specialists, few have the opportunity to develop the broad, balanced managerial perspective required to manage a multi-strategic business. As a consequence, we find business organizations frequently managed in a lopsided way and reflecting the background, interests, and points of view of the particular management group in power. A shift in the power structure can result in dramatic changes throughout the entire organization.

SUMMARY

In this chapter we have reviewed the dynamics of business, the underlying strategic considerations, the way in which organization develops, and the common patterns of organization and administration. We have devoted considerable attention to what might be called the "anatomy" of business organization, the formal structure conceived by management and around which work activities are organized and administered. However, the formal structure is only part of the total picture. It describes only management's idea of how the organization ought to function. In order to understand the business organization as it really operates, we must focus attention on the behavior of employees within the system of work. In the next chapter, we shall analyze the dynamics of human behavior and the basic concepts of human relations which we shall use over and over again in describing employee behavior and attitudes throughout subsequent sections of this book.

2. THE DYNAMICS OF HUMAN BEHAVIOR

WE HAVE seen that the patterns of organization and administration developing in business are determined to a considerable extent by the strategic aims of management. The adjustment of employees within the system of work, however, is determined largely by personal and social needs. This chapter will be devoted to a brief elaboration of the key ideas about the attitudes and behavior of employees which will be utilized throughout the remainder of the text. We are not attempting here to develop a completely systematic statement about human behavior. Our only purpose is to describe certain concepts which have proved useful in analyzing human relations in industry.

FEELINGS AND EMOTIONS

We cannot understand employee attitudes and behavior without some understanding of the nature of feelings and emotions. Perhaps the most important element involved in all human relations is that they evoke feelings among people. In one sense, feelings are the prime movers in all social interaction. Without feelings, employees would never become hostile to management, would never restrict output on the job, and would never develop grievances. Without feelings, also, employees would never have the ambition to succeed, would never invent new ways of doing things, and would never co-operate wholeheartedly in the achievement of the over-all goals of an enterprise. It is characteristic of humans that they size up the world around them in terms of their feelings and attitudes. Their behavior is directly related to their evaluation of their environment in terms of the feelings and emotions which this evaluation evokes. The demands of the world around them play on their emotions like a bow on a violin. They react in any situation in terms of the discord or harmony of the music thus created.

23

How One Employee Views the World

The relation of inner feelings and emotions to outward behavior and attitudes can best be shown by a fictional example of one day in the life of a rather introspective factory employee whom we shall call Joe. Through this account, you will observe not only that Joe does certain things but that he has feelings about them, too, which sometimes are outwardly expressed and affect his behavior.

Joe has just entered the factory gates. He is hurrying because he is late. He missed the 7:20 A.M. streetcar. "Damn the streetcars anyway," he mutters to himself. "Why they have to travel in bunches, I'll never know. If I miss one bunch, the next ones don't come along for fifteen minutes. Then I'm late. Must be some ex-admiral is running the system now, the way they go in for convoys." He chuckles a little over his own joke but then remembers that the boss doesn't like people to be late, and he starts feeling defensive again.

By this time, he is in his section of the factory area and nearing the time clock. The boss is standing beside it, examining the timecards which have not yet been punched in. He shakes his head thoughtfully as Joe comes up and snares his own card from the rack. "The old man is mad," thinks Joe; but he mutters, "Good morning." The boss simply glances at him without answering his greeting. He is preoccupied at the moment with wondering how much work he can get out of the crew with four men absent.

Joe goes over to his machine and thinks to himself. The old man *is* mad. They never stop to realize that a guy may have a reason for being late. They all have cars. They don't have to worry about this damn streetcar system.

The day passes with the whirr and clang of machinery. Joe likes the machine, its rhythmic beat, and its smooth operation. He feels a certain pride about his job. Took him a number of years to work up to it. A lot of guys would trade places with him.

Later, Joe is still hard at work. He glances up to see the plant superintendent standing in one corner of the department with the boss. "Boy, there's a guy with a lot to do," Joe says to himself. "Just wanders around and watches the rest of us work. Whatta life! Oh, oh! He's coming over this way. I'd better look busy." He plunges into his work with gusto. As the superintendent pauses near his machine, he feels a certain tension. "Jeepers, you don't suppose they're talking about my being late. Well, of all the . . ." But the superintendent moves on and finally leaves the department. Joe feels relieved. A good time for a smoke. He shuts off his machine and heads for the washroom.

On the way to the washroom there is a bulletin board which Joe generally hurries by without a second glance. This time, however, there is a bright poster on it, occupying about half the available space, which catches his eye. It is a poster adapted from one of the company's advertisements appearing in a national magazine. It makes him feel good to work for a company which makes a well-known product. He has no trouble explaining to his family and friends what it is he works on.

The washroom is the scene of a lively discussion. Several of the boys are arguing about the recent labor contract. Joe lights up a cigarette and joins in. "The trouble is . . ." says Joe, exhaling an atomic explosion of smoke, but he never finishes his statement. The personnel manager has just come into the washroom. He is making his weekly inspection—always inspects the washrooms personally because "a clean washroom is very important to employee morale." The conversation dies as the personnel manager sees them standing near the open window. He shouts a little too enthusiastically: "How's everything going this morning?" A few of the employees say, "Fine"; but their response is somewhat subdued compared with their loud arguments of a few minutes before. The others nod pleasantly enough but continue to smoke in silence. The personnel manager tries again. "Nice weather!" They all agree that it's nice weather, but one by one they pinch out their cigarettes and go back to work. The personnel manager moves to the next washroom, thinking, "You've got to keep close to your employees."

We could follow Joe through the remainder of his workday, but there is sufficient evidence in these few episodes to illustrate the point. Joe is a sentient being; he feels. He has certain feelings of defensiveness when he comes to work late. He feels anxious when he has to face the boss at the time clock. He has negative feelings about the superintendent and all these "guys who don't have anything to do but wander around and watch other people work." He feels anxious when the superintendent moves over near his machine. He feels relieved and wants a smoke when the superintendent leaves the department. He feels pleasantly cordial and at ease in the washroom with the boys. He feels restricted and constrained when the personnel manager moves on the scene. Not only does he have feelings with reference to other people; but he has feelings about his machine, which is a symbol of his own success, and about the poster on the bulletin board because it, too, is a symbol of importance to him.

It is apparent that Joe's work life is a veritable network of feelings which add meaning to the events occurring around him and determine his attitudes and behavior. As a matter of fact, the life of any employee in the work place has meaning to him only in terms of his feelings about it. As administrators or students in the field of human relations, we cannot begin to understand the behavior of employees unless we think in the language of feelings.

The Observation of Feelings

If the feelings of people were immediately apparent, a good deal of the bungling in human relations would never happen. We would see the results of our actions at once and would modify them to fit the situation. Unfortunately, feelings are not so easily observed. For one thing, some people just are not aware of the feelings of others unless they are expressed openly. The utter bore whom you meet on the bus and who insists upon talking incessantly to you about various topics of no importance to you is completely unaware of your lack of responsiveness; nor does he observe from any of the clues you offer him that your most fervent desire is just to sit quietly and read your evening paper. Such a person is much too concerned with his own feelings to notice those of anyone else. Indeed, anybody who becomes preoccupied with his own feelings, for whatever reason, is not observant of others.

In our little story of Joe, you will remember that the boss was so preoccupied with his production problems that he was barely aware of Joe when he punched his timecard and said, "Good morning." Furthermore, Joe was so defensive and concerned with his own feelings at the time that he himself was in no position to analyze the boss and his feelings of the moment. Everyone can become preoccupied in these ways and wall himself off from even the most obvious behavior around him.

There are other reasons, however, in addition to self-preoccupation, which can interfere with our ability to observe the feelings of others. One of the most important of these is our relative concern with the other person. Some people are of great importance to us; others, of less significance. The big boss, as he walks through the plant, often is hardly aware of the rank-and-file employees. However, if the corporation president confronts the superintendent, he becomes keenly aware of him. The importance of the other person can make a big difference in our sensitivity to his feelings.

Probably the biggest reason why many of us pay little attention to the feelings of others is that we are simply not trained to be alert to them. In fact, in business, we are often trained to a directly opposite point of view. Business is generally regarded as "practical and logical" and outside the realm of personal feelings and emotions. Being "businesslike" means keeping one's attention entirely on the formal aspects of doing business and not permitting oneself to become diverted by personal needs and the "perversity" of human nature—even in ourselves. This kind of thinking has a long history in the business world; it has become so ingrained in management's thinking that it constitutes one of the most significant barriers to the development of good human relations in the industrial world.

Expression of Feelings

Even if we become alert to the feelings and emotions of others, we cannot always observe them. They are often expressed in subtle and fleeting ways, in a quick glance, a sharp remark, a posture, gait, opinion, etc. For the most part, people hide their feelings. They hide them because they have been taught to keep them to themselves, particularly in public. The person who is quiet and retiring in the work place may be "hell on wheels" in the privacy and intimacy of his own home. More than this, people hide their feelings because they fear the reactions of others or are afraid of hurting others. Finally, it is apparent that most people are not themselves fully aware of their own inner emotions, particularly the deeper ones, and cannot express them directly even if they wished.

All of these difficulties in observing the feelings of others, however, do not make the task insurmountable. Simply becoming alert to expressions of feelings—even if you cannot accurately label them—provides a wealth of information about human relations. It helps to ask such questions as: Why do people talk and act as they do? What is the meaning of their behavior in terms of probable feelings? Why does this student always sit in the last row in the classroom? Why does the professor always put his foot up on the chair when he lectures? Why does another student always insist upon talking whenever there is open discussion? You may not be able to provide precise answers; but you will certainly become aware of various degrees of anxiety, tension, defensiveness, aggression, hostility, and lack of control in others.

Nondirective Interviewing

Observation of the feelings and emotions of others can be extended through a method of interviewing known as nondirective interviewing. This kind of interviewing is the same as that used by psychiatrists and clinical psychologists in the diagnosis and treatment of emotional disturbances. It has also been utilized extensively by sociologists and anthropologists in field studies because of its advantages in delving behind the manifest content of what people say and in gaining insight into latent feelings and hidden meanings. It is not our intention here to describe in detail the method of nondirective interviewing. However, the serious student of human relations should acquaint himself with this technique since he will find it especially useful in analyzing the feelings of others.[1] Most of the observations about human relations included in this text are based on data obtained through nondirective interviewing.

SOCIAL ASPECTS OF HUMAN BEHAVIOR

Thus far we have been discussing the feelings and emotions which develop in the individual as a consequence of his interaction with the world around him. We have seen that human beings generally are active forces—units of psychic energy, if you will—seeking satisfaction, relief from frustration, adjustment, support, self-realization, peace of mind. The most passive employee in the work place has internal energies. He is not just "sitting there," as you might think, but has a definite awareness of himself in relation to the passing parade of events. He feels, strives, thinks, forms attitudes, seeks adjustment, tries to express himself; and, in whatever ways seem appropriate to him, he seeks to achieve some kind of psychic equilibrium. His passivity itself may only be an expression of internal needs.

In his efforts to gain personal satisfaction in the social environment, the individual, by the time he is an adult, develops a reasonably consistent pattern of behavior which represents his efforts, through time, to order his life's experiences into an integrated system of feeling, thinking, and acting. He acquires ways of handling his interpersonal relations. He develops certain notions about himself—who he is, and where he fits in the scheme of things. He gains a sense of identification and can distinguish his "kind of guy" from others. He develops specific manners of living, dressing, eating, and acting, which constitute his way of life. He acquires beliefs, sentiments, and ideas about the world around him—its values, morals, sacred symbols, sanctions, etc. And, no matter what patterns of behavior he develops, he continues to search for situations in which he can achieve some degree of satisfaction and to reject, in a variety of ways, situations which create frustration, insecurity, and self-depreciation.

As we all know, the satisfaction of the individual's needs, interests, and drives must be secured in a social environment. Very early in life, the individual learns to direct his attention to the people around him, through whom he must seek to allay his needs for food, security,

---

[1] See F. J. Roethlisberger and W. J. Dickson, *Management and the Worker* (Cambridge, Mass.: Harvard University Press, 1939); Carl R. Rogers, *Counseling and Psychotherapy* (Boston: Houghton Mifflin, 1942); and also Chapter 18 in this text.

personal comfort, growth, and self-realization. He redefines his basic physiological and psychological needs into social terms. He strives to gain acceptance, love, sense of belonging, and an assured position in the social group—whether it be his immediate family, play group, or class in school. Moreover, he grows and develops through identification and integration of the attributes and characteristics of people around him. Life becomes an eternal game of seeking personal satisfaction through others—a never-ending quest for psychic equilibrium and self-realization—in an environment where you must compete with others for these satisfactions. Although the individual as he matures becomes less and less dependent on his immediate social environment, nevertheless, his relations with his associates at home, in the work place, and in the general community remain very important to him. The same striving for love, sense of belonging, recognition, and assured position continues.

Influence of Social Structure

It is obvious that a person's associations will have a strong influence on the pattern of behavior which he develops. His associations provide both the social environment in which he must work out his personal needs and also the stuff out of which he ultimately weaves the fabric of his life. It is important, therefore, to know something about the structure of society and the patterns of human interaction and association which develop within it.

A society is not just a group of people thrown together in haphazard array. One has only to fly over the country in an airplane to observe some of the obvious aspects of man's design for living—the neat patches and squares of his farms; the geometry of his towns and cities; the connecting rail and highway arteries which proceed purposely and aggressively across plains, across rivers, and over, around, and through mountains; and the corpuscular trucks, automobiles, buses, and trains moving through the arteries from one urban concentration to the next. Even the airplane, flying through uncharted skies, follows man-made, though invisible, highways. There is no question that human society is patterned and structured, but from eighteen thousand feet in the air, we see only the superficial aspects of its design.

Moving closer, we can observe institutions like the family, the school, the factory, the church. We can see neighborhoods which are parts of communities—which in turn are parts of towns and cities—

which are parts of states—which are parts of regions—which are parts of nations. We become aware of all kinds of systems of human interaction, all welded together in more or less consistent fashion. Moreover, within each of these systems, there is an obvious internal structure. People perform different functions and are related to one another in specific ways. Within the family, for example, there are the father, the mother, and the siblings of different ages, each performing different functions and each behaving in particular ways with regard to one another.

For the purposes of this text, there are only certain aspects of social structure with which we are concerned. First of all, social structure determines the individual's associations throughout his life. His patterns of interaction are described by his family, his friendship groups, his neighborhood, his place of work, his church, the region in which he lives, and the nation of which he is a citizen. Knowing where he fits in each of these systems of social interaction provides excellent clues to the pattern of attitudes and behavior which he is likely to develop. Social structure not only determines with whom the individual will interact but also the nature of the interaction, the kind of demands, expectations, and relations of reciprocity which develop.

Secondly, while social structure creates similarities in behavior, it also creates differences. Society is characterized by differential perspectives, attitudes, and ways of behaving, from group to group and from individual to individual. Differences create the need for communication, understanding, and co-operation on the one hand and the potential for conflict and disunity on the other.

Third, it is characteristic of human society that it is ordered, not only on a horizontal plane, but vertically and hierarchically as well. Every human society, no matter how egalitarian, appears to develop a status system, in terms of its values, with different positions in the society being accorded greater prestige and exercising greater influence. The status system introduces factors of higher, lower, and equal social positions. We find this phenomenon occurring not only in the broader community but within the family, the church, the school, the corner gang, and the factory as well.

Fourth, social structure is relatively stable. It achieves a certain equilibrium which evolves slowly. One of the reasons for this relative stability is the fact that people identify their personal needs, interests, and ambitions with particular positions in the social structure. Their whole way of life—their system of security and satisfaction—is bound up, in this way, with the structure of society.

Fifth, the social structure, and the system of interaction which develops, constitutes an integrated, functionally related whole. In this respect, a society is an extended counterpart of the system of behavior achieved by the individual to satisfy his personal needs, interests, and ambitions. It reflects some of the same characteristics. It is reasonably consistent; you cannot change one part without affecting the rest; it evolves slowly, integrating the new with the old; it tends to resist change. It is the inner man externalized and exhibits the same processes of the human mind.

Finally, the social system is sanctioned by all kinds of sacred symbols, rituals, ceremonials, religious and philosophic notions, and value systems which support and reinforce the particular way of life that develops.

Dynamics of Social Behavior

Within the social structure, one of the principal preoccupations of the individual is deciding where he fits and where others fit in relation to him. It is characteristic of humans that they are continuously feeling each other out to determine just who they are in the social scheme of things. There is good reason for this "feeling out," since expectations, demands, and social behavior in general are largely determined by the social positions occupied by the interacting parties. The individual acts differently in relation to persons in higher positions than he does with subordinates in the social hierarchy. He behaves still differently in relation to associates who are more or less on the same level. He reacts differently to the minister than he does to the local bartender. He responds differently to his sister than he does to the girl next door. In short, he must define the situation socially before he knows how to feel and act. He must know the function or role of the other individual in the society and also his status in the social hierarchy.

It can be seen that much of what takes place in any social system is symbolic. It has meaning over and beyond what is happening from a purely functional standpoint. Indeed, stripped of all its strictly human trappings, a society is simply a system for conceiving and training its children and for feeding and sheltering its members. Superimposed on these basic phylogenetic and physiological activities is a social organization with a myriad of socially defined relations which have symbolic meaning to the people within it. In order to understand human behavior, therefore, it is obvious that we must look to the social meanings of the events which transpire.

When we consider that the structure of a society not only shapes the way people behave but also thrusts them together in various combinations, we begin to get a feel for the dynamics of social behavior. The whole life of the individual is bound up with his efforts to achieve some kind of personal adjustment and equilibrium as, say, a husband, father, member of the working class, punch press operator, member of a fraternal order, etc. In all of these roles, he must continuously adjust his behavior to meet both his own internal needs and the expectations of others.

IMPLICATION TO HUMAN RELATIONS IN INDUSTRY

We are now in a position to describe some of the implications of the dynamics of human behavior to an understanding of human relations in industry. The industrial organization is a social system involving positions and patterns of interaction which bring people of different backgrounds together into relationships which have, or develop, social meaning and significance to the participants. The industrial organization has both a formal, or manifest, social structure and an informal, or latent, social structure. The formal structure is what appears on the organization chart; the informal is what appears when we look behind the organization chart and view the organization as it actually functions.

A key aspect of the social structure of industrial organization is its status system—the formal and informal system of rankings from the president on down. The status system determines where the individual fits in the structure, and the prestige and recognition which he secures, as well as the influence and power which he exercises. Another important aspect of the social structure of the industrial organization is its various functional activities—its division of labor, which determines the job interests of employees, where they fit in the system of work, and which groups employees of like interests and background together. Many of the attitudes and patterns of behavior which employees share in the work environment are directly influenced by the functional activity which they perform and by the relation of this activity to other functions in the organization.

The dynamics of human relations in industry are intimately bound up both with the status system and the division of labor. It is in the social structure, largely circumscribed and defined by these two factors, that the individual attempts to work out the necessary adjustments which he must make to achieve personal satisfaction and equanimity. The remainder of the text will be devoted to an elaboration of the common patterns of behavior which develop among employees in this process of adjustment to the demands of the work system.

THE WORKER AND HIS SOCIAL BACKGROUND

Before proceeding to a discussion of human behavior in the industrial setting, it would be helpful to describe some of the attitudes and ways of behaving which the worker brings with him to the work place from the broader community of which he is a part.

The American Culture: Basic Sentiments

Among the attitudes which every person in our society learns early in life are the basic American sentiments which most of us hold to be immutably true. These sentiments in a sense constitute our national "religion." They color our notions of how we ought to act in our relations with one another and what we can expect out of life. These are the sentiments we learn in our homes, in our schools, in our churches, from history, from our national heroes, and from our national ceremonials and symbols. Although they are vague and sometimes ill-defined, they constitute powerful motivating forces in all areas of our society. If these sentiments are frustrated in the work situation, hostility, insecurity, and anxiety are likely to be created among employees.

Because these sentiments are so much a part of our national "religion," we will elaborate on them here only at the risk of being accused of maudlin sentimentality and Fourth of July speech-making. Their significance, however, has been borne out in practically all research in human relations. If you read between the lines of industrial relations research, you cannot help becoming keenly aware of the pattern of expectations and sentiments which characterize the American worker on all levels.

This pattern of basic sentiments was dramatically revealed in a study of several thousand comments made by employees in an extensive survey of their attitudes and opinions about their work environment. Their comments were made in answer to a completely open-ended question: "What are the best and worst things about your job and company?" The most intriguing thing about the answers was the extent to which they reflected basic American ideals concerning the rights of the individual in a free society. Indeed, the attitudes expressed sounded exactly like a résumé of what any American citizen expects out of life and in his relations with others in the broader community.

This study and others have revealed that many of the sentiments of American workers revolve around their notions of authority. It seems apparent that a nation such as ours, which was founded in revolt against authority and has developed a political system which attempts to limit arbitrary political control, would also train its citizenry to be suspicious of arbitrary authority wherever it might occur—whether it be in the community or the workplace. It is not, therefore, difficult to understand why employees in industry are continuously scrutinizing their supervision and management and reacting adversely to it whenever it becomes arbitrary, unilateral, and tyrannical. It is not that the American worker is anarchical by nature. As a matter of fact, he is quite willing to co-operate with others in getting a job done, provided that the leadership is democratic and not domineering or restrictive.

In light of these sentiments, the reactions of many employees in the work situation become readily understandable. Douglas McGregor points out that the "outstanding characteristic of the relationship between the subordinate and his superiors [in industry] is his dependence upon them for the satisfaction of his needs. Industry in our civilization is organized along authoritative lines."[2] Power in an industrial organization emanates from the top, quite the opposite of our political system. Decisions are made and passed down to the rest of the organization through the many layers of supervision. Refusal to follow orders in most industrial organizations is generally grounds for immediate dismissal. In this respect, an industrial or business organization is more like an army than a democratic political organization. It is like a nation that is always at war and never enjoying the luxury of peace. It is action-conflict oriented; decisions must be made immediately and without a great deal of debate and wrangling. And well they should be, too; for, if decisions were made in a business as they are in Congress, it would be in the hands of the receiver before important questions of policy or procedure were answered. Nevertheless, centralized authority such as that found in business and industrial organizations runs contrary to the basic sentiments of American workers, who are

---

[2] See Douglas McGregor, "Getting Effective Leadership in the Industrial Organization," *Journal of Consulting Psychology*, Vol. VIII, No. 2 (1944), pp. 55-63.

taught, as McGregor points out, that they are supposed to stand on their own feet and not be solely and completely dependent upon higher authority. As a consequence, supervision and authority in business must be handled with finesse and considerable awareness of the volatile nature of the relationship. The fact that this is not being accomplished everywhere in business in spite of the emphasis placed on supervisory training is evidenced by the extent to which many of the grievances and complaints of employees revolve around the kind of supervision they receive.

Supervision and authority involve more than the personal relations that exist between the boss and employees. The supervisor should, of course, be friendly and understanding. But there are other factors—perhaps more subtle, yet none the less significant—which are related to the employee's attitude toward authority. One of these is the notion of "freedom on the job," which is sometimes expressed as a "feeling of individual responsibility." It is surprising the extent to which this attitude is expressed, even by employees on the lowest levels in the organization. It can range all the way from a desire on the part of the employee for freedom from close supervision and restrictive job demands to abstract concepts of "free enterprise," freedom from governmental control, and free markets. However it is expressed, it is the same basic sentiment—the same notion of being allowed to stand on your own feet and do the job in your own way.

Industrial relations research has shown that the productivity and morale of employees improves to the extent that they are allowed to participate in decisions that affect them on the job. Case after case has demonstrated that employees respond more willingly and with greater enthusiasm and effort if they are allowed to take part in what they are doing and have at least a modicum of control over the environment that affects them. This reaction of employees is founded on the basic sentiment of a great majority of employees that they are supposed to stand on their own two feet and not depend on others to make decisions for them. All of the studies of improved morale and productivity among employees, resulting from allowing them to participate in decisions affecting them in the workplace, are merely illustrations and examples of the importance of this basic orientation of the American worker.

Other expressions of the American worker's attitude toward authority are found in their demands for fair treatment from their superiors, for the right of appeal in the event that they do not get fair treatment from lower-level supervision, and for freedom of expression in the workplace. Fair treatment is a concept which is strong in the thinking of Americans. If you wonder about this, go to any ball park and listen to the reactions of the audience when the umpire makes a "bum" decision! The "rules of the game" are very important to the American worker. If you have it coming to you, you take punishment without complaining; but, if it is the result of a "bum" decision, you make "plenty of noise." The right of appeal is closely allied to our notions of fair treatment. Our court system is an obvious manifestation of our basic sentiments in this regard. In industry, however, oftentimes there is no appeal from decisions made by management. This situation becomes particularly oppressive when decisions are made without reference to policy or past practice.

The Land of Opportunity

Most Americans have during their lifetimes received strong doses of the "rags to riches" dream. America, the Land of Opportunity, where the immigrant boy can work his way up from the streets of New York to economic and social success! America, where the Cinderella fantasy actually becomes a reality for the beautiful girl of the lower classes who marries the rich man's son! Much of our escapist literature deals with this theme. It is taught to children in grammar school and is still being taught in one form or another when they graduate from high school or college. That this sentiment should have an important effect on the thinking of employees is not surprising. Indeed, there are few things more frustrating to the average worker in America than the feeling that, no matter what he does, he does not have a chance. The feeling is important, in fact, even to those who personally have no desire to move up the line. The most unambitious person still wants to feel that, if he did put forth the effort, he could rise in the social and economic hierarchy. Many people, though they have no aspirations for themselves, do have hopes for their children. The idea that the children should have more opportunity and success than their fathers is strong in America. It is part of our "third generationalism" which has seen each new generation better integrated into American society than the preceding one.

Our attitudes toward opportunity tie in closely with our feelings about progress. It is accepted in this country that each new generation as a whole should live better than the last. The notion of a constantly rising standard of living is taken for granted by management and worker alike. It is to be expected that each decade should find us with better housing, better refrigeration, better clothes, more wealth per family—no matter what its station in life. The idea of a rising standard of living is reflected in the continuous cycle of demands for increased earnings in industry. No one expects our economy ever to stagnate on any one level; the growth curves must be ever upward. The "rising standard of living" idea also emerges in the worker's expectation of constantly improving working conditions. The notion that each new generation of workers should work under better conditions than the preceding one is hardly a radical notion in American thought.

The American worker also expects a degree of security from his work life. This is not the paternalistic brand of security which industry has, on occasion, tried in the past and found wanting. The security which the American worker expects runs something like this when expressed in his terms: "Any man who wants to work for a living should have an opportunity to work"; "Any man who has worked all his life for a company deserves some recognition"; "No man should be unemployed through no fault of his own." In other words, the American worker typically wants security in the feeling that he can make his way, achieve a certain material and spiritual satisfaction in life for himself and family, and hold what he has gained if he is willing to put forth the effort. The management representative who feels that the average American worker thinks the world owes him a living is as wrong as the union representative who feels that the American worker is more strongly motivated by a desire for welfare security than anything else. Both are dead wrong. Just give the worker reasonable economic stability with an opportunity for an increasing standard of living and you have answered a major portion of his security demands!

Regional Differences in Attitudes and Behavior

The previous section has dealt with cultural sentiments which characterize the great majority of Americans on all levels in our society. Management and the worker can agree in these sentiments, even though variously expressed. However, we are all aware of differences in attitudes and behavior among the various segments of our population. We are aware, for one thing, of regional differences and differences in attitudes between those who have been brought up in rural areas and those who were brought up in the cities. Morale surveys have shown that these regional differences can have an important effect on the attitudes of employees toward management. Extensive studies show a decided relation between employee morale and the regional location of the organization surveyed. Morale tends to be very high in the South but low in the older industrial centers of the East. One study was made in the retail stores of a large merchandising organization. Since the employee policies were applied by this company on a nation-wide basis and, also, since management in each unit was generally comparable, it was felt that the differences in morale could only be accounted for by broad regional differences in attitudes. Other studies have shown that employees who were brought up in rural areas seemed to be more willing to accept management's "point of view" and the demands of the organization than urban employees. However, employees reared in rural areas such as Tennessee, where there are strong kinship ties, have shown an unusual independence in their attitudes toward management and organizational demands. These employees often are far more concerned with kinship ties back home than with their ties to the industrial organization where they work. The situation is typified by an incident, reported to one of the authors, of an employee in a Detroit factory who left a note pinned on his machine: "Have gone home to help with the spring plowing. Back in May."

Social Class in America

However, the most significant differences in attitudes among employees do not arise from regional differences. Actually, social class differences within a single community are far more important in creating differential attitudes and behavior among people. This may come as a surprise to those of us who think of democratic America as classless. However, a number of recent studies of American communities, ranging all the way from a tiny rural village to much larger urban centers, show a well-defined class system. In general, the pattern follows similar lines from one community to the next, although there are some variations. At the top of the heap are the "old families"—the "aristocracy of birth and wealth," as Professor Warner and associates put it. These are the people whose families have occupied positions of power and prestige in the community for generations. They inherit their status by birth, that is, by belonging to the right families. They

---

[3] See W. Lloyd Warner, *American Life: Dream and Reality* (Chicago: University of Chicago Press, 1953), for a detailed description of the class system in America.

live in large homes or mansions in the most exclusive neighborhood in town. They go to the church with the highest social rating and belong to the best clubs. They are arbiters in social affairs, and their presence at a dinner party can make it a social success. Altogether, their status and position in the community is assured; although others of lower status may resent them, they nevertheless recognize them as the "old aristocracy" or "social people."

Below them is another small group of people with whom the old families are willing to mingle but do not accept completely. These are persons who have the money and the manners to live like the aristocracy, but they and their families have not been "in society" long enough to "rate." They are, in the sense, the "new aristocracy." Their attitudes are described by Professor Warner *et al.* in *Social Class in America*.

> Except that they aspire to old-family status, if not for themselves then for their children, these men and their families have a design for living similar to the old-family group. But they are consciously aware that their money is too new and too recently earned to have the sacrosanct quality of wealth inherited from a long line of ancestors. They know, as do those above them, that, while a certain amount of wealth is necessary, birth and old family are what really matter.[4]

Clearly separated from the "aristocracy," and not necessarily particularly impressed by it, is another somewhat larger group of "respectable" and relatively well-to-do families "frequently associated with an expression of moral attitudes and with definite conceptions of the positive value and important role of wealth."[5] This group constitutes the upper-middle class of the communities studied. It is among the wealthiest groups in the community, but it places no great importance on family background or lineage. Individual wealth is regarded as far more significant, and special value is placed upon rigorous adherence to religious and moral precepts. These are the "solid, respectable" members of the community who are active in civic affairs and very often "front" for the upper classes in community activities.

The three groups just described represent the top crust of the communities studied. Although they include only one-sixth or less of the total population, they hold most of the positions of respect, power,

---

[4] W. Lloyd Warner *et al.*, *Social Class in America* (Chicago: Science Research Associates, Inc., 1949), p. 12.

[5] Davis, Gardner, and Gardner, *Deep South* (Chicago: University of Chicago Press, 1941), p. 68.

and prestige. In some of the newer communities which have been studied, there was no distinction in the upper class between the new families and the old. Because of the relative newness of these communities, it is to be assumed that an "old aristocracy" had not yet had an opportunity to develop in these places. Nevertheless, the distinction between a "society" group and the upper-middle class was still made.

Below the top crust is the "common-man" level, composed of clerks, small tradesmen, foremen, and a few skilled workers at the top, and then moving down through the "respectable" working class to the very poor and shiftless at the bottom. The top of the common-man level is the lower-middle class, which reflects the moral precepts and way of life of the upper-middle-class group. They think of themselves as being like the upper-middle class but lacking the money to live like members of this group. " 'We poor folks' and the 'other poor people like us' make up the lower-middle class. But, 'it shouldn't be that way,' they think. 'The people who are up are there mainly because they have money,' they insist."[6]

The lower class of all the communities studied was made up of two more-or-less distinct groups: the "respectable" working class and the "shiftless no-accounts." The "respectable" working class constitutes the "poor, but honest" workers—mostly semiskilled and unskilled employees in industry, who work steadily and make a real effort to provide for their families. They are much less likely to ascribe any moral values to the social hierarchy that they observe in their own communities. The people who are "up there" are there simply because they have more money, not because they have worked hard, saved their money, and generally followed the principles of the Protestant ethic. Nevertheless, these people have aspirations in the American tradition, if not for themselves, at least for their children. Professor Warner has demonstrated clearly that they have "feelings about doing the right thing, of being respectable and rearing their children to do better than they have."[7]

At the very bottom of the social hierarchy are those persons who are completely economically insecure and lacking in a desire to get ahead. In one sense, they can hardly be regarded as being integrated into the community at all; in fact, they often show a disdain for the values of the upper classes and for the government and laws created

[6] *Ibid.*, p. 69.

[7] Warner, *et al.*, *op. cit.*, p. 15.

by these classes. Unlike the group just above them in the social hierarchy, they have no regard for the mores and institutions of the middle class.

On the basis of studies made in a number of communities throughout the country, a clearly defined class system of five or six levels is evident, as shown in Figure 5.

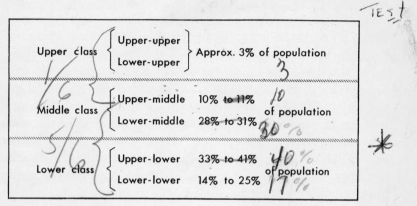

FIGURE 5.—Class Structure of American Society

Significance of Class System in America

There are a number of reasons why the class system in America is significant. First of all, it is not just a theoretical grouping of people ranging from those who have the most money down to those who have the least. This kind of grouping is simply a statistical exercise that has no bearing on the behavior of people. The important thing about a class in society is that class members tend to participate socially only with those who are in their class. They see members of their class as "people like us," "people who think and live like we do." While there is some overlapping of class membership and participation in most forms of organization and social activities, there always exists the awareness of the class status. Furthermore, to refer to a person's class position is really to refer to his whole way of life—the social environment which shapes his attitudes and expectations and which determines the way he lives and spends his money.

All these differences among the diverse social classes of our society do not mean that there are no attitudes which all or most citizens share, or that there is no participation whatsoever among members of several social classes. Earlier in this chapter we have reviewed a number of sentiments and basic beliefs which a great many Americans of all walks of life hold to be true. There is an American pattern which apparently cuts across class lines; and although it is variously interpreted at different class levels, it is nevertheless sufficiently distinct to bind our society together and provide the value system in terms of which we view and solve our life problems. In one sense, you can say that class attitudes are secondary to national sentiments, at least in times of important crises. Nevertheless, the significance of class attitudes and behavior should not be underestimated, for they determine our way of life in the workplace as well as in the community.

Although the different social classes do not frequently mingle socially, they do participate together in various civic and business organizations in the community. It will be noted that these organizations are relatively formal and are built around specific interests. Churches, associations (like the American Legion and the Chamber of Commerce), and fraternal orders (like the Moose, Elks, and Masons) bring persons from various class levels together in mutual participation and association. The middle class, however, represents the "great joiners" in our society. The upper classes and the lower-lower classes participate to a much lesser extent.

Industrial Organization and Social Class

It is apparent from the foregoing discussion that one of the characteristics of business and industrial organizations is that it brings together persons of varying class backgrounds and with diverse attitudes, sentiments, and values. In one Midwestern community which was studied, the range of classes represented in the main industry of the town was from the lower-lower class to the upper class. The distribution of workers in each class was as you would expect. The majority of the lower-level jobs were held by lower-class persons. Higher-level jobs were occupied by persons who were higher in the social scale of the broader community. Office workers, for example, were all lower-middle class or higher. Management was recruited entirely from the upper-middle and upper classes.[8]

The significance of this class distribution of employees within the factory or industrial organization hardly needs elaboration. Because of differences in values and sentiments among the several classes, misunderstandings can easily occur. An example of this is upper-middle-class management's tendency to use money rewards and financial in-

[8] See W. Lloyd Warner and Associates, *Democracy in Jonesville* (New York: Harper & Bros., 1949).

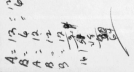

centives as a primary motivating force among rank-and-file employees. A good deal of this overemphasis on financial incentives can be directly attributable to management's middle-class background. By the same token, the failure of these incentives actually to provide motivation among many lower-level employees is evidence of the differing values held by the two classes. The typical factory worker is far more concerned with his relations with his fellow employees than with earning an extra dollar or two under a piecework system. Unless the entire group is motivated, it is unlikely that the individual worker will step out of line to increase his own take-home pay.

Management's concern with the moral virtues of hard work, thrift, and all of the other essentially good attributes of the moralistic middle class of our society can also create problems of misunderstanding and poor communication among the various class groups in our society. This is especially true in dealing with underprivileged workers who, often as not, are unambitious, irresponsible, and shiftless from the standpoint of middle-class standards. Studies have shown that the lives of many of the lower elements of society are geared to a life of insecurity. Being threatened with discharge or actual loss of job causes no great concern among these employees, as it would among middle-class employees. In fact, it fits in pretty well with what they expect out of life, living, as they do, in an insecure, unrewarding world.

The values which the underprivileged worker holds are not evidence of basic psychological disabilities or inferior capacities, as many management representatives and supervisors believe when confronted with the problem. Allison Davis points out that the attitudes and value systems of these employees are not a result of inferior breeding or bad stock. "The habits of 'shiftlessness,' 'irresponsibility,' lack of 'ambition,' absenteeism, and of quitting the job, which management usually regards as a result of the 'innate' personality of the underprivileged white and Negro workers, are in fact *normal responses* that the worker has learned from his physical and social environment. These habits constitute a system of behavior and attitudes which are realistic and rational in *that environment* in which he has been trained."[9]

Management's ability to understand and communicate with the lowest levels of workers is limited. However, the majority of workers are members of the so-called "respectable" working class or of the lower-middle class. Here management finds its values to be far more

---

[9] Allison Davis, "The Motivation of the Underprivileged Worker," *Industry and Society*, William F. Whyte (ed.) (New York: McGraw-Hill, 1946), chap. v, p. 86.

successful as a motivating force. In retailing, where a large percentage of the sales personnel is middle class in background or aspirations, the problems of management are considerably lessened. Employees in these organizations generally accept the values of management. The ideologies of management with reference to the operation of the business generally make sense to them. Furthermore, their behavior and interests make sense to management, too. The problem of two-way communication under such circumstances is much simpler.

Changing Patterns in the Industrial Community

The problem of class differentiation and its concomitant effects within the industrial organization itself is being further enhanced by changing patterns in the industrial community. Not so many years ago, the owner of the factory or business was not only the manager of the business but also a leading citizen in the town or community in which the organization was located. He was a man whom everyone knew. People, even in the lower levels of the community, felt close to him and recognized the role he played in the total community life. But more important than this, they knew he was part of the community and that he was controlled, partly at least, by the laws and values of the community.

Warner and Low describe this kind of owner-manager-citizen integration as it occurred in a New England town in the early days of the shoe industry:

> In the early days of the shoe industry, the owners and managerial staffs of the factories, as well as the operatives, were residents of Yankee City; there was no extension of the factory social structures outside the local community. The factories were then entirely under the control of the community; not only the formal control of city ordinances and laws, but also the more pervasive informal controls of community traditions and attitudes. There were feelings of neighborliness and friendship between manager and worker and of mutual responsibilities to each other and to the community that went beyond the formal employer-employee agreement.[10]

This same kind of situation has been observed more recently in a Midwestern town. Here the owner-manager was not only a leading citizen of the town and state but he was a person who was able to mingle on all social levels—in the local taverns, on the street corners, in the factory. He would be likely to meet some of "his boys" in the

---

[10] W. Lloyd Warner and J. O. Low, *The Social System of the Modern Factory* (New Haven: Yale University Press, 1947), p. 108.

local bar, get into a rousing conversation with them, and invite them to his own home for a "nightcap." This kind of behavior had a strong integrating influence not only within the factory organization but in the town as a whole. The owner-manager's ability to communicate up and down the line, to understand and be understood, was just short of phenomenal.

This pattern, though it still persists in many communities, is changing. More and more, the managers of industrial enterprise, even in smaller towns, are not born and bred in the community in which the enterprise is located. They are more often outsiders, brought in because of their experience and technical knowledge. As such, the problem of integrating into the community, becoming part of it, and wielding the kind of influence over rank-and-file employees which is characteristic of the owner-manager-citizen has become exceedingly more difficult.

The effects of this change in pattern is well illustrated in industrial conflict situations. In such crises, the lack of integration of the new management class becomes dramatically apparent. In Warner and Low's analysis of the strike situation in the shoe industry of a New England city, they show that the rallying point of the conflict was around the symbol of outside management. They say in this regard:

> As the vertical hierarchy of the factory system extended to executive offices in New York, even the local factory managers came to be, for the most part, "outsiders" and members of ethnic minorities. They had their factories in the town and some of them drove down to work in the morning and left at night. The workers knew or felt that the forces that controlled local men would not control these outsiders. The vast network of relations and memberships that made the former owners local leaders, as well as local manufacturers, had been reduced to a purely economic one of employer and employee. It was that and nothing more. It is small wonder that the workers during this strike "gave the horse laugh" to the managers when they talked about being good fellows.[11]

A somewhat similar situation was observed during a strike in a smaller Midwestern city where management was composed entirely of persons from outside the community. In this strike, the split occurred almost entirely between the outlanders and local people. During one phase of the strike, the management of the company attempted to move a truck containing equipment belonging to another company which had secured a court order demanding its delivery. While the

---

[11] W. Lloyd Warner and J. O. Low, "The Factory in the Community," *Industry and Society*, William F. Whyte (ed.) (New York: McGraw-Hill, 1946), p. 40.

truck was being loaded, a small group of pickets gathered at the gates. When it looked as though management really intended to move the truck, some one of the pickets called up a few of the boys who were not on the picket line. From all over the city, automobiles converged on the factory; many employees came with their wives and children, driving their automobiles in front of the gate and defying management to move the truck.

In the meantime, management representatives were inside the factory discussing the age-old problem of law and order. Someone thought of calling the local police. The sheriff was nowhere to be found. Finally, one of the deputy sheriffs agreed to come over; but, when he arrived, he did little more than exchange the time of day with the local union representatives, who were his friends and neighbors. Management never succeeded in moving the truck.

The battle cry of the strike eventually became: "We won't go back to work until they send the Hoosiers back to Indiana." It so happened that there was a large section of management which had worked together in a factory in Indiana. Striking employees were ready to send all management representatives "back to Indiana" whether they had originated from that state or not.

There has been an increasing concern in larger companies with the problem of integrating the management of local units into the community in which they are located. One company gives definite instructions to its managerial employees about becoming a part of the local community. Participation in community affairs is regarded as an important part of the manager's job. This same company is careful to pick managerial personnel for jobs in local communities where they are likely to fit in and be accepted.

In big urban centers, the separation of management and the workers in the broader community is even more complete than in the smaller towns. Executives in the large metropolitan centers no longer live in the communities where their businesses are located or where their employees live. Instead, they have concentrated in suburban areas or middle-class neighborhoods away from the industrial communities of which they are a part. As a result, in most industrial areas the industrial and business leadership plays little or no part in political and civic affairs. It is as though each group lived in a different social world, with no common meeting ground except within the formal system of the factory. It is not difficult, under these circumstances, to understand why the relation between management and the worker has been reduced to a purely economic one in many of these areas. Another important aspect of the industrial community is its constant turnover of residents, particularly in the large industrial centers and during a period of expanding production. Moving "up and out" is the pattern in American life. This means that industry must constantly recruit new workers to fill the lower-level jobs. With immigration from Europe being reduced to a trickle, compared to the early part of the century, most new workers are coming from the South and Puerto Rico. In many cases these migrants have different racial backgrounds from previous members of the community, besides being of a lower social class like all industrial migrants. The twofold impact of lower class position and racial difference has had a disintegrating effect on older communities. Social unrest and tension are common during the period of readjustment and integration. The same kind of problems have been reflected in many industrial organizations.

SUMMARY

We attempted, in this chapter, to elaborate briefly the key ideas about human behavior which will be used throughout our analysis of human relations in industry. We discussed the importance of looking behind the overt behavior of people to their underlying feelings and emotions. We saw that we could begin to understand the meaning of human behavior through the language of feelings. We found that the social aspects of human behavior were of special significance in analyzing human relations in industry. Since human beings live in a social environment, they redefine their basic needs into social terms. They strive to gain personal satisfaction and psychic equilibrium in their relations with others. As a consequence, the world around them takes on meaning in terms of its social significance to them.

We discussed the notion of social structure and saw that this structure defined and circumscribed the system of social interaction which develops among people. We reviewed the implications of these ideas about society and the social nature of man in reference to human relations in industry. Finally, we discussed the effects of external community factors on the social behavior of employees outside the work place. We discussed a number of the basic sentiments and behavioral patterns which people share rather broadly and which they bring with them to the workplace.

3. DIVISION OF LABOR

THE division of labor of an organization is logically related to its goals and its technology. It obviously is not by chance that every manufacturing organization has a production department, engineering department, and accounting department; nor is it by chance that the two principal functions of a retail store are merchandising and operation. These functions are essential to conducting the business. They are logical developments from the over-all goals of the organization and the way that organization is attempting to accomplish those goals. This, of course, is why the same types of organizations exhibit similar functions whether they are located in Chicago, Illinois, or Alexandria, Egypt.

In addition to its logical relation to the goals and technology of the organization, the division of labor is also dependent upon the size of the organization. The larger the organization, the finer the breakdown of jobs and positions in the organization. In smaller organizations, one man or one small department may perform a myriad of functions; in larger companies, these activities may be divided among several departments. The tendency very definitely is for employees and departments in larger companies to be responsible for narrower and narrower segments of the functions of the organizations. Organizations of the same type and size will generally have a similar division of labor.

EFFECT ON HUMAN RELATIONS

One of the important significances of the division of labor is that it places employees in a special set of relations with one another. Employees are bound together by mutual needs and by the demands they make upon one another, growing out of the jobs that they are called upon to perform. The production worker, for example, by the very nature of his job wants the necessary materials to perform his job efficiently when he needs them. Already you can see that he will be

49

making demands on the floor boys or central trucking or the supervisor to secure for him the things that he requires. If there is a breakdown in the flow of necessary supplies, he will react to it in one way or another. Likewise, the production worker wants efficient operating tools and equipment at all times. He is, therefore, continuously making demands on the maintenance workers and the setup men. Also, because of the nature of his work, the production worker is interested in securing a rate on his job which will permit him to earn a "fair" return on his efforts without "killing himself." A certain set of relations, therefore, builds up between him and the rate setter.

Stresses and Strains

Every job, every department in an organization, by the very nature of the functions which it is called upon to perform, develops a certain set of demands on other jobs and departments in the organization. Out of these demands grow many of the stresses and strains and the potentials for conflict which are characteristic of industrial organizations. Instead of worrying about the flow of work in the organization, management should be more concerned with the flow of demands, for it is out of these that most of the potential for conflict among employees will arise on all levels in the organization.

Studies by William F. Whyte in the restaurant business demonstrate clearly the significance of flow of demands to potential conflict among employees.[1] In his *Human Relations in the Restaurant Business*, Professor Whyte points out that the demands in the restaurant start with the customer, flow back from there through the waitress and pantry, and ultimately reach the kitchen. At each point along this chain of demands, friction can develop. It can develop between the customer and the waitress, the waitress and the counterman, the kitchen runner and the cook. If the personal needs of employees along this chain do not permit acceptance of the formal, organizational demands being made upon them, open conflict will develop and the efficiency of the organization will suffer. Thus, Whyte shows that the efforts of the waitresses in one large restaurant to initiate action and make demands on the men working on the counter resulted in conflict because the men, who were trained socially and culturally not to accept orders from women, had difficulty in adjusting to the demands made upon them by women in the work situation. In the same way, the

---

[1] William F. Whyte, *Human Relations in the Restaurant Business* (New York: McGraw-Hill, 1948).

kitchen runners, who were of very low social status in the restaurant, came into continuous conflict with the cooks who were of very high status. The cooks simply could not accept a low-status youngster shouting orders at them no matter how dire the need was from the work standpoint.

As the division of labor in an organization becomes more complex, it can be seen that the demands become correspondingly proliferated and intense. To take an example again from the restaurant business, the small lunch counter, compared to the larger restaurant, has practically no problem of co-ordination. In the small lunch counter the cook, counterman, and waiter are all one and the same person. In the larger restaurant, there may be four or more job positions between the cook and the customer. Furthermore, each one of these positions may be occupied by five, ten, or more different personalities. The potential for conflict is multiplied tremendously. In the small restaurant, there is no difficulty in seeing the relation of the demands of the customer to the activities of the organization. In the larger operation, however, the original demands of the customer come through so many hands that they become confused with other demands operating in the organization.

It is apparent from this that the potential for conflict among employees increases with the complexity of its technology and its size. In both cases the division of labor is increased and the demands intensified. Evidence of the effects of size and complexity upon the morale of employees can be found in morale surveys conducted by the authors and by others. In these studies, size alone was especially significant, larger organizations of the same type tending to have lower morale than smaller organizations. Complexity of technology and division of labor seemed even more important. In our surveys, factories generally had lower morale among employees than retail stores. Certainly foremost among the factors causing these differences in feelings and friction among employees was the greater problem of co-ordination which existed in factories as compared with retail stores. In retailing, the manager only has to be concerned with the co-ordination of merchandising activities and with operating. In the factory, the manager must be alert to the problems and demands of manufacturing, engineering, methods, maintenance, inspection, sales, and what have you. He must be able to co-ordinate these demands to develop a working team. In effect, the retail store manager is running a two-ring circus, while the factory manager is confronted with six or more rings. Unfortunately, also, he often is not sufficiently well trained to administer as complex an organization as this. However, given the same caliber and quality of management, employees of retail stores will always have higher morale than factory workers simply because the potential for friction is so much less.

Types of Relations among Departments

Important also to the potential for conflict among employees are the types of relations which exist among departments. Several dimensions are important here. One is the actual extent of relations which exist. It is apparent that some departments or groups of jobs are in continuous relations with one another and that others practically never come in contact. We have seen some organizations where departments exist side by side but with no functional relationship between them at all. The potential for conflict in such cases is, of course, practically nil. Other organizations constitute an intricate web of relations so that each department is variously related to practically every other department in the organization. The potential for conflict here is considerably incremented.

The nature of the relations which exist between departments is also exceedingly important to the potential for friction among employees and the type of problems which will arise. The authors have been able to distinguish four such relations which appear to characterize all organizations. These will be discussed in the following paragraphs.

LINE RELATIONS

The line organization of any company is usually thought of as that department or set of departments which is involved directly with the principal functions of the company. In a factory, the production departments represent the line organization. The sales department may represent another line. In a retail store, the merchandising and selling functions are the line activities. In a restaurant, the flow of work from the kitchen to the customer is the line. All other activities in the organization are more or less built around the main line of work and are auxiliary to it. However, the distinction is not always clear. A developmental engineering department may, in one sense, constitute a line activity even though it is generally thought of as a staff activity. The development of new products is, of course, an important and direct function of any manufacturing organization; as such, it is not auxiliary to the production departments, and therefore is a line function. In general, a developmental engineering department is set off by itself in the organization. It comes into contact with the line only during the period of initial construction of the new product.

Another difficulty in defining line activities is that, within a staff department, there may be activities which constitute a line function for that department even though the department as a whole is an auxiliary activity. In a personnel department, for example, the employment procedure may be a line function within that department. The relations between employees working along that line will be similar to those between production workers. In the same way, in an accounting department, there is a line of activity which will relate employees in a certain way, one to the other. The important thing to remember here is that we are discussing the relations that exist among various jobs and departments. Whereas the department as a whole may be a staff activity, nevertheless, within it, there may be activities which are related as in any line organization.

The line organization develops a special orientation toward the rest of the organization because of the nature of its activities. Perhaps this orientation can be described best by saying that employees in the line at all levels feel that they are "doing all the important work" in the organization. Most other activities in the organization are thought of by this group as service activities of varying degrees of value to the line. What happens between various service and administrative control departments and the line organization will be discussed elsewhere. In this section, we are primarily concerned with what happens between line organizations and within a single-line organization.

Relations between Line Organizations

It can be readily seen that the principal source of friction and conflict between members of rival line organizations revolves around the question of who is doing the most important work. Since each line organization feels that its work is the most important, difficulties can arise whenever one makes demands on the other. The conflict which often develops between the sales and production departments of a factory is a good illustration of this. From the production department's standpoint, the sales department is forever going out and making promises to customers, either in regard to the construction of an item or to delivery dates, which "no self-respecting person, if he knew anything about production" would ever do. From the point of view of the sales department, the production and manufacturing divisions of the organization are always giving them a hard time because "they don't seem to realize that if the company doesn't get sales, there just won't be any production to holler about." And so goes the argument swinging back and forth, very often depending on how prosperous the times are—that is, if times are bad, sales are regarded as most important; if good, production gets the nod. Very often, too, the resolution of conflicts such as this one depends on the orientation of management. Studies have shown that some management is sales-minded and some production-minded, with very definite effects on the nature of the business that develops. It has been found that production-minded management is particularly interested in securing large, long-term contracts with big merchandising firms. This solves the sales problem for them and, at the same time, permits the operation of a relatively stable and efficient production organization. Sales-minded management, however, is not at all interested in large, long-term contracts but prefers smaller contracts with many customers. The reason for this is simply that the executive enjoys sales contacts. The more, the merrier! As one said, "If I had to give up selling, I'd just die." By the same token, such a company is less concerned with stable, efficient production.

Conflict can also develop between developmental engineering departments and production departments. Here the conflict is not so much a question of whose activity is the most important but of who knows the most about production. The engineer's knowledge is highly specialized and professional, generally gained through formal education and training. He is trained in general principles, while the shop-worker has the know-how that comes from actual and direct experience in the factory. It is apparent that there is potential for conflict between them that only careful handling can prevent.

In retailing, the two principal line activities are merchandising and operating. The merchandising organization is concerned with the problem of buying the right goods and selling them. The operating people are responsible for all the other activities of receiving and shipping the merchandise, control of store equipment and properties, problems of personnel, and so on. There is potential for conflict between these two line organizations on all levels in the store where the cleavage exists. The buyer, for example, may decide that he needs four more display tables and an additional employee in order to achieve the sales quota that he has set for himself. The operating manager, however, may decide that the store cannot spare him four additional tables and, furthermore, cannot increase its payroll costs at this time. So, the conflict starts—where it ends depends again on the orientation of management and on the economic times. Retailers tend to follow bullish and bearish trends like the market. In good times, any "wild" scheme in merchandising goes. But, in bad times, the close, tight operators reign supreme.

It can be seen that conflict between rival line organizations can arise over the two questions, "Who is doing the most important work?" and "Who knows more about the work that is being done?" Now we will turn to a discussion of what happens among employees within a line organization.

Relations among Employees in the Line

The essential feature of line activities is the flow of work. One person performs one operation and passes on the products of his efforts to someone else. The activities of these workers are generally logically connected, at least in terms of the job to be done. The separate operations constitute a series of interconnected steps leading to a final product. In relatively simple organizations, the employee can see the relation of his work efforts to the creation of the final product. He knows that he must receive work in process from his fellow worker, perform certain operations on it, and pass it along to the next person. He knows that he must keep up with the others or they will all fall behind. He sees the importance and significance of working together as a team. The work makes at least some sense to him.

It can be seen that, in simple organizations of this type, there is a potential for co-operation on the job. The problem of co-ordination is reduced considerably, particularly if the breakdown of jobs along the production line is necessary and sensible. However, in many organizations, the line is not nearly so simple and uncomplicated as this. The original self-explanatory logic of the line, which is understandable to everyone involved in it, becomes lost in a maze of complications. This can happen in two ways. First, the line of activity can become so long and the steps along it so minute in importance that the employee feels only his complete insignificance in the total effort. He is no longer working on a significant unit of production. Moreover, he shares his responsibility with so many others that his job seems small indeed. The logic of the line and the need for co-operation is, therefore, lost to him.

However, mere extension of the line and the overelaboration of steps along it are not nearly so bad as the complete elimination of the logic of the line. In a number of organizations, this has been done, leaving the individual worker isolated and performing completely meaningless activities. Perhaps the best way to describe this situation is by means of diagrams. In the set of diagrams shown in Figure 6,

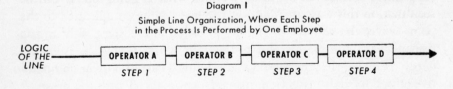

Diagram I

Simple Line Organization, Where Each Step
in the Process Is Performed by One Employee

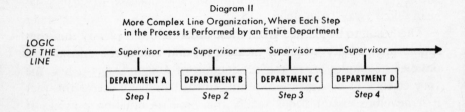

Diagram II

More Complex Line Organization, Where Each Step
in the Process Is Performed by an Entire Department

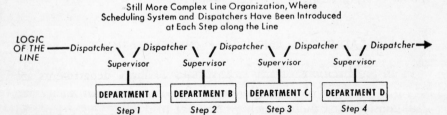

Diagram III

Still More Complex Line Organization, Where
Scheduling System and Dispatchers Have Been Introduced
at Each Step along the Line

FIGURE 6.—Logic of Line Tends to Be Lost as Organization Becomes More Complex

Diagram I represents a simple straight-line production setup. In Diagram II the organization has been increased in size so that each step in the production process is now performed by an entire department of employees. It can be seen that the logic of the line has been moved up to the supervisory level. The employees no longer participate in it; the potential for co-operation which existed when only one man occupied each step in the process is gone. Now the co-operation of employees at each step along the line must be secured by constant explanation of the logic of the process to them by the supervisor and by plain and fancy urging. The problem of co-ordination has been considerably increased.

Diagram III represents another complication of the line. Here the logic of the line has been broken still further by the introduction of dispatchers who guide and control the movement of raw materials and work-in-process through the line. Under these circumstances, the supervisors themselves begin to wonder what is going on. It can be seen that, in this way, the logic of the line can be complicated to the point where the activity of the organization makes sense only to top management. Employees down the line work almost in isolation, hardly realizing that the job they are doing is part of a great co-operative effort. In such a situation, management is faced with the prospect of trying to create team spirit among employees when the obvious and apparent need for co-operation and co-ordination of efforts has been taken away from them.

The lesson to be learned from these observations is plainly this, that simple line activity which is meaningful and enlists the efforts of a number of employees in the production of a significant item is the very essence of co-operation. Management can make use of this fact if it develops organizations where this kind of situation prevails. It can, however, completely eliminate the benefits to be gained by the self-explanatory logic of line activities either by extending the line too far or by isolating employees completely from it.[2]

ADVISORY AND STAFF ORGANIZATIONS

In all organizations of any size, various auxiliary departments are set up as an aid to the line. Among these auxiliary departments, we shall consider first those which give advice to the line and attempt to help with difficult problems where specialized assistance is presumably needed. Personnel departments and engineering departments partially fall into this category. The members of these departments are regarded as advisory experts from outside the immediate shop organization, who come in either when difficulties arise or when changes are contemplated. However valuable and necessary they may be, therefore, they are not the ones who ultimately have the responsibility for getting the work out. And as a rule, the more efficient the shop or-

---

[2] For an excellent study of the relation of work effort and level of co-ordination to employee morale, see Richardson and Walker, *Human Relations in an Expanding Company*, Labor Management Center (New Haven: Yale University, 1948).

ganization and the better it handles its own problems, the less need there is for the technical staff. Setups of this type almost inevitably lead to friction between the advisory and line organizations.

Each advisory or staff organization is prone to see the work of the line in terms of its own special functions and to be very critical of any failure of the line to follow its suggestions or directions. The engineer has an eye out for any possible improvement in equipment or methods, and complains that the shop foremen and workers are ignorant, stupid, and unco-operative about such changes. The personnel man is always on the watch for improper treatment of employees and complains, no doubt with some justification, that shop foremen are indifferent to the workers or object to following correct practices in hiring, firing, and promotion. Thus each directs his attention to only a limited aspect of shop activities, and each is looking for trouble or chances for improvement, since it is largely through such changes that he justifies his existence.

People in the shop, on the other hand, feel, with equal justification, that the staff members are all riding their own special interests, that they are more concerned with making a showing personally than with helping to get the work done, that they do not realize the pressure the shop is under, and, all in all, that they are not as smart as they think they are. The shop foreman has to deal with the job as a whole. He has to get the work out; and, by the way, he has to struggle with technical difficulties, enforce safety rules, and take into account dozens of other factors in everything he does. It is not surprising that he often resists suggestions from staff members and is annoyed when they seem to expect him to drop everything else when one of their specialists comes around.

Engineers and the Shop

Between the engineering organization and the shop, antagonism is especially common. The engineers usually look down on the shop-workers as being of lower status, uneducated, and "sot in their ways"; while the shop employees consider the engineers too theoretical, filled with book-learning, very impractical, and altogether obnoxious with their superior airs. When the engineers have the responsibility for developing better products or manufacturing methods, they are in the position of imposing changes on the shop almost constantly. Every time they make any improvement, it is likely to mean that the shop people have to learn new work habits or change their accustomed routines, and the established status systems and systems of interaction between workers may be upset. For example, an improvement in method which would eliminate certain skilled jobs would mean that some workers would have to change to other jobs perhaps at lower pay, and at the same time it might remove the goal that some of the younger men were working toward. Another change might result in new and tighter rates, which would mean either harder work or lower earnings for the group.

The various functions of the engineer all put him in a position superior to the shop people. He is either proposing changes which may be rammed down their throats whether they like it or not, or he is finding things wrong with the way they do their job, or he comes in with his superior knowledge to straighten things out that have gone wrong. Even if he is acting as trouble shooter, they would much rather handle the problems themselves than call him in, since they feel that too much reliance on him may be interpreted by their bosses as meaning that they cannot handle their jobs. (An engineer who sits around waiting for the line supervisors to call on him for help is usually not kept very busy.)

We do not mean to imply that there is always conflict and antagonism between engineers and the shop, because in many instances there are cordial and co-operative relations. In any shop group, however, there are innumerable tales, or we might say myths, illustrating the ignorance and impracticality of engineers, and frequent complaints about the new ideas the engineers dream up. On the other hand, every group of engineers has its own tales about the stubbornness and lack of co-operation in the shop. There is so much of this that we may conclude that there is inherent in the relation between an engineering organization and a shop organization a basic conflict, so that members of each group identify themselves with their fellows and are opposed to the other group.

Not just with engineers but in their relations with staff experts generally, the shopworkers and foremen are usually on guard. Even when maintaining friendly and co-operative attitudes, they are often on the alert to protect themselves against undesirable changes and resent any attitude of superiority. In many cases there is open hostility toward a staff man which shows itself in a negative attitude toward all of his suggestions, covering up anything which he might criticize, or finding reasons why co-operation is impossible. Sometimes the resistance to him takes the form of putting off the execution of any of his ideas, of not wanting to try things out, or of refusing to do anything except under direct orders from their superiors. At best, a staff man is in a difficult position. To get things done, he must always work through the shop organization, and especially through the foremen, who are the ones to put his ideas into practice. And, no matter how good his ideas may be, their success or failure often hangs on the willingness and ability of the shop foremen and workers to carry them out in actual practice. There are, in fact, plenty of cases in which sound ideas failed because of the indifference or opposition of the shop organization. And when he meets with active opposition, the staff man's position becomes even more difficult. He often feels blocked in everything he attempts; everything moves terribly slowly; and he finds himself in an agony of frustration.

An Outsider in the Shop

Another factor which adds to the difficulties of the staff representative is his position as an outsider in the line organization. Because of this he is always under suspicion. If he is coming right into the work situation, watching the work and the workers, in touch with what is going on, he is a potential threat, since he provides a channel of communication upward which is not controlled by the line. As a part of a staff organization, he can effectively short-circuit the line and carry criticisms of the line organization up to the top of the structure without detection. This is a very real problem to the staff specialist, too, because he must not only get his ideas across to the line but must keep his own boss informed of his activities and show what a good job he is doing. This means that he has to report on the problems of the line organization to show how he is spending his time. Inevitably, then, he becomes a channel through which shop problems are passed up through the structure and are short-circuiting the line. For example, a foreman finds that a certain process has gone wrong and he calls in an engineer to help straighten it out. The difficulty seems to lie in some short cuts which the workers have been trying to get away with, and the foreman would hate to have his boss find it out, as he would be blamed for laxness in his supervision. So the foreman says nothing up the line and hopes that he can get by. The engineer, however, tells his boss what he has been doing. They discuss the cause of the difficulty, and his boss complains that they are spending too much time fixing up things that would never happen if the shop foreman followed the engineering instructions. The next day, in talking to the superintendent of engineering, he uses the incident as an illustration of the kinds of unnecessary difficulties they have to deal with. The superintendent of engineering, when lunching with the manufacturing superintendent, asks him why he cannot make the foremen follow instructions, and recounts the incident. The manufacturing superintendent then puts his subordinates "on the pan," first for letting such a thing happen, and second for not keeping their superiors informed on what is going on so that he has to learn about his own job from outsiders. Such a situation seems to justify shop suspicion of staff experts and shows just how much of a threat to the shop they may be.

Judging Staff People

The problem of justifying their existence, of showing that the work they are doing is actually worth the expense, is often a serious problem, especially with large staff organizations. The individual members, as well as the organization as a whole, often show concern as to how management evaluates the organization or how the superiors judge the individual. An engineering organization may be judged by the number and value of the improvements they introduce, or by the number of problems they solve. A safety organization may be judged by the decrease in accidents. And since much of the showing they make depends upon the acceptance and co-operation of the shop organization, they are likely to feel that their success is blocked by the indifference and obstinacy of the shop. In some cases the relations with the line are seriously affected by the manner in which the staff people are judged either by their immediate superiors or by top management. For example, an engineer whose job is evaluated on the basis of the improvements in shop equipment and methods which he develops may find that he is competing with shop-workers or foremen. Engineers are often accused of stealing bright ideas from shop people and presenting them as their own; and engineers say that the shop people do not have the technical knowledge to make even a really good idea work and that their ideas would never amount to anything without the engineers. In one instance a shopworker developed a simple but important improvement, submitted it through the plant suggestion box, and received considerable recognition. The engineer who had been assigned to developmental work in that department was called in by his superiors and bawled out for not making the improvement himself. As he told it to a friend, "I was told that it was my job to make these improvements, and I shouldn't let the shop have all these bright ideas. It made our organization look bad, especially when such obvious improvements got by us." Inevitably, such attitudes lead to competition rather than co-operation.

Desire for More Authority

Because of these conditions, the staff experts are apt to feel that they should have more power and authority to force the shop to accept their ideas or to co-operate in their work. They are also prone to react to resistance by "going up the line" with complaints and demands for co-operation. Almost every staff man at times dreams of being able to demand the co-operation of the shop foremen and workers. And almost everyone has at times been guilty of going over the heads of the shop foremen with complaints and criticisms. Unfortunately, there is no authority that can force co-operation, and any such attempts to force it tend to increase the difficulties. An example of this was seen in the case of a very unpopular safety engineer who always had an authoritative manner toward the shop foreman. He would inspect a department, list everything which he could find wrong, and then, instead of taking it up with the foremen and letting them straighten things out, he would go higher up and report on the terrible conditions. He himself was always complaining about the un-co-operative attitude of the shop. He complained that there had to be a club over the foremen to get the safety rules enforced and that he could not understand why management did not back him up more. As a result, the entire shop organization disliked him. They did not want to have him around; they never asked his advice or told him anything. On one occasion he brought a division chief down to inspect the shop on a Saturday morning when the place was shut down and the foremen were not present. Apparently the division chief felt that he could not refuse; so he accompanied the safety man, who listed every instance of poor housekeeping, safety hazards, improper machine guards, and so on. On Monday morning the division chief had a meeting of his department chiefs and foremen and told them of this inspection. The entire group was furious, even though the division chief told them that he understood the situation and was not criticizing them, that he was just cautioning them to try to improve conditions before they all got in trouble. They felt very strongly that the safety man had been snooping behind their backs and had not given them a chance either to correct or to justify the conditions before calling in the division chief.

While the desire for more authority is especially strong at the lower levels of the staff organization where members are in direct contact with the shop, there are similar feelings at all levels. There is a tendency, therefore, not only on the part of the individual experts but of the whole organization, to be pressing management constantly for more and more authority and power. Then, too, since each organization is concentrating on its own specialty, all are constantly struggling to increase their effectiveness in their own field. This often results in a tendency for each staff group to try to increase its size, to add more and more specialists, and to impose more and more of its point of view upon the entire company. This leads to a lot of competition between staff groups, even though they have quite different functions. Each is likely to be critical of the others, skeptical of their value, and jealous of any group which seems to be getting unusual recognition or growing rapidly.

Internal Structure of Staff

In their internal structure the staff organizations tend to be quite different from the ordinary shop organization. Even in very large plants the staff organizations are much smaller than the shop units and usually have a shorter supervisory hierarchy. Individual engineers, for example, may report directly to a department chief without the intervening supervisory level, or the department chief may report directly to the plant manager. Furthermore, the number of individuals reporting to any one department head are much fewer than in the shop, so that each individual has much more contact with his immediate superiors and even with higher levels. This has the effect of bringing the individuals closer to the higher supervisory levels, often develops feelings of being close to management and of identification with management and its objectives, and generally adds to their feelings of superiority.

Because of the nature of their work, the staff men are apt to have more formal education than people at comparable levels in the shop organization. They often have college educations and even graduate training and are generally looked upon as being superior in intellect to the foremen and workers. The need for special technical training means that people are usually recruited for staff jobs from outside the plant rather than from the shops. As a result, there is no channel through which the shop people can rise from the ranks. This means that the staff organizations are differentiated from the shop not only by their functions but also by the kind of people who are selected to perform these functions.

This selection process tends to bring in at the bottom of the staff organizations a group of young college graduates, often with degrees in engineering or science, thoroughly drilled in the logic and point of view of their particular field. These newcomers usually run into difficulties in their relations with the shop. There are the young engineers, for example, often fresh out of college, who are in constant contact with the shopworkers and supervisors and who try to give them technical assistance. And there are the young personnel men, often without actual factory experience, who try to tell the old-time shop foremen how to handle personnel problems. Being young and ambitious to make a showing and get ahead, these young experts tend to become very aggressive toward shop people, to be critical, and to indulge in pleasant daydreams of having the authority to "tell that stubborn old so-and-so in charge of the X Department just what he has to do and no back talk." Inevitably the experienced shop people look upon these as "not-yet-dry-behind-the-ears youngsters," long on book-learning and short on judgment, who are more interference than help. In their turn, the young people feel constantly frustrated in their efforts to put their knowledge to use; and in their attempts to get the shop to change its ways, they feel that they are beating their heads against a stone wall. They look upon themselves, furthermore, as future executives, as the cream which is bound to rise to the top. This tends to strengthen their feeling of being part of management and their acceptance of management's aims and point of view. At the same time, it makes them impatient with the shop people, those "unintelligent" people who do not accept the ideas and reasoning which to the young experts are so clear as to be obvious. They are often impatient, too, with the slow processes of advancement and part of their feelings of frustration are translated into antagonism toward the shop organizations which block their ideas and prevent their getting suitable recognition.

In some staff organizations which have been well established over a long period of time, there may be two groups of people at the lower levels. One is a group of older people who have been in the organization a long time but who have no college training. Often these people have been brought in from the shop in the early development of the staff organization because of their practical knowledge of shop work. They may be experienced mechanics, tool- and diemakers, or others with extensive practical knowledge and skill. Their limited technical training, however, in many cases serves as a barrier to further advancement, and they remain for years at the lower levels in the staff jobs. The other group is composed of young people like those just described above, highly trained specialists, often just out of college, who start at the same level as the old-timers. They usually advance rapidly because of their education. These two groups are generally mutually antagonistic and split the organization in two. The non-college old-timers feel that their practical knowledge is not given adequate recognition, and the college group are scornful and impatient of them because "they don't know anything and haven't gotten anywhere." The older group tends to be antagonistic to management—or at least toward the top of the staff organizations—and does not share in the feeling of identification with management and acceptance of its logic to the same extent as the younger fellows. Often they identify themselves much more with the shop and sympathize with its general antagonism to "the young punks out of college who don't quite know what the score is."

Personnel and the Line

The personnel department often finds itself in somewhat the same position as the engineering staff in its efforts to have its ideas and suggestions adopted by the line organization. Like the engineering people, personnel representatives deal with a special problem which is just one of the concerns of the line supervisor. Furthermore, because of their specialized training, they can observe all sorts of personnel mishandlings in the line organization. They are, therefore, considerably troubled about the lack of ability shown by line supervisors in their handling of human relations. These same supervisors, however, often feel that the personnel department wastes its time with "Sunday school stuff" and has no awareness of the practical problems of running an organization.

In some respects, the personnel department is in an even more difficult spot than the engineering department. The work it is doing is usually less well established in the thinking of top management. As a consequence, it is much more concerned with its status in the organization as a whole. Much of the work of personnel departments is designed to impress management that it has a job to perform. This work takes the form of projects of various kinds so that something can be shown management whenever questions about personnel activity arise.

Whether or not these projects contribute in any way to the over-all efficiency or well-being of the organization is often not a consideration.

Like other staff departments, personnel departments frequently attempt to take over various functions of the line in order to insure that personnel matters are handled correctly. Very often this usurping of line functions is accomplished by the establishment of red tape and procedures covering personnel handling. When everything of this nature must clear through the personnel department, the line becomes saddled with red tape and loses its ability to make important decisions with reference to the employees that it is supervising. The personnel department under these circumstances ceases to play an advisory role in the organization and is actually performing administrative functions for the line.

Wastes are a big problem of organizations — take this on as a project.

4. DIVISION OF LABOR—CONTINUED

SERVICE ORGANIZATIONS

Nature of Service Organizations

SERVICE departments differ from advisory departments in an organization in that they perform some direct and needed service for the line; their work is tangible and necessary. Unlike advice, these services cannot be turned off and on by the line. The line has to have them. A department like the maintenance department in the factory falls into this category. Employment activities in the personnel department are of a service nature, and the purchasing department is also a service organization. Warehousing, customer delivery, mechanical repair units, receiving—in fact, practically all nonselling departments—are service activities in retail stores.

It can be seen from the nature of service departments that problems of various kinds can arise between these organizations and line departments. A number of these problems hinge on the fact that the line departments initiate action for, and make demands on, the service organization but, at the same time, do not have authority over it. Although the service organization must meet all reasonable demands made upon it and cannot easily refuse a request for service, nevertheless it can decide when it will meet these demands. Many intense conflict situations in industry revolve around this crucial issue. Because the line cannot obtain services when it feels that it needs them, it accuses the service department of hampering and bottlenecking production. It takes the attitude that the service organization does not have the interests of various line departments at heart. The service department, on the other hand, is of the opinion that the line department has a interest only in its own problems and is not at all concerned with the over-all problems of the organization.

Problem of Scheduling

The proper scheduling of service is, as a matter of fact, a real problem for service departments. It actually is difficult to determine which

67

department has the greatest need for service and should come first. There are various ways of handling this problem of scheduling. The simplest is, "First come, first served!" But there are always special requests, and handling those is usually a headache. Very often, the determination of who should come first is made in terms of the relationship between the service department supervisor and the supervisor making the request. If this relationship is friendly, then the service department supervisor is likely to give his friend priority. Cries of favoritism are thereupon heard ringing throughout the line organization. Another basis on which priorities are granted is in terms of who screams the loudest. Under such an arrangement, the supervisor who is most capable of dramatizing his need for service and who shouts loudest for help gets what he wants. This situation lends itself neither to good feeling nor well-balanced service activities.

Management on higher levels is in a position to gain priority for its pet projects over any lower-level demands. Top-level administrators, as a consequence, are often impressed with their own leadership ability because they can get things done so easily while lower-level supervisors struggle around with the simplest of problems. One manager thrived on this evidence of his ability. "Why can't these foremen get anything done around here?" he was frequently heard to say. "I told Pete two weeks ago to get that junk cleared out of his end of the department. Today, I finally had to do it myself. Called the maintenance department, and they had it out of there in two hours. You'd think these foremen would exercise a little initiative." Of course, the facts of the matter were that Pete had made the same request of the maintenance department on three occasions, and had practically pleaded on bended knee; but all he had gotten were promises which were never fulfilled.

Because service departments are on the receiving end of the demands constantly being made in the organization, a certain frustration develops. No one likes to be told incessantly to "do this and do that." It is like living with a nagging wife; even the most docile husband will snap back on occasion. Very often service department employees are quite critical of the line organization. This is true because usually the service employees are experts in their own field, and they can see careless mistakes and poor planning in the line organization which result in more work for them. "Why don't they take care of this equipment? They must beat this stuff with sledge hammers," is one remark not infrequently heard. Or else, "You'd think they'd plan their work better. They wait until the last minute and then expect us to pull them out of a hole."

Effect of Different Lines of Authority

The problems between service and line organizations are considerably enhanced and magnified whenever each organization reports through a different line of authority. Under these circumstances the line department cannot easily get the help of higher authority in securing services which it feels are necessary. Furthermore, the service department is not close enough to the line department to understand its problems fully. In one manufacturing organization, the maintenance department reported directly to the general manager of the factory. The plant superintendent had no authority to demand service for the production departments. Actually, the relationship which developed was unfair to both supervisors involved. Throughout the line departments, there was considerable criticism of the maintenance superintendent. They felt that he played favorites, continuously and unfairly criticized the line, and carried stories to the general manager. In one sense, these criticisms made by the line organization were true. The maintenance superintendent was in a position to observe many of the mistakes and problems of the line organization. Furthermore, he was in a position to carry his views direct to the top man in the organization who, in his turn, was eager to receive them and use them to stimulate line supervisors to greater effort and improved skill on their jobs. The pattern was not, however, organizationally sound and was finally resolved by placing the maintenance department under the direct supervision of the plant superintendent, who was also in charge of manufacturing.

A similar situation occurred in a merchandising organization. The functions of this organization were to buy, receive, store, and distribute—at the proper time and in the proper quantities—soft-lines merchandise to retail stores throughout the country. Most of the lower-level activities in the organization, of course, were devoted to the receipt, storage, and distribution of merchandise. Originally, each merchandise department was set up to mark and ticket its own merchandise, then to store it, and finally to assemble it for distribution to the various stores in accordance with a centralized distribution plan and also in accordance with special requests from the stores. Under this setup, the merchandise department was able to work together as a unit in meeting seasonal demands and any special requests from the stores.

However, the operating division of the organization sold management on the idea of centralizing all marking and ticketing operations. This was going to improve the efficiency of these activities by bringing all employees performing the same functions together in one place, scheduling their work more intelligently, and utilizing their time more completely. When this was accomplished, the new marking and ticketing department became a service department with reference to the original merchandise departments. On routine orders, all went well; but the moment the merchandise departments started making demands for merchandise out of its proper order, the fight started.

Usually the requests for special handling were made by one of the girls from the merchandise department involved. These girls were placed in the position of attempting to initiate action for the supervisor of the new service department. The results were appalling from a human relations standpoint. First, the supervisor did not, under any circumstances, like to have his system for handling incoming merchandise disturbed. Special requests meant bringing in merchandise out of order, with all the extra work and diminished efficiency that this involved. Second, he certainly did not intend to have his neat, well-organized department thrown out of gear on the say-so of some little "pipsqueak" from another department. After all, he reported through the operating department, which was primarily concerned with efficiency and saving money, "If you let the merchandising departments push you around, why, they would be asking for special handlings all the time," etc., etc. The end result was that the girl went sobbing back to her own supervisor and he emerged forthwith to do battle for the honor of his departmental womanhood (not to mention his departmental needs). The argument that followed, and the shouted accusations and counteraccusations which accompanied it, was dramatic evidence of the problems which line departments can become involved with in their relations with service departments.

CONTROL ORGANIZATIONS

Activities and Functions

Accounting or cost control, rate setting, and inspection comprise another group, which may be thought of as control functions. Except in large concerns, these are not usually set up as three separate and distinct organizations. On the basis of their functions, however, we shall discuss them here as three types of control systems, without regard to their exact positions in various plant organizations. These control organizations do not actually control operations in the shop directly, but they supply the basis for management's evaluation and control of shop performance. The accounting or cost control organization, for example, is constantly checking up on the performance of the shop and reporting to higher executives about it. Management relies on its reports to judge how well the shop is performing in terms of production and costs. The piece-rate organization has the responsibility of setting the rates which serve as a control over labor costs and which are another standard by which management evaluates the shop.[2] The inspection department must pass on the quality of the products, and its reports serve as still another measure of shop performance.

All these various reports on costs, quality, performance, earnings, and so on, serve to pull together in a highly condensed form certain information concerning the way the shop is operating, for the use of higher supervisors and management. On the basis of their interpretations of these reports, management judges how things are going, puts pressure on the shop organizations, and makes decisions regarding shop activities. The proper interpretation of such reports is one of the skills that executives must develop, since it is important for them to understand just what the figures mean in terms of the way the shop actually functions.

Anticipating Control Reports

Since it is evaluated largely on the basis of these reports, the shop is inevitably concerned about them, how they will be interpreted, how management will react to them, and what the consequences will be. Shop supervisors want to be able to anticipate all such control reports. They want to know, at least approximately, what is going to go up the line, especially for those reports which are most used by management. Supervisors are also interested in understanding the

[1] Almost invariably, even in small plants, there is an accounting system which is separate from the shop organization. Inspection, however, is usually part of the shop. Rate setting usually comes under the accounting or engineering organizations, and only rarely achieves the status of a separate organization.

[2] The functions and problems of rate-setting organizations will be discussed in a later chapter on wage systems.

methods by which the figures are gathered, so that they may keep alert for any errors and, when possible, control the figures themselves. In other words, the shop bosses want to know just what the reports will mean to them and how to beat the system. As we shall see in a later discussion of piece rates, the foreman often tries to control the job in order to maintain straight-line earnings, as a means of protecting himself from criticism or questions from above. The same is true of any other report which goes up the line; if it is used as a control report by management or if it is examined and questions asked about it, the foreman tries to see that only harmless figures go up. In the case of reports which go in on regular dates, for example, such as monthly reports, a foreman likes to know about where his department stands before the report is compiled, so that he can try to correct any adverse conditions. If a company is trying to cut down on raw-material inventory and places great stress on monthly reports of raw material on hand by departments, then just before the inventory period each foreman starts keeping his own private check on raw materials and tries to reduce his stocks to a minimum. Once safely past that period he will let his stocks build up again.

If the foreman can anticipate any such reports, he can not only plan his work so that the figures will be what his superiors like, but, in case of adverse changes or any conditions which might be questioned, he can prepare his answers safely in advance. Thus, if he sees that his group will show a drop in piecework earnings which he cannot avoid, he will have his explanations prepared even before the earnings report is released. In many cases, he not only prepares his story but passes it up to his boss, so that he, in turn, knows what to expect and what answer to give. In fact, it is considered very important that the foreman warn his boss of any important changes which will appear on any reports. This is then passed up the line for at least a few levels, so that when the big boss gets the report, everybody is ready for his questions. In that way all levels can show that they are on top of their jobs and know what is going on in their organizations.

This need to anticipate the reports often leads to a lot of informal record keeping on the part of the foremen. In some cases a foreman himself may keep a few records which give him the needed information, but on other jobs there may be so much work that he has a clerk just for this purpose. In one company where piecework earnings reports were used as an important control, it was informally expected that the foremen pass on their estimates of the earnings for their groups a few days before the actual accounting figures were released. A study of this company showed that every foreman had some form of informal records, usually duplicating in a rough way the actual accounting records and requiring as much as the full time of one clerk for each department. In other words, there were two sets of records of piecework earnings, one the extremely accurate accounting figures and the other the rough records from which the foremen made their estimates. While the informal records seemed rather unnecessary and quite expensive, the foremen felt that they needed them in order both to control their groups and to warn their superiors as to what to expect at the end of the month. These needs are so great that there is probably no way to eliminate completely this kind of informal record keeping.

Accounting and Cost Control

The systems of accounting and cost control arise directly out of the economic logics. These systems provide a method by means of which practically everything—the buildings, machines, tools, materials, labor, and so on—is reduced to a common denominator of dollars and cents. Thus they provide a basis for comparison of the most diverse activities or for combining them in various ways. In effect, they provide a means for adding horses and cows to bushels of oats and bales of hay, or for comparing one to another. Thus through a cost report, management can compare the performance of the department making heavy castings with that of the final assembly department, or it can combine them all into one report to show the performance of the entire plant for any given period. This seems rather obvious and is usually taken for granted, but back of all cost control lie a number of assumptions which have their effect upon the way people act on the job.

Because cost reports are frequently used as a sort of score sheet for the shop organization and its segments, the supervisors tend to run their jobs with one eye on these reports. If labor cost per unit of output appears on the reports, the foreman watches his labor costs; and as long as they stay within limits acceptable to higher management, he feels at ease; when they go beyond those limits, he tries to dig up an acceptable excuse. Thus such reports set the operating goals for the shop and set the standards of proper performance. As a result, we see foremen and higher supervisors devoting their attention to meeting the requirements of the score sheet rather than to actually improving the job. As long as these requirements are met, they seem quite willing to coast along keeping everything stable. In fact, we may conclude that the average shop organization tends to seek stability—to level off and hold everything steady—and does not have within itself the pressure to lift performance to higher levels. Top management, however, as we have seen, is always concerned with raising the level of performance and uses the cost reports as a pressure device to stimulate the lower supervisors to this end. These supervisors, in turn, often react by working out devices to protect themselves from this pressure with a minimum of disturbance to the equilibrium of their organizations. For example, we see foremen juggling the records or shifting people around to cover up, when one part of their job is "going in the hole." Often the supervisors are not primarily concerned with doing the job the best or cheapest way, but with doing it in the way that will look best on the reports.

Although cost reports are a useful tool for management, it must be remembered that they provide an oversimplified picture of what is going on. To have a report showing that the cost per unit of output has increased 1 per cent over the preceding month may provide management with something very concrete and simple with which to put pressure on the manufacturing organization. Nevertheless, behind such figures lie all the problems and difficulties with which the organization has to struggle, all the delays beyond their control, as well as all their own mistakes in judgment. And if top management takes the cost reports as the sole measure of performance and gives no consideration to all the difficulties which may arise, the lower levels feel unfairly treated. This is generally recognized by top management; they know that to interpret the reports properly and to be fair in their demands upon the shop, they must be able to read between the lines and not just take the reports at their face value. This usually means that they must have some acquaintance with the way the shop works and with the difficulties it faces, and must keep informed as to changes in its situation.

Many companies use a budget system in which they make an estimate of the needs of each department and set up a budget based on these estimates. Thus, they make an over-all estimate of the needs of the business and the funds to be spent during a period, and then distribute the funds to the various departments. This may be further broken down into details of the way in which the funds are to be spent, such as: so much for direct labor, so much for indirect labor, so much for materials, tools, repairs, and so on. Under such a system, and especially where there is a detailed breakdown of the budget, each department operates within a framework of anticipated expenditures which do not always fit changing conditions. When management readily approves variations from the budget, this does not present much difficulty; but when it tries to adhere pretty closely to the budget, many problems arise. For example, if a punch press department has almost exhausted its monthly budget for tool repairs, it may be forced to delay necessary repairs until the next month. This often results in makeshift repairs by the department itself in order to save sending the tools to the regular toolroom, or it may mean using tools beyond their period of efficient operation. This, in turn, may decrease the output for those tools or increase the defective parts. This may lower the earnings of the operator or cause him extra trouble with the job, which, in turn, annoys him because he can see no reason for not having the tools repaired when needed. Also, such makeshifts often result in things being done in more expensive or less efficient ways, even though it does keep the budget looking right. In any case, having to subordinate the needs of the job to the needs of the cost control system is always annoying to the worker and the foremen, who are acutely aware of the inefficiency and waste of such practices.

While the whole system of cost control and its reports is a constant threat to the peace of mind of shop supervisors, there is rarely open antagonism and conflict between the two organizations. The cost control procedures are highly systematized and reduced to simple routines of paper work, much of which is done by clerks. These systems depend very little upon personal contacts between foremen and accounting people for the collection of data, which frees them of one source of possible friction. As a result, because there is little personal interaction, there is much less friction between the shop and the accounting organization than between the shop and the average staff organization. In some cases, however, the way the cost control system is set up gives rise to friction between segments of the shop organization. For example, where there is strong emphasis upon scrap losses, there is always argument as to who is responsible. Often defective work in one department may not appear there, but may cause work in some other department at some later stage to be junked. In such cases, there is always the argument as to who is actually responsible and to whom it should be charged. And each department is always suspecting the other of trying to do a little "chiseling" by passing on defective work rather than junking it when found, or by trying to pass the blame back to someone else. Thus, it is often found that the particular cost control system, or the emphasis it places on various items, has far-reaching effects upon the attitudes of the workers and the relations between various departments.

Since the accounting and cost control system, especially in large plants, involves a great deal of routine clerical work, these organizations are usually larger than the staff organizations and often parallel the shop organization in number of levels. In the large accounting organizations where much of the work has been reduced to simple routine operations, no great skill or understanding of accounting methods is required of the clerks. In smaller organizations, there is less routine work, and even the clerical workers may need to have an understanding of the system as a whole. In either case, the average clerical worker needs to know little beyond the mechanics of the accounting system itself.

The accounting organization offers opportunity for many of the younger people from worker families to move to the often-coveted white-collar or office status. Many of the jobs can be handled by any alert high-school graduate, and others may require moderate skill at typing or operating business machines, such as comptometers, calculators, or adding machines. This makes it relatively simple for any ambitious youngster either to start directly in this work or to prepare for it through brief evening-school courses. In the past, the desire for these jobs has been so great that most accounting organizations, as well as most office work, have a starting rate no higher, and sometimes even lower, than the starting rate in the shop.

To the youngster with college education, however, especially if trained in accounting, the average accounting organization is discouraging. If he comes into a large organization, he starts at low pay, is thrown into a lot of routine work which others with no college education can perform as well as he, and he feels that his talents are wasted. Furthermore, he is often working under supervisors who have little or no theoretical training but who have grown up in the organization and know its routines thoroughly. This gives him a feeling of isolation, of not having opportunity to display his learning and talents. A small organization is often more satisfactory, since it offers more variety of activity and more opportunity for contact with higher levels, which relieves some of the feeling of being completely lost in a huge organization.

Inspection

Inspection is another type of control which is also important to the shop and with which it has considerable contact. The inspector's job constantly puts him in the position of telling the shop what is wrong with its work. He points out mistakes and defects in the products and reports such mistakes to his superiors; and, in a piecework system, he directly affects the pay envelope. Also, in many plants his reports on quality are one of the control reports which top management watches closely and which are, therefore, a constant threat to the shop.

Because of these functions, there is likely to be a sharp cleavage and considerable friction between inspection and the line organization. The workers and shop foremen rarely regard inspection as a friend; they are apt to be critical of the way it does its job; they argue over its standards, and disagree with many of its judgments. This is especially apparent when inspection involves the judgment of the inspector rather than precise standards of measurement. In such cases the shopworkers and foremen are likely to complain that the inspector uses poor judgment, that he discards parts which to them appear perfectly adequate, or that he is trying to hold them to standards that are impossible to maintain. Of course, when inspection is primarily a matter of the inspector's judgment, he can be tough or easy on the shop; and, unless they question every judgment, they have a hard time defending themselves. A case of this was described by a foreman of a finishing department, who said:

We once had an inspector in here who was a terrible grouch and always made it as tough as possible. Once we had a job putting a baked enamel finish on some metal panels about five feet long and a foot wide. We would spray the enamel on one side, rack them up flat on a truck, and shove the truck into the baking oven. When they would come out, this inspector would tilt each one up to the light, and if he would see even one dust speck, he would send it back; said the specifications called for perfectly smooth finish. Well, our spray room and oven weren't in too good shape and it was almost impossible to get one completely dust free. It was crazy to be so strict; it was only a protective enamel for an inside surface that was never seen, but this guy didn't care. Finally we got the engineers to look at the job and they told him it was good enough the way we were doing it.

Inspectors often feel superior to shopworkers and express attitudes of superiority, which increases the friction between the two groups. Most inspection people feel that they are always fighting with the shop in order to maintain the quality of the products and the reputation of the company. They feel that the shop people are only concerned with their own selfish interests and want to make a showing in output or earnings at the expense of quality and that it is up to the inspectors to keep them in line. Furthermore, they often feel that the shop is not to be trusted but must always be watched with suspicion —attitudes which are often shared with other groups, such as safety engineers, cost control people, and rate setters.

The shop cannot feel that they are through with any job until it has been passed by inspection; but, once passed, their responsibility is ended. In many cases, they feel no concern for their work beyond getting it past inspection. If inspection is lax and passes products that will not work, that is no concern of the shop and may even be their good fortune. If they can "pull a fast one" and sneak some defective parts past inspection, that may even be considered a good joke on inspection. As a result, we often see considerable scheming by the workers, and even foremen, to "beat" inspection. When the quality reports are used by management for control, it becomes important for the shop to keep defective work down. One way to do this is to see that defective work does not go to inspection but, rather, that it is either repaired or junked before inspection sees it. Sometimes the department maintains its own informal inspection of the work either by the workers or by the foremen. For example, the foreman may make a rough check on the work, either during processing or before it goes to inspection, and, if there seems to be a lot of defective work, he may go over the whole job carefully. Sometimes he will sort over a bad lot of parts and send only the good ones up to inspection. In these ways he can keep his workers on their toes with regard to quality and keep some control over their quality reports.

Under individual piecework, inspection has an important influence upon the earnings of the individual worker. The work of each individual must be counted, and the inspector's records become part of the accounting routine by which the worker is paid. This tends to increase the possibilities of friction between the inspector and the individual worker and stimulates the worker to try to figure out ways of slipping poor work past inspection. The functions of piecework as a wage system and the problems involved will be discussed in some detail in a later chapter.

If, as sometimes happens, the inspectors and shopworkers are on friendly terms, the inspectors may help the shop make a good showing by turning back defective work without reporting it. In such cases the inspectors will call the workers' attention to any recurring errors, will send defective parts back for repairs or to be junked by the shop, or may even make slight repairs or readjustments themselves when they have time. These inspectors are always well liked by the shop and usually have little difficulty in getting the shop to accept their judgment. Sometimes this sort of alliance between workers and inspectors goes on even without the knowledge of the shop foreman and serves to protect not only the shop organization but also the individual worker from his boss. The extent to which such co-operation can flourish, however, is usually limited by the way the inspectors are judged by their own supervisors. In many cases the work of the inspector is judged by his reports of defectives found and by spot checking his work to see if defectives are getting past him. If he does not report any defectives, the assumption is either that he is not doing his work carefully or else that the shop is turning out such perfect work that it does not need inspection. If check inspections show that there are not any defectives, then they may decide either to do away with that inspection or put it on a sampling basis in which only so many pieces out of every lot are inspected. If they find the inspector has been working closely with the shop and turning back all the defectives without reporting them, they feel that he has somehow betrayed his own organization and superiors. In any event, he has to report some defectives in order to keep his boss from looking too critically at the job he is doing.

In general, inspectors rank somewhat higher than shopworkers; and inspection organizations, as a whole, have status superior to the shop organization. This probably arises partly from the fact that the worker is, in a sense, directly subordinated to the person who checks his work and decides whether it is good or not. Also, most inspection jobs are lighter and easier than the shop jobs, so that the inspectors can dress like the office workers. Because of this superior status, inspection work often offers a chance for a minor degree of mobility from the shop. It does not ordinarily rank high enough to attract people with special training or with a desire for office status, however, since its work is done in shop location and to the office people it still ranks with the shop.

INFORMAL RELATIONSHIPS AND ORGANIZATIONS

So far, we have been considering the groupings, divisions, and relationships which grow out of the formal organization and are largely defined by the way the organization is put together. In addition, there is the more spontaneous type of groupings which arises out of the daily contact of people. This "informal" organization is an important element in the whole structure and is one of the major objects of the social environment in which each individual spends his days.

Patterns of Interaction

When we speak of a factory as a system of human relations, we mean, in part, that the individuals in the system are brought together into frequent interaction with each other. This interaction is not a matter of random contacts but, to a large extent, has a definite pattern, and may even be a habitual routine. Thus, every person has a fairly definite pattern of interactions which relate him to certain others in the structure. Contacts outside of this pattern are generally infrequent and limited. Of course, much of the interaction is determined by the work itself, as, for example, the contacts between superior and subordinate for the purpose of giving instructions or communications regarding the work, or contacts between helper and machinist as a result of their working together. On the other hand, there are innumerable contacts which are not directly necessary to the work, such as morning greetings, chatting about outside affairs, joking and "horseplay," and gossiping about what goes on around the plant. These all go to complete the pattern of daily contacts and interaction which help make the factory an integrated social system.

When we look at all the human relations in a factory, we see that each person fits into a pattern in which he has a lot of contact with a few people, a little contact with some more people, and practically nothing at all to do with most of the others in the plant. In other words, people fit together into groups. Within a group there is a lot of interaction, and between groups there is little. Thus we can think of any organization as being broken up into a myriad of groups of workers—some large, some small, some following formal organizational lines, some groupings of people who work together every day, some groups-within-groups, and some embracing a whole plant division of workers. An individual usually has some feeling of belonging or identification with the group or groups into which he fits. He may hold attitudes of antagonism or friendliness toward certain other groups, or he may express beliefs and sentiments which are common to his group with regard to the work, the company, or anything else in the work environment. Thus we find that much of the work behavior of the individual is an expression of his place in the group or groups to which he belongs.

These groups are not all clearly defined or separated from one another, by any means, and there is a great deal of overlapping. For example, the six girls who work side by side on the assembly conveyor form a work group, and four of them may be a social clique who get together outside of the factory. At the same time, they all probably have a strong feeling of belonging to the department as a whole and have only very limited contacts with people in other departments. Going still further, they all probably feel themselves members of a still larger group composed of all shopworkers, as opposed to office workers.

Formal Organizations and Informal Relations

In talking to the members of each division of the organization, it is seen that each member has feelings of identification with his own particular division, usually has a high degree of interaction with his fellow members as compared with members of other divisions, and may express fairly uniform attitudes toward the functions and behavior of the members of others. In many cases, well-developed patterns of antagonism are found between such major divisions, with each being very critical of the others and defensive of their own organization. Generally, there is a sharp cleavage between the staff and line organizations, growing out of their difference in function.

Within each of the larger organizations, too, there are further subdivisions which, in turn, are groups. The maintenance department, for example, feels itself different and separate from either production or inspection, and usually has quite definite attitudes toward these other groups, although all are part of the production division. At this level in the organization, there is likely to be conflict between the production and inspection departments, arising out of the fact that inspection must pass on the work of the production department and decide whether it is acceptable or not. This frequently puts inspectors in the role of critics, and nobody loves his critics.

In one small factory some of these conflicts, antagonisms, and cleavages along organizational lines were observed in extreme form. An observer described the factory and some of its groups and discords as follows:

The organization described is one that has grown over a long period from a small beginning to a present group of about 400 employees. . . .

There are several vice-presidents in charge of departments, and some men heading up smaller departments who have not yet been given any title. . . . The many departments making up the organization are like separate nations, the department executives standing against each other, demanding more in the way of salaries for their people, and more in the way of service from other departments. This causes friction and rivalry between heads of departments and constant problems for the office manager and personnel director. . . .

Mr. K. is a vice-president in charge of the largest department—65 men and women. He does not seem to consider that he is vice-president for the whole organization; his department is all that matters. His people are higher paid than those in other departments. He thinks the service departments—typing, dictaphone, filing, mailing, etc.—operate for his benefit alone; and if their results do not suit him, he does not hesitate to tell them so, in no uncertain terms. The result is that there are really two organizations—K's department and the rest of the office. To illustrate, this year his 65 people are having their Christmas party on the twentieth by themselves, and all the other departments—300 people —are having theirs on the twenty-second. Mr. K. explained: "Mr X. [the president] knew I wanted a separate party, so he didn't insist on a general office party." The office manager commented: "K. could sell X. a gold brick any day. . . ."

Then there is the little vice-president who started as an office boy forty years ago. Great rivalry exists between this one and Mr. K. as to whose department makes the most money, which is closest to Mr. X., etc. For weeks they are not on speaking terms, and the slightest concession from Mr. X. to either of them is likely to start another war.

Even when conflicts and antagonisms do not actually exist, lines of cleavage tend to develop between organizations, so that their members remain as distinct groups. For example, in one instance two separate organizations each occupied half of a large room. In the center of the room, members of each organization were seated back to back at adjacent rows of desks, only a few feet apart (Fig. 7). In spite of the physical proximity, there was very little interaction between these individuals beyond a polite good morning or occasional comment. Al-

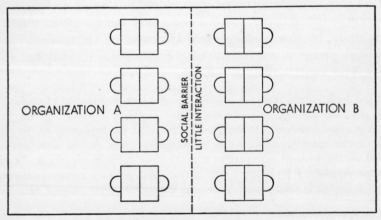

FIGURE 7.—Floor Plan of a Workroom

most never were there any long conversations or gatherings between members of the two groups. Within each group, on the other hand, there was a great deal of interaction both on the basis of the work and for purely social conversation. In this case it was apparent that the formal organization itself set up a wall between the two groups in spite of the fact that there was no apparent feeling of conflict, antagonism, or defensiveness. Furthermore, there was nothing in the attitudes of the superiors in either organization to prevent them from mingling. There seemed to be merely a distinct feeling of indifference of the members of each organization toward the others, with the result that there was very little interaction of any sort.

When there is conflict or competition between supervisors or superiors in different organizations, as, for example, in the case of the vice-presidents described above, the barriers between the members at the lower levels are strengthened. In such cases, subordinates tend to have feelings of anxiety over any contacts with the other organization. They wonder what their boss will think if he sees them talking to someone from the other group; they avoid social contacts which might be observed by the superiors; or they feel it necessary to explain any such contacts to the boss. The result of this is to limit all forms of interaction and to isolate the groups from each other, even though they may be seated almost side by side.

Cliques

Within the nonsupervisory group in any organization, there are forces acting to split it into smaller groups, too. Often such lines of cleavage may follow functional lines as in the case of a clerical organization in which typists formed one group and file clerks another. In one study, by Roethlisberger and Dickson,[3] of fourteen men in a small work group, it was found that the group was divided into two cliques. This was described as follows:

On the basis of the material just reviewed some conclusions can now be drawn as to the informal organization of this group of workmen. In the first place, it is quite apparent that the question raised at the beginning of the preceding section must be answered in the negative: these people were not integrated on the basis of occupation; they did not form occupational cliques. In the second place, it is equally apparent that there did exist certain configurations of relations in this group. With one exception, every record examined

---

[3] F. J. Roethlisberger and W. J. Dickson, *Management and the Worker* (Cambridge, Mass.: Harvard University Press, 1939), pp. 508–10.

seemed to tell something about these configurations. Whether the investigators looked at games, job trading, quarreling over the windows, or friendships and antagonisms, two groups seemed to stand out. One of these groups was located toward the front of the room, and the other toward the back. "The group in front" and "the group in back" were common terms of designation among the workmen themselves. The first of these groups will be designated as clique A, the second, the group toward the rear of the room, as clique B.

What was the membership of these two cliques? This question can be answered only approximately. Clique A included W1, W3, W4, S1, I1, and clique B included W7, W8, W9, and S4. W5, S2, and I3 were outside either clique. With W2 and W6, however, the situation was not so clear. W2 participated in the games of clique A, but beyond this the similarity of his behavior to theirs ceased. He entered very little into their conversation and tended to isolate himself from them. Much of his behavior suggested that he did not feel his position in the group was secure. He was the only wireman in soldering unit A who traded jobs with S4, the solderman in clique B, and he traded jobs with his own solderman more than anyone else. In so far as the social function of job trading was to differentiate wiremen from soldermen, this could be interpreted as meaning that W2 felt rather keenly the necessity of constantly emphasizing his position by subordinating the soldermen. Taking all the evidence into consideration, then, it may be concluded that W2 was not a bona fide member of clique A. W6 tended to participate in clique B. He was continually "horsing around" with the selector wireman and had relatively little to do with the members of the clique A. That he was not entirely accepted in clique B was shown in many ways, chief of which was the way in which clique B co-operated in resisting his attempts to dominate anyone in their group. Yet he participated in clique B much more W2 did in clique A. It may be concluded that although W6 tended to participate in clique B, he was still in many ways an outsider.

As a means of summarizing the results of this inquiry, Figure 45 [Fig. 8] has been prepared to represent diagrammatically the internal organization of the observation group. The soldering units into which the members of the groups were divided are shown by the three rectangles. The two large circles demarcate the two cliques. There were three individuals, I3, W5, and S2, who were clearly outside either clique.[4] The line around W6 has been made to intersect

---

[4] "Perhaps a word of caution is necessary here. When it is said that this group was divided into two cliques and that certain people were outside either clique, it does not mean that there was no solidarity between the two cliques or between the cliques and the outsiders. There is always the danger in examining small groups extensively, of overemphasizing differentiating factors. Internal solidarity thus appears to be lacking. That this group, as a whole, did have very strong sentiment in common has already been shown in discussing their attitudes toward output and will be brought out more clearly in the next chapters. It should also be said that position in the group is not so static as one might assume from this diagram. Had the study continued longer, membership in the cliques might have shifted. Also, if the group had been larger, or if the group had been allowed to remain in the regular department, it is quite probable that the people who appear as outsiders here would have formed cliques with others who had similar sentiments" (*ibid.*, p. 510, n.).

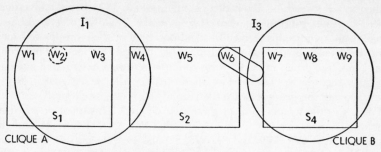

FIGURE 8.—"The Internal Organization of the Group"
"Bank Wiring Observation Room"

that of clique B to indicate his partial participation in it. The instability of W2's position is indicated by the broken circle around his number.

That the members of clique A regarded themselves as superior to clique B was indicated in many ways. Clique A did or refrained from doing things which were done by clique B. They did not trade jobs nearly so much, and on the whole they did not enter into the controversies about the windows. Clique A engaged in games of chance, whereas clique B engaged often in "binging." Both groups purchased candy from the Club store, but purchases were made separately and neither clique shared with the other. Clique A bought candy in small quantities, whereas clique B bought a less expensive kind in such large quantities that W9 one time became ill from eating too much. Clique A argued more and indulged in less noise and horseplay than clique B. The members of clique A felt that their conversations were on a higher plane than those which went on in clique B; as W4 said, "We talk about things of some importance."

Horizontal Cleavage

In many cases, too, we see horizontal lines of cleavage between the vertical levels within an organization. The most common point of cleavage of this sort is between workers and supervisors. This separates them into two antagonistic groups, with the workers feeling that it is necessary for them to unite in defense against excessively critical or demanding foremen or other supervisors. This defensive attitude of the workers causes them to avoid contacts and interaction with their superiors, makes them withhold information, cover up mistakes, restrict output, and devise a variety of protective measures. Foremen usually respond to such behavior by critical attitudes, avoiding social conversation, and restricting contacts to those required by the work. In such cases, we find contacts are kept at the "strictly business" level, and then they are filled with feelings of suspicion and criticism, so that the contacts are uncomfortable for both sides. Such horizontal cleavages are not, however, confined to that level but may occur at any point in the hierarchy. In some cases, foremen group themselves with the workers in opposition to higher levels. A striking instance of this was observed in the following case:

Department chief A was new to the organization, having replaced a man who had been very popular with both the foremen and the workers. A was very hardboiled in his manner, critical of the way the department was running and wanted to make a lot of changes. Foremen B and C had had long experience in the department, worked together well, and were popular with the men. The department had been running very smoothly; they objected to A's criticisms and rebelled at the changes. There soon developed open friction, with A in opposition to B and C.

D was a production control man reporting to the production control organization, but handling the planning and scheduling of work for this department. He was not of supervisory rank, but his particular job gave him status well above the ordinary office worker. Because of his job, he was well informed as to how work was progressing in the department. Also, he had once reported to A when A had been in charge of a production control department.

As friction developed between A and his foremen, interaction and communication diminished. The foremen admitted that they were always afraid of A's criticism and avoided him whenever possible. One of them said: "If he comes around, we find some excuse to be busy somewhere else. If he is at his desk, we stay out on the floor; if he is in one end of the department, we go to the other end. We never tell him anything unless he asks us and try never to discuss the work with him. We all went to a department party the other night, and if we were at the bar and he would come up, we would walk away."

As this blockage developed, A turned more and more to D as a source of information about the department. The foremen in turn reacted against D who, they felt, was carrying tales to A about the department and was, therefore, not to be trusted. They also felt that D was trying to gain favor in the hopes of

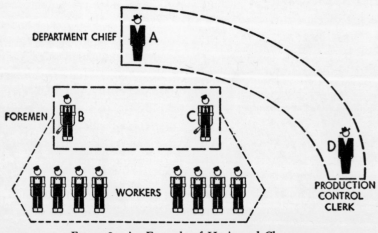

FIGURE 9.—An Example of Horizontal Cleavage

being promoted to C's job, since A had threatened to get rid of C if he failed to do a satisfactory job. As a result they would have nothing to do with D beyond what was necessary for the job. Thus the department was split into two antagonistic groups, A and D who were friendly and working together, and B and C who worked together and were friendly with each other but would have nothing to do with A and D. The workers were not directly involved, but they shared the antagonism toward A and were therefore loosely grouped with B and C whom they liked and trusted [Fig. 9].

5. AUTHORITY SYSTEM AND CHAIN OF COMMAND

As we have seen, the man-boss relationship is one of the basic elements in an organization. The concept of supervision in which one person directs others is fundamental to the system of division of duties and responsibilities. Basic, also, are the different roles and expectations for supervisor and supervised. Thus the supervisor has a primary responsibility for getting a job done. And he is expected to get it done according to the standards and requirements set by himself or set by the organization.

In addition, he has *secondary responsibilities* which control or restrict the way he must function in getting the job done. He may have to keep within certain costs, see that safety requirements are met, abide by union contracts or personnel policies, etc.

As a supervisor, he does these things by influencing those under him. He must direct them, judge them, motivate them, etc. And unless he can do that effectively, the job does not get done. However, the supervisor expects certain things of his subordinates:

1. They will accept his right to give orders, to judge, to direct
2. They will obey the orders, or at least try

In turn, the *supervised* have certain responsibilities and expectations. They have the *responsibility* for trying to carry out the orders. They expect that the orders will be:

1. Understandable
2. Possible
3. Reasonable
4. Related to their job and the work situation

They also expect that they will not be held accountable for failure if the job is not understood, is impossible or unreasonable, or is beyond their ability.

Now these expectations are basically part of our culture—we all grow up in a society which teaches us what these roles are and what we can expect of either supervisors or subordinates. Thus the idea

89

that the boss has the "right to give orders" is merely an expression of an established social code of behavior. Furthermore, the obedience of subordinates is also part of the social code.

We have, then, the situation in which the boss gives orders because his role, or his job, requires that he give them; and the subordinate obeys because his role requires acceptance of the boss's right to give orders.

One thing is clear—the obedience to the boss is not solely a matter of giving in to a superior force. While the boss has at his control certain power of rewards and punishments, he has far from absolute power. He can hardly "make" anyone do anything, and the extent to which he can try to force obedience is controlled by custom, by rules of the organization, and by the climate of opinion within the work group itself. Thus, in reality his authority over others rests not in the power which is placed in the position, but in the acceptance of that authority by subordinates.

In spite of the general acceptance of the authority relationship, it is clear that not any order nor any act of the boss is accepted. In fact, the problem of how to get subordinates to do what you want them to do is a constant problem with any supervisor. How do you get them to come to work on time? How do you get them to do more work? How do you get them to obey the rules? How do you get them to talk less and work more? The supervisor's primary preoccupation is with how to get people to do things. Nevertheless, careful observation in almost any work situation will show that there is a vast body of acceptance of orders and of general obedience to the rules and directives set by management and imposed or enforced by the supervisors.

Turning now to the chain of command, we see that it is through the linkages of this man-boss relationship that the top man is linked with the bottom. Every person except one within the structure has a boss; and every boss, in turn, has his boss, until finally at the top of the heap we find that rare and practically sacred individual, the president, the owner, the big-shot-who-has-no-boss. (Of course, even presidents have their boards of directors; but a director is a different sort from your personal boss, who seems to be ever present, asking questions and "breathing down your neck.") In most companies or factories there is one Big Boss and below him rank after rank of smaller bosses down to the very bottom, where we find those unfortunates who have no one to boss, those who are so numerous and so unimportant that their names never appear on the organization's charts—the workers.

The Supervisory Hierarchy

The whole structure forms a neat pyramid, with the Big Boss at the top and each rank of lesser bosses increasing in numbers as they decrease in importance, until at the bottom of the supervisory structure there is the largest and perhaps the most misunderstood group, the foremen or first-line supervisors. The whole forms a status system with all foremen having a rank superior to the workers, all the next level outranking the foremen, and so on.

Although each department chief outranks every foreman, it does not follow that a foreman will take orders from any department chief or even from any superintendent. (At least in theory they do not, but it is pretty hard to say "no" to a superintendent.) Instead, each person has his own personal boss to whom he looks for orders and instructions, for praise and criticism, for rewards and punishments. This extends on up to the top, so that each person is linked up to the Big Boss through a series of these man-boss relationships. This forms what is known as "the line of authority," or "chain of command" in the army. Since each level has more persons in it than the level above, each boss, as a rule, has more than one person reporting to him. This gives the fan-shaped pattern so well known on the formal organization charts, with a number of lines of authority merging at each level until finally they all merge into the supreme command of the Big Boss.

Just as the lines of authority converge toward the top of the structure, the lines of interest and attention converge also. In fact, everyone seems to be looking upward with his attention focused upon the people above him and especially upon his boss. His boss is the man who hands out the orders, assigns him to his work, gives him a pat on the back for a good job, and passes on a good word for him to the "higher-ups." And his boss is the man who can give him a dirty job to do, criticize him for doing it poorly, and give him a bad name up the line. His boss is his link with those above him in the structure. Thus the likes and dislikes of the boss, his moods and opinions, his comings and goings, his least comment and gesture, or the way he is distracted by that cute little redhead from the next department, all these are subjects of interest to his subordinates. Each subordinate is concerned over just how his boss feels about him. He wonders if his work is satisfactory, if he makes a good appearance, if his boss thinks he talks too much or not enough, or if he knows just what his boss does expect.

While each boss is thus the center of attention from his subordinates, he in turn is busy watching his own boss and wondering about him. As a result, he tends to look upon his subordinates in quite a different way. He rarely worries about their opinions of him; he does not lie awake at night wondering if he acted like a fool in front of them; he does not treasure their words of wisdom or of praise to be retold at the dinner table. He does not even remember that he is the center of their attention, and he is likely to be annoyed with them if they are upset by his indifference or demand a lot of his time.

Thus we have a series of man-boss relationships in which each person is intensely concerned with how his boss judges him and at the same time is busy judging his subordinates. Each is constantly looking at his subordinates, trying to determine how well they are doing their jobs and how they might do better work; and each is constantly being irritated and disturbed when they fall short of what he thinks they should be doing. At the same time his concept of the job is constantly being mixed up with what his boss will think and what *he* expects, until "doing a job" often becomes a matter of "doing what the boss thinks is good." Often this concern is not merely with what the boss expects in terms of the work itself but also with what he thinks is "proper" behavior. As a result, the boss at each level is constantly judging his subordinates not merely in terms of the work accomplished but in terms of "what would my boss think if he saw them?"

Now one fundamental concept of formal organization is that responsibility is drawn together into fewer and fewer hands as we progress from bottom to top of the organization. Thus, each supervisor has responsibility for the work of, and supervision of, several subordinates but has only one boss. As a result the man at the top has only a few whom he holds responsible and through whom his influence and authority reaches down into the depth of the organization.

Fundamental to this supervisory-subordinate relationship is the belief that superior status attaches to the one who gives orders. Thus the supervisor outranks his subordinates—in fact, he is referred to as the "superior." And "Who is your superior?" is understood to mean "Who is your boss?" This basic relationship establishes the fundamental status system of the organization, with each link in the chain of command seen as a unit of status. This is best seen in military organizations, where each position, or "rank," is clearly described along with all the appurtenances of title, insignia, uniform, etc. In such situations, each individual clearly understands where he fits, both in terms of status and in terms of giving and receiving orders.

This chain of command also forms the primary channel of communication for the organization. This provides the series of relationships through which the commands of the Big Boss are carried downward through the structure to its most distant points. And it is also up this line that information is carried back to the Big Boss, so that he is kept informed as to the progress of the work or of significant occurrences. Thus, one of the major functions of the line is that of providing channels of communication extending from top to bottom throughout the structure.

The Limitations

It is not, however, the simple, direct channel of communication that it is often thought to be. By its very nature as a linkage of man-boss relationships, it has a number of peculiarities which affect the quality, accuracy, and speed of its transmission. In fact, much of the transmission is so difficult that it is rare for a superior who is several steps removed from the work level to have a comprehensive knowledge of what goes on in the shop. Such a statement may offend the many top executives who speak with glowing pride of how close they are to the work level, of how their subordinates trust them and tell them all. In any sizable plant, however, where there are hundreds or even thousands of workers at the bottom, it is obvious that the man at the top cannot possibly be kept informed of every detail. His knowledge of the work situation must be limited to only certain kinds of details or general information. The movement of information from the bottom to the top must be limited, and what goes up must be carefully selected. Ideally, only those things are communicated to the Big Boss which are necessary for his decisions or which will help him to perform his special functions. Actually, this ideal is rarely achieved, and often important information never arrives at the top, or a lot of small details clutter up the channels.

Although this is a two-way channel with information moving both up and down, there is a striking difference between the kinds of information which go each way. From above comes, "The boss wants to know . . . ," and "The orders are . . ."; while from below comes, "This is what happened . . . ," "These are the difficulties . . ." and "Here are our successes or our alibis. . . . Rare are the occasions when direct demands move up the line from the bottom or explanations for failures move down from the top. (Remember that we are talking about the flow through the line of authority. Other systems of communication will be discussed later.)

The line as a channel of communication has an important function in two kinds of relationships: first, between each person in the structure and his job; and second, between each one and his boss. Probably everyone is aware of the first function and each one does communicate to adjacent levels the obvious things they need to know to do their jobs. Because this function of communication through the line is more or less effective, the system works, people do their jobs, and goods are produced. The second function of line communication is often ignored or misunderstood, however; and because it is overlooked, the man-boss relationship is often so unsatisfactory as to seriously impair efficiency and co-operation.

Communication Down

Because of the nature of the man-boss relationship, because each person is so dependent on his boss for recognition and communication up the line, because each person is so sensitive to his boss's moods, opinions, likes, and dislikes, there is often much confusion and misunderstanding in communication down the line. Since everyone below him is constantly trying to anticipate his wishes, trying to read his every word and gesture, the boss does not always have to put into words his ideas and what he expects of the job. But as a result of this extreme sensitivity to the boss, there are, in any work situation, frequent misinterpretations, and the problem of impressing the boss sometimes becomes more important than getting the work done.

For example, we see the superintendent passing through the shop convoyed by the foreman. Being in a jovial mood, he makes a conversational comment that "the girls seem happy this morning, the way they are talking and laughing." The foreman thinks, "Is he hinting that I shouldn't allow them to talk? Does he think I don't keep proper discipline? Those girls ought to have sense enough to stop talking and act busy when he's around. Maybe I better move Mary off by herself because she always gets the others started talking." The boss leaves, quite unaware that his comments have been interpreted as criticism. As soon as he is gone, the foreman bawls out the girls for talking and not paying attention to their work; he moves the Marys around, and it is weeks or even months before the final ripples of disturbance have died down.

Or, again, the foreman may come in some morning with a slight indisposition or with family matters on his mind, and he does not notice Joe, who is standing near the aisle. Joe, of course, was all set for the usual, "Good morning, Joe. How's everything?" Now he's all upset, and he thinks, "What's wrong? Wonder if he's sore about something. Did I do something wrong? Wonder if he saw me kidding with that new girl yesterday and got sore about that." For the rest of the day Joe is so busy trying to figure out what might be wrong that his mind is only half on the job. Finally the boss speaks to Joe about something in a very matter-of-fact way. Joe heaves a sigh of relief and says, "Boss, when you didn't speak to me yesterday, I thought you was sore about something." And the foreman thinks, "These guys are just like a bunch of kids. Just because you don't go around waving and smiling all the time, they think you're sore at them. I wish they would grow up and pay as much attention to their jobs as they do to those little things."

Distortion up the Line

At the same time, and also because of their sensitivity to the boss and their dependence on him, there is a good deal of distortion of the facts in communicating up the line. Along with a great concern for "giving the boss what he wants," there is a constant tendency to "cover up," to keep the boss from knowing about the things that go wrong or the things that do not get done. No one wants to pass bad news up the line, because he feels that it reflects on him. He is supposed to handle his job so that there is no bad news; he has to give his superiors the impression that he is handling his job efficiently. As a result, he does not go running in to tell the boss what a poor job he did or how stupid he was. That is, he does not unless he thinks someone else will get to the boss first with the story. And when he does have to break some bad news to the boss, he will probably have gotten everything fixed up or developed a good alibi for his failure. In this way, people at each level develop methods of defense, often complicated and ingenious, by means of which they protect themselves from criticism from those above. For example, we may have the following interchange between a department chief and one of his foremen:

DEPT. CHIEF: "How are things going in your place, Joe?"

FOREMAN: "About as usual." (*Thinking*, I wonder what's on his mind. Maybe he would like to know about our output.) "Looks like we will finish that last order for the Model X gadgets this week. If we do, we will beat our promise by about three days." (*Thinking,* He ought to be pleased to hear that, especially after our slow start on that job. Guess I won't mention the trouble we've been having with the Model B, where the inspectors threw out half that first lot. Think we have it licked, but I would rather not worry him with it until we are sure.)

DEPT. CHIEF: "That's fine. Glad to see that job out on time. How's the new Model B order coming?"

FOREMAN: (*Thinking,* Oh, oh! What brought that up? Maybe he's been talking to inspection. Thought Jim would keep his mouth shut. He knew I was getting that fixed up.) "Had a little trouble on the first lot. Final inspection found some of them out of adjustment. We had to make some changes." (*He explains the details of the change at length.*) "Think we have it licked now but won't know until tomorrow."

(*Thinking,* That ought to show him that I'm on top of my job. Maybe I ought to tell him about my argument with the foreman of the machine department yesterday, just in case Bob takes it up with his boss. Then my boss will want to know all the answers, and I don't want him coming back asking why I don't tell him about these things. And I don't want him to think I'm not trying to co-operate with the other departments.)

"Say, here's something that came up yesterday. You know Bob in the machine department furnishes us with the base plate for Model N gadget. Now that's a tricky job and he wanted to make a few small changes that would make it easier for him, I tried to show him why we couldn't use them that way." (*He gives a technical explanation.*) "I would have liked to help him out because he's been having a lot of trouble on that job, but I just didn't see how I could do it. Maybe the engineers ought to take a look at that model."

DEPT. CHIEF: "Yeah, you're right. You couldn't do anything. If Bob's boss comes to me, I'll suggest that we get the engineers to try to straighten out the job. Well, glad everything is going along all right. So long."

FOREMAN: "So long." (*Thinking,* Guess he really didn't have much on his mind.)

In such contacts we see the subordinate constantly selecting what to tell the superior, trying to anticipate what the boss wants to know or what he may want to know later, trying to present things in such a way that his boss will feel that things are not too bad, or, if they were, that they are now under control, and trying to give him good news and take the sting out of bad. And the boss goes away from such contacts feeling that he knows what is going on, that he has his finger firmly on the pulse of the shop.

Filtered Information

Thus we see each individual in the line acting as a filter who sorts over the information coming to him and carefully selects what he will pass on to his boss. The boss always responds most favorably to good news, and so there is a tendency for good news to go up the line quite easily and rapidly. Information as to improvements in output, quality, costs, and so on are transmitted readily from level to level; and as it goes, it leaves everyone with that self-satisfied feeling, the I-gave-the-boss-some-good-news-and-he-was-very-pleased-and-thinks-I'm-fine-and-maybe-he-will-tell-the-big-boss-what-a-good-job-I-did   feeling. On the other hand, bad news meets certain barriers; everyone is reluctant to communicate his mistakes or failures. The what-will-the-boss-think-of-me feeling acts as a brake upon full and rapid reporting of things which go wrong. It encourages delays; it fosters alibis; it develops skill in the tactful presentation of bad news.

Take the case of Bob, foreman in the machine department, when he suddenly discovers that he does not have enough bronze rod on hand to complete the order of part number X37A22 for the end of the week and that it will keep two hand screw machines going steadily to make delivery on time. So he talks to Charley, the machine operator who came to him asking for the rod:

BOB: "Are you sure there isn't any of that rod over in the rack? When we started on this job, I checked the storeroom records and there was plenty on hand."

CHARLEY: "There sure isn't now. You remember when we first started on this order somebody gave us the wrong specifications and we turned out a lot that had to be junked."

BOB: "That's right. Well, I'll call the stockroom and get some more over right away." (*Thinking*, I sure did slip up on that. I completely forgot to order more rod.)

(*He calls the stockroom.*) "I'll need two hundred pounds of that ⅜ths bronze rod for part number X37A22. We're in a rush for it, got to get the order out right away and a couple of machines are waiting. Can you get it right over?"

STOCKMAN: "Sorry, we are out of that rod. Won't be able to get it in before Friday. Why didn't you call last week?"

BOB: "Can't you get hold of any before that? If I don't deliver those parts before Monday, the gadget assembly department will be tied up."

STOCKMAN: "We'll do the best we can, but don't expect it before Friday. Why don't you guys give us a little more notice instead of waiting until your machines shut down and then expecting us to do miracles?"

BOB: (*Thinking*, This is a terrible note! I slip up on ordering that rod at the one time the stockroom is out of it. Why can't they keep some stock on hand instead of trying to work from hand to mouth. Just trying to make a good showing by keeping down inventory and they tie up production. They ought to realize that they are there to help the shop, not to give us all this trouble. Wonder what I can do now. The boss sure will give me hell when he hears this. Maybe I ought to check with Joe in gadget assembly to see how many parts they have on hand and how long before he will need more. Maybe I better let him know what's happened so he will know what to expect. Maybe he can plan his work so the people on that assembly job can do something else for a few days.

But if I tell him what's happened, he will tell his boss, and his boss will jump on my boss, and my boss will jump on me for letting this happen and not letting him know. So before I tell Joe anything I better tell my boss. Maybe if I tell him, he can tell Joe's boss, and I won't have to say anything to Joe. Joe's going to be plenty sore anyway. He got kind of hot the other day when I tried to get him to let me make some changes in the base plate for that Model N job. Seemed like he was just being stubborn. Wonder if he might have enough parts on hand so he could just go along and say nothing about this affair. If I knew he had enough, I just wouldn't say anything and take a chance on getting some to him before he runs out. I'm afraid to risk it, though, without being pretty sure, because if he did have to shut down, my boss sure would raise cain. Yeah, and Joe called the other day to know how we were coming on that lot we delivered yesterday, said he didn't want to get caught short. But Joe always does that. He starts crowding you for things long before he actually needs them. He seems to think no one will keep their promises unless he rides them. If I ask Joe how much he has on hand, he will suspect something and I will have to tell him.

Guess I better not take a chance on Joe. I will have to tell my boss first. But gee, how I hate to tell him! I know just what he will think. I know I should have remembered to order more when we spoiled that first run, but I was so busy getting caught up that I forgot. Anyway, you never would expect the stockroom to be out of a standard item like that. And if they ran this place right, they never would be. But my boss won't care about that. All he'll think is that I must be asleep on the job. He expects me to keep track of everything; and if I have to do the stockroom's job for them to keep my job going, he expects me to do that. What will I tell him, anyway, that won't make me look like a fool who doesn't know his job? Maybe I better not tell him now. It won't hurt to wait till tomorrow, and maybe then the stockroom will know when I can expect the rod. Maybe they will do better than Friday, and I might squeeze by. When I do tell the boss, I want to be able to tell him just when we will be able to start on the job again, and maybe I can plan it so we won't hold up the assembly. Guess I will wait till tomorrow and see what I can figure out.)

And Bob spends the rest of the day in a state of jitters trying to figure a way out of the predicament, or at least a partial solution which he can present to his boss when he finally is forced to tell him. He goes home that night with a terrible grouch, is cross to the children because they are so noisy, gets annoyed with his wife because she seems so cheerful, can hardly eat his supper, sleeps poorly, and hates to go to work the next morning. Such is the human element of communication up the line.

The Boss's Interests

Since the subordinates are interested in giving the boss what he wants to hear, any signs of interest in certain aspects of the work tend to stimulate the flow of information concerning them. If the general foreman expresses interest, or merely curiosity, concerning a new machine or process, or concern over some problem, or interest in some worker, then in every contact with the foreman the boss is likely to hear something about the object of his interest. If he has looked on some new worker with favor, the foreman is likely to find some complimentary things to say about the worker; if the worker is learning the job rapidly, the foreman reports that he is a whizz; if he is slow but friendly with the others, he gets along well; if he is just average, he is coming along well; and so on. If the general foreman did not think so much of a new machine the engineers wanted them to try out, the boss hears critical remarks. If the machine does the work, the operators find it hard to operate, or they cannot seem to get the hang of it, or the controls are wrong and it is tiring. If it does a poor job, then it is just a piece of junk and never will be worth anything. Furthermore, the minute the boss shows a loss of interest in such details, he stops hearing about them. The moment he responds with obvious boredom or lack of interest his subordinate is likely to sense it and to drop the topic and hunt around for something else to take its place.

As a result of this tendency, the boss may receive a considerable amount of minor and unimportant details about a few aspects of the job. Besides, since such information is usually conveyed merely for the purpose of interesting the boss, it is selected and faintly colored to fit that purpose. Thus he gets snatches of slightly distorted information which makes him feel that he is keeping well informed about what is going on. (Many executives may feel that such a statement does them a gross injustice and that *they* really do know all about their organizations. If they are at the intermediate levels in the structure, however, they will probably tell you confidentially that the Big Boss really is not in close touch with the job and its details.)

Since these selective processes are working in all communication from each subordinate to his superior, the taller the supervisory structure, the more filter stations the information must pass through before it reaches the top. Thus, for a small concern with only two or three levels, there is much less selection than for a large concern with five or six levels. Then, too, the larger the concern, the larger the mass of details at the bottom, a mass which is beyond the powers of any one individual to comprehend in its entirety. Between the sheer volume of detail to be selected from and the successive stages of selection at each level, the man at the top ends up with only a vague and highly generalized picture of what is going on.

Keeping the Boss Informed

Everyone in the supervisory structure expects certain kinds of information from his subordinates; and while the precise details vary with the nature of the job and of the individual, there are certain general types of information which all desire. For one thing, almost everyone in the structure wants to be informed concerning those things about which his boss will inquire. Nothing is more disturbing than to be forced to admit ignorance to your boss regarding events in your organization. When he calls you in and asks, "What about the trouble on X job yesterday?" and you have to reply that you did not know of any trouble there, you immediately feel that you have failed, that the boss is annoyed, and that he thinks you are not on top of your job. On the other hand, when you can reply to his question with a detailed statement of the trouble, you feel that you have impressed him with your alertness and ability, have relieved him of any concern about the way you are handling the job, and have generally been a success. There is nothing quite so satisfying as having the right answers for the boss, and having them on the spot without having to say, "I'll look into it and let you know."

Because of this, every subordinate is expected to be on the alert for those things which his boss should know in order to be able to give *his* boss an answer. If the foreman hears that the union is going up to the president on that case which has been kicked around in the department for the last two months, he warns the department chief. If there has been friction with some other department which is likely to be carried up the line, he warns his boss. If the monthly cost report will show some item out of line, the foreman warns his boss. Whatever happens that may get up the line without passing through the successive levels must be anticipated and each level warned.

The line of authority is, then, a channel through which information moves by fits and starts, is sifted over at each level, and is, to a large extent, dependent upon face-to-face communication. This means that the larger the organization and the more levels in the supervisory structure, the slower the flow of information either up or down the line. (I tell my boss something and he sits on it a day or so before he tells his boss, and so on until it may be weeks before something gets through from bottom to top, that is, if it does not get completely lost on the way.) To be sure, there are types of information or certain conditions when items may go bounding up to the top with very little delay. In any case, it is the type of channel which tends to limit the flow of information, slow it down, or censor it; and the longer the channel the greater these effects.

48 T-F

Social Classes
%
Identify Emotions (types)
Feeling & Sediments
common example
Central ✓
Staff ✓
line ✓
Service

status   line
                          Service

boss
general level   status

wage rates

method of paying

shop - office status

seniority

jobs

men - women

negro - white

6. STATUS AND STATUS HIERARCHIES

THE IDEA of relative status, of who outranks whom, is a basic ingredient in our society. Furthermore, it is not a concept which can be readily eliminated or ignored, even though it seems counter to our basic tenet that "all men are equal." We see it in the home, where parents are the superiors of the children, and the older child is superior to or "ahead of" the younger. And the child looks forward to being an adult, the youngest wants to catch up with the eldest, etc. We see it in every organization; and in every community there are those who, by virtue of formal position, ability, birth, possessions, or luck, are looked on as being in some way above or superior to others. We hear it expressed in a myriad of phrases, such as "leading citizens," "no-accounts," "upper crust," "ordinary folks." All this tells us that even in America we have, not a system of pure equality, but one in which there are great differences in social status.

Now there are two kinds of status relations. One is that of the subordinate to his boss, or the enlisted man to his commanding officer. This status relationship involves not only a general difference in rank—the officer is always thought of as superior to his subordinates —but also the right to give orders. It is always connected with specific positions in organizations in which superiors give orders to subordinates. This relationship comprises the chain of command.

The other type of status relation does not involve the right to command. It merely expresses a concept of relative positions, of who outranks whom. For example, an upper-class executive is felt by the community to be somehow superior to the "po-white" fisherman; he will be deferred to in many ways, while the fisherman will be ignored; yet the executive, merely because of his high status, has no "right" to give the other orders.

Any organization chart is a diagram of positions occupied by individuals, and each person is identified by his position. Thus John Jones, a machinist, becomes a different person in the organization when he becomes John Jones, a foreman. Furthermore, these different positions fit into systems of ranks, or status hierarchies, in which one is seen as superior to another. These systems are most clearly seen in

103

military organizations, where differences in rank are carefully spelled out so everyone can know who outranks whom.

The supervisory structure is, then, a status system in which it is accepted as a matter of course that each level has more status and prestige than the ones below it. In fact, the words used in discussing it show this status factor. We speak of superiors and subordinates, of higher and lower levels, of up and down, of above and below—all of which imply differences in rank in such a structure. The problem of status or prestige does not end with this simple supervisory hierarchy, however, but intrudes itself into all sorts of situations and in innumerable guises. In fact, the matters of relative status, of where each person fits in terms of it, of how each compares with others, present some of the most interesting and, to those involved, some of the most annoying and painful problems of people at work. Certainly, if no one was ever bothered by the status of himself or others, life would be much simpler for everyone.

As we have seen, the chain of command establishes the most clearly defined hierarchy, with the supervisor outranking the supervised. Now differences in rank extend beyond the command, or supervisory relationship, so that all foremen are considered superior to all workers just as all officers outrank all privates. Thus we have rank hierarchies based on ideas of relative position rather than on face-to-face relationships. And these types of status systems, which are very widespread both within industry and in society generally, have great influence on human behavior. In this chapter, we will examine some of the common types of status hierarchies and their significance in the work situation.

Shop-Office Distinctions

In the first place, we find the important status distinction between shop and office or "white-collar" jobs. Despite the talk about the "dignity of labor" and the pleasures of working with your hands, there is an almost universal feeling that the office jobs are in some sense "superior" to the shop jobs and that the person who runs a typewriter or adding machine has a higher status than the person who runs a drill press. This feeling was well expressed by a girl working on a shop job, who said:

> I'd really like to work in the office. Isn't it funny the way office people treat factory people? I don't see any difference between them myself, but the office people think they are so much better than the girls who work in the factory.

Lots of them have the same education as the office girls, and we are just as refined as they are. They seem to think that factory girls are loud and rough, but there are just as many girls in the office who drink and smoke and are immoral as the girls in the shop. It just seems that having an office job makes them feel that they're better than we are. I've seen the difference in some people I know. One who came from a farm in Missouri went to school and got an office job. Well, she talks about her office job as much as she can and isn't near as friendly as she used to be. We don't have anything to do with each other any more.

I've noticed it with other girls too. I'll meet them at church and they ask me where I work. I tell them. They ask if I work in factory or office. When I say factory, they say, "Oh," and then ask me if I don't get tired of it, and ask me if it's dirty. Then they take every chance to talk about their office jobs.

My mother feels the same way as these people do. She says that since I've worked in the factory I've gotten more boisterous. I talk in a louder voice, not as refined as I used to be. Well, you don't like to hear those things. You don't like to feel that something's happening to you.

In this interview, an important characteristic of the status system was expressed, that is, the fact that the person who occupies the higher status position tends to identify himself with the status of his position until it becomes a part of him which he carries into all his contacts with those of lesser status. Thus the girl who had obtained an office job began to draw apart from her former factory friends, and the factory girl was looked down upon by the office girls whom she met in church. And so the status of one's position is not something which is shed when he leaves his job; it is carried with him into all kinds of situations.

This interview also shows the general feeling of superiority which the higher-status group has toward the lower. Not only is their work felt to be of a higher order of importance or value, but they are superior beings. The office group tends to look down upon the shopworkers as inferiors in mind, manner, and morals. The shopworkers have grimy hands and poor taste, they say; they are loudmouthed and use coarse language; they are less educated, or at least less intellectual. Although these attitudes of office workers may seem to be extreme expressions of feelings of superiority, similar feelings are expressed by every high-status group toward their "inferiors." Executives have something of the same attitude toward foremen, foremen toward workers, the old-timers toward the newcomers, the skilled workers toward the semiskilled. In fact, we can safely say that everyone in a factory busies himself from time to time with looking down on someone, looking up to someone, or assuring himself that, in spite of what certain others think, he is just as good as they are. As the girl in the interview said, "We are just as good as they are," and in the next breath voiced her doubts.

Status and Wages

The rate of pay or earnings is, of course, another important source of status differences. This is quite in keeping with a business or factory as an economic enterprise in which everything is supposedly evaluated in terms of money. Thus the higher the pay, the higher the status of the job or the individual. The ten-thousand-dollar-a-year man is far superior to the five-thousand-dollar man, or the dollar-forty-an-hour shopworker is superior to the eighty-five-cent man. In the same way, the job that pays a dollar-forty an hour is superior to the eighty-five-cent an hour job. ("Superior" in this sense does not always mean more desirable, since individual tastes in jobs vary considerably.) As a result, every work situation in which there is a gradation of wages has a status hierarchy revolving around these wages and one which is readily upset by any changes in the wage structure. There is also a status system based upon the different kinds of jobs found in any work group. As a rule, the jobs requiring the most skill are at the top and those requiring the least are at the bottom, although other factors may enter in to disturb such a simple arrangement. For example, a job which receives a great deal of attention and recognition from the boss may become the superior job even though other jobs in the group require more skill. Sometimes, too, jobs acquire status because they are always held by long-service people who receive recognition because of their service.

Seniority and Status

Seniority forms the basis for other status differences, with the old-timers feeling that they are somehow superior to the young people and newcomers. In most stable companies there is a feeling toward long-service people something like the attitude toward age which we find in our society generally. The youngsters are thought of as lacking in knowledge and understanding and are expected to give recognition and deference to their elders, while the very old have a place with certain rights and privileges because of their age. The special privileges of old-timers were demonstrated by the nurse in one factory. We quote from an observer's notes:

In a plant which had, before the war, found it necessary to employ only one nurse, the expansion due to the war brought the need for more nurses.

The original nurse had been with the company thirteen years. Then a male nurse was hired for the 4–12 shift. And when a 12–8 shift started, he was transferred to it. Two more nurses were hired, and since none of them wanted to work 4–12 all the time, it was agreed that they should alternate.

The nurse who had seniority took one turn at the afternoon shift and then refused to work it again. The doctor and the personnel manager agreed that she need not take her turn; and the other nurses, although they resented this evident favoritism, seemed to feel that it was done because she had been with the company so long.

Organizational Differences

There are also status differences among organizations, and in any plant there are usually certain organizations which are generally thought of as superior to others. The shop-office distinction accounts for some of this, as the strictly office organizations are usually superior to the shop organizations. As a result, a typist or file clerk with the shop department is usually thought to have a "poorer," that is lower-status, job than the typist or file clerk in an accounting department. Also, organizations such as engineering or sales, where much of the work requires technical skills or special training, are usually of status superior to shop or accounting organizations. In all such cases the feeling of superiority does not remain merely the prerogative of the salesmen or engineers but carries over even to the most routine jobs in the organization. The office boy in the engineering department, for example, is likely to feel superior to the office boy in the accounting organization.

Occupational Hierarchies

We have seen how certain types of jobs carry differences of status. However, this extends often to very elaborate rankings in which there may be recognized differences between many jobs. Thus in many of the skilled trades, we find the hierarchy of apprentice, journeyman, master. In these, a man's position is based upon his progress through a clearly defined system of training and experience.

In addition, we see differences in rank between jobs based on the levels of skill required, such as the semiskilled versus skilled worker. Or the simpler machines are lower than the complicated machines. Or the job that requires long training outranks the one that requires little training. In general, all jobs in a plant can be placed on a scale which expresses the general beliefs as to where each fits in relation to the others.

As we have seen, many of the status systems are based on the characteristics inherent in the work organization. Supervisory rank, levels of skill, wage differences, etc., are largely defined within the organization. However, there are other types of status which are general to the society and are carried over into the work situation. In communities where the particular hierarchies do not already exist, they do not appear in the local industries.

Men versus Women

In our society, women are traditionally defined as the "weaker sex," subordinate to the male. This traditional role of subordination and inferiority is carried over into the work situation. Women's jobs are thought of as simpler, requiring less skill, or in some way unsuitable for men. And attempts to place women in jobs habitually defined as men's work meet with considerable resistance from men. Also, the man who is placed alongside of women, doing the same work, feels that he is degraded.

Negro versus White

Here again we find status differences between the Negro and the white existing in our society. This is expressed in the most extreme form in the deep South, where the Negro is thought of as socially separate and inferior. There he is generally restricted to the lowest status and lowest paid jobs and is rarely permitted to occupy a supervisory position over whites. And while the system is less rigorous in the North, many of the same attitudes and restrictions still exist.

Complicating Factors

These status systems are not nicely co-ordinated, however, so that the older person always gets more money, has the better job, or is higher in the supervisory structure. We see old-timers in some of the poorest jobs at the lowest pay. We see bright young executives who, with only short service, have climbed high in the supervisory ranks. We see office jobs paying less than shop jobs, or skilled workers earning more than their foremen. We see innumerable complicating factors, so that it seems impossible to present a simple picture of the status relationships between individuals within any plant or even in any one department.

We do find, however, that there is a feeling that these various status systems *should* be co-ordinated. This is most strongly expressed in the idea that superiors should earn more than their subordinates. Generally in the supervisory structure wages rise rapidly as you go up in the structure, and it is usually felt to be wrong for a foreman to get less pay than his subordinates. There is also some tendency for wages to increase with age, and a feeling that this should be so, especially when the rate of pay is not rigidly tied to the kind of job. Also, the more highly skilled jobs are often held by the long-service people who have worked themselves up. Interestingly enough, the status difference between office and shop is usually not recognized in pay, especially at the lower levels. Apparently the office jobs are sufficiently attractive, especially to girls, that they are preferred even if the wages are lower, so that in many organizations we find these "better" jobs being paid considerably less than the others.

"Placing" People

A matter of common interest and concern to everyone in the factory is the problem of "place" in the social organization. Everyone wants to know where other people "fit" in terms of the functional relations of the work and, what is to many even more important, in terms of the status systems. The newcomer is always faced by the questions, "Who are you?" and "Where do you fit?" In fact, one of the important aspects of getting acquainted on a new job is the process by which the newcomer finds out just where he belongs. He learns with whom he will work and what their relationship is to him and to each other; he learns who are his superiors in the line of authority, who can give him orders and who cannot, to whom he should defer and whom he can ignore. All this is the real function of much of the introduction and conversation which often takes place when a new worker comes into a group. For example, the foreman brings a new man over to Joe Blow on the dinkus assembly line, and the conversation goes like this:

FOREMAN: "Joe, this is Jim Blank, who is going to work on this assembly. I wish you would show him how to do the job." (Telling Joe that Jim is new and inexperienced on the job.)

JOE: "Howdy, Jim. You ever had any experience with dinkus assembly?" (Trying to place Jim a little more accurately.)

JIM: "No. I been on a drill press in the gadget department for a couple of years." (Letting Joe know that he is not entirely a greenhorn and has had experience on machines, as well as service with the company.)

JOE: "You did? Why I worked over there when I first started eight years ago. Is old Jake, the foreman, still as 'sour-puss' as ever?" (Telling Jim that he need not feel that two years of service amounts to much and that he knows about the gadget department also.)

JIM: "Well, Jake's a pretty decent guy after all, even if he does act sour at times. I kinda hate to leave the department, but work was getting slack on the drill presses." (Showing a little annoyance at Joe's implied criticism of the gadget department, and also telling Joe that he had not left to get out of the place or because they did not want him.)

JOE: "Yeah, I used to like Jake and hated to leave there myself." (Sensing Jim's irritation and trying to express a common attitude.)

Scenes such as this occur constantly; and in every one the individuals are consciously or unconsciously telling each other just where they fit and how they feel about it, and at the same time finding out about each other. When making introductions or when talking about newcomers, there is this same emphasis on "placing" people. Once the individual's place has been established, however, interest in him and gossip about him shifts to other topics.

Symbols of Status

Because of the importance of status, the individual himself is greatly concerned that he be placed properly, at least not in a position inferior to what he actually occupies. The private may be amused to be mistaken for a lieutenant, but the lieutenant who is mistaken for a private is really burned up. Undoubtedly, that is one of the important functions of military insignia. In industry people feel much the same way, with the result that almost every large plant has developed its own insignia, its own set of symbols by means of which everyone can be placed properly in the status system. In general, these symbols are not the simple and obvious types evolved by the Armed Forces but are much more subtle and indirect. The sort of clothes you wear, the desk you sit at, the position of your desk or workbench, the machine you operate, and many other things may indicate status. In fact, these things are often so indirect that the outsider is not aware that such a symbol system exists at all. Many executives, too, deny that there are such systems; but usually these denials are coupled with an assertion that, even if they do exist, they are wrong and should be abolished. Unfortunately for such a point of view, there is no way to stop people from trying to place one another or to keep them from being concerned about their own status.

Because of the importance of the distinction between shop and office, there is a strong tendency to differentiate between them in many ways, each of which becomes a symbol to indicate the position of the individual. While the nature of the work usually leads to a separation between office and shop groups, the separation itself becomes an important symbol of the difference in status. As a result, most office workers are upset and feel that they have lost status if they are moved from an office location to a shop location even though there is no change in the job. In most large plants where there is a separation of the office and shop organizations, there are usually separate washrooms for the office people; and any attempt to have the office people use the shop washrooms, or to bring shop people into the office washrooms, meets with strong resistance from the office people. To be forced to share lockers or washrooms with these "uncouth and inferior" people is a bitter pill to the office people. In such instances, all sorts of complaints are voiced about the crowded washrooms, about how untidy the shop people are, about how they throw paper towels or cigarettes on the floor or leave the washbasins grimy from their dirty hands, or about their bad manners and unrefined language. This whole attitude was well expressed in the behavior of a typist who had been transferred from an office location to the same work in a shop: rather than use the shop washrooms which were adjacent to her new location, she would walk across a building and up a flight of stairs to a washroom used by an office group.

In many companies there is a payroll distinction, too, between shop and office, the shopworkers being paid by the hour and the office by the week. Since both groups are actually paid every week, there is no obvious difference; yet the different payrolls assume the status differences of the two groups. And to move from the hourly to the weekly or salaried payroll is a step up in the world. In some cases this difference may be accentuated by having different time clocks or a different payday for each group, so that there remains no doubt as to where a person fits. Separate time clocks or paydays are, of course, usually thought of as devices to assist the payroll department in preparing the pay checks, or to spread the work load a bit; but it is surprising how often such devices get mixed up in the status system and become status symbols in themselves. And once they become status symbols, any attempt to change them meets with strong resistance from the people.

An almost universal characteristic of all types of status hierarchies is that certain prerogatives accompany high status; and as one ascends in the structure, he acquires certain rights and privileges which are denied to those below him. Some of these rights have to do with the symbols of status themselves. As one is promoted, he acquires the right to display the insignia of his new place. Others are much more tangible rewards, such as increased freedom from restraints, special rights, additional pay, and so on. For example, the following situation was observed in one small plant:

As more machines were added to the departments, the girls who had the best records in attendance and production or showed aptitude for mechanics were made adjusters. This was considered a promotion, although there was no increase in pay. They had a small measure of authority in that they were responsible for seeing that the operators turned out perfect work and for adjusting the machines to make this possible. Since the adjusters operated the machines during the regular lunch period, they ate alone. There were no bells to ring to signify the beginning and end of their lunch period; so they took a few minutes extra. Although everyone knew about this, nothing was said, so the adjusters felt that they were a little above the ordinary workers.

These symbolic distinctions are well shown, too, in the shop-office division, with the office usually having definite privileges denied to the shop. For example, office workers frequently have a longer lunch hour than shop; they may be free to leave their desks to go to the washroom whenever they please, while the shop is limited to fixed rest pauses. Through the device of the weekly pay, the office workers may take time off or come in late without penalty, while the hourly paid shopworkers are usually paid only for the time they are actually on the job.

It is interesting that foremen are generally on the weekly payroll and so are grouped with the office people. It appears, then, that the ordinary factory is split into two groups, one of which is composed of the hourly paid shopworkers, the other of the weekly paid office workers and the entire supervisory staff. The nonsupervisory office workers, furthermore, tend to think of themselves as akin to the supervisory and executive group rather than to the shopworkers.

Within the office group itself, there is usually a high development of status symbols. Almost anything in the work situation seems to have potentialities for becoming such a symbol, whether it be a desk, chair, telephone, location, arrangement of furniture, or whatnot. For example, a telephone directory usually becomes a sort of *Who's Who* which reflects status more than phone calls. Whether you have a telephone on your desk, or share one with the next desk, or have none at all may be a direct reflection of your status and is usually interpreted that way. In one large organization, desks were an important symbol: the lowest clerical workers worked at tables, the next level had single-pedestal desks with one bank of drawers, the supervisors had larger, double-pedestal desks wth two banks of drawers, and so on, up to the plant manager, who had a great big desk of fancy woods. In such a system, to give a man a promotion without the proper desk would have given rise to elaborate speculations as to whether he really rated the title or just what was wrong. It would be like promoting a lieutenant but telling him that he would have to still wear his lieutenant's bars, that he was not really a captain yet. The emphasis on these status symbols in one small factory was described by an office worker, as follows:

This same vice-president has three assistant vice-presidents in his department besides his department manager. He gets them increasingly large bonuses each year. He can't give them all private offices, so he gathers them all into one special corner of the office away from their secretaries, gives them each a desk *and* a table and more space for visitors. Their desks have leather desk pads with green blotters instead of the usual rubber mat, and, on the whole, he keeps them happy. But if one of them were to get a bronze wastebasket, they would each have to have one.

In the same way, offices for executives become important symbols of status. In most large organizations there are certain superior offices which, because of size or location, are preferred. Usually these better offices are occupied by the top-ranking men in the organization and reflect their status. Other offices may fit into the status pattern on the basis of their proximity to the "brass hats." Thus the office next to the president is superior to the one down the hall. Where offices occupy several floors of a tall building, the higher offices usually have the most status. The manager or president usually occupies the top floor, and the lesser officials are found somewhere below. In such cases, moving to a higher floor is getting up in the world in more ways than one. The importance of location as a status symbol affects the people who work for executives, too, so that their secretaries, stenographers, and even their office boys, feel very strongly the status significance of working on the top floor or in the office next to the president's suite. This was described by a girl in the personnel department of one organization, thus:

Then there is the social problem caused by the physical layout which comprises three floors. The executives' offices are on the tenth. (This is special!)

Several departments, including accounting and payroll, are on the ninth. (This is O.K.) There is the eighth floor, with dictaphones, typing, filing. (This is Bargain Basement!) The girls on the eighth feel that the girls on the ninth and tenth look down on them. The secretaries on the tenth floor are supposed to be pretty high-hat. Girls on the ninth beg to be transferred "upstairs."

Among shopworkers, on the other hand, there is not quite so much emphasis upon status symbols. In general, a person's position in the shop is pretty clearly shown by the work he is doing. The man operating an automatic screw machine is obviously different from the sweeper or material handler, the machinist is superior to his helper, and anyone familiar with shopwork can place people easily in the general status system. This does not mean that shopworkers are not concerned about status, but merely that the work itself provides fairly obvious status insignia.

With office people, however, as pointed out, the symbols of status are often a major concern, and changes in them are sure to create disturbances. To account for such emphasis is difficult, but we may present two possible hypotheses. In the first place, the office and supervisory groups probably contain more people who want to improve their status. And these people naturally want to display evidence of any gains; they want people to know where they belong. At the same time, the nature of office work is such that all jobs look alike from a distance; people sitting at desks writing and shuffling papers may be either important executives or the most unimportant clerks. For that reason, it becomes important that the superior people acquire symbols to distinguish them from the rest. (And everyone gets upset if the new clerk gets the desk by the boss or one by the window.)

These status symbols are a constant source of conflict and anxiety. Each watches his equals lest they acquire symbols which he lacks; each longs to have the choice office or the large desk and schemes to get it; each judges the importance of his job by symbols which go with it. As a result, every change in arrangement, every movement of people or organizations, may upset the status systems and cause trouble.

An Example of Status Problems

A situation involving status problems, changes, and disturbances in one small factory was described by a personnel officer, as follows:

Fred J., aged 45, was one of the most capable all round machinists in a tool industry of about 350 employees. A year and a half ago he was placed in charge of a night shift in the approximate capacity of superintendent. The night shift had just been started, and none of the day foremen who might have been eligible for the job seemed to want it.

The initial night force was small, but it grew rapidly to a total of 125 employees. The top management never made a clear announcement of Fred's position as superintendent. He had the duties of a superintendent except that one department operated at night as an independent unit. No clear directive was given to the effect that Fred was in complete charge, although it was intended that this should be generally understood up to the point of his being responsible for all night activities except in the one independent department.

A great deal of antagonism having the appearance of jealousy immediately developed among the foremen of the day shift. The day superintendent likewise seemed to resent the fact of there being another superintendent in the plant. He would often challenge Fred's right to deal with operational matters that extended through both shifts. In a showdown between these two, Fred answered the challenge by saying, "All right, let's go up to George's (the general manager's) office right now, and I'll apologize to you in his presence." The offer was declined.

Characteristic expressions of the day foreman in referring to Fred would run somewhat along the lines of "that fellow that's on nights. . . . I don't know what you'd call him. . . . He ain't a superintendent, and I wouldn't even call him a foreman."

The management says that, had they clearly designated Fred as a superintendent, they would have had a blowup. They had to place him where they did because the job had to be done and there was no one else in the place who would take it and would have their confidence to the same extent.

Over a period of sixteen months Fred seems to have been winning his battle slowly. But the whole thing has been marked by a good deal of antagonism, frequent ignoring of notes left by Fred for the day supervision, and quite obvious buck-passing, such as the charging of scrap against the night shift when portions of it belonged unmistakably to the day shift.

In one instance Fred had one of his night operators mark each piece he turned out, a piece which was being produced by both shifts. In the inspector's reports on rejects, all the scrap was charged against the night shift. Fred examined the rejected pieces, found that his man's symbol was not on them, and demanded of the inspector, "How come?" The inspector explained: "The day superintendent told me to charge them that way."

4 C.A.
4 Emb B
4 Hist 0
4 Gen
3 SW B
3 SW B
3 Aut · B
3 Ann. B
2 Sem B
3 ROTC B

7. SYSTEMS OF COMMUNICATION

COMMUNICATION between people is essential to any group activity. In a sense, we might consider communication as the element which makes any form of organization possible. Without it, there could be no common understanding, no co-ordination of efforts, no direction or control. Communication, in this sense, is more than the written documents or the verbal commands. It is the whole complex system by which information of all sorts is passed back and forth throughout the organization. Part of this system are the formal orders, both written and verbal; part are the records and reports from various sources; part are the idle conversations and gossip; part are the queries and responses from one part of the organization to another.

Just as with the organization, we see the patterns of formal communications which have been established to serve the needs of the organization. In addition, there is the vast system of informal communication which arises spontaneously and is not subject to control. It can be understood and used, but it cannot be abolished. At the same time, it often fills a gap not provided for in the formal system; it takes care of unexpected situations; and without it, the organization could scarcely function.

If we examine the communication activities within an organization, we see that much effort is devoted to vertical communication, both up and down and through several channels. First there is the communication (discussed in Chapter 5) up and down the chain of command. This provides the primary channel for communication downward, for purposes of direction and control, and upward, for information as to what is happening in the organization. Some of this is highly formalized in the form of written orders and reports, but much of it is informal and verbal.

While the chain of command can provide top management with information of many sorts, it is not usually expected to be the source of many types of routine reports. For example, management desires regular information on costs, quality, production, sales, etc. For such information, it usually does not look to the chain of command nor expect each supervisory level to collect the data from its subordinates

117

and pass it on to its superiors. Instead, there will be a system established which collects the data, organizes it into the proper form, and passes it directly to management. Thus, a report on the number of units produced may be compiled from the records and passed on to management without going through the hands of the supervisors. Or a report of number of units failing to pass inspection will be taken from the inspection records. In the same way, the accounting, or cost control, system keeps elaborate records from which they can report to management such items as costs on direct and indirect labor, overtime, material, repairs, etc. Often these can be shown for specific jobs, individual departments, or various time periods.

This kind of information can be considered as control information, since from it management can watch the functioning of the information and can judge its performance. In effect, it is the score board on which the hits, runs, and errors are reported. From it, management knows when and where it should dig into certain problems or situations. And without it, management would not know how the game goes, or who performs well or poorly.

This control information may be originated in many ways and handled through several organization channels. It is largely compiled from data existing at a low level in the organization. If, for example, it is a report on man-hours worked on certain jobs, it will be compiled from work records filled out at the work level by the workers, supervisor, timekeeper or clerk. If it is a report on purchases, it may be compiled from records of purchases in the payroll department.

Generally the cost records and reports are the most important and widely used of this control information. However, the basic data is accumulated, is collected according to systems established by the accounting department, and is passed into its hands for processing into the appropriate reports. Thus labor costs may start with records filled out by the worker and approved by his foreman. The form of the record has been established by the accounting or cost control department, which seeks to standardize records for the whole organization. Once the record leaves the foreman, the future processing is beyond his control, and he may never see the final reports compiled from it.

Here we have a flow of information which bypasses, or "short-circuits," the line. Instead of each link in the chain having the opportunity to see and interpret the information, it moves directly to management. This by-passing is not confined to control reports, however, but may occur both informally and through certain other formal systems. For example, it occurs when a worker with a complaint goes in to see a superintendent instead of his foreman or department chief, or when an engineer takes up some problem with a higher level before consulting the foreman on the job. In all such cases the line supervisors may feel very insecure, since their superiors will learn things about the work which have not first passed through the line and of which the line may know nothing. This information may give rise to criticisms or questions which the lower levels are not prepared to answer. There is nothing better for producing insomnia than to think the boss knows something about the job that you do not know and is going to ask questions that you cannot anticipate.

So we see that the accounting or cost control systems provide a one-way channel for communication, but the information leads to action on the part of management. This action usually flows back down through the chain of command. Thus, a cost report showing excessive costs in a certain manufacturing department will stimulate the vice-president in charge of manufacturing to ask questions or give orders which move, step by step, down to the guilty department, until action is taken within the department either to justify the costs or to take corrective measures. Therefore it becomes important to each foreman and department head to anticipate such occurrences and to be prepared for the repercussions. Some of the techniques of such defenses will be discussed later.

Another channel of communication leads directly from management to workers, foremen, or other specific groups. Such communications may be through letters, memoranda, bulletin boards, or verbal expression at meetings, or, in some cases, over a loud-speaker system. In these instances, management—often top management—is seeking to communicate information, to give statements of policy, or to express management attitudes. Through such direct communication, management seeks to reach and influence the rank and file. Thus, when business is slow and orders are off, they may want to keep the workers informed of any change in the situation, and of what management is doing to get more business. Or when new policies are put into effect, they may want to be sure that all have been informed. Also, in case of conflict with the union, they may want to present management's side of the case.

The union provides a special channel for communication from workers to management and, to some extent, from management down to the workers. As we will see in Chapter 9, this is an especially important channel for certain types of information and often bypasses the chain of command. It is not, therefore, a channel controlled or directed by management or supervisors.

It is clear that the bulk of the formal communications serves to keep management informed. Also, most of the regular communications in a large organization deal with general information rather than specific details. For example, accounting reports generally present information from many sources, combined and condensed into certain patterns; and a report showing the ratio of sales expense to total sales is a highly condensed summary of many transactions. Thus management is constantly interpreting this generalized information and making decisions which may not be appropriate to many specific situations concealed within the general pattern.

When management wants information on specific situations, it relies on requests either through the chain of command or through the special information-gathering groups, such as cost control or accounting. However, these details are not called for unless attention has been drawn to them for some reason. In general, management relies on its subordinates to spot these situations requiring detailed attention. Thus management often requests special details when subordinates have drawn its attention to a problem situation.

These communications work to serve what management sees as its needs in running the organization. There is little provision for communication to management from the individual. For example, the plant manager may see his department heads daily, and they have opportunities to discuss their ideas and problems. The foreman, however, may only rarely see the manager and has little chance to express his ideas. If he wants to communicate something directly, he can only do it by taking extraordinary steps and by passing his general foreman and department head. The worker is even more remote and finds it even more difficult to communicate directly.

Communication between Organizations

Much of the communication between organizations is through the "channels," that is, up the line of one organization until it reaches the individual who is at the top and then back down the line of the other organization (Fig. 10). This is the formal, correct, and "safe" procedure. When followed, each level is informed and can control what is passed on to the next, and there is no danger of "short-circuits." There is also, however, some direct communication between the lower levels of the various organizations which does not go up the line.

Each type of communication between organizations has certain characteristics and certain difficulties. In a large organization, for instance, communication is often so slow that it seriously slows down the job. For example, take the following not too hypothetical case:

Joe, foreman of the Assembly Department, thinks it might help him to plan his work if he could have a little advance information on the progress of the work in the Machine Department on some of his piece parts. He would like to have regular weekly reports from the Machine Department, and he decides to ask his boss about it. His department chief thinks that it is a good idea and says he will take it up the line. The department chief waits a couple of days until he has a chance for a long talk with the division chief, when he presents the idea. The division chief says it sounds good to him, and why not bring it up in the weekly meeting of his department chiefs next Monday to

FIGURE 10.—Communication through Channels

see if something can be worked out. Next Monday the idea is discussed, and the department chief of the Machine Department says it sounds as if there might be possibilities. But, he says, it will put additional work on his foremen; so he would like to talk it over with them first. The division chief thinks this sounds reasonable, and so the next day the idea is presented to the Machine Department foremen by their department chief. They complain that the idea sounds good but is not so simple as it might be, since they do not ordinarily keep just the proper records to give that particular information. To do it accurately, they say, there will have to be additional records, which will mean additional clerical help—say about ten man-hours a week. The department chief then goes back to his boss and says it cannot be done unless they can arrange for this additional help. The division chief agrees to this, and the next day he tells the Assembly Department chief that the plans are being worked out to get the information. Finally, several weeks after he originated the idea, Joe is told that it will be carried out.

While communication directly across from one foreman to another is much quicker and simpler, it is likely to be limited because of each foreman's concern over his relations with his superior. If Joe talks to Jim about difficulties he is having, and if Jim repeats it to his department chief, and if the department chief mentions it to Joe's boss, who has not yet heard of the difficulty, then the boss questions Joe, and both of them are apt to be disturbed. One of the important principles of communication up the line, as already pointed out, is to be sure that you keep your boss informed about anything which he may hear of from other sources, so that, when these things are mentioned by others, he is able to talk about them intelligently. Since the movement of information out from the work situation through any other channel than the line is likely to place the higher levels in an uncomfortable position, all such flow is limited.

Written Communication

Written communication in the form of letters, memos, reports, records, instructions, and so on, plays an important part in the total process. Practically all communication through the accounting system is in some written form which can be retained for future reference. Also, anything from the top which becomes part of the formal instructions, rules, or policies is almost always in written form. As a rule, such written material has a permanence lacking in the strictly verbal communications. Thus, everyone keeps a file of correspondence, reports, memoranda, and so on, in which he keeps everything he receives and everything he sends out.

Written communication, however, is slow and time-consuming, compared to verbal communication. You want to get some information from someone in another department; so you dictate a memo and then wait for a reply. Your correspondent receives the memo and sooner or later dictates a reply. Or if you are at one of the lower levels without a secretary, you scribble out a note and try to get some typist or secretary in the department to type it for you. Or if you are one of those who came up the hard way, without benefit of formal education, and feel somewhat sensitive about your use of English, you just do not write anything you can avoid and trust to verbal communication. In any event, five minutes' conversation is more effective for the interchange of ideas or information than six weeks of correspondence, and it is only when there is serious antagonism or conflict between two individuals that they depend upon writing for much of their communication.

"The Grapevine"

Within any factory, too, there is also a large amount of what may be called "informal communication" which is not following the channels or any formally designated patterns and which is concerned primarily with the human relations of the work situation and serves the needs of the people rather than the needs of the job. This is what is commonly referred to as the "grapevine," and in most places comes to be an accepted feature of the system. Usually it is nothing more than the passing-on of information from one friend to another without regard to any formal organizational lines. Often there is a clique of secretaries to the top executives who keep each other informed as to what is going on. Sometimes there are luncheon groups of supervisors from various departments which enable them to trade news of changes and developments, and of rumors or gossip about what is going on throughout the company. Individuals have friends in various organizations, from whom they can get off-the-record information and keep in touch with those organizations, and to whom they are careful to give similar information and informal reports.

The successful operation of the grapevine, however, is dependent upon the discretion with which each person uses the information it brings him. If Jim tells Joe at lunch that his department is having trouble on a certain job, and Joe goes around talking about the trouble that Jim is having, it usually ends up with Jim being mad at Joe and feeling that he cannot trust him. And from then on, Jim either avoids Joe or is careful not to tell him anything that should be treated confidentially.

SUMMARY

Such a description of the complications and limitations of communication, especially through the line of authority, might give the impression that communication between levels in the industrial status system is completely ineffectual. Actually, of course, this is not true.

People at the bottom of the structure do produce the goods, and those at the top do control that production and maintain their authority over those below. The point to be made here is that, because of the nature of the man-boss relationship, because it and other status relationships in the system are not clearly recognized and understood, communication sometimes actually interferes with satisfactory work relations and effective production, even though it is thought of as facilitating these things.

8. THE FUNCTIONS AND PROBLEMS AT EACH LEVEL

SO FAR we have been looking at supervisors as a uniform group, all part of a status system and part of a communication system, all links in the line of authority, and all having the same kind of role in an intricate linkage of man-boss relationships. When, however, we examine the kinds of work they actually do at each level of supervision, and the kinds of relationships they have with others, we see that there is a shift in activities and job functions from one supervisory level to another up the line. A superintendent does not have the same function as a foreman. He doesn't have the same job, or the same contact with the work situation, or the same relationship with the workers. His attention, power of authority, and feelings of identification are different from those of a foreman.

Suppose we consider again a representative hierarchy for a concern in which we have a president, superintendents, division chiefs, department chiefs, and foremen, as five levels of supervision. In such a factory the foremen and department chiefs are usually located at desks in small office spaces in the work location in plain sight of the workers. The division chiefs, superintendents, and president are located in private offices on the top floor of the building, away from the noise and dirt of the work location.

THE FOREMAN

Daily Activities

Most of the daily activities of the first-line supervisor are related directly to the work and the workers. He is on the floor, actually seeing that work gets done, a good part of the day. Usually he spends a few minutes at his desk looking over the work schedules or orders for the day and the records of deliveries for the day before. Maybe he consults with other foremen, or with his department chief, about plans for the day. He then goes out on the floor for the rest of the

125

day. Or he may start the day by walking around the shop, seeing that everyone is getting started on his work, perhaps answering questions, giving instructions, and then go back to spend some time at his desk. Throughout the day he usually spends most of his time on his feet, moving about the floor, keeping in contact with the workers and the work, listening to problems, making decisions, and directing the workers. He does not wait for his group to come to him with problems, but tries to keep in touch with them and available at all times. He also spends some time with other foremen in the department and may join them at rest periods for a smoke and a cup of coffee or have lunch with them. He may spend a little time with his department chief whenever he is available, and may show him various jobs or discuss problems with him.

From this we see that the foreman, who is usually considered the first level of management, is the one who has the most direct and detailed knowledge of the job and the workers. He is the one who has the most frequent contact with the workers. He plans and directs their work; he checks and judges their work; he maintains discipline and enforces the rules. To the workers he is the one who gives orders, who rewards and punishes. And it is through him that all the pressures downward through the structure, all the demands and orders moving down the line, are transmitted directly to the work group.

Orientation and Perspective

Out of his intimate relationship with the work the foreman develops an orientation toward it which is different from that of the rest of the hierarchy. In the first place, his attention is focused on the everyday details; he sees all the immediate difficulties and the complexities of getting the work out; and he usually knows a lot about the workers and their attitudes. As a result, he tends to be impatient with higher levels or with staff people who try to generalize on the basis of partial knowledge and make decisions which affect his job. He frequently feels that his superiors impose tasks on him and on his group without trying to understand the difficulties of his job. He feels that it is easy for them to say "do this" or "give us this information," but that he is the one who has to carry out the orders and still keep the job going.

Since he controls his job primarily through direct knowledge of the details, he feels little need for records or reports. He tries to know what is going on when it happens rather than learn about it later through reports. In many cases he is expected to collect data and prepare reports which his superiors then use to put pressure on him. He is impatient, therefore, of elaborate reports or paper controls, since they tend to keep him at his desk away from contacts with the job and since they mean extra work and may mean more pressure from above. Also, he knows the inadequacies of such records and is critical of decisions based upon them. Thus he always prefers the job on which records and reports are kept to a minimum and can be taken care of by some clerk so that he does not have to do paper work himself.

Attitudes and Identification

When we talk to foremen about their jobs, their superiors, and their subordinates, we see a variety of attitudes. In some cases they have strong feelings of sympathy with the work group, a sort of identification with the workers in which the foreman acts as though he were one of them and is constantly defending them both from his superiors and from outside organizations. In such cases, there is usually a very friendly and informal relationship between the foreman and his group. They may joke together, and the workers feel free to discuss their personal and work problems and to voice their complaints. Generally, in this situation there seems to be very little barrier between them because of difference in rank, and the foreman maintains little social distance or distinction between himself and the group. Many of these situations are characterized by a much greater distinction between the foreman and his department chief, and sometimes there is a very strong barrier between these two levels. In such cases there is little interaction between the two, and the foreman may actually avoid contacts and force the department chief to come to him. Also, the foreman will try to keep the department chief away from his group, try to be present when he is around the work situation, try to cover up mistakes, protect individual workers from his criticism, and otherwise try to build strong barriers between them. He will resist demands for changes from above, always finding reasons for not accepting them or for their failure if they are forced upon him. Such situations are diagrammed in Figure 11.

The opposite of this situation is the foreman who has a strong identification with management and his superiors and holds his subordinates at a distance. He tends to be critical of the workers, feels that they are not dependable or are not trying to do a good job, and

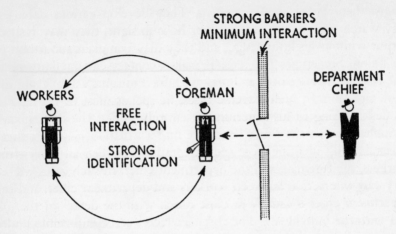

FIGURE 11.—Foreman Identified with Workers

is not interested in them as individuals. They feel that he is aloof and disinterested, and they hesitate to talk freely to him or to discuss problems with him. When together at department parties, neither he nor the workers feel comfortable, and they tend to stay apart. He is likely to seek out contacts with his superiors, both on the job or outside. He is often concerned about his relationship with his department chief and always tries to make a good impression. Thus there is a situation of close relationship between foreman and department chief and considerable distance between foreman and worker (Fig. 12).

In this type of situation the workers feel forced to be on their guard against their foreman and think of him as someone who is

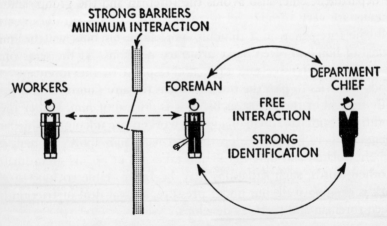

FIGURE 12.—Foreman Identified with Department Chief

against them rather than for them. They develop various defenses; they watch their behavior whenever he is in sight; they may restrict output without his knowledge; and they may complain about him to the union. Sometimes the tension makes contacts so uncomfortable that even he is aware of it and may withdraw to some extent from the work situation. In such extreme cases, he spends most of his time at his desk, talking to his superiors, or entirely out of the department.

Sometimes, on the other hand, we find a situation in which there is very strong identification and integration between all three—the workers, the foreman, and the department chief. In such cases we see very easy interaction between workers and department chief, and the department chief is usually in close touch with the details of the job and with the individuals. The foreman feels very comfortable under these conditions, does not worry about the presence of the department chief, and does not need to cover up mistakes or try to protect the group, since the boss can be trusted. In many instances of this kind, the whole department stands as a unit against outside pressures or against demands from above. Probably these are the most comfortable and satisfactory work situations for the foreman and for the workers.

Sometimes we see a foreman who is isolated from both his department chief and the work group. In these cases, there is considerable avoidance on the part of all concerned. If the job will run with a minimum of direct supervision and interaction with the workers, the foreman may stay out of the group most of the time and stay away from his department chief, too. As long as the work goes all right, the department chief also avoids the foreman and the group, and all contacts are very formal and uncomfortable. If the job does not go well, the foreman is in a difficult spot, since his boss will be quite critical of him and often make arbitrary demands. At the same time, the group is defensive and does not respond to the foreman's demands. He tries to pass the buck to them for any failures and is generally critical of them; just as his boss is critical of him. Under these conditions, both the foreman and the workers are uncomfortable; and whenever there is pressure on the foreman from above, he feels extremely isolated and defenseless and takes it out on his subordinates. In other words, such situations may be fairly stable so long as the work is running well; but under pressure, a great deal of friction between foreman and workers develops.

The Forgotten Man

Because of his position at the bottom of the management hierarchy, the foreman often feels that he is the forgotten man. He rarely participates in the making of decisions or the determination of policy, and often he is not well informed as to the why and wherefore of such decisions. All too frequently he knows only that management has decided to do thus and so and, in many cases, expects him to put the decision into action. While theoretically his ideas or sentiments are communicated up the line and are taken into account when management makes decisions, he knows that, actually, they only get through to the top in a very hit-or-miss manner and rarely influence decisions or policy. Certainly he almost never has the satisfaction of communicating them directly and seeing that they are actually considered. Of course, management occasionally makes the gesture of consulting the foremen, but usually all it amounts to is to call them together after a decision has already been made and to go through the motions of talking it over with no real idea of changing if the foremen object. Such meetings are often thought of as an attempt to "sell" the foremen on management's decisions rather than as an honest attempt to let them join in making the decisions.

All this does not mean that foremen necessarily think that they are qualified to make the decisions which top management must make. While top management often talks of them as being part of management and expects them to identify themselves with the interests of the company and of top management, they do not feel that they really "belong." They feel that they are expected to take whatever is handed down to them from above, no matter how arbitrary it may seem to them or how difficult it may make their jobs.

Management's Ideal

Nevertheless, top management is frequently concerned about the attitudes of the foremen. Management often feels that the foremen are incompetent and need more training, that they do not identify themselves with management, do not understand and accept the aims of management, and do not carry out decisions. Top management's ideal of a foreman is one who thinks much as they do, who understands their problems sufficiently to accept their decisions without question, and is a "good soldier"—that is, one who accepts orders and carries them out without question or reservation. Yet, often it is the actions and pressures originating at the top which create doubt and uncertainty on the part of the foreman, prevent him from becoming identified completely with management, and make him feel insecure.

Foreman and Morale

As we have seen, a foreman is in constant contact with the workers and has the responsibility of putting into action many of management's policies and decisions. Thus he is, to a considerable extent, the one who interprets management to the workers; he is, to a large degree, the only representative of management with whom the workers have much contact; he is the one who imposes management's controls upon them. For this reason he has an important influence upon their attitudes toward the job, the management, and the company generally. He is the one who can most directly affect their morale and loyalty. While his importance to employee morale has long been recognized, recent studies have shown that in many respects he is the most important factor in the work situation. For example, in a preliminary report on extensive research conducted by the Committee on Human Relations in Industry of the University of Chicago, the author reported as follows:

Some of the things which stand out quite clearly are the factors which are especially significant in determining the attitudes of people toward their jobs. In general, it appears that a few factors in the work situation are generally responsible for active enthusiasm or dislike, while other factors play a much more passive role.

It is important to note that these active elements are those things involving the individual's relations with others on the job. The things that really "burn 'em up" are the things the boss says or does, or the things that go on in the gang, or the way other employees act toward them. And they respond with enthusiasm to the congenial group and friendly boss. This was well shown by the statement of an industrial truck driver:

"I've had a lot of different jobs; I've worked in lots of factories, but I've never seemed to feel quite right about them somehow. I mean that I never cared much about the job; it was just something I had to do. But this is different. I've never been on a job before where the men help one another the way they do out there. Why, if one man is done with his work, he doesn't sit down and wait for something to turn up like they do on most jobs. He goes and helps somebody else. And the men will ask someone to help them, and I never seen one of them get turned down. Everybody always seems to want to help everybody else. And sometimes when I don't have anything to do for a minute or two I go over and watch one of the machines and the fellow who runs it, he'll explain it to me and tell me how it works. That's something I never seen them do any place else."

It is quite clear, furthermore, that of all the relationships within the work situation, the relation with the foreman or immediate supervisor is the most critical of them all. This is nothing new and is often expressed in the statement that "the foreman is the front-line personnel man." It is interesting, however, to see the strong emotional significance of this relationship as it is expressed in interviews. For example, a former machine setter with ten years' service left his job to take one for less pay and said:

"On that job there wasn't a day went by without the foreman would have some crack to make just to get your goat or just to be mean to you. He's supposed to be the foreman, but as far as I can figure he didn't do nothing but go around making everybody sore. If you'd ask him some question about the work, something about one of the machines or something like that you wanted to know, he'd look real nasty and he'd say, 'You're the operator. What d'ja want me to do about it?' And then he'd walk off; he'd never give you any help. 'You're the operator,' he'd say. 'What d'ja want me to do about it?' And that's all he would ever do for you.

"But if you'd argue with him about something or make some suggestion or something, he'd tell you to just mind your own business and do your own job. 'I do the thinking around here,' he'd say. 'You just tend to your work and I'll do the thinking for all of us.' He does the thinking! Huh! Yeah, the heck he does. All I can see that he ever does is to go around pickin' on everybody.

"And when you go over to ask him a question, any kind of question—Well, maybe it does sound a little dumb or something, but you're sincere when you ask it and it's something you want to know—but he'll just make fun of you for asking it and say the question again, mocking you, and not give you any answer to it. He could never give you a polite answer, always got to be something sarcastic, so that you get so you don't want to have to talk to him about anything if you can help it. And you get so when you see him coming you get all nervous and wonder what's coming now. What kind of a nasty crack he's going to make this time.

"When you get someone like that around you all the time it makes you get so you don't want to go to work at all. Some jobs you get up in the morning, and you feel like going to work; you feel good about it and you're glad you got a job and that you're going to it. But this job, I got so I'd lie in bed in the morning and think, 'If I just didn't have to go to work, if there was something the matter with me so I wouldn't have to go, if I could only think of some reason for staying home today!' I'd just wonder to myself, 'Now, what's he going to think of today? What's he going to find that he can pick on?' And then I'd start worrying. And by the time I'd get to my breakfast I didn't even want to eat. And I'd just sit there trying to figure out some way I could get out of having to go down there; but there never was. You gotta work; if you have a job you gotta go to it."

When we seek to determine the effects of such things as employee benefits, vacations, good working conditions and all the morale building devices, we immediately find ourselves in a region of vagueness and contradictions. While the interviews were with all kinds of people from a wide variety of companies, there was little spontaneous talk about such factors in work situations. Even with workers from companies which were well known for their advanced personnel systems, it was rare to have enthusiastic talk about these matters. What people seemed most concerned about, what they really wanted to talk about, were the matters of their daily relationships with their boss and fellow-workers. Furthermore, where there was some show of enthusiasm for company policies or benefits, it was always coupled with statements about it being a friendly place to work or having a swell boss. In fact, if the supervisors were fine and fellow-workers friendly, almost anything might be referred to as showing what a fine place it was. For example, in some cases, after praising the boss, the individual would make some such statement as, "The company is really interested in the workers. Why, you know they give us a ten minute rest period every morning and afternoon, and recently they put in a vending machine so we could buy a coke during rest period."

Closely related to this problem of the attitude of workers towards their jobs is the problem of turnover. In considering this we found it useful to think of the work group as being subject to a number of forces, some of which tend to hold it together and others of which tend to force it apart. Furthermore, it is clear that some of the forces operating arise from the outside society and are not readily controllable by management. On the other hand, many of the forces arise within the work situation itself and can be influenced or controlled by the management of the individual concern.

When we examine present conditions we see that the war has set in motion a variety of disrupting forces which increase the rate of turnover. Obviously, unless such disruptive forces are compensated for by the cohesive forces within the work situation, there is bound to be a sharp increase in turnover. Unfortunately, the effects of wartime expansion and conversion have also increased the disruptive forces within the work situations, with the result that turnover has increased excessively.

Discussion with people concerning why they do or do not change jobs has shown several things. Just as their attitudes towards their job is strongly influenced by their relations with their superiors and with fellow-workers, also their decisions as to whether to stay or leave often hinge on these relations. As in the interview quoted, it is apparent that unsatisfactory relations with the boss constitute a powerful disruptive force, while the foreman who is liked is an equally powerful stabilizing force. To quote a worker who had made several changes in the last few years:

"You know why people are changing jobs? It's simply because jobs are plentiful and people don't have to take a pushing around by these dumb grafters who call themselves supervisors. Sure, when times are tough a man has to work at his job whether he likes it or not; he has to take it. But why should he today. You know, it's a funny thing, but when you work around here and there and see how people are treated, you get so you enjoy telling a foreman to go to—it's fun.

"My present boss I would do anything for simply because he is the only man who has ever shown any confidence in me. It's the one company I worked for where a man in supervision shows some consideration for the people under him. I think the entire management shows that attitude. These companies are always talking about backing up the foreman, yet the only backing that really means anything to a foreman is the backing of the men under him. What good does it do the company to be constantly backing up the foreman if that foreman has a big turnover or can't get the cooperation of his men? My boss never has to ask the company to back him up, because he has the backing of the men. I would do anything for him and so would the other guys."[1]

THE DEPARTMENT CHIEF

The activities, attitudes, relationships, and functions of a department chief are usually quite different from those of a foreman. As we have seen, he is not so close to the actual work even though he sits nearby. He usually spends more time at his desk, reading reports, going over and signing various papers, preparing memoranda to his boss. He spends much more time out of the work location, in the division chief's office, in conference with other department heads, or with engineers, inspectors, or other staff people. He deals with many of the relationships with other departments, and he may be active in co-ordinating the work of his department with that of others.

Since he is not directly in control of the job, he relies to a considerable extent upon reports from his foreman for his knowledge of what is going on. He usually expects his foremen to keep him informed daily as to the progress of the work and as to any significant occurrences, especially anything about which he may be questioned by his division chief. Thus he is constantly gathering information from his foremen which he uses in his contacts with superiors or with others. The foremen may report to him any failures of delivery or faulty materials from other departments, and he can then use this information either in contacting the other departments or for communication to his boss. He pays more attention to formal reports, too, such as cost, quality, or earnings, than does the foreman. On the whole, he relies on his foremen's verbal reports to keep him in touch with the job, and thereby expects to have a general idea of how the department is getting along before the formal control reports appear.

Perspective and Participation

Department chiefs generally identify themselves with management much more than foremen do. They seem to be much more "manage-

[1] Burleigh B. Gardner, "A Program of Research in Human Problems in Industry," *American Management Association, Personnel Series Number 80* (1944), pp. 35–38.

ment minded"; they show more interest in costs and efficiency; and they accept the rules more completely. This may be the result of their separation from the work itself, plus their increased participation in planning, co-ordinating, and contacts up the line. In general, the broadening of participation, so that the individual has to become familiar with problems of co-ordination beyond those of his immediate organization, seems to shift his orientation so that he thinks more like management and sees the more general problems. Furthermore, the department chief is likely to participate in discussions with both division chiefs and superintendents. He may be called in to discuss proposed policies, changes in practices, technological developments, and so on. He has more opportunity than the foreman does to voice his opinions, to see the processes of decision-making, and possibly to influence them; and he generally has more of a feeling of being a part of management.

Relations with Workers

To the workers the department chief is the highest level of authority readily available with whom they may have fairly frequent contact and to whom the foreman must turn for decisions. He is the highest level of "visible" authority, and to many he is the "boss." While they recognize that he is subordinated to the higher levels, he is still the one who transmits the demands from above the department. He has the final say on most matters concerning them and may overrule the foreman. Because of his location in the shop, the barriers to approaching and contacting him are much less than with higher levels of supervision. He is someone they can get to. But, at the same time, actual interaction with him is considerably less frequent than with the foreman. He is not the one who constantly watches over their work; he is not ever present, "breathing down their necks" all day long as the foreman is. As a result, if he is friendly and has an approachable manner, they may often feel that he is more understanding and sympathetic than their foreman and that he can be trusted to be fair with them even if their foreman cannot. On the other hand, if he is forbidding and critical, he may be the focus of their complaints and may be thought of as the source of everything that goes wrong on the job. If he is friendly, they feel that they can speak to him if their foreman is too disagreeable and that he will fix things up. If he is unfriendly, there is no escape from an unpleasant foreman; there is no one in authority to whom they can turn for help.

On his part, the department chief usually has quite a different attitude toward the workers than that of the foreman. The foreman has to deal directly with the workers in his efforts to get the job done; he must deal with them each individually; he sees their faults and errors; and, when things are going badly, he is apt to be irritated and critical of them. The department chief, however, usually thinks of the foremen as being the ones responsible for the work and even for the behavior of the workers. When things go poorly, he blames the foremen rather than the individual workers. Even when the workers break the rules, he is likely to blame the foremen for not maintaining discipline. Thus each level wields authority over the one below; and, under this direct pressure, friction is likely to be generated. At the same time, the department chief can remain aloof and friendly to the workers without becoming involved in frictions between them and the foreman.

THE DIVISION CHIEF

At the division chief level, we move into the area of invisible authority. The division chief sits in an office away from the shop. He has little firsthand contact with the job and may appear among the workers only infrequently. He really is in the realm of the "big shots" and the "brass hats." And not only is he far from the work, but the gap between him and the department chief, or what has been called "social distance,"[2] is likely to be greater than between any other two levels. The marked cleavage between these two levels was noted by Roethlisberger and Dickson in the Western Electric study.[3] As they point out, however, this does not mean that there is more conflict and hostility between these two levels. It does mean that there is a greater difference in sentiments and interests with the change from visible to invisible authority.

[2] a) "The concept of 'distance' as applied to human, as distinguished from spatial, relations, has come into use among sociologists, in an attempt to reduce to something like measurable terms the grades and degree of understanding and intimacy which characterize personal and social relations generally" (Robert E. Park, "The Concept of Social Distance, "*Journal of Applied Sociology*, VIII [1924], p. 339).

b) "If, as we shall assume, grades of understanding and intimacy between persons or groups, or between a person and a group, are dependent upon the degree to which they share the same sentiments and interests, 'social distance' measures differences in sentiment and interest which separate individuals or groups from one another or an individual from a group" (F. J. Roethlisberger and W. J. Dickson, *Management and the Worker* [Cambridge, Mass.: Harvard University Press, 1939], p. 359 n.).

[3] *Ibid.*, pp. 359–60.

At the division chief level we really come to the management group. Division chiefs are away from direct contact with the work level; they cannot just step out into the shop to see how things are getting along, the way a department chief can; and they are not generally concerned with the details of one small part of the job or with the work of one group. They sit at their desks and gather their information through reports, memos, and conferences with their department chiefs. They concern themselves with problems of coordination and planning for their divisions and with liaison with other divisions. They rely to a great extent upon cost and performance reports and usually have charts showing various measures of performance so that they can keep a close watch on any changes. They are likely to be very cost-minded and to be constantly after their departments to keep costs down or to keep within the budget.

While the division chief level is getting into management, this is not really top management. The primary concern of a division chief is with running the job, keeping the pressure on the shop departments, and keeping a close watch on the controls. He does not spend his time with future planning, with policy-making, or with major decisions. We might say that the focus of his attention is downward upon the job; and he often resents too much change or interference coming from above, since these things always disturb the equilibrium which he is attempting to maintain in the job.

THE SUPERINTENDENT

At the superintendent level, we really reach top management. Supervisors at this level usually constitute the "staff" of the president. They sit in on decisions of policy; they participate in the planning; they must concern themselves with the future. In dealing with the job they are even less concerned with details, and even more concerned with the over-all situation, than the division chief is. They do not feel that they must keep up with a mass of everyday details, but rely on their subordinates for that. And when, as often, they have to make decisions about specific situations, they expect their subordinates to bring them such details as are pertinent and must be considered.

Diverging Points of View

In many companies a sharp cleavage can be found at about this level. The striking thing about such a cleavage is the sharp divergence in point of view and attitudes between the executive, whose attention seems to be directed downward and who is always thinking in terms of his organization and is engrossed in the problems of its operation, and the higher-level executive, who thinks more in terms of the company as a whole and all its extended activities and relationships. In some cases this cleavage appears just above the superintendent level, between president and superintendent; often it is particularly striking between the president and the superintendent who is in charge of the manufacturing organization. In other cases the greatest divergence is found just below the superintendent, between superintendent and division chief; this is particularly true in large companies with an extended supervisory hierarchy. Because this cleavage seems to appear with equal frequency at either level, either just above or just below the superintendent, it is difficult to talk about superintendents as a uniform or general group.

Identification with Work Group

On the one hand, we find the superintendent who is looking downward, identifying himself with the work group, sympathetic with his division chief, and impatient with the Big Boss, who seems to be more concerned with his luncheons and clubs than with running the business. These attitudes seem to be especially marked when there is a great difference in background or industrial experience between a superintendent and the man at the top. A manufacturing superintendent, for example, is often an old-timer who has risen gradually through the ranks of the manufacturing organization and has spent his whole life in that setting. Higher executives, on the other hand, have frequently risen through other channels, such as engineering, sales, or accounting organizations, or may have been brought in from other positions or locations. Such divergence in background seems to sharpen the differences which arise out of their positions and functions in the structure, and frequently results in mutual feelings of irritation and exasperation. The superior thinks that his subordinate is hardheaded and "sot in his ways" and that it is impossible to get him to accept new ideas or see changing conditions and adapt himself to them. He has an excessive tendency to cling to the old ways and to stay in the same old grooves, thinks the top executive. At the same time, the superintendent feels that his superior is trying to change things just for the sake of change, that he does not see the difficulties or the effects of these changes upon the work. His superior seems to be always critical, when the superintendent wants merely to be left alone to run the job and see that the work gets done. As a result, we often find this type of superintendent on the defensive, trying to protect his organization from the demands of the Big Boss, reducing interaction to a minimum, and generally trying to erect a protective wall around himself and his group, much as division chiefs and department chiefs do. And how this annoys the Big Boss! As one top executive said:

For all the influence I have, you would never know that the plant is part of the company. Why, if I go into the plant for anything, I hardly get in the door before the superintendent is standing by my side, and he stays with me until I leave. And I know that I only get to see the things that he wants me to see. And trying to introduce any changes seems a hopeless task; it's like pushing against a stone wall. Even when he seems to agree to something, it goes only slowly and halfheartedly, and there are a dozen things wrong with it.

And yet the plant runs well in terms of getting production and making money. There isn't any major thing to complain about. But we feel that it isn't going ahead. Instead of constantly improving the plant, the processes, or their organization, they are just marking time. While it seems to be going along all right now, we are afraid of what it will be in a few years, and we want to see it improving so it can meet whatever comes.

We have just been sitting tight and trying to make a few changes gradually, and I think we are making some progress, but it is awfully slow. I suppose the only way to do anything with it very rapidly is to go in and tear it limb from limb and put it back together the way we want it. But the situation isn't bad enough to justify that, and that would mean the end of the superintendent; he would just have to quit along with a few others. We would much rather handle it without taking such drastic steps.

Orientation

On the other hand, there are many superintendents who are oriented like the president, who look outward to problems of public relations, governmental regulations, and all the various external things which affect the functioning of a business. They are often active in outside affairs, attend meetings and luncheons, belong to business organizations, take part in community affairs, and in various ways extend themselves beyond the walls of the plant. In such cases, there is likely to be the same antagonism, the same social distance, the same mutual feelings of annoyance between superintendent and division chief as that described between president and superintendent above. And, as at the higher level, these feelings are intensified when there is a marked difference in their backgrounds—when the division chief is the one who came up the hard way and the superintendent the one who came in through staff organizations or from outside.

THE BIG BOSS

Outside Activities

Top management, and especially the very top (the president or in larger companies the works manager or the plant manager), faces certain problems which are of little concern to those lower in the structure. In the first place, the top executive is constantly concerned with the position of the company in the entire industrial and economic system and with co-ordinating its activities so that it will meet competition, survive social, economic, and political changes, and generally maintain itself as a going concern. This means that he must keep informed on a whole range of matters in the outside world, must be evaluating them in terms of their effect upon his concern, and laying plans or making changes in the internal activities to meet these conditions. As a result, he is constantly seeking information through various sources. He reads newsletters, market reports, and technical journals, and follows the financial pages carefully. But, often, even more important to him is a knowledge of what other businessmen are doing and how they are interpreting the course of events. So he belongs to businessmen's clubs and attends dinners and meetings where he will be able to exchange ideas and information with others on his own level. These contacts often make it possible for him to act in harmony with other top executives as a group, either through conscious effort or, more often, unconsciously, merely by following the example of a few leaders. These groups in which he moves are, furthermore, an important part of his social environment; they become the groups he feels identified with; they are his kind; and inevitably he tries to maintain his position among them. This means that he often acts and talks in ways which he thinks will be acceptable to the group, or tries to gain their respect for his judgment and abilities, or tries to increase the standing of his company in terms of size or prestige in its field.

These activities of the top executive are very important to the concern as a whole, since they provide the basis for many new decisions which affect the future adaptation of the organization to the total society, and which may even determine its future existence. Similar contacts or information at levels below the president and sometimes his immediate staff have much less significance, since the fundamental decisions flow from the top down. Thus, while it may be of vital importance for those at the top to be well informed on national and world affairs and well integrated into groups at their own level, it is not especially important for those at lower levels; and, as a rule, their attention is directed inward toward the details of the company rather than outward to the external world.

Maintaining Equilibrium

Another major concern of the top executive is that of maintaining an effective equilibrium and balance within the company. One of his aims is to develop an organization which functions smoothly with little friction, which has an adequate equilibrium so that the company can sell its products at a profit, and which is sufficiently stable to function with a minimum of attention from him. When he has such a situation, he can devote his energies to other things, and especially to relations with the outside world without worrying over the details within the walls. Probably almost every president longs to have just such an organization, and probably few of them attain it.

The Big Boss must continually concern himself, too, with keeping what he considers a proper balance of all the parts of the structure. Since every organization within the company is concerned primarily with its own function, each constantly acts as a pressure group demanding that its point of view and ideas be given more consideration, that things which hamper its activities be changed, that other organizations give way to it, and that it be expanded or improved so that it can do a better job. Thus the accounting organization will be in love with its own theories and systems; it will want to have better methods, more records, closer controls, and will frequently feel that all other activities should be subordinated to its routines. To other organizations it may appear that the accountants think the business is being run for their own exclusive benefit. In the same way, however, the engineers seek to improve and expand their activities, seek more authority and control, and try to subordinate the shop to their ideas. The personnel organization struggles to build up its functions too, and so do all the other organizations and every segment of them. The man on top has to be judging the total situation constantly. He must decide just where to limit the functions; he must decide on size and cost for each, balance the demands for control and authority, and not let one take over the place to the detriment of the company as a whole.

As part of the pressures from the different segments, there are also frequent frictions and conflicts between them, many of which are carried up to the top executive for settlement. Thus, he must not only try to decide on and maintain the proper balance among the segments, but he must also preserve harmony and co-operation among them. All too often these conflicts between superintendents are communicated to lower levels and thus increase the friction and instability of the organization as a whole. For this reason it is extremely important that the president pull his top executives together into a smooth-working, co-operative group.

Keeping in Touch with the Company

Although much of the top executive's attention is focused outward, it is still important for him to keep well informed about how things are going in the concern. For one thing, it is important for his own sense of security, since, if he feels any doubt about the way the organization is functioning, he develops anxieties which harm his relations with his subordinates. Also, if he is to be able to make proper decisions, to settle conflicts, and generally to function properly, it is necessary for him to have adequate information. For this he relies on both formal reports, such as costs reports, and on verbal communication from his staff. All reports, especially the highly formalized cost reports and production records, present quite a problem in interpretation, since they are extremely oversimplified condensations of very complex data; and to know what they mean requires a detailed knowledge of the work and all conditions which might affect it. In fact, a great deal of the verbal communication of subordinates usually has to do with the interpretation of these formal, written communications. In their efforts to be informed, therefore, the top executives are constantly asking their subordinates for reports covering many types of activities.

Top management in general is always interested in raising the organization to new levels of performance. The top executive likes to see new records set for output, quality, cost reduction, and so on, and is frequently trying to work out new methods for producing such improvements. He is interested in learning of new incentive systems, or new technical developments, or better control methods which can be used to produce these results. Also he is constantly using the various reports as a basis for stimulating performance. Thus, nearly every plant has certain reports which lower levels think of as "batting averages" or "score cards," since top management uses these figures as a method of comparison between organizations. By such comparisons, the president often attempts to develop competition between units and to keep them all trying to improve.

Besides trying to improve performance by putting pressure on the organizations, management also seeks improvement through changes in organization, personnel, control methods, and so on. Many internal changes, too, grow out of the need to adapt the organization to changes in the outside world. In many cases management faces the problem both of deciding what changes will make a more effective organization and of handling the change in such a way that it will not cause serious disturbance in the organization. For example, a certain change in organization which appeared to be an improvement might so disturb the supervisors as to ruin the morale and efficiency of the entire group. For that reason, top management must try to anticipate the results of even the simplest changes and must take whatever actions may be necessary in order to make the changes successful.

Top Management and the Workers

It is clear that, as you move upward in the structure, the frequency of interaction with the workers decreases. In fact, it drops off sharply above the department chief level simply because there is little opportunity for those located away from the shop to have casual contact with the workers. Of course, many executives make a point of chatting with some of the workers whenever they visit the shops, but actually such contacts are likely to be infrequent and limited to only a small portion of the workers. The president who walks through the shop every day and speaks to a few of the old-timers may feel that he is "keeping in touch." Actually, such contacts are usually somewhat artificial and rarely are extended to new workers. Certainly in any plant with several hundred workers, it becomes impossible for the president to spend the time necessary to really maintain contact with all the workers. This means that his knowledge of the attitude of the workers is based principally upon what other people say it is.

In spite of the little interaction, or perhaps because of it, the workers often look to top management as being fair-minded and sympathetic. In part, this seems to arise out of the fact that a worker often receives a sympathetic hearing and gets action when he does approach the man at the top with a request or complaint. If Joe, with twenty years of service, works up enough courage to go to the Big Boss and complain that he thinks it is not fair to give all the better jobs to new men without giving him a chance, the Big Boss is likely to think only of Joe and the way Joe feels without knowing the factors in the situation which made the foreman decide not to put Joe on the job he wants. Even if he realizes that there may be more than meets the eye, he can be friendly and soothing and say that he will talk to Joe's foreman about it. And Joe goes away feeling that the Big Boss is certainly a fine man. Furthermore, when the executive asks about the case, the foreman may either give Joe the chance he wants, in which case the Big Boss gets the credit; or the foreman may show why it cannot be done, in which case the foreman gets the blame from Joe. This sort of thing does not happen often, of course; individual workers only rarely step out of bounds to take their troubles to the president, or to the plant manager, or even to the superintendent or division chief. If many such things were placed in the Big Boss's lap, he would probably be forced into the position of backing up his foremen and would no longer be thought of as such a fine man.

In order to retain some contact with the worker, and especially to provide a channel for complaints, many top executives maintain what is referred to as an "open-door policy." This merely means that they announce that they will talk to anyone in the organization at any time, that any worker can come up and see them about anything without asking permission to do it. While the executives are sincere in their attitude of wanting workers to come to them with complaints, unfortunately such a device does not work. In the first place, the fact that the worker has to take the initiative, that he has to go out of his accustomed environment into the office and approach the Big Boss, blocks such action except under very exceptional circumstances. Usually a worker has to be really "burnt up" about something and has to have reached the point where he feels he is ready to risk anything to get a hearing before he will take such a step. And with the men at the very top, who have secretaries to protect them from informal contacts, the barriers are even greater. Of course, under such a policy a few workers may get through to see an executive, giving him a feeling of being available to the workers and of being in touch with what is going on. If he would only note how few such contacts he has in any given month, however, and consider how many workers there are, he will realize that any belief that the open-door policy really works is more wishful thinking than actual fact.

9. THE UNION: ITS FUNCTIONS AND PLACE IN THE STRUCTURE

A LABOR union is ordinarily thought of as something extraneous, an excrescence upon the structure of industry, rather than as an integral part of it. Actually, a union can be as much a part of the total structure as an engineering or accounting organization. Probably the fact that it usually arises out of the desires of the workers rather than as a decision of management leads to the belief that it is something apart and outside. From our point of view, however, whatever organizations or groupings exist within any given plant organization are all equally parts of the structure of that plant. This does not mean that the plant could not function without any one of its parts. The fact is that the one basic relationship in a factory is probably that of workers at work, producing goods. All other organizations and relations are built upon this; but they are, nonetheless, integrated parts of the whole plant structure.

Internal Structure

The internal structure of the large labor organizations, such as the Congress of Industrial Organizations or the American Federation of Labor, is quite complicated; but the structure of the local unit in any one plant is usually fairly simple. In one medium-sized plant, for example, the local union consists of four status levels: the chairman, members of the executive board, stewards, and all other members (Fig. 13). All of the offices are elective, and all are held by regular shop employees. Any complaints or grievances may be taken directly to the stewards, members of the executive committee, or the chairman. Since all the officers are working in the shops, they all have direct contact with the other workers. In fact, each one, regardless of his position in the union hierarchy, functions as the steward for the shop department in which he works.

A complaint from a worker is generally handled first by his steward, who takes it up with the foreman. If it cannot be settled at that

145

level, the steward may contact the next level of supervision directly. But if it is necessary to go higher, the complaint is turned over to the executive board, who carry it higher up, according to the procedure agreed on in the contract between the company and the union. In some cases the chairman may delay formal action and may take up

FIGURE 13.—The Structure of a Union Local

the complaint unofficially with the higher levels of the company in order to give supervision time to work out some satisfactory settlement.

The Functions of a Union

Union organization often develops as a result of management's limited point of view and of restricted communication within the structure. In the supervisory ranks the whole focus of attention is upon getting the job done and upon conditions affecting the job. This leads to a habit of thinking of the workers as merely tools, merely means to the real goal—production. The attitudes and problems of workers are likely to be treated as unimportant compared to the job, and workers feel that management is indifferent to them. They feel that their future, their rewards, and their satisfactions are controlled by a management which is basically indifferent to them and their desires. Furthermore, because of their subordinate position at the bottom of the hierarchy, they feel blocked and helpless to get anyone to listen to them. The line of authority is their one accepted means of communication with management. This means that their immediate supervisor, the foreman, is the one to whom they have to take their grievances. The way in which the complaints are handled and the satisfactions they receive are dependent upon the effectiveness of the immediate supervisor in carrying them up the line. If he is indifferent, they do not feel free to take their problems above him except as a most reckless venture. If he is sympathetic, they know that he may be blocked by the indifference of those above him.

With a union, however, the situation is considerably altered. The union is the workers' own organization; it is concerned with what they think is important; the focus of its attention is on the workers, not on the work. The existence of a union gives the workers a feeling of unity as a group, which makes them feel protected and courageous. As individual workers, they hesitate to stand up for their rights against their bosses; and when one does occasionally, the others look upon him as brave, but foolhardy. But as union members, with a group behind them to back them up and protect them, they can speak without fear. Furthermore, their immediate supervisors are not then the only ones to whom they can go with their complaints; they can take their grievances to their union representatives and expect to get some action.

Some of the situations and worker feelings which stimulate demands on the union are shown in the following statements by employees:

1. I feel so badly I could scream. With my service and the way I'm pushed around! I complained to the union representative and he said he was going to take it up with the big boss. I'm not wasting my time talking to any supervisors any more, because they don't do a thing for you.

2. I didn't get a raise this time. I sure was hurt about it. They never call me up and tell me anything about the job; yet I don't get a raise. I come in every morning; I'm never late; but I never get anything for it. I'm going to talk to the shop steward.

3. I'm back here and it sure gripes me. There are still men over me there with shorter service than I have, but they transfer me. It means a cut of $5.00 a week for me. I saw my union steward this morning and complained to him.

In all these statements the employees feel that they have been unfairly treated and that they must look to the union to defend their interests. In the first statement the employee feels that his superior cannot or will not correct the situation and that the union will take the complaint to the Big Boss. In the second statement the operator seems to feel completely ignored, since he gets neither a raise nor any recognition for his faithful service. As these statements suggest, the attitude of employees toward the union and the extent to which they feel the need of a union is frequently closely related to the effectiveness with which the line handles work dissatisfactions.

Even those who are not especially ardent union members recognize that it is only as a group that they dare to stand up to the boss. As one worker said,

> I ain't too sure about the union. I guess it's all right for some, but I can't see it does me much good. Of course, if you've got a complaint it's better to have the union to go to the boss with you. It's hard sometimes to get the boss to listen when you have to go to him all alone and lots of people are afraid to do it. With the union, you know he will pay some attention and not push you around.

Union Communication

Besides giving them this feeling of strength as a group, the union has a variety of other functions for the workers. Most important, it has highly formalized procedures by means of which it can bring its demands (the workers' demands), directly to top management, if necessary, and thrust its point of view upon them without being delayed and blocked by intermediate supervisory levels. Through its stewards and other officials, it serves as another channel of communication through which information can move up through the structure even as far as top management. Unlike other channels, however, communication through the union is not controlled by management. The union is not trying to satisfy the demands of management for information; it is not trying to give management only the "good news"; and it is not trying to protect itself from management's criticism. On the contrary, union communication is seldom simply for the purpose of keeping management informed, but it is predominantly concerned with bringing *to* management criticisms of the way line organizations are functioning and demands for changes. In this respect, the union is unique in the industrial structure. In all the other organizations in the structure the great bulk of communication takes the form of information moving *up* and criticisms and demands moving *down*. Communication upward through the union, however, serves to put pressure on management and supervision and sets in motion changes in activities in a way that other forms of communication fail to do. Significantly, however, the union cannot make the decisions or actually take the action necessary to solve the problems about which it complains and makes demands. It acts largely as a mechanism for getting supervision's attention to employees' interests, insisting on decisions, and speeding up action. Decisions and final action must come down the line from above.

Union communication may cover a wide range of subject matter and is, in fact, almost as versatile as the line of authority in this respect; but unlike the line, it is always directed toward the workers' interests rather than toward the job and the effect of things upon the work. A foreman reporting to his boss on some difficulty in the shop is thinking mostly in terms of what it means to the job; a shop steward reporting on the same incident to the union is thinking of the workers' attitudes and feelings about it. When both of these reports are passed on to management, one through the line and one through the union, then management must examine the situation both from the point of view of the work and from the point of view of the workers.

The union, too, serves to speed up action on worker requests and complaints, either by speeding up communication upward through the structure or by "short-circuiting" the line. In many cases, as we pointed out in an earlier discussion of communication, worker requests move very slowly up the line; and waiting for action may seem interminable. The request or complaint is viewed with less and less interest as it goes up the line and gets farther removed from the work situation; each level of supervision feels that it is rather unimportant, and each one either neglects to act on it or passes it on to his superior without making a decision. In all such cases the entrance of the union into the situation speeds up the processes of communication and decision. The union does not have to wait for things to move up the line through the normal routes, but can go directly, without waiting, to any level. This fact speeds communication up the line especially at the lower levels of supervision, where they do not have the authority to make the decisions. If the union should go to a higher authority with a request which has not already come up the line, then the lower levels are "on the spot" for not having kept their superiors informed. For that reason, the moment a case goes to the union, the news is passed up the line in a hurry. For example, a worker feels that he deserves an upgrading to a higher grade of work, and he requests it of his foreman. The foreman feels that the change is not justified, or at least that it will not benefit the job, and so he refuses, or puts it off and forgets about it. The worker, however, is not satisfied and he goes to his shop steward. The steward sees the foreman and says that he thinks the request is justified. The foreman then either grants the request, refuses it, or says that he will have to con-

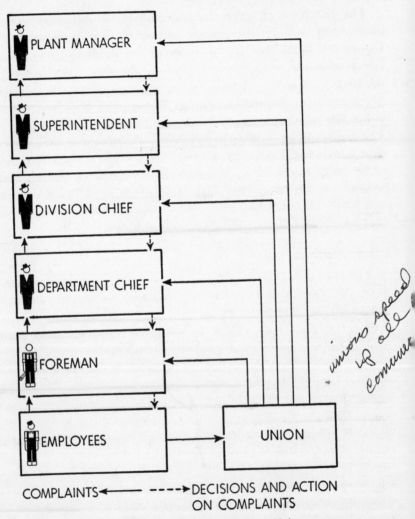

FIGURE 14.—Communication through the Union

sult with his boss, depending on his authority in the matter. Unless he has the authority to allow the change and does allow it, he will inform his boss of the incident, presenting his side of the story and his excuses for not acting sooner. This is imperative, because his boss must be informed before the union goes to him with the request. At higher levels, or whenever the supervisor can make the decision and is merely "stalling" because of indifference or lack of attention, the union may serve to hurry his decision, not necessarily by actually going above him, but sometimes merely by the fact of having the ability to go above if he does not act.

The functions of union communication, as compared with communication through the line of authority, can be diagramed as in Figure 14. Solid line arrows indicate the channels through which information and complaints may pass up the line; dotted arrows show decisions and action moving down. With a union, the employee is not limited to communication up through the line but may go to either his supervisor or his union representative with his problems. The union can go directly to any level and force it to deal with problems which might never get through the line; and when there is delay or blockage at one level, the union can short-circuit the line and take problems to the next level. It will be noted, however, that decisions and action do not come from the union but from management and are passed down through the lines of authority.

Union Organization

The union has relationships and internal problems of organization quite different from the other organizations. In the first place, there is little of the concept of authority in union relationships. The chairman is not the "boss." He does not give orders or make decisions which can be imposed on those below him. He does not directly control the distribution of rewards or recognition for the individuals. In contrast to the line, where supervisors are selected by their superiors, union officials are elected by, and are therefore responsible to, those below them in the union hierarchy. Besides this, or perhaps because of it, the union also lacks the elaborate system of rewards and punishments which a line organization usually has available. The average union member accepts the union activities as useful but incidental to the work. His daily life, his hopes, and expectations are centered much more around his job than around the union. His eye is on his boss for approval or criticism, not on his steward. He may be critical of his steward, but he does not especially care what the steward thinks of him; recognition from the steward does not give him the same satisfaction as recognition from his boss; and criticism from the steward only makes him mad.

For the most part, workers judge the union by results; and the individual worker often thinks in terms of satisfaction for himself, more than for workers as a group. In many cases, workers complain that the union is incompetent or lacks the power to get effective results for them. In other cases—and this is one of the severest criticisms—they believe that the union is indifferent to them and does not try to get results. These critical attitudes toward the union are illustrated in the following quotations from dissatisfied workers:

1. If anyone such as a union steward comes around, I'm going to mention that I'd like a transfer. A. doesn't pay any dues because she doesn't belong, but I pay my $2.00 a month and don't get a thing out of it, and she gets a good job.

2. I don't even make $45.00 a week after all my service. That's no salary for a man with a family. We had a union meeting last night about the percentage here. It's no good. All the fellows are kicking. I didn't go myself, didn't feel as though I wanted to. How can a fellow support a family on a salary like that? They ought to do something about me. What good does it do to complain, though? They don't do anything about me.

3. The steward was down to see me and said the superintendent was going to fix me up with something good. I said he doesn't even know me; he walks through here and never recognizes me. As far as I'm concerned X and his union can go to hell! I'm a fool for paying them $2.00 a month!

4. We're supposed to hear something from the union this week. I suppose we'll get knocked off on it. I don't think they can do us any good. I think we were foolish to make a kick at all. They just sit around and talk about it; it doesn't make any difference to them. They don't seem to care whether they help us or not.

5. That damn union is no good. We took our kick up to them and got nothing. In fact, they made it worse for us.

The union does not, of course, spend all its time on the complaints and grievances of individual workers but is constantly keeping an eye on company policies and practices and suggesting or demanding changes to benefit workers as a group. Besides this, the union is always pressing management for uniformity in practices. Thus the union seeks uniform wages for comparable work throughout a plant, and it asks for uniform methods in upgrading, transfers, and so on. If one department introduces rest periods, the union may request them for the entire plant; if one group changes its starting time, the union may ask that others do the same. This pressure for uniformity becomes especially noticeable when one union has organized several plants of one company. Then, any change in one plant may lead to requests for similar changes in the others. Under such conditions, management is very careful about making any changes or improvements in one location which it is not willing to consider for all the others.

Foremen and the Union

The ability of the union to go over his head on any problems or complaints puts the foreman in a difficult position. Since he is the one who has the most direct contact with the workers and who is constantly controlling and directing them, many of their complaints and dissatisfactions arise out of his actions and decisions. Without the union these dissatisfactions usually have no effective outlet and are not an immediate threat to the foreman, since few workers have the temerity either to "tell off" their boss or to go over his head with their complaints. The foreman can, therefore, concentrate on getting the work done and does not have to worry much about how the workers feel. Once the union comes in, however, he is forced to think in terms of satisfying both his superiors and his subordinates. He has to give attention to the workers as well as the work, and neglect of either may bring criticism from above. Thus he is, in a way, caught in the middle between his superiors and his subordinates. This situation often gives a foreman feelings of great insecurity; he feels that he is losing his authority and control. If many of his decisions are taken up by the union and then overridden by his superiors, or if the union gets favorable action on requests which he has turned down, he feels that his superiors are not backing him up and that the union is running his job. He is likely to feel, too, that his superiors will listen to the union while they ignore him, which is certainly true in many cases. Such situations and attitudes make the foreman's position an unhappy one, especially if he is having difficulties with the job or has an aggressive steward.

It should not be assumed, however, that blockages or difficulties with the union always occur at the foreman level or that they occur only at that level. In some cases the foremen, and even higher supervisors, are aware of employees' sentiments and do whatever they can at their level. Sometimes, however, the foreman himself feels frustrated in his attempts to get higher levels to recognize the workers' problems and help to solve them satisfactorily. Then he may recognize the fact that the union is more effective than he is in overcoming blockage in the line and getting the attention of higher levels. This is illustrated in the following statements by supervisors:

1. These guys had quite a kick. They took it up to the union and argued about it. They talked to me about it first, but there wasn't anything I could do about it. After all, there's a limit to my authority; so I told them that's the way things are; so they went to the union with it. After all, what've they got a union for?

2. I suppose you've heard about the rumpus we've been having. What the union is asking for is that we increase their rates. That sounds reasonable enough to me, but it's up to the guys upstairs to approve it. I can't get Mr. X to approve it because he's leaving and says it's Mr. Y's job, but Mr. Y won't do it until he takes over. As a result we are getting pushed around by the union, and, of course, we can't tell the union what's holding it up. They would be shocked to learn that the bigshots are handling it like that.

In some cases, where a department chief is being dilatory or indecisive, the foreman can get action by merely mentioning that the question has been referred to the union. In other cases, foremen deliberately let complaints that might easily be settled by the line go to the union because they believe that the union can get action more quickly and easily. In extreme cases they may even encourage the union to take up matters which would not ordinarily interest them, or about which workers have not complained much. For example, a foreman may think that his shop needs better lights, but he has been unable to get his superiors to approve the expense of the change. A discussion with the shop steward about the "lousy lights we got" and a little complaining about not being able to get anything done about it, and soon the union may present a complaint about the lights. The idea of foremen using the union in this way will probably be shocking to management, but it does happen sometimes. And when it happens, it can always be traced to some blockage in the line which prevents the foremen from getting things done through the regular channels.

Management and the Union

It will be apparent from this discussion so far that the union differs sharply from other organizations in the industrial structure in several ways, most particularly in its relations with management. To begin with, the union's orientation and point of view is opposed to that of management, of staff and control organizations, and of most supervisory levels in the shop organization. All of the union personnel—its members and its officials—are workers; and all of its attention and activities are directed toward worker interests; whereas all the other organizations or groups are oriented toward satisfactory production of goods or some special phase of it. In the second place, the union has quite different procedures for communicating its point of view to management. We have seen how each of the other organizations struggles to get the attention of top management, each working through the lines of authority, each striving to force its interests on its superiors, while the executives weigh, select, eliminate, or pass on the demands. The union, on the other hand, working through the formalized contract negotiations and grievance procedures, can bring its demands to bear directly upon top management without censorship or control by the intermediate levels. This is true whether they are dealing with particular cases in grievance procedures or with general principles.

Unlike the other organizations, then, the union is not controlled by management and management cannot protect itself from the union. In the other organizations, the hierarchies and lines of authority serve not only as channels of communication but also as layers of insulation by means of which top management protects itself from many problems and demands originating at the bottom of the structure. A request for a new machine in the shop, for example, seldom reaches top management via these channels. The request is either granted or denied at a lower level, and there is usually no recourse, no formal procedure by means of which it can be carried to higher authority. In contrast to this, the union offers a relatively open pathway to the top, and management cannot be insulated against it.

The chief function of the union is to force management to consider the effects of company policies and practices upon the workers. It is the function of management, on the other hand, to decide on these policies and practices and to give orders about them. In this role, top management may be seen as dictator; and it often assumes an attitude of complacent omnipotence, passing down decisions and orders with the assurance that there can be no repercussions from below, since it is safely insulated from any backfire up the lines of authority. In view of this, it is not surprising that management is often reluctant to accept either the union's point of view, its ability to short-circuit the line, or its pressures. In many cases, top management believes that consideration for the worker, his attitudes and satisfactions, is irrelevant and even detrimental to the main objective of getting the work done cheaply and well. Even when it is recognized that worker satisfaction is essential to maintaining efficient production, management often resents having the fact "rammed down its throat" or decisions forced upon it by the union.

Once top management has accepted the point of view and powers of the union, however, it usually sees the union organization as a useful part of the total structure. If worker attitudes must be considered, management usually finds it simpler to have one organization which can present a composite of these attitudes. And it is easier, too, to deal with a small group of union officials than with a mass of individual workers when discussing complaints, company policies, or changes in practices. In this particular the union can function like the other organizations in the structure, assembling and selecting from a mass of detail the significant matters to be presented to management, and aiding in the interpretation because of its knowledge of these details. Even here, however, there is an important difference between the union and the other organizations. When the others have brought information to top managment and helped to interpret it, then management makes the decisions and gives them back down the line as "orders." The union, however, does not take orders from management. When union officials take information to top management, they are "consulted," they may make suggestions, and may even be asked for advice. Thus, management can say to the union: "We are planning to make these changes. How will they work from the employees' point of view?" Or the union can say to management: "There are certain practices which are hurting morale, and something should be done about them."

The union is also expected to help management in carrying its decisions back down to the workers. When management and the union have come to an agreement about a matter, the decision or statement of changes is passed down from management to the work level through the regular channels. But the union is expected to explain and justify the decision to the individual employees and to smooth the way for its acceptance. Since the union officials are elected by the workers and are the workers' representatives, management quite naturally expects, too, that the workers will accept the decisions about which the union has been consulted and has agreed. If, for example, through the collective bargaining process, management and the union have reached an agreement as to wages, seniority rights, or shop practices, it is expected that the union will explain the agreement and that the workers will accept it. Unfortunately, this does not always happen; and either individual workers or groups sometimes refuse to accept the agreements, especially if they mean a compromise for the workers. (One is reminded of our state and national legislative processes, and of how often people refuse to accept and abide by the laws which are passed by their elected representatives.) When workers do refuse to accept these joint decisions, management is usually outraged, not only at the individual offenders, but at the whole union setup. Once a matter has been settled with the union representatives, management feels it should be settled for good and all. For this reason, management often prefers to deal with a "strong" union which has the backing of most of the workers, which is, in reality, representative of the workers and which can actually smooth the way for acceptance of union-management agreements.

Union Officials

Union officials are an interesting factor in the effective functioning of the union, both in its relation to the workers and in its relations with management. Just as the effectiveness of the line in dealing with problems of the work or workers is in large part dependent upon the receptivity of supervisors at each level and their ability to make decisions or carry the problems on up, so the effectiveness of the union is largely dependent upon the ability of its individual representatives. And just as a worker's attitudes and relations with his foreman often set the tone for his feelings toward the whole company, so his attitudes toward his steward often determine his evaluation of the union as a whole. Thus the steward who is indifferent to the complaints or requests of his people often arouses antagonism, not just toward himself, but toward the whole union organization. As the irate worker quoted above said, "As far as I'm concerned, X and his union can go to ———!"

Unlike supervisors in the other organizations, the union officials, as we have pointed out, do not have either the authority or the status of the boss. The workers, whether union members or not, do not have to take orders from the officials, and, for the most part, are quite indifferent to them unless they have some grievance. Furthermore, except for a relatively small group of full-time officials, the union does not offer a way of life, a job with a pay check, to which the individual can devote all his energies, and it does not offer economic re-

Nature is political for union bosses pointed

wards or status. The union official is just another employee, with his own job and his own problems and career to think about. His duties to his fellow workers as their union representative do not make his personal situation as a worker any less pressing, but may, in fact, add to his difficulties.

All these factors have a significant influence upon the kind of individuals who become active in the union. Generally, the ambitious worker who is progressing satisfactorily, and especially the one who expects or hopes to move into supervisory ranks, feels little need of union support or protection and may even sympathize and identify himself with management instead of the union. Some believe, too, that to be active in the union will antagonize their superiors and lessen their chances of promotion. These ambitious ones make very poor stewards, when they do occasionally accept the office out of a feeling of duty. They are more concerned with their own future than with the interests of other workers, and they are reluctant to criticize their superiors or be too aggressive in contacts up the line. One such steward explained his feelings thus:

I've had a feeling, and I've also heard from a lot of the other stewards, that once you get to be a steward you never get a raise. If I thought there was any truth in that, I would quit this job right away. No sense in me sticking to a steward's job if I can't get a raise out of it. I actually heard a lot of the stewards talk like that. Why is it I can't get something better around here?

. . . I'd like to get something I really like. After all, I've got twenty years' service and I wouldn't want to stop at $70.00 a week. That's why if I thought being a steward kept me from getting a raise, I'd get out of this as fast as I could.

. . . . I don't mind the job at all. I've learned a lot on it. But if it is going to hurt me, I'd get out of the union tomorrow.

In other cases, earnest employees, working hard to make a showing on their jobs, feel that they do not have time for union activities. These, too, are ineffectual and promote antagonism to the union if they become stewards. Their preoccupation with their own jobs, their reluctance to discuss union matters on the job, and their concern with proper shop behavior, all tend to keep them away from the people whom they are supposed to represent, and force the other employees to take the initiative in bringing matters to them. One of these stewards explained his position:

When they brought that thing up to me about the low earnings, I intended to take it up. First three guys came over to me, and then five more, then seven more, and finally I said, "Hey, let's not have any more of this up here." I told them we could have a meeting over at headquarters, so that's what we decided to do. I figured, let them have their meeting. That way they can raise their opinions and let off steam over there. I haven't got time to listen to that stuff during working hours, especially when they pile over here to see me. That looks very bad on the job.

. . . I don't spend hardly any time on union activities during working hours. I have a lot of new people in here that I should be contacting to try to get them to join up. I just don't feel as though I ought to spend the time on it.

In other cases there are the older, skilled workers who feel that they have made satisfactory progress and who are, in many cases, the spokesmen or leaders of their work groups. They are likely to feel that the union has little to offer them, or, sometimes, that the union is a fine thing for the others but that they themselves do not have time to be active. Like the other indifferent ones, they sometimes accept jobs as stewards through feelings of duty or because they think the wrong people are running the union. Usually they soon grow tired of the duties and drop out "to give some one else a chance."

On the other hand, many stewards and other union officials are very active and enthusiastic members who are aggressive in upholding what they consider the "rights" of the workers, who take seriously their duties as representatives of the workers, and who are very critical of stewards who approach supervisors timidly or not at all. Something of their attitude was expressed by one steward, who said:

It is hard for me to know when they really have something to complain about. After all, I have to go up the line with some of these things, and sometimes I am not so convinced that the employee has a squawk coming. But I carry it along just the same because I feel that I owe it to them because of my job as steward. These guys that are indifferent to their responsibilities give me a pain in the neck.

Often the person who is dissatisfied with his own situation, who is very critical of management and the work generally, who is a "sorehead" or "griper" in the eyes of the foremen and management, is very active in the union and becomes a steward or higher official. The workers often feel that such a person will put up a better fight for their interests than one who is less critical and accepts conditions. Such a steward, however, who is aggressive, antagonistic, and inclined to belligerence, generally rubs foremen and management the wrong way; and they invariably feel that he is prejudiced and unreasonable.

Problems of Stewards

Another problem of union personnel is that the officials change quite frequently, especially the shop stewards. This means that, at any given time, a great many union stewards are novices who have not established relations with the workers as their representatives and who have not devised techniques for dealing with supervisors. It means, too, that supervisors and workers are continually having to deal with new stewards who are unfamiliar with procedures, who do not know what has gone on before, and who, therefore, have a lot to learn before they can function efficiently. Very frequently, neither the union organization nor management have the benefit of a stable group which, over the years, constantly improves its understanding of the problems and its skill in handling them. Each time there is a change in officials in the union, there is a resulting period of tension and adjustment—with the new officials feeling inept; the workers, doubtful and anxious; and management inclined to be irritable—until satisfactory and familiar working relationships are developed again.

Some workers do, of course, remain active in the union over a period of time, and some rise in the union hierarchy. And just as there is a shift in understanding when a shopworker is promoted to foreman, so the union member who becomes an effective and active shop steward changes his point of view. As a mere worker, even though a union member, he generally thinks of problems of the work, or policies, or management's decisions primarily in terms of himself. His attitude toward the whole work situation is personal. If Joe gets a better job on the basis of seniority, Charlie may feel that he is being treated unfairly because he is a better worker than Joe. But as a shop steward, Charlie has to think about Joe's promotion not just in terms of himself but in terms of Joe and all the others in the work group. He has to consider, not just the promotion of Joe, but the matter of policy and fairness for the whole group. If there are complaints, he has to hear the foreman's side of the problem, too, and try to understand it. To be effective, he has to know the foreman's problems, too, as well as the workers'—why the foreman does the things he does and what pressures he is under.

The steward who is conscientious often meets complications in trying to represent a whole work group fairly, and he sometimes gets mixed up in their personal relationships, especially where there is disagreement in the group. As an ordinary worker, he can enter into an argument and take sides; but as a steward, he is likely to be caught with both factions expecting him to represent them. Frequently a suggested change in practice will benefit part of the group and be to the disadvantage of the rest, and the steward has to decide whether or not to press for such a change. For example, in a department working on shifts, the morning shift started at 6:00 A.M. and the second shift ended at midnight. Some of the people on the first shift complained that they had to get up too early in the morning and wanted to change their starting hour to 7 o'clock. This seemed reasonable until the steward discussed it with workers on the second shift. They were strongly opposed to the change because they would not get through work until 1 o'clock instead of midnight. If the steward then officially requested the change, the second shift would be down on him; but if he did not, the first shift would feel that he was not representing them properly. In another case, one group of workers complained that it was unfair for them to be kept on a type of machine which was harder and more disagreeable than a slightly different type of machine which another group used. They requested that all workers be rotated on the different machines. Here, again, the steward had to decide whether to request a change which would improve conditions for part of the work group at the expense of the rest.

After experience in trying to work out problems like these, trying to improve conditions and relieve conflicts, and acting as go-between from workers to management, union officers often begin to change their point of view about the problems and what to do about them. Especially when dealing with a management which is honestly trying to work with the union, the officers sometimes begin to understand management's problems and point of view and are more sympathetic with its difficulties. They begin to see why it is impossible to adjust the system to satisfy each individual demand; they see the limitations of legal restrictions, of wage ceilings; they learn something of the complexities of planning the work so that things go smoothly. And with this broader point of view and understanding, they often find that they have difficulty in explaining their actions to the groups which they represent. They are making decisions based on an understanding which the others lack, and because of this lack the others cannot accept their reasoning. As a result, the officials sometimes become annoyed with the people they represent, begin to think critically of them as dumb or hardheaded, and complain that they are unreasonable. As one steward said, "You know, some of these people are funny. No matter what you do for them, they still blame the union and never give us credit. Some of these guys don't appreciate the position the company is in. The company is really nice to us guys; they give us a lot of consideration."

10. UNIONS AND THEIR STRUCTURE

ORIENTATION OF UNIONS

WE HAVE so far discussed unions as part of the social system of the business or factory. In this sense they are as much a part of the total structure as any other formalized set of relations within the organization. In addition, however, they are generally something more than just another segment of the particular firm or a special set of relationships within it. In most cases today, the local unit which exists within the plant is one segment of a much larger entity. For example, the local union in the XYZ Company may be one unit of the United Auto Workers, CIO. In effect, the individual worker is a member and participant in two systems which are built around the work situation and affect his attitudes and behavior in it. One is the formal system set up and controlled by management, and the other is the system set up by the workers themselves.

These systems differ in certain important aspects, and out of these differences arise many current problems and conflicts. First, there is a basic difference in their purposes and objectives. The business firm or factory arises in an effort to produce goods or sell goods or services and to do these things in the interest of its owners or managers. On the other hand, the union arises out of the feeling of the rank and file that they must protect themselves against exploitation by the managers.

Crusading Spirit

Not only does the worker believe in the union as a protective device, but he also feels strongly that the union provides a way in which he can fight back. It is thought of as the means for battle, for standing up for the rights of man, for meeting power with power. And out of all these feelings there often emerges a crusading spirit, which seeks through the union movement to build a better world for the common man. This crusading spirit has been strong throughout the history of unionism and reflects itself in many ways. For example,

163

the union movement has its heroic figures, its folklore of oppression and conflict, and its songs. And every good union leader is expected to know these things, to know the history of unionism, and to think of it as a movement. Thus, he often feels he is part of something greater than himself, something for which he may be called on to sacrifice his own personal welfare and to do it willingly.

Of course, such nobility of motive is not characteristic of all union leaders, but it must not be overlooked that this is the general concept of how they *should* feel and act. This is shown in the fact that in any union education program there is great emphasis upon the history of the union movement, with proper attention to the great conflicts and the great martyrs.

We might contrast this with our concept of the executive and his education. No business school seems to imbue its students with a feeling that they are going out to build a better world. They do not feel that they are part of an important movement. They rarely know much about the rise of modern capitalism; and certainly they do not study it in the context of conflicts, of heroes and marytrdom, of songs of hope and defiance. Instead, they learn that they are going out to get ahead in the world, to compete individually, to manipulate people and things for their own success. Thus, few go out with any feeling of becoming part of an important world where the things they do will matter to anyone but themselves.

Nature of Authority

Next, there is a difference in the nature of power and authority. In the business organization, the formal authority rests at the top. The boss has extensive powers of decision and action vested in him by virtue of his position and reinforced through both custom and legal forms. He is placed in his position through decision of those higher in the formal system. The union, however, is in theory and, to a considerable extent in practice a political system in which the rank and file select their officials, who are then accountable to them for all actions and decisions. Thus the union leader rises to his position through his ability to gain the support of his fellows, while the executive rises through the approval of his superiors.

In a sense, both executive and union leader rest their authority on the same base. As Chester I. Barnard[1] points out, all authority rests

---

[1] Chester I. Barnard, *The Functions of the Executive* (Cambridge, Mass.: Harvard University Press, 1938).

upon acceptance by subordinates, who can always choose whether or not to obey orders. However, management cherishes the belief that the orders from the superior should be obeyed merely because he is the boss. Within the union the leader is thought of as looking after the interests of the rank and file and as carrying out their desires— not as someone with the right to give them orders. Thus, custom and belief affirm that the boss is expected to give orders, and disobedience may be punished. With the union leader, custom and belief hold that he is the servant of the group, and he is not expected to give orders.

This concept of the role of the union leader at times creates peculiar problems. Although he may have the official right to negotiate contracts, settle grievances, and whatnot, merely getting him to agree does not guarantee that the group will accept. Thus we see the dilemma of dealing with John L. Lewis. He and the mineowners cannot agree on a contract; so the coal miners strike. The government threatens to invoke its powers, and he tells the miners to go back to work; but they refuse to go. Does this mean that he has "lost control" and is no longer accepted as the leader? Or does it mean that the miners interpreted his order as a mere formality which he did not really want obeyed? About all the court could do was to determine whether he had really tried to get the miners back to work. If he had really tried, then he was not responsible for continuance of the strike. Thus, in negotiating with any union, the problem is not only that of obtaining a settlement to which union officials will agree, but also that of obtaining one which their people will accept.

This condition is often very trying to the executive. He is accustomed to dealing with people who can make decisions and commitments. When he signs a purchase order, he expects that the seller can deliver or will be penalized for not delivering. But when he makes an agreement with a union leader, whether he be a shop steward or the president of the nation-wide organization, he cannot be certain that the agreement will stick. He begins to feel that he is dealing with untrustworthy people, people who do not have "the strength of character" to make a decision and stick to it.

Union leadership sometimes uses its position of "political" authority to very good advantage in order to get action from management in tight situations, particularly where there are no-strike agreements. If necessary, union leadership can always threaten management with loss of control over membership: "The fellows out there are pretty hot about this and unless something is done, I can't guarantee what will happen." Unauthorized work stoppages are not uncommon in a situation like this, and management never knows for sure whether union leadership actually has lost control or whether they are simply being put under pressure to take action on a grievance.

STRUCTURE OF UNIONS

There are two basic types of union organization: the craft or trade type and the industrial type. The craft union limits its members to people of one particular activity or skill, i.e., carpenters, truck drivers, boilermakers, etc. All members in a locality may belong to the same "local"; but they usually work for a lot of different companies, and changes in place of employment do not affect union membership. The union officials thus deal with many different managements in representing their members. This is the traditional organization of the American Federation of Labor.

The industrial union is based upon the organization of all the workers in a given plant or company. The general tendency is for the "local" to consist of employees of one company, and for its officers to deal only with the one management but to represent all the variety of occupations and people. However, movement of workers from one plant to another means a change in their union affiliation; even if it is the same larger union, such as the United Auto Workers, they change to another local. This is the basic pattern of the Congress of Industrial Organizations.

Local Unions

One important characteristic of the craft unions is their focus on one specific activity or skill. For example, the plumbers' union is concerned with plumbers, their economic welfare, and the preservation of their jobs. Therefore, their officials not only battle for higher wages but seek to control competition by restriction of membership. They also try to prevent other craftsmen from doing plumbers' work and to limit the use of technical improvements or mass-production methods, etc. New developments in materials often give rise to jurisdictional disputes as to which craft has a right to the job. For example, should new aluminum window frames be installed by carpenters or by sheet-metal workers?

These attitudes are quite understandable when we consider the significance of his trade to the skilled craftsman. He has spent years in learning his trade; often he has progressed through an apprentice system which required several years of training before he could receive the rating of carpenter, electrician, or toolmaker. His sense of achievement and his status as a worker are identified with his trade. As a result, he is concerned with the preservation of his trade and of his place in it. Furthermore, he identifies himself not only with his trade but also with the union which represents it, and it only. In *his* union he does not concern himself with those of different skills or no skills at all. He does not have to accept those outsiders or submit to their dictates. His is a union of the elite, his fellow craftsmen. Thus, often his bonds with his union are stronger than the bonds with the company; and if his union says strike, he strikes.

The industrial union presents quite a different picture to the craftsman. Within it the lines of loyalty are to his fellow workers in the company, and to all workers, not merely to craftsmen like himself. Furthermore, he is subordinated to the mass of lesser men, the unskilled and the semiskilled. In such a situation he often feels that he is not given the consideration, or the respect, that is his due. The union is not primarily concerned with his problems or with the preservation of his trade and his way of life. As a result, it is often difficult for the industrial union to gain the support of the craftsmen, and sometimes they may even remain an actively rebellious group.

The strictly craft type of organization presents certain difficulties when applied to workers in modern industry. When a plant is organized along strictly craft lines, it means that every skilled group is represented by a different union. At the same time, a large part of the workers who do not fall into craft categories may not belong to any union. However, within the factories the craft unions have become more and more complete industrial organizations. In some cases a union may organize one section or department in a factory and represent all the workers in it. In other cases the same union may represent an entire factory, while in still other situations it may retain its strictly craft characteristics and represent only craftsmen. For example, in one factory there are four different unions. The International Moulders and Foundry Workers have all the workers in the foundry; the International Brotherhood of Blacksmiths, Drop Forgers and Helpers represent the forge shop; the International Association of Machinists represents the bulk of the workers, including assemblers, warehouse workers, tool- and diemakers, machinists, etc.; while the International Brotherhood of Firemen and Oilers represent the small group of boiler-room employees remaining.

It is interesting to note that, where a factory is organized by several different unions, consistent action and solidarity among the several unions is achieved not only through formal means but, more especially, by informal processes. In the plant just mentioned, the formal methods of attaining uniformity and solidarity are, first, by having a joint grievance and bargaining committee and, second, by having an agreement whereby no one of the individual unions can go out on strike without the acquiescence of the other unions involved. These formal methods, however, would not be adequate to keep all four unions working together if it were not for certain informal processes. Usually one or another of the chairmen of the grievance or negotiating committees of the respective unions will emerge as the informal leader of the joint committee. He will become the spokesman of the entire group of committeemen. In their negotiations with management, his views will generally prevail. If conflict develops between management and the unions, management sees him as "the man to beat" in the situation. Very often management feels that the elimination of this informal leader, who spearheads the demands of the several unions, will weaken the position of the unions in their negotiations. It seems obvious to management representatives that he is the driving force behind union demands, because he is the one who is always pushing the demands, speaking for the others, raising grievances, and "telling management off" when things are not going right. The other committeemen seem so meek and mild, so reasonable, in comparison with him. But the supposition that his removal will ease the conflict between management and the unions and strengthen management's position can be completely erroneous. If he actually is removed, another of the committeemen will emerge as the spokesman and the "man to beat." In one situation a management representative said, "You know, it's funny. Joe used to be such a nice guy. But now he's just like that so-and-so we used to have around here," and he mentioned the informal leader who used to spearhead union activity in the plant a few years before.

The Larger Structure of Unions

Except for a relatively few small "independent" unions, the local is only one segment in the larger structure of either craft or industrial union. Above the local, with its stewards, committeemen, chairmen, and other officials, rises the superstructure of the larger union officialdom. While there are varying patterns, there is generally a regional organization, with an official responsible for the locals within his area, and above this official there are one or more levels. In addition, the different unions are largely grouped together into the still larger structure, such as the CIO and the AFL.

At the local level the officials are often working members; that is, they are actually workers on the company payroll. If the local is large and active, it may have one or two officials who devote all their time to union affairs and are paid entirely by the union; but even so, they often must maintain the fiction of being employees of the company. Above the local level, however, all officials are full-time union employees; in union slang they are the "pork choppers" who live off the members. This higher level is, in effect, the real management group of the union and is concerned with the effectiveness and success of the union as a whole and not merely with the success of one local. Thus, just as in business management, as a person moves up in the union hierarchy his responsibilities widen in scope and his concern shifts from the problem of the small unit to more general problems. Thus, at their higher levels we see men concerned with general policy, with over-all tactics, with manipulating public sentiment or political influence. We see them trying to convince the locals that they should accept guidance and should follow the broader union policy for the good of the whole. Even as management often restricts or limits a department for the good of the whole company, so this top union leadership may call on the locals to sacrifice their own desires for the larger good.

In large unions, the structure of organization can become very complex. In the usual international union, you find at the top a president and a secretary-treasurer; these are the two top-status, full-time positions. In addition, there are a number of vice-presidents who are chosen generally by region or industry and who may or may not be full-time officials. Very often the vice-presidents are in charge of the organizing activities and union functions for a region or industry. In addition to these positions, there is also an executive board which usually consists of the president, secretary-treasurer, and the vice-presidents, but which in some unions also includes additional persons, who are elected. Also, there may be a board of trustees, consisting of several elected members, whose function is primarily that of auditing and checking on the financial affairs of the union.

All these official positions are filled by election, but below this level are a number of staff positions which are generally filled by appointment. In most cases, international representatives are appointed by the president, subject to the approval of the executive board. The duties of the international representatives are to organize new locals, represent the local during the initial stages of organization, organize district councils, and continue to represent isolated locals. In general, the international representative is chosen from those business agents or local union officials who have demonstrated that they have the interest and ability to operate on a broader level.

Below the international representatives are the rank-and-file unions, consisting of locals and district councils, where all officials, including business agents, are, for the most part, elected directly by the workers. The district councils and locals are generally small recapitulations of the international, in so far as official positions are concerned. On the district level, there is a president, secretary-treasurer, and executive board. The business agent is not an officer in the local union. His is the only full-time position, however; he is paid by a per capita tax on the locals plus, usually, a sum from the international, so that the international is able to maintain some financial control over his activities. The local consists of a president, vice-president, recording secretary, financial secretary, treasurer, and other minor official positions. It, too, has an executive board and board of trustees with an auditing function.

The typical union organization is relatively amorphous and uncontrolled. Although it has a definite pattern that repeats itself from one union to the next, it does not have the semblance of machinelike precision and military authority that is characteristic of many business organizations. A great deal of authority and decision making in unions has to be passed down to the lowest levels.

For example, international representatives have to make decisions in terms of the local situation. In most cases they cannot check with higher officials, simply because those officials are in no position to judge the merits of the case without going into all the facts. As a consequence, international representatives operate very much on their own; in fact, they are expected to do so and are selected by higher officials with this in mind. One top official of an international was reminiscing about his earlier days as an international representative and was reminded of what the president told him when he first went on the staff: "When you're out in the field, don't run to us. Remember it is a local proposition that we know very little about. Your judgment must prevail. Don't worry if you make a few mistakes. You won't hear from us. But if you make a lot of them, we'll send you a telegram and let you know you're through. And, Brother, you can pay your own expenses home!"

In view of this relative local freedom and autonomy which prevails throughout union organization, it is natural to wonder about the problem of control. First and foremost, there is a written constitution. No one anywhere may deviate from the constitution. This is the law, and one of the important functions of the executive board of the local is to interpret local union action in light of this law. Furthermore, at regular intervals there is a national convention which meets to decide policy but which also functions as an integrating device that draws the locals together and gives them a uniformity in thinking and action which might not otherwise occur. The international representatives, in moving from one local to the next, also provide a means of communication which binds the membership together. And, finally, there is always an official publication which helps to integrate the thinking of the membership.

UNION LEADERSHIP

Local Level

When an individual moves up through the ranks of the local into the top group, he enters a different world. At the local level he generally had his regular job, and his union activities were separate. Furthermore, he could still think of progress in terms of the work and the company hierarchy and could say: "You have to be careful or you hurt your chances of getting ahead." But once he moves out of that, the union and its activities become his job. There are no longer conflicting loyalties or conflicting ambitions, and he can throw himself completely into the task of building the union.

Also, the local official maintains his position directly through support of the local membership. While the approval of the superior officials can be helpful, with or without it he must sell himself to his fellow workers. As long as they are with him, no one can put him out; and if they turn against him, no one can keep him in. Thus, if he wishes to maintain his position, he must deal with the political problem of satisfying the majority of those whom he represents, of doing those things which they see as his duties and responsibilities, and of serving them in the ways that they think they should be served. If they are suspicious and hostile toward management, he must express this suspicion and hostility in his dealings with management. If they feel that certain customs or rights must be maintained, he must lead in their defense. And he must speak for the aggrieved individual, as well as defend the interests of the group.

This makes him appear as a mere puppet being manipulated by the group. And in some cases this is almost true, since some stewards think of their role as merely that of "grievance men." As one said, "All I do is take up grievances to the bosses. It doesn't matter whether I think it is right or wrong; I take it to the foreman and put up a fight." Such a steward sees his role almost as that of a lawyer, who does not judge the cases but merely tries to win them.

In general, the stewards or other local officers do not see their role as such a simple one. Most of them try to take a position of active and effective leadership. They are not merely there to fight the battles of individual grievances but also to guide and direct the group. They watch for grievances and inform the individual when he has one. They argue with foremen or management over what they see as injustice. They seek to arouse the group to defend its rights. They counsel the group on what they consider a fair deal. And when it comes to open conflict, they are the ones who plan and organize the strike and try to hold the workers together for the battle.

Furthermore, it is those local officers who display this ability to lead the group who move up into the higher union positions. This movement does not take place merely through ability to get the support of fellow workers. Even when he moves to an elective post, the strong man in one local cannot be well enough known in other locals to draw a majority of the vote. Therefore, he must have the assistance of other established officials, who must handle the political maneuvers necessary to elect the man they want. And in selecting their men they generally pick those whom they feel will be able to take positive leadership in dealing with the local unions. They want men who have the ability to organize a plant, to negotiate with management, and to make a contract work.

Higher Levels

Since a local officer only moves up through some form of higher sponsorship, he must then maintain good relations with his superiors in the system. Especially at the level of international representative or business agent, he cannot maintain his position merely through rank-and-file support. Therefore, he rapidly becomes involved in elaborate patterns of interpersonal relations and loyalties, and even intrigues. For, in many unions, even as in many business organizations, there are complex sets of cliques struggling for influence, position, and power. In such a system the victory of one clique often leads to wholesale elimination of others, and the security of an individual often hinges upon the survival of the group with which he is identified.

This union management structure always presents quite a different pattern from business management. Even with appointive positions, the lines of authority are not so sharply defined, and the autocratic use of authority cannot be so readily developed. Even the best intrenched top leaders must generally maintain the attitude that they are responsible to the group. The representative or business agent who deals directly with the locals must be especially careful not to act as though he had authority over them or can tell them what to do. Thus, his accomplishments depend upon his ability to gain the acceptance of others over whom he has no formal powers of punishment.

With the industrial unions, the primary jobs at the level of district representative or business agent are either servicing the established locals or organizing new ones. The servicing consists mostly in keeping in close touch with the locals, participating and even leading the discussions with management over grievances, negotiating new contracts, and so on. Through all this the district representative must keep in close touch with the sentiments of the local members so that they feel he understands their problems and is really fighting for them. At the same time he tries to get them to accept general union decisions in such matters as the kind of demands they will make to management, policy in respect to types and length of contracts, incentive systems, benefits, and such. Also, he must try to get their acceptance of what he considers "fair" offers by management or to stop their making unreasonable or unworkable demands.

In general, in the established locals the union representative wants things to work out fairly smoothly. He does not want his locals to be constantly quarreling with management or making extreme demands which lead to long, drawn-out negotiations or strikes. For one thing, such difficulties require too much of his time, and with several locals involved he cannot give them all the attention they expect. Besides, if they lose out after periods of conflict, they are prone to blame him for their failures and demand that he be replaced. Therefore, he prefers to have everything work out with a minimum of open conflict. But, conversely, if things go so smoothly that the local groups feel no need of his help, he will feel that he is losing his position of leadership. Thus, he faces the dilemma of keeping things peaceful and, at the same time, convincing the group that it is his skill in dealing with management which keeps it that way.

The job of an organizer presents quite a different problem. He may be given the responsibility for organizing new locals in a district, or he may be assigned to one large company. He must contact the workers, evaluate the strength of antagonism to management, and seek out the complaints or other factors which can be used to stir the workers to action. Then he must plan the campaign, enlist the co-operation of workers, prepare publicity, hold meetings, and give speeches. This is the job for a person skilled in sensing and stirring the emotions of the group, who can arouse them to a sense of wrong and of persecution and can then direct these feelings into necessary action.

The effective organizer is often the militant leader who burns with indignation at the wrongs the workers suffer and sees management as the hostile oppressor. When management has been callous to the welfare and feelings of the workers, such a leader can often rouse the workers to rebellion and lead them in battle. When, however, the battle is over, the union is established, and a contract is signed, then he is often less effective than a calmer or less colorful person. For one thing, in the heat of the conflict, strong feelings of hostility develop on both sides; and these feelings cannot be dropped overnight. As long as such hostility is strong, it is difficult to develop comfortable working relations between the union and management. Many union leaders recognize this and know that after the battle the militant organizer must often be replaced by a different type of person, a person who can represent reasonable compromise and co-operation to both workers and management.

As the union leader moves from the local level into the full-time union job, he tends to separate from the rank and file. No longer is he one of them, coming to work with them, putting on his overalls, and spending his day among them. Now he is a "big shot" who wears a suit and hurries from one place to another, from union meetings to conferences with management. Furthermore, he tries more and more to direct the workers' thinking, telling them what they ought to do, what union policy is, and so on. Even with the popular leaders, who have strong support from the rank and file, there still develops a feeling of distance and separation which grows stronger with time.

When management is friendly and discusses matters with the union official, he may be placed in a precarious situation. If he is convinced that management is sincere, then he may try to co-operate in working out problems; and the decisions then become joint decisions which he must help to carry out. In many such cases the rank and file begin to feel that he is getting to think like management and is neglecting their interests, and they become antagonistic to him. In some cases, he may react with criticism of the rank and file and feel that they are "dumb" because they cannot see things as he sees them. Once such attitudes develop, he loses touch rapidly with the attitudes of the group and has difficulty in maintaining his influence.

Who Is the Union Leader?

What kind of people rise to positions of union leadership, and why? To begin with, it is clear that the rewards of a union career are different and in some respects meager, as compared with careers in management. For example, at the local level the officials frequently are paid nothing beyond reimbursement for time lost from their regular jobs. At the higher levels, union salaries are modest, compared with executive jobs in industry. Yet, even without salary the official is expected to work almost day and night.

At the local level, we see a variety of motivations which induce an individual to take on such duties. In many cases, individuals treat it almost as a civic duty: they believe in the union and feel that they must do their part. Many with such attitudes serve only when there is no one else willing, or when their friends insist; and many of these will serve for a time and then happily relinquish the position. In fact, they often express the idea that they have done their share and someone else should now take over. While such men may serve ably, they rarely rise to higher union posts or care to make their careers in the union.

There is another group from which many leaders come, however. These are the able and ambitious men who feel trapped in their jobs and can see no future opportunity. In their frustration they turn to the union, both as a way of fighting back against the system which has trapped them and as something to take hold of which will give scope to their abilities and bring them recognition. Many of these people were active in developing the CIO and rose to top positions in it. Many of them, in fact, were moving toward management positions; they were planning on college and careers as business or professional men, but they were trapped by the depression and turned to the union movement instead.

Take the case of one able district representative for a powerful industrial union. His father was a foreign-born, semiskilled factory worker. The boy had a good high-school record, and his parents encouraged him to plan on college. After high school he decided to work for a year to save money for college, and he took a job in the same plant with his father. Then the depression came. The plant laid off many workers and cut wages of others; the father was laid off; and the boy stayed on to support the family. Conditions at the plant became worse, with more wage cuts. Finally, in desperation, the son and a group of his friends—other young men like himself—called a mass meeting, and in a short time they had the plant unionized. He and several of the original group have stayed active in the union and now hold important posts.

In such cases, we see ambitious men, who in other circumstances might rise through the ranks of management, make their careers in the union instead. In fact, the union is just about the only route to recognition and status in those companies which recruit men for management positions through the colleges and so block mobility for the poorly educated workers. It sometimes happens that these workers come to the attention of management only by demonstrating their ability as union leaders, and are then offered supervisory or personnel jobs.

It is significant that, where all mobility from below is blocked, the ambitious men either get out or fight. In very small companies with a limited supervisory and management staff, the tendency of these workers is to recognize the limitations and leave; in larger plants, they often turn to the union. Often, too, when opportunity is blocked in this way, it is not only the ambitious workers who rebel but also many who lack drive and ability. In such cases you see men who would not try very hard to get ahead complaining that they "have no chance around here."

Another type of union leader is the man who is very agressive and rebellious. He is likely to be very emotional, quick to resent those in authority, suspicious of all their acts. He is willing to voice his suspicions and resentments and is not afraid to "stick his neck out." When the group is hostile to management and feels maltreated, he is the perfect spokesman for their resentment. His own fervor not only expresses their feelings but also helps to fan the fires of suspicion. Besides being an effective local leader in times of strife, such a man often rises into higher union ranks in periods of rapid growth, when crusading organizers are needed.

Sometimes, too, in local unions you find the apathetic steward or officer. He lacks the zeal or interest to work hard at his position. He is often critical of his fellows, "doesn't have time to listen to their gripes." This is the man who was pushed into the job because no one else wanted it. He may have had an idea that he would get some acclaim or recognition from his fellows, but he lost interest when he found that he received more gripes than praise. He is not one to hold the position long except through indifference of the group. The minute they feel the need of an effective leader, out he goes.

Within many of the younger industrial unions there is still another type of official. This is the intellectual type, usually fairly young and with a college education. These men have not risen out of the rank and file but have worked directly into the higher levels. This invasion became possible during the rapid expansion of the CIO unions. During that period, most of the leadership was relatively young and inexperienced. They lacked well-established organizations, and they welcomed almost anyone who wanted to work hard in the interests of the union. Furthermore, with the pressure of organizing large groups of workers who had never belonged to unions, there was a great need for effective educational and informational services. Research and educational positions were established in many unions to provide information on economic or other matters, to set up union newspapers, to prepare publicity, and to start union education programs. These positions were frequently filled by these intellectual recruits. Other intellectuals became active in strikes or organizing campaigns and gradually made a place for themselves.

To the young liberals the vigor and crusading spirit of the CIO during the depression was very attractive. Then the business world was clothed in gloom, and there was talk of a "maturing economy" in which individual opportunity was waning. In the union movement, by contrast, there was a spirit of achievement. They were forging a better world; they were going to bring a new hope and vision to the common man and save our economy from itself. So, to the union movement flocked those who sought a leadership and a destiny, who wanted to find something worth struggling for. Many able and effective leaders developed from this group.

Another group which turned to this new union movement were the radicals, especially those who saw the Communist party as the savior of the common man. The local Communists saw this as an opportunity to attain leadership and control which could be used to aid the party. With this motive they tried to move their members and supporters into top union posts, and in some cases they were extremely successful. Gradually, however, the less radical leadership began to strengthen its position and began to oust the clearly pro-Communist leaders. This shift was probably partly due to lessened need for the extremely radical and crusading leaders for purposes of fighting management. At the same time, a growing hostility toward Russia gave the more conservative leaders a chance to attack them as pro-Russian and anti-American.

CONCLUSIONS

The union serves a direct function for the workers in enabling them to fight back against the pressures acting upon them through the management hierarchy. Through the extended union organization the workers can bring influences from the outside world to the process of dealing with management. Because of its extension, the union is able to press for uniformities among companies in wages, policies, and other factors. Thus, it serves as an equalizing influence while maintaining pressure to keep the general level of wages, benefits, and working conditions ever improving.

In addition, the union is an organizational entity with a life of its own, independent of the companies with which it deals. Its existence depends upon its function of dealing with management, however; and unless this function retains its significance for the workers, the union suffers. The significance of its function is clearest in times of open conflict, when union enthusiasm and solidarity are usually at their height. However, constant open conflict cannot be maintained, for at some point the workers go back to work and hostilities are submerged. From then on, the union has to struggle to maintain its importance and to stay alive as an organization. This struggle lies behind the constant demands for union security in the form of closed shop or maintenance of membership contracts.

Part and parcel of this struggle is the battle put up by the union leaders to retain their positions. Though the union movement has the spirit of a crusade, the unions provide an organizational framework in which able and ambitious men seek success. Whatever their reasons, these men have prestige and careers at stake, and they are as wholeheartedly devoted to being a success as any ambitious executive. Out of this competition, strong men often rise who are able to maintain their positions through a combination of personal leadership and political skill.

At the same time, this struggle often leads to difficulties which are especially annoying to business management. The executive is annoyed by the constant play for the attention of the workers, and he objects to having contract negotiations or grievance hearings used for union political maneuvers. He feels that he is caught in activities which are unfamiliar and even immoral.

In spite of the difficulties, however, there is a growing understanding on the part of executives toward the problem of the union. More and more companies are developing patterns of union-management co-operation. Many are proving that there can be many areas of mutual co-operation and that solutions can be found for the areas of disagreement. Out of these developments there may come a better understanding of the way to industrial peace.

C.I.O. Dates back to 1930's

Chapter 19

11. WAGES AND WAGE SYSTEMS

THE CONCEPT OF WAGES

ONE thing that practically everyone in industry has in common is that they work for pay.[1] In fact, the majority feel that pay is the only important reason for working, or, at least, for working at their particular job for their particular company. Many are the pleasant daydreams of inheriting a million dollars, telling the boss just what he can do, and disappearing from the job forever. Wages, in fact, play such an important part in the lives of people that it sometimes seems as if the mere fact that people are paid to work is the source of more problems and difficulties than any other one factor.

Management Looks at Wages

To the owner or manager of a business, wages are a necessity; they are the price he must pay to get people to work for him. In a sense, labor is to him a commodity which must be purchased just as he purchases coal or copper or other materials. In this sense the payment of wages is a simple economic transaction which may be governed by the same reasoning or logics as any other purchase, in which one endeavors to obtain the greatest quantity and highest quality possible for his money. Out of this comes the idea of a "labor market" in which employer and employee bargain over the services, or in which there are established scales of prices for various grades and types of the commodity. Unfortunately for the potential employee, he is like the farmer with a truckload of ripe tomatoes; if he does not sell today, the tomatoes will not be worth anything tomorrow.

Actually, to the employer the labor he purchases is not a simple commodity such as a sheet of steel, which he can buy according to certain specifications as to size, weight, strength, and chemical com-

[1] We are using the word "pay" as synonymous with wages or salary, but it should be noted that there is actually a certain amount of prestige or status difference in the terms. Executives usually receive salaries, and wages or pay are usually reserved for those at lower levels.

181

position—all of which can be tested beforehand and which can be expected to remain stable. Labor as a commodity is even more perishable than the load of tomatoes, since it is the ability of a person to do work, and since this ability may vary from day to day and may be affected by all sorts of things. Management generally recognizes this and thinks of wages, not just as a payment for a simple commodity, but as a means of stimulating the individual to be a better and more effective worker. It feels, too, that the wages should promote a feeling of loyalty toward the company and enthusiasm for the work. Labor is not, then, like the load of tomatoes, because the tomatoes do not care whether their price is high or low and they cannot be motivated to make more or better soup.

In setting the pay scale for jobs, management generally wants to keep the wages "in line" with what others pay for similar work. If they are paying much above what seems to be the generally accepted rates for a job, they feel that they are being very generous and fear that they may be wasting money. Many companies, however, pride themselves on paying above the average and justify it on the grounds that to pay high wages gives them the pick of the available labor supply and promotes loyalty and efficiency among their employees. Others feel that if they are paying the going rate on the jobs, then their wages are "fair" and the workers should have no complaints. Still other companies make a practice of paying no more than they have to, and they feel that unless they keep wages down they will have difficulty in meeting price competition on their products.

Determining how much to pay for a job is often a very haphazard procedure, especially in companies which do not have a union contract. You need a drill-press operator; so you hang out the "Help Wanted" sign; and when a drill-press operator comes in, you offer him about what you have been paying others for similar work. Or else you call a friend in another plant and ask what they are paying drill press operators at present. Or, if you want to be really "scientific" about it, you conduct a wage survey and compare your wages for various jobs with the wages paid by other companies. Or perhaps you make use of similar surveys conducted by groups of companies, trade associations, and so on. In any case, you come out with some idea of what the market is and what you may expect to pay.

A great many wage surveys ignore efficiency and productivity in their determination of the proper wage for any job. They arrive at the supposed market value of a job, expressed solely in cents per hour or dollars per week or month, with no correction for the fast or slow worker. In general, the assumption is that their figures are based upon average performance, but they do not specify just how much output should be expected for the wage. It is almost as if they quoted a market value for a commodity without considering quality. You pay a lathe operator so much an hour, and it is up to you to determine what is a proper day's work and to see that you get it. This is in keeping with the way most people look on jobs and on wages. For example, almost everyone has certain ideas about the value of various jobs. They think of a job, such as typist, toolmaker, or office boy, as paying about so much; and the person who is paid more or less than these amounts is considered well paid or underpaid. Very rarely do they think of differences in pay for similar jobs as being a result of differences in individual ability or effort. They do not think that Mary is paid less than the "fair" rate because she is not worth it, but only because her employer is a cheat who is taking advantage of her.

Wage Differentials

For factory jobs or all jobs requiring the use of tools or manual skill, there is a rough relation between the skill and training required and the wage. Thus the skilled worker is paid more than the semiskilled worker, the machinist more than his helper, and the machine operator more than the laborer. This relationship is, of course, a rough one and may be affected by other factors, as, for example, in certain jobs which have carried prestige and corresponding high pay over a period of years even though technological changes have reduced the actual skill required by the job.

If we look at the wage structure of any factory, we see that the wages themselves form a hierarchy which conforms roughly to the general status hierarchy and which usually forms a similar pyramid, with the majority of the people at the lowest wage levels and the head of the concern and the top executives in the highest wage levels. Thus the wages of the individual tend to place him in the general status hierarchy in relation to others. There is, in fact, a strong feeling that an individual's wages *should* reflect his status in the structure and that it is therefore "wrong" for a supervisor to earn less than his subordinates or for a person to be promoted without being given a raise.

In most companies we find that the wage structure divides the people into two major groups, usually referred to as the hourly-rated people and the salaried people. This usually conforms to the office and shop division, the factory workers being paid on the basis of the number of hours they work, and the office or white-collar workers being paid by the week or month. Thus, we see a separation between people who work for "wages" and those who work for a "salary." As a rule, foremen and supervisors are placed in the salaried group. In addition to this major division, many large concerns further divide the salaried group, placing the higher levels in a separate group from the ordinary clerks and stenographers. Usually this division is reflected in differences in payroll and accounting procedures, and it may follow along strict lines of amount of salary or upon differences in function. In one company the division is based upon amount of pay; all salaried people who earn above $400 a month are paid once a month and are referred to as "monthly rated people," and all others are "weekly rated people." The top group are thought of as executives and are not required to punch a time clock. In another company, all executives and foremen are paid on what is called the "main office payroll," and their checks are sent out from the headquarters of the company rather than being made up in the individual plants. Such divisions are themselves status groups; and to move from the hourly to weekly payroll, from weekly to monthly, from plant to main office, is felt to be an increase in status, something which merits congratulations from the group and something to tell the wife with pride.

One interesting aspect of the division between hourly rated and salaried employees is that the groups generally have sharply different functions in the structure and that, within each group, there is a wage hierarchy which is quite independent of the others. The hourly rated people are shopworkers who are directly engaged in the manufacturing processes. They are the skilled and unskilled workers who run machines, handle tools, wear overalls, and get their hands dirty. In contrast are the salaried people who work with papers, handle the mechanics of controls, and tell the other workers what to do. They are the typists, secretaries, accountants, supervisors, and executives; they wear the clean clothes and the white collars.

The rate of pay of salaried people is not necessarily higher than the hourly rated people, however, in spite of their being a higher status group. In fact, in the lower levels the office workers may earn no more or perhaps less than the lowest level of shopwork. For example, office boys or file clerks may be paid at rates as low as, or sometimes lower than, the lowest shop wages; and a boy or girl just out of high school can often earn more by starting work in the shop than in the office. There are, then, two separate wage hierarchies, and the status of the individual is determined by his position in these hierarchies as well as by the actual level of his wages. Thus the young fellow in an accounting job may feel that he has advanced over his father, even though his father earns more money as a machine operator in the shop.

Maintaining the proper wage differences between jobs is one of the problems of management. Those jobs whose wages are "out of line" in the status hierarchy, in the thinking of either the operators on those jobs or other workers, will be a source of complaint and trouble. For example, if you pay a helper as much as the machinist he works with, the machinist thinks either that the helper is overpaid or that he himself is underpaid. In fact, examination of any work group shows a fairly definite hierarchy of jobs; and if the wages for different jobs vary greatly from this accepted scale, the workers feel that the wages are "wrong."

In order to maintain a wage structure in which different jobs maintain the proper wage relationship to each other, many companies use a system of "labor grading" or "job evaluation." In these systems, jobs are graded on the basis of such factors as skill, education, learning period, and responsibility, so that they can be arranged on a scale ranging from the job having the most requirements to that having the least. At the same time, a wage scale is established with the highest-rated jobs in the top pay grade and the lowest-rated jobs in the lowest pay grade. Then the pay for any job will be determined by its place, as established by its evaluation. Such systems provide a systematic means of comparing one job to another or of placing a new job in the established hierarchy.

From the point of view of management, such systems are expected to serve two purposes. In the first place, they are expected to prevent complaints from workers or from unions that certain jobs are not paid properly in comparison to others. Undoubtedly, the systematic grading of jobs, if used consistently, does prevent serious variations in pay between jobs. If, however, the particular system does not place jobs about where the workers think they belong, the system itself will be the source of friction. For example, in one case where a job evaluation system was introduced, the grading of jobs reversed the relationship between two jobs, so that the job which had always been thought superior and more desirable was placed below the other job on the wage scale. This gave rise to so much friction and dissatisfaction that the management was forced to restore these jobs to their accepted relationships.

Job evaluation serves a second purpose for management as a means of establishing proper control of labor costs. By careful analysis of the jobs and comparison with similar jobs through wage surveys, it is possible to set rates which presumably approximate the "market value" of the work. Thus, if other companies are paying one dollar and twenty cents an hour for jobs with such-and-such requirements, the company is able to show that one dollar and twenty cents an hour is a fair wage for all their jobs having these requirements. This, in effect, prevents individual bargaining on jobs, a practice which often tends to push jobs out of line. For example, in large concerns it is customary for the executives to ask for raises for their secretaries; and because some executives are more aggressive or cleverer at justifying such raises, a great discrepancy results in the pay of secretaries on comparable work. Eventually someone investigates the pay of secretaries; some cost-minded top executive is shocked by the high salaries paid to some; and the company puts in a form of job evaluation by means of which secretaries can be graded and their salaries kept within certain limits.

The Worker and His Pay Check

To the wage earner his pay check is something much more complicated than money in his pocket or payment for services; and his attitude toward the fairness and adequacy of his pay is affected by many factors both within the factory and in the larger society. To begin with, as we have pointed out, his wages tend to place him in relation to all others in the factory system and, so, to direct and limit his relations with them to some extent. His place in the wage structure affects his attitudes and relations to Joe and Jim who work beside him, to the new man who has just started on the next bench, and to the women who are learning to run certain machines. At the same time, his ideas of what constitutes a fair or an adequate wage are, in part, a reflection of both these attitudes and relations and of his place in the wage hierarchy. This is particularly apparent when he or another worker associated with him is given a raise. When a raise is given to one worker in the group, that one usually feels that he has been set apart and is somehow above the rest. The others feel slighted, think they should have raises too, and assure themselves that they are just as good as he is. They all feel vaguely that they have lost status in relation to this one, and the effect is much as if everyone had been given a cut in wages except him. Their idea of a fair wage changes immediately, and all feel that what is fair for him is fair for them all. Very rarely will they admit that the other is a better worker, and they may claim that they have not had an opportunity to show their ability or to develop it as he has. In any case, the supervisor has on his hands a very dissatisfied group who are likely to turn against the favored one.

Besides these personal attitudes, there are some general beliefs among workers about the fairness of wages and job differentials. As we have pointed out, it is not considered fair to pay a machinist less than his helper or a foreman less than his workers. Sentiments toward length of service—either on the job, in the department, or in the company—also affect attitudes toward pay. A new man, for example, can not be brought into a job at more pay than others already on that job without causing resentment and dissatisfaction. Old-timers and experienced workers believe firmly that they should be paid more than newcomers or beginners. And the man who spent years as an apprentice feels that he is worth more than the man who learned the job through some speeded-up training program.

Another important consideration for the wage earner is the effect of his pay upon his life outside the factory. The size of his pay check has a very real influence upon his place in the community. It may limit and determine the kind of home he has, the neighborhood he lives in, and the friends he may acquire; and it is frequently a symbol by which others place him in the status system of the community. For instance, rent is often thought of in terms of a week's pay for a month's rent, so that a man earning $50 a week is likely to live in a neighborhood where he pays $50 a month for rent. As he increases his earnings, he will probably move to higher rental areas, where he can live according to his income. The man who makes $40 a week and lives in a $50 neighborhood often feels that he cannot quite keep up with his neighbors and is likely to think that his wages are inadequate.

An individual's ideas of an adequate wage are, then, a reflection of what he expects in the way of living conditions and comforts, association with others, recreation, and social place. His concept of an adequate wage is actually more a part of the way he thinks about himself and his whole way of life than a part of the job he does. From his point of view, an adequate wage is one which enables him to live in the kind of neighborhood, among the kind of people, to which he feels that he belongs. He should be able to have a car if the others do, wear the same kind of clothes, eat as they do, entertain in the same way, and generally spend his money as his friends and neighbors do. If his earnings do not permit these things, he worries about his relationships and his place in the neighborhood or community, and he thinks that his wages are inadequate and unfair. For example, a college graduate, son of a professional man, living in an upper-middle-class neighborhood, would feel that the $60 a week earnings of a shipping clerk were completely inadequate, since they would not enable him to maintain his accustomed relationships and activities in his community. On the other hand, a high-school graduate from a tenement neighborhood, whose father is an unskilled worker, might feel that he was doing well to make $50 a week.

In evaluating the fairness of his job and his pay, a worker does not usually think of it in terms of what the work is worth on the labor market, or in terms of what is fair pay for that kind of work, but in terms of what is fair pay for himself. In other words, an individual thinks of himself as having a certain value, quite aside from any particular job. This same attitude is seen when, for example, a highly skilled man is put on a less skilled and lower-paid job for some reason. He invariably feels that, since he has the ability to do more skilled and more valuable work, he should be paid accordingly. This does not mean that he thinks the job is worth more; in fact, he may quite agree that the job is only worth so much. It does mean that he has certain ideas of his own worth and of what wage he must have to maintain his established relationships and feelings of status.

Sometimes a wage may be adequate and still not be considered fair. There is, as we have pointed out, a rough correlation between status in the work hierarchy and rate of pay. In the community outside the factory, both these things—the kind of job he does and the size of his pay check, as demonstrated by his spending—are indications of the individual's status and importance at work. Each group in our society has certain ideas about what is a fair income for "people like them"; and members who earn less than is "proper" for their group generally feel sensitive and insecure, try to conceal the fact from their friends, and think that their rate of pay is unfair. Even an individual who has other income than his pay check, who has no actual financial difficulty in meeting the economic standards of his friends, is usually ashamed and apologetic if his wages are much below theirs. If his rate of pay does not indicate a work status comparable to that of his friends and neighbors, he may feel that it is unfair, even though he does not "really need" the money.

MERIT-INCREASE SYSTEMS

Management's Point of View

Management is inclined to believe that money is the principal motivation of people in industry and that, by proper manipulation, wages can be the most effective incentive to better work and greater production. Many top executives even assume that all difficulties between people at work, all problems of co-operation, can be solved by the proper wage formula. They believe that the economic difficulties of paying high wages in the face of stiff price competition is all that stands in the way of their having a loyal, enthusiastic, and efficient force of workers. As a result of such beliefs, the matter of proper wage policies and systems is of great concern to management. Probably every factory or business is interested in obtaining maximum results from the money spent, and is, therefore, always interested in wage systems which will provide effective incentives to their employees. Out of such interest a wide variety of wage systems have arisen, each one usually based on a few simple assumptions concerning the way in which money can serve as a motivating factor. The simplest system is that which may be called the "merit-increase," or "merit-raise," system, in which wage increases are granted at the discretion of management or other supervisors on the basis of an individual's performance and his value to the company. In theory, management, or its representatives, is watching the performance of every worker; and as one improves and demonstrates his increased value to the company, he is rewarded by an increase in his wages. Also, as one backslides and decreases in efficiency or value, his wages are cut. Such a theory puts management in the role of the all-wise and all-just, weighing every act and meting out rewards and punishments accordingly.

The individual working under such a system, whether a shopworker, supervisor, or executive, is expected to be earnest and enthusiastic because he knows that he will receive a wage increase if he improves his performance. He should be enthusiastic in co-operating with others for the good of the job and the company because such co-operation will be noted and rewarded. He should be constantly trying to increase his knowledge of his own job and of others; he should be interested in the success of the company. He should not be critical of the policies or decisions of management but should be a "good soldier" and do his best to carry out the orders. If he does all these things well, his superiors will know it and reward him accordingly.

The Limitations

Unfortunately most such merit-increase systems have certain "bugs" in them and do not seem to work quite according to theory. For one thing, there are usually limits to the amount management will pay for any one job, so that the job one is on sets the ceiling beyond which he cannot go, no matter how much he improves. A janitor, for example, is usually paid less than a machinist; and no matter how hard the janitor works or how he improves his efficiency, he will probably never rise to the wage level of the skilled machinist. This means that, to rise beyond the limits set by a given job, the individual must move on to a higher-rated job. Since this movement is limited by the openings available, and since the higher-rated jobs are usually fewer than the low-rated jobs, it is obvious that hard work and self-improvement are not an automatic passport to continued wage increases.

Economic conditions further affect the merit raises. When times are good, management may be very generous with raises; but when business is bad, raises may be few and far between, because management believes that raises are an increase in costs which cannot be permitted under such conditions. The result is that, when business is bad, the wage progress of an individual is usually very slow, regardless of how much he improves his efficiency; while in good times he may progress rapidly with comparatively little effort toward improvement. To the worker who progressed very slowly to the top level for his job during bad times, it usually seems very unfair that people coming in during good times rise to his level very quickly.

In companies which have periodic rate revision, the amount of raises at any one period is continually being adjusted to meet conditions at that time. Top executives look over their budgets, estimate how much increase in payroll can be allowed, and decide that increases can amount to only a certain percentage of the total payroll for this period. The foremen's recommendations, which are usually too high for these estimates, will then be trimmed to fit the required percentage. In this way, management maintains the necessary control and, at the same time, gives the impression to the lower levels that a raise is not something to which they have a right because they have earned it but is something which may be given or withheld at the discretion of management.

Evaluating the Workers

The problem of evaluating the individual workers presents one of the most difficult and complicated problems in any such system. In the first place, there is the problem of what the executives expect from the individual. For what are they paying? Do they judge the individual's value solely on the basis of quantity of work produced, or will they pay for willingness to co-operate, for conscientious endeavor, for loyalty, dependability, and so on? And then how do they measure these things on which they base their increases? If output is the chief criterion, what happens to the fellow who sacrifices output for the sake of good workmanship, or who co-operates with others in the interest of the job as a whole, even though it cuts down on his own output? And what happens to the fellow who increases his efficiency very rapidly until he reaches his maximum and then cannot show further improvement, although he works at that same level of efficiency year after year? And what do you do for the conscientious worker who goes along, year after year, taking whatever job is given him without complaint, doing them well if not brilliantly, accepting the judgment and decisions of his superiors without question or doubt, and generally doing the best he can? Every worker knows what happens to him: he goes just so far and then stops getting raises.

In theory, merit increases are an expression of the increased value of the individual to the company and should, therefore, have little relation to what others do. Actually, there is considerable confusion when deciding upon the merits of an individual; and he is not measured against any absolute yardstick of value or by any set standards to show degrees of improvement, probably because such standards of measurement are almost impossible to devise. As a rule, an individual is compared, not with any scale, but with his own past performance or with the performance of others. Thus the individual who has shown pretty clear-cut and obvious improvement in performance may be judged deserving of a raise, or the one who is the most efficient of a group may be thought to deserve a higher wage than the others. There are, then, two different merit-raise policies. In one case, a person is working against his own past record and will be given a raise if he beats his own performance. In the other, members of the work group are competing with each other, and the one who does the best work gets the raise.

To further complicate the evaluation of individual workers, in many or even most jobs there is no simple way in which performance can be measured. This is especially true of office work or jobs that are quite varied in nature, so that the worker does not repeat the same routine operations over and over. Even where output can be measured, such as on routine machine jobs, it is still necessary to set up routine procedures for measuring it before output can be used as an absolute basis for determining increases. As a result, decisions as to merit are very often based upon the judgment of the boss. He gives raises—or recommends them—where, in his best judgment, they are deserved; and if a worker does not deserve a raise, he does not get one. In large organizations there is the added difficulty in that the immediate supervisor, especially at the foreman level, cannot make the final decision but must get approval for raises somewhere up the line. And when, as sometimes happens, some of his recommendations are turned down by those higher up, the foreman is furious but helpless. Probably the only thing which can make him madder is to have his superior give out merit raises to people whom he has not recommended.

Generally, merit raises are not based on simple clear-cut criteria but are affected by a number of different considerations. In some cases they seem to be given in response to pressure from the individuals. Joe, for instance, goes to his boss and says that he is dissatisfied and discouraged, that he has been working for two years without a raise, and that he feels his work has improved a lot and he is sure that he is doing better work than some of the others who are making as much as he is. He adds that the cost of living has gone up and that he had an offer of a better job elsewhere. The foreman thinks that Joe is a good worker who is conscientious; he has shown improvement and really deserves to be making more than that loudmouthed "griper" Jim. It is hard to replace men now, anyway; so he gives Joe a raise on the basis of merit. (There is always some doubt that such raises should be called "merit" raises.) The next day Joe tells the group that he got a raise, and Jim and the rest all ask for raises within the next few weeks. The foreman may give out a few more, and then his boss begins to ask questions about the sudden burst of improvement in the work group, since he has noticed little change in the cost reports. At that point the foreman stops giving raises and tells the group that he cannot give any more until they show him that they are really improving, that he only gave raises to those who were the most deserving. After that, it is likely that two or three fellows who have not had raises for some time will go out and get other jobs; or they may complain to their union steward, who will start working on the foreman.

In other cases, however, the wage policy is much better organized, and definite procedures are set up for the evaluation of the individual and the granting of merit increases. Some companies have periodic rating periods, at which time each supervisor must consider the work of each of his subordinates and make recommendations for merit raises. In some cases this is done individually, according to the time a person started with the company, so that a new employee is rated, for example, at the end of his third, sixth, and twelfth months of service, and annually thereafter. In other cases the entire company goes through a rating procedure at fixed dates, so that everyone is judged, and all raises given, at the same time.

Merit raises, no matter how they are handled, usually cause disturbances in the status relationships in the work group. By giving one worker a nickel raise for merit, even though deserved, and withholding it from another, the foreman or management is saying, in effect: "Joe, you are a better man than Jim, more valuable to us, and we think more of you." And Jim feels not only that Joe has received recognition but that, in a sense, he himself has been criticized, that his quality and worth have been questioned. When Joe tells his wife that he got a raise because of good work, she tells the neighbors proudly and repeats what the boss said to Joe about his value to the company. Jim's wife, on the other hand, wonders why he did not get a raise and is ashamed to tell the neighbors. She scolds Jim for telling her that he has been getting along all right, or she takes it out in being mad at the company and at his boss for not giving him proper recognition; and she is sure that that fellow Joe with the "snooty" wife must have a "pull" somewhere.

In theory, if raises are given for improved performance, then pay cuts could be given for poor performance. Actually, such pay cuts are very rare unless the individual is so poor that he is demoted to another job. This means that, as long as he stays on the same job, a worker will maintain whatever pay level he has reached. While this is not very logical from the point of view of costs, the sentiments are so strong against such penalties that few companies attempt to use them. A practice of giving cuts regularly would probably upset the morale of the entire group, since a cut in pay is a very serious blow to an individual's feelings of worth and to his status, relative to others in the group.

Another basic difficulty in the systems of merit increases is the implicit assumption that supervisors or management can make an accurate evaluation of the performance of an individual, relative to either his past performance or the performance of his fellows. Such an evaluation assumes that they have all the facts concerning his actual work and will consider the difficulties he encounters and the many factors which affect his work. It assumes that they can be very wise and just in their evaluation of the total situation and completely fair in their decisions. It assumes that they will not be influenced by prejudice, personal likes or dislikes, or friendships and that decisions will be based upon what a man does, not on whom he knows. Unfortunately, it rarely works that way, because there are always many intangible things which influence judgment and decisions; it is always easier to decide in favor of one person rather than another; and it is always difficult to make decisions which are completely fair to all those involved. And for the person who does not get a merit raise, even a fair decision is painful and difficult to accept.

There is, furthermore, in most work groups a certain measure of distrust of the ability of management to administer a merit-rate system fairly and satisfactorily. In some cases there is a strong distrust of the intentions of management, a feeling that no plan proposed by management would ever work to the benefit of the workers. The common complaint against almost any system of merit raises is that the foremen fail to evaluate people properly, that they play favorites or overlook the people who do not complain and make demands, that they do not take the proper factors into account, or that their superiors have these failings when they overrule a foreman who is trying to be fair. In other words, they do not trust their superiors as all-wise judges able to decide fairly for all.

In general, merit-increase systems are much more popular with top management than with foremen and other lower supervisors. Frequently, the big bosses are people who have come a long way on ability and merit. They believe firmly that an individual should be able to get ahead by hard work and application and that one who does do better than his fellows should be properly rewarded. Furthermore, since many of them have been motivated by a desire to get ahead, they often think that all others either do or should have the same drive and that they will respond enthusiastically to an opportunity to gain recognition. As a result, they believe that a merit system will be welcomed by the majority of workers and that it will offer management a powerful tool by means of which they can motivate their people to build a more effective organization.

Foreman's Point of View

For the foreman, however, it is often a different story, especially when he does not have final authority on raises. He would like to be able to reward his people properly at his own discretion; but he knows that final decision is in the hands of his superiors, who are often more concerned with costs than with rewarding the faithful. He realizes that wages play an important part in the status equilibrium of his work group and that careless adjustment of wages may create serious problems, problems with which he may have to deal for months to come. He knows that, no matter how conscientious he may be in granting raises, there will always be some who see only their own side and are critical and dissatisfied. Many foremen, in fact, would rather not have a merit system, since it so often engenders complaints and criticisms. One company, for example, had regular rate reviews at six-month intervals, when the foremen made their recommendations for raises. If times were bad and only a few raises were given, the workers who did not get them felt that it was unfair; if times were good and raises were generous, there were less complaints, but there were always some who felt that the foreman had been unfair in the amounts given, even if there was a general uniform increase for the whole group.

The Union Preference

As a result of all the complications and attitudes toward merit raises, it is quite common for unions to oppose such systems. In some cases, as one of its first moves, a newly organized union tries to force management either to do away with the system or to set up careful controls over merit raises. Even where merit raises have been in use for years, union officials usually respond to the flood of complaints after every raise period by demanding either drastic modifications in the system or its elimination. In its place they usually prefer a system in which raises are based upon service and are not dependent on a foreman's judgment. In such a system the progress of the individual within the rate range for his job is a matter of "right," and he does not feel that he has to play up to his boss in order to get ahead. Obviously, such a plan lacks the incentive features which are supposed to lie in the merit increases, but it is simpler from the point of view of the foremen and generally more satisfactory for the workers.

PIECEWORK SYSTEMS

Piecework is another wage system which is often in high favor with management. It is just what the name implies: a worker is paid according to the amount of work turned out, and the more he produces, the more he is paid. Such a system should provide the maximum of direct monetary incentive to spur workers on to greater and greater effort. In its simplest form, management establishes the amount it will pay for each unit of output, or each piece; and measurement of the output of the individual determines his earnings. It is very simple and direct in its basic principles, but it becomes very complicated in actual application.

This system has considerable appeal to certain of our ideas of what is fair, and especially to the idea that the individual who works hard and produces should be rewarded. As we have seen, to reward these hard workers through merit increases is a very difficult problem, and it is inadvisable to punish those who do not produce. All this is solved theoretically by piecework; when they work hard they get paid for it, and when they do not work hard they do not get paid. Each member of a work group will work out his position in the wage system without being dependent on the judgment or good will of his boss. Furthermore, the system itself is supposed to supply all the necessary incentive, so that the boss does not have to stand over his people and by weight of authority, threats, or kind words struggle to get them to do a fair day's work.

From the point of view of management, this system has the advantage of not only stimulating output, which it actually does, but of being an effective control of labor costs. When a rate is set for a given job, that fixes the amount which will be paid to the workers. Thereby the labor cost can be known before the work is actually done and will not be dependent upon the ability of the foreman to get the work out of his people. In actual practice it is not, of course, quite this simple; but, on the whole, it provides a much simpler control over labor costs than other methods. With such a system, however, there can be no savings in labor costs by improving the efficiency of the workers without cutting the rates, but that is a problem to be discussed later.

Piecework Variations

There are a number of variations of piecework systems. In the simplest of these, there is a price set for each unit of output; the output of each worker is measured, and he is paid accordingly. The rate itself is usually based on a determination of the expected output per hour of an average worker and the hourly rate for jobs of that level of skill. If, for example, it is estimated that an average operator can turn out ten units per hour, and if it is a semiskilled job for which you would pay $1.20 cents an hour, then the rate would be set at 12 cents per unit; and if the worker turned out twelve units, he would earn $1.44. Although all workers have an hourly rate which applies when they are not working on piecework, it does not affect their earnings on a piecework job of this kind. The 75-cent man who turned out twelve parts an hour would earn just as much as a 90-cent man who turned out the same amount. Thus the high-rated, experienced machine operator who was placed on a bench assembly job might actually earn less than the low-rated girls with nimble fingers who habitually worked on bench assembly. From the point of view of labor costs, with such a system it does not matter whether the worker is on a job fitted to his particular level of skill; but it does matter to the worker. Therefore, the machine operator usually insists that he be given jobs with rates such that he can earn more than the girls on bench assembly, so that he can maintain his proper place in the status system. In other words, the operators will not allow the piecework system to function so as to reduce the wage differentials between the top and bottom of the job hierarchy.

In most piecework systems today the operators are guaranteed their hourly rates. That is, they will be paid their hourly rates no matter how low their output. This protects them in case there are changes in the job, poorly set rates, or in case they are changed to new jobs. It puts a floor under their "take-home pay" and relieves some of their anxiety over changes which would lower output. It also sets a minimum level of performance as a goal for the foreman to shoot at. Since his labor costs will be high until his workers are earning their hourly rates, he prods the workers whose piecework earnings are below; and if they do not improve, he will want to get rid of them. In some plants there is a rule that a worker who does not reach this acceptable level of output within a certain period will be discharged.

Another variation of the piecework system is group piecework.

Here the group, rather than the individual, is the unit for measurement of output and payment. Although each job may have a rate on it, no record need be kept of the work of each individual but only for the group as a whole. In calculating the earnings, the group is credited with all the work turned out, and this is distributed among the workers in proportion to their hourly rates and time worked. Thus, every member of the group shares with the others and is interested in the way the group as a whole works. This is expected to encourage group unity and co-operation and to develop group discipline over slow or lazy workers. In this system the hourly rates become important because they directly affect earnings; the earnings of each individual in the group are determined by this hourly rate, relative to the others, rather than by his efficiency.

Another variation is the use of "time" rates, in which the rate is set in units of time rather than in units of money. In the preceding illustration, for example, the rate which was set at 12 cents per unit under money rates, would be 0.1 hour per unit under time rates. If the operator turned out twelve units per hour, he would receive credit for 1.2 hours of output and would be paid 1.2 times his hourly rate. In this system the hourly rate again directly affects earnings, since the 90-cent man who turns out twelve units will earn $1.08, while the 75-cent man turning out the same amount will earn only $0.90. This protects the high-rated worker who may be placed on low-rated jobs and maintains the differentials in earnings between low- and high-rated people.

Limiting Piecework Earnings

It might be supposed that piecework would provide an opportunity for the worker to increase his earnings far beyond the normal level of pay for his particular job. Actually, however, this is not the case, because on most piecework jobs there is a clearly defined ceiling beyond which the worker does not attempt to push his output and earnings. From the point of view of management, there are two concepts operating to prevent unlimited increase of piecework earnings. In the first place, the worker on straight daywork is expected to do a fair day's work, which is somewhere near the upper limits of his capacity. Piecework is looked on as a device for stimulating him to give that extra push, to extend himself to the limit; and the limit should be only a moderate increase over what can be expected of him without the extra incentive. In some cases the possible increase is assumed to be only 15 per cent, but in others it is supposed to be 25 per cent.

Furthermore, in keeping with the general point of view concerning labor costs, if a worker on a certain job is earning far above the accepted daywork rate for the kind of work, management is likely to feel that they are paying too much for the job. This is especially true when there is no generally recognized standard of output by means of which management can compare its labor costs for the job with the labor costs of other companies. Since this is true of almost all jobs, there is usually a feeling that you are paying too much if your workers earn a great deal more than workers on comparable jobs in other companies. If other companies can get people to do those jobs for so much less money, there is no need for you to pay more.

Setting the Rates

The key problem in any piecework system is the setting of rates. This may be done in a number of ways, the simplest of which is to have an experienced foreman estimate either what the rate should be or how much hourly or daily output should be expected. If the job is not a new one, the rate can be based on average figures of past performance. Such methods are at best rather inaccurate and are not often used. In order to obtain more accurate rates, methods of time and motion study have been developed by means of which the proper methods of doing a job are determined and the exact time necessary is measured. In theory, proper study will produce an exact rate which is not a product of judgment but is the result of "scientific" measurements. Such rates are supposed to be so exact that all variations in earnings on a job will be the result of differences in skill or effort of the operators. Furthermore, with such accurate rates there should be no cases of excessively high earnings or low earnings, and labor costs can be held firmly in line.

Unfortunately, this ideal of completely accurate and "fair" rates is probably never achieved. There are always what the workers refer to as "fat" or "loose" rates, on which it is easy to make high earnings, and "lean" or "tight" rates, which are hard to make. This is a continual source of dissatisfaction on the part of the workers, since the men fortunate enough to be on jobs with fat rates can earn more with less effort than those on lean rates. This leads to friction and quarreling within the group; and if the foreman controls the distribution of jobs, he is continually being accused of playing favorites in the way he apportions the fat and lean jobs.

This problem of fat and lean rates is a source of concern to management, too. As we have seen, if the rates are too fat, management feels that it is paying too much for the work. This, combined with the friction which arises in the work group, makes foremen and executives all feel that it would be desirable to keep rates "in line," that something should be done about rates which are too fat or too lean. While the workers also feel that something ought to be done about the lean rates, they are bitterly opposed to any change in the fat rates. There is, in fact, a common belief that the principal function of piece rates is to enable management to get more work out of them for less money. As a result, management is always welcome to increase any lean rates, but cutting fat rates is considered a very despicable act. Indeed, rate cutting often leads to strikes and labor troubles and is outlawed in many union contracts. Many piecework systems guarantee no reduction in rates without a change in methods, that is, a change in the way the work is done. This does not prevent management from increasing rates whenever they feel it is necessary, nor does it prevent the workers from asking for increases when they think a rate is too low.

Individual piece rates are likely to require elaborate systems of records and controls. If the work is broken down into simple units, each performed by separate workers, then a rate must be established for each unit. If, for example, the processing of a particular part requires grinding of a rough casting, drilling two holes, and tapping the holes, then the work may be broken down into three operations, each handled by a different operator, and there may be three separate piece rates. Furthermore, it is necessary that the parts each operator processes be inspected to see that the work is done properly and counted in order to determine his earnings. Under some conditions, piece rates may be impractical because of the difficulty and expense of either setting the rates or of maintaining the system.

In group piece work the problems are somewhat different. In some cases, all the group may be on the same type of operation, such as drill presses; but in others the group may perform a sequence of operations on the same objects. In the first case, the rates are set as in individual piecework; but in the second, the rates may be set on the entire sequence rather than on each separate operation. Then the work can be measured and inspected after the final operation rather than at each stage, since the group performs all operations within the sequence. This reduces inspection and counting costs, and the larger the group the cheaper and easier it is to administer.

With group piecework the earnings of the individual and his status in the group are directly affected by his hourly rate. When they are paid on a money rate, however, the distribution of hourly rates within the group does not affect labor costs but affects only the distribution of piecework earnings within the group. Changes in hourly rates can, therefore, be made without affecting costs, and there is a tendency for management to be fairly lenient in giving increases in hourly rates. Any such change does affect relations within the group, however; and when one gets an increase in rate, he increases his earnings at the expense of those who are not increased. With time rates, on the other hand, the labor cost under group piece rates is directly affected by the hourly rates of the members of the group. As a result, management is much more careful in the way it gives out raises, since every raise increases not only the earnings of the individual but also the labor costs of the job. This is considered fairer to the workers, however, since a rate increase for one worker does not penalize the others.

RATE SETTERS

Activities and Functions

In a shop that uses piecework, rate setters have a very important role; and because of their activities and functions, they may be seen as a control group. Rate setting determines labor costs of the products; it has direct effect upon the earnings of the workers; and their piece-rate earnings reports are in many plants an important source of information for management. The man who sets the rates is the one who can keep costs down or let them go up; he makes the rate fat or lean for the workers; and he gets the blame from either side or from both when the system does not work. In large plants there is usually a piece-rate organization which is set apart and functions somewhat like a staff organization. When a new job is brought into the shop, members of this organization are called in to set the rate; and once the rate is set, the accounting routines do the rest without further aid from the piece-rate organization. Thus the rate setter seldom goes into a department where everything is running smoothly and where there are no changes, but spends most of his time where there are new jobs or where rates are in dispute. In effect, his presence is a sign of difficulties or change in the shop.

Relations with the Shop

One of the outstanding features of the relations between the piece-rate organization and the shop is the constant suspicion and antagonism between the two. Interviews with workers show a consistent suspicion of piece rates and rate setters. This is so widespread that it seems almost to be one of the attitudes which is transmitted from parent to child among workers and is not necessarily learned from experience in the work situation. For example, it has been observed that young people on their first factory jobs show concern and slow down their work when a rate setter comes into the department. As a result of this distrust, workers carefully regulate their work pace and work behavior whenever a rate setter is present.

The foreman usually shares the suspicions of his people and sides with them against the rate setters. From his point of view it is important that the rates be fair or even fat, since then his people can make satisfactory wages without difficulty or complaints. He must see that there is slack in the job to take care of delays, breakdowns, or other emergencies without affecting either output or earnings, so that he can make the proper showing on the earnings reports. He is constantly in the position of defending his group against the piece-rate organization. He often feels that he should study every rate before it goes into effect; that he must look for errors in it especially of operations overlooked or difficulties underestimated; and that, if there is too much trouble in making the rate, he must demand a review and insist that it was set too tight. And if the earnings drop on new jobs, he usually excuses himself on this ground, complains that the rates are too tight, and wants his boss to do something about them. As a result, the foreman and his superiors frequently find themselves in conflict with the piece-rate organization.

For his part, the rate setter is prone to be critical and suspicious of the shop. He often suspects that the workers are trying to put something over on him; he feels that he is really looking out for the interests of the company, while the foreman is more concerned with keeping his people satisfied than with keeping costs down. This becomes especially apparent when there is a large piece-rate organization. Then the rate setters can associate with their own kind and sometimes tend to draw away from other organizations, to eat and play in isolation together, and to put up a defensive front toward the whole shop organization.

Rate-Setters' Logics

Every piece-rate organization has a very definite set of beliefs regarding the function of piece rates in general and its own organization in particular. They have firm convictions about economic motivations and the way wage incentives should operate. Usually they accept as self-evident the theory that the desire for more money is the strongest motivating factor for all people, including shopworkers. Furthermore, they usually believe that the proper wage incentive should overcome problems of lack of co-operation, restriction of output, poor morale, and so on. They feel that, since the opportunity to earn more money is such a boon to the workers, piece rates and their services in setting rates should be welcomed by workers and shop supervisors. Therefore, when they meet with antagonism and suspicion, they are likely to think that the shop people are ignorant and uncoperative and "don't know what is good for them." When a rate does not work, that is, when the shop claims that it is too tight and that they cannot make any bonus on it, rate setters are inclined to believe that the failure is due either to the shop supervision, which does not organize the work or keep the job going smoothly, or to the attitude of the workers, who will not co-operate. The fault must be in the shop, never in the rate. Probably most rate setters or wage-incentive men will feel that this is an unfair accusation or even a misrepresentation of their attitudes. They are convinced that they reach their conclusions through sheer logical examination of facts and that the attitude of the worker represents a lack of understanding of piecework and a pigheaded refusal to accept the good intentions of the piecework organization. Among themselves they may admit the existence of tight and loose rates; but according to the logics of rate setting, such rates are mistakes and should not exist. However, in the face of the general suspicion, antagonism, the widespread restriction of output under piece rates, and the frequency with which wage-incentive systems fail to work satisfactorily, it might be well to re-examine some of the logics of human motivation and try to see a more complete pattern of why people act the way they do.

Large piece-rate organizations sometimes develop both a high degree of interaction as a group and a uniformly defensive front toward outsiders. Under such conditions they tend to be suspicious of members who become friendly with outsiders, especially with shop people. A rate setter, for example, who develops very friendly relations with a certain shop department may be suspected of buying this friendship by setting fat rates on the jobs in that department. His superiors may feel that such friendships will prevent him from being objective in his rate setting and will make him prone to accept shop complaints about the rates without examining the merits of the cases critically. In other words, it is often felt that a rate setter cannot be both friendly to the shop and loyal to his own organization. It is probably true, in actual fact, that the rate setter who is friendly with the shop is more sympathetic with the shop's complaints about rates and with their ideas of fair rates than the rate setter who does not like the shop and is suspicious of their ideas.

Such attitudes are, however, contradictory to some of the basic assumptions of piece rates. Piece-rate organizations, as mentioned earlier, usually take the position that rates can be set so accurately that, for a given expenditure of energy, an experienced worker will earn exactly the same amount on different jobs—in other words, that earnings on different jobs will vary directly with the ability and effort of the workers and that there need be no fat or lean rates. This belief is often expressed in the statements that rate setting is a "scientific measurement" of the elements that go into the job and that it is completely "objective." It is thought to be in a class with other forms of measurement which can be reduced to simple operations in which the judgment of the operator plays little part. Unfortunately, and inevitably, with any except the simplest sorts of operations under most uniform conditions, the rate setter introduces into the rate many of his personal judgments regarding such matters as what constitutes an average worker operating at normal speed, what variables to take into account, or what unusual conditions must be allowed for. If rate setting were the completely objective procedure which many claim it should be, furthermore, then there would be no need for concern over friendships between rate setters and the shop, since the work could always be checked by examination of the objective evidence, or another rate setter working independently would always get the same answer.

One effect of the assumption that rates can be set which will be exact and scientifically accurate is to stimulate the search for better methods and for more accurate work. As a result, modern rate setting has moved far from its earlier methods. There have been elaborate studies of the motions required to do certain jobs; there have been detailed measurements of various motions; there have been careful techniques of measurement devised. This has led to more uniformity in rates and has reduced the possibility of excessively fat or lean rates. At the same time, this produces a tendency for the rate-setting organization to increase in size. In their attempts to do a better job they tend to increase the intensiveness of their work and expand their force, adding more specialists along with more elaborate techniques. Thus, as with other staff and control organizations, their preoccupation with their own special field acts as a pressure toward both refinement of techniques and expansion of force. And over a period of time we see that this pressure is blocked by management. At some point the big boss has to say no, and the organization is filled with feelings of frustration and anxiety.

An Illustration

The following excerpt from a study of one factory shows how one wage-incentive organization operates, and illustrates some points of this discussion:

The organization has certain beliefs which it uses to explain its activities; and these have become identified with the organization itself, so that any admission that the concepts are inadequate would be an admission that the organization itself is inadequate. One of these is the belief that piece rates are wage incentives, that they are a means of getting the employee to produce more because he will be paid more. While they recognize that piece rates may be thought of as a cost control, they feel that such functions are incidental to their primary function as wage incentive. Furthermore, the piece rate is regarded as a product of scientific measurement which is something final and absolute; and if the rate setter applies proper techniques, he will arrive at the correct rate for the job.

While they admit within the organization that a rate is "out of line," they always look on such as a failure of techniques rather than as any failure in their basic assumptions. These admissions of failure are found only when rates are "fat." Apparently, no rate considered "tight" by the shop will be admitted to be other than the exact rate for the job. Thus "fat" rates are mistakes, and "tight" rates do not exist as far as the organization is concerned.

The rates in this plant are supposed to be set with a 15 per cent incentive. That is, a group working at maximum efficiency should earn 15 per cent above the base rates. Since there are admitted to be individual differences in skill, there is expected to be a possible variation from this of 10 per cent so that the groups should earn between 5 per cent and 25 per cent. Actually, there is a great variation from this ideal with some groups going "in the hole," that is, earning less than their base rates, and others earning 70 per cent or 80 per cent.

Since these extreme variations are considered to be "wrong," the organization must find acceptable explanations for them. And to be acceptable the explanations must fit the concepts of the organization. For example, a department which was on a fairly new job was running far "in the hole." This was at first explained on the grounds that the group was inexperienced in the work and that the job was poorly organized. As earnings rose gradually over a period of time, this was pointed out to prove that the rates were correct. When improvement stopped with the earnings still below the base rates, the piece-rate organization claimed that the workers and foremen were unco-operative and were not trying to increase earnings.

In another case, there was a group with extremely high earnings on a job which had been running without change for a number of years. Since this suggested that the rates were wrong, the piece-rate organization made a careful study of the job, with the idea of finding changes in methods which would justify changes in rates or else finding an acceptable excuse for the high earnings. The job was such that no changes in method seemed possible; so under company policy the rates could not be changed. The organization prepared an explanation, which was announced to all rate setters. They explained that the workers were all men with long experience on that job and were unusually efficient. Furthermore, they took special pains to learn all the instructions on the job, would even take the blueprints and instructions home and memorize them in their spare time. Thus they could work steadily without stopping to read the instructions or check the prints.

For smaller deviations from what were considered the proper earnings, there were a few stock explanations. When only a little above 20 per cent or 25 per cent, the groups were spoken of as efficient; and if earnings were low, the group was called inefficient in terms of poor organization or supervision or inexperienced workers. When earnings went much above 25 per cent, they explained that there must have been changes in methods of which they had not been notified.

The higher levels in the piece-rate organization kept a close watch over the piecework earnings of every shop department as one of their controls over the functioning of their own organization. If there was any sharp change in earnings for any department, someone from the organization would go to the shop foreman to investigate the cause. Regardless of the explanation given by the shop, it was restated in keeping with the concepts of the piecework organization. For example, in one case there was a sharp drop in earnings in a department having a combination of machine work and assembly work. The foreman explained that the machine rates were tight and the assembly rates loose, so that any change in proportions of work affected the earnings of the department as a whole; and for that month most of the work had been in the machine section. In reporting back to his superior, the investigator said the drop in earnings was due to the relative inefficiency of the group on machine work. Nothing was said about fat or lean rates.

Rate setters are aware of the antagonism of the shop and sometimes remark: "Those guys are lazy and don't like us because we make 'em work." In one case where a group was having trouble in making the rates on a conveyor assembly job, the rate setter pointed out to the foreman that the workers would slow down the conveyor when they could not keep up. He suggested what he called a "slacker-proof" conveyor which could not be controlled by the workers. The foreman replied that the idea might work but that he could get the same results with a horsewhip. The rate setter said he was wasting time trying to help out the shop foreman and might as well give his idea to his superiors and get credit for it.

Another type of defensive behavior was shown when the company decided that the foremen should be given a better understanding of the piecework system. A series of meetings were arranged at which supervisors from the piece-rate organization would explain the system and answer the questions of the shop foremen. In preparation for this the piece-rate organization prepared a series of questions which might be raised, and the higher levels worked out the acceptable answers to these questions. Copies of the questions and answers, which were called "The Bible," were given to the supervisors, who were to attend the foremen's conferences so that they might all give the proper answers to any questions.

12. WAGE INCENTIVES AND RESTRICTION OF OUTPUT

To THOSE who hold to the theory that economic motivations are the principal motivations of all workers, wage incentives—and especially piecework—appear to be the perfect solution to many of the problems which plague management. If one accepts the idea that to each worker nothing is so important as the opportunity to make more money, then any system which would enable him to earn more should be received with enthusiasm. Some theorists have even felt that workers were so "money hungry" that they were likely to overwork themselves on piecework. Actually, such simple faith in the incentive value of piecework has rarely been justified in actual practice, and we are forced to conclude that individual motivation is a much more complex matter than the theories imply.

RESTRICTION OF OUTPUT

Careful observation of many work situations makes it quite clear that restriction of output in some form exists in practically every plant, on all sorts of jobs, and under all kinds of payment systems. It is so common as to be taken for granted by most experienced workers; and one of the first things the man on the new job wants to know is: "How much is a day's work?" The newcomer who does not abide by the accepted standards of the group usually has it called forcibly to his attention. In fact, it often happens that such limitations are much more strictly adhered to on piecework than on daywork.

Concepts and Beliefs

On nearly every job there is some concept of a day's work which serves as a standard of performance for the group. It is rare to find a job on which the only measure is "as much as you can do"; almost always there is some definite amount against which an individual can measure himself. To understand restriction of output, it is necessary to

209

understand how these standards become established and what ends they serve for the group.

One of the most important factors in limiting output is the general suspicion which workers have of the motives of management. Especially when it comes to output, the workers feel that management is primarily interested in getting more for their money. Almost invariably they look on piecework not as a means for them to earn more money but rather as a method by which management can get more work out of them. Such attitudes are usually justified, too, since management does quite consistently look on piecework, or any wage-incentive plan, as a system for increasing the efficiency of the workers. The important thing about these attitudes of workers is that they so often feel that they cannot win in the long run but that they will end up by doing more work without significant gain in wages. Workers believe, too, that if their earnings are too high, their rates will eventually be cut. This is quite consistently believed, even when management has assured them that no rate will be cut without definite change in method. Even where there are union contracts protecting them against rate cutting, workers still cling to this belief; and almost every experienced worker can tell of cases from his own experience when rates have been cut.

In the case of straight day wages or daywork, the fear is that any increase in output over what is customary will make the boss expect them to do more work all the time. If one worker exceeds the others, they all feel that his record will become a goal which they will all be expected to reach. Thus, the more one does, the more is expected of him; he just cannot win.

Establishing Ceilings

Out of all these expectations, quite clear ideas inevitably develop as to how much output is proper or "safe" for any job. On daywork jobs, it is expressed in units of output—so much is a day's work. One executive told how he learned this fundamental truth when he took his first job on the line gang of a telephone company. He said: "The first day I was on the job they put me to digging post holes. I was a young punk just out of college—ambitious, and eager to win approval. So I was really getting those holes dug when an old-timer came over and said, 'Hey, Bub, three holes is a day's work.' So I saw the light and dug three holes, no more."

With piecework, especially where the individual handles a variety of work with different rates, the day's work is usually expressed in terms of earnings rather than in units of output. If $1.50 an hour is considered the proper earnings, each worker will watch to see that his output does not exceed that amount. If he is working an eight-hour shift, then, when his earnings amount to $12, he will stop work and kill time; or he will help someone else, or hold over any additional output for the next day.

The way in which these ceilings are established is often not very clear and may involve a number of factors. On any new job, one of the first questions the workers ask of the foreman is how much output is expected. Then, after they have worked on it for a time, there gradually develops some idea of what can be thought of as a fair day's work; usually this is kind of a balance between what the foreman would like to have and what the group finds it possible to do. If they find that they can come up to the foreman's expectations without too much effort, they may soon level off at that point. If his sights are pretty high, they may level off somewhat below that point and may resist any further efforts on his part to increase output. He may then gradually modify his demands until they reach an agreement on what he will accept and what they will do. All this goes on rather under cover—with the foreman prodding them to do more and with the group finding all kinds of reasons for not being able to do it—until finally an agreement, often unstated, is reached.

In many cases the ceiling on piecework earnings grows out of the general idea of a fair wage for the type of work. When earnings rise much above what is generally accepted as a fair wage, the workers begin to wonder what management will think about it; they wonder if they have not gone far enough and soon begin to restrict. A few comments about the possibility of management cutting the rates, and the ceiling is soon fixed.

In some cases the accounting routines have been observed to set a very definite ceiling on piecework. In one piecework system, which was mentioned earlier, it was believed that 25 per cent was good earnings; and anything above that must be due to exceptional circumstances. While a few jobs showed earnings over 50 per cent, they were viewed with considerable concern by the rate setters, who felt that the rates were out of line. They further assumed that any earnings above 100 per cent were impossible; and when the records showed such high earnings, it was assumed that there was either an accounting error or else the worker was putting something over. For that reason, no payment of over 100 per cent could be made without the specific approval of the superintendent, which meant that all such cases would be investigated. As a result, the foremen let the workers know that it was best not to earn as much as 100 per cent; 95 per cent was all right, since it would be paid automatically without discussion; but 100 per cent meant that the superintendent would be asking questions and looking on the department with a critical eye, that the rate setters would be looking the job over, and that the accounting organization would be checking over all records—all looking for something wrong. Inevitably, no worker earned 100 per cent; that was the absolute ceiling and nobody would think of violating it.

Controlling Output

Usually a work group likes to keep the output level at a point where the individual can maintain acceptable production without too much effort. This does not mean that the workers prefer to just loaf on the job. Actually, most workers prefer not to kill time deliberately; but they do not want to be under too much pressure. They also like to feel that, if they have trouble with the job or are not feeling well part of the day, they can speed up and can make up losses later. In other words, they like to have something in reserve for emergencies; and this reserve means a work pace and level of output well below what is easily possible for the fastest workers in the group.

The control of output usually lies in the hands of the work group. They come to an informal agreement as to how much is a day's work and then exert pressure on the individuals to see that they all abide by the limits. As we have seen, a new worker is informed of these limits, and they usually police him to see that he accepts them. If he does not, he will likely become an outcast, will be the butt of jokes and "kidding," may have difficulties with his tools or his work, and will have his life made unpleasant generally. Most workers soon succumb to such pressures and accept the dictates of the group, or else they become so unhappy that they quit the job. The "rate buster" is, in fact, almost always a source of friction and a center of disturbance —so much so, that he is often not even liked by the foreman in spite of his high performance.

In many instances the foreman knows that there is restriction of output and accepts it as a matter of course. In fact, as long as his group is performing to the satisfaction of his superiors in terms of output, costs, or however they judge him, he is not apt to be very concerned over a certain amount of restriction. As long as the group works together smoothly, turns out the work expected of them, and responds to any emergency demands, he is perfectly willing for them to go along at whatever pace suits them best. He himself may, in fact, limit their output if he thinks any increase will call undue attention to the group. Just as in the case where earnings exceeding 100 per cent were investigated, the foreman is ever on the alert to prevent anything from calling excessive and critical attention to his group; and if high output or earnings may do it, he will act to limit them. He may do this directly by telling the operators what the ceiling is, or he may do so by manipulating the work. If he thinks that the high output of a rate buster may call attention to the customary ceiling of the group, for example, he may keep moving the rate buster around on different jobs to prevent his developing speed on any one; or he may give him the jobs with the lean rates or put him on daywork jobs. Such practices are, of course, viewed with horror by higher executives or by rate setters, but they are perfectly natural adjustments to the pressures under which the foreman must operate.

Output Records

The concern of either the workers or the foreman over attracting undue attention to the group often results in the control of output. For one thing, high executives, in watching the various reports, usually question any sharp fluctuation from normal or any changes which run counter to what they expect. Output records based on department or work group are usually watched closely; and in the case of piecework, there may be records of the average earnings of the group. As a result, the foreman is likely to be questioned concerning sharp or unexpected fluctuations in these records. In case of a drop in either output or earnings, he may be criticized for failing to keep the job running smoothly; or in case of a sudden jump, executives may wonder why he has not kept output at these levels before and may expect him to keep it up in the future. To avoid this, he prefers to have the job run pretty evenly with little fluctuation or with only those fluctuations which are obviously due to changes beyond his immediate control and for which he will have adequate alibis. Thus, the "straight-line" output, or earnings, records are to the foreman and the work group the "safest" and the most desirable.

To maintain such straight-line performance is not so difficult on long-running jobs—that is, jobs in which the same operations on the same products are performed day after day. In such jobs, the workers can perform the same operation over and over, and an even work pace can be maintained. On irregular jobs, where different parts or operations are met with daily, there may be a constant shifting of workers and work pace. In any case, the foreman will try to keep some sort of records so that he will know just where he stands with respect to maintaining a straight-line output record. He prefers to have the average work pace at a level where he can, if necessary, call on the group for more output without too much resistance. Under such conditions he can maintain an even record, in spite of difficulties or delays, by taking up a little slack in the system.

A good example of this was observed in a department working on group piecework and making electrical switchboards. The orders were usually for relatively small lots, so that the workers rarely worked day after day on one routine operation but were constantly being changed from job to job. Two important control reports were the monthly piecework earnings of the department and the monthly "fall-down" report, or record of orders not delivered on the date promised. The manufacturing interval on many of the orders was fairly long, and the delivery dates were not very tight; so they did not have to rush each order out as soon as received but could plan the work over several weeks. The foremen in the department always tried to organize their work with these two reports in mind and, during the month, would keep informal records to show where they stood on the orders which had to be delivered that month and where they stood on their cumulative piecework earnings for the month. Thus, if they were falling behind on an order, they might shift a lot of the workers onto that job and let some other less-pressing job wait. In this way, they could make deliveries on time and stay off the "fall-down" report. At the same time, they would watch piecework earnings, especially after the middle of the month; and if it looked as if they were falling behind, they would shift their people onto the simple orders, which could be rushed through in time to clear inspection and be paid for on that month's piecework. Or they would put as many as possible to work on the final stages of work in progress in order to get it finished that month. If they seemed to be ahead on their piecework earnings, they would put the group on the difficult jobs which would not be completed that month; or they would take them off the final stages of work and put them on the beginning operations of jobs just starting. This would stop the movement of finished work into the inspection department and accumulate unpaid-for time in work in progress. By close watch over the details and careful juggling, they were thus able both to make deliveries and to control the piecework earnings, so as to prevent serious fluctuations.

In another department, the foreman used individual output records as a method of keeping track of what was going on. He had each operator turn in a daily report of all the work he did. Each operator had to show the job he had worked on, the quantity of parts used, and the time spent. This was a sandblasting job on which each operator might work on one job all day or on eight or ten small jobs, each with a different piece rate. The operators had a definite idea of a fair day's work, and before they turned in their output records they would carefully figure their earnings for the day. If too low, they would claim some lost time; or if several were on the same job, the fast workers would let the others have part of their output. If too high, they would either "give it away" or just not report part of the work actually done. This did not affect their earnings, since it was group piecework and since they were paid on the basis of work actually finished and delivered to inspection, rather than on the operators' reports. However, the work shown on the daily reports was never quite what was accounted for by inspection. While they approximated a straight-line output record, they were careful not to show the same earnings day after day. They said that the foreman knew that no one could work at a perfectly even pace on that job; so if they maintained a perfectly even straight-line record, he would know that they were making it "with the pencil" or controlling it in other ways. For that reason they always saw to it that their reports fluctuated slightly from day to day in order to "give the boss what he wanted."

In this same department it was interesting to see how the concept of the proper learning curve for a worker on a new job operated. One old-timer had been brought in from another totally different job and put on sandblasting. He had had experience on sandblasting years before and picked up the work very rapidly. He watched his daily reports very carefully, however, and showed only a moderate increase each day, even though he was well below what was considered a fair day's work and was not working very hard. When asked about the work, he said that he could have reached the average output within three days but was careful not to progress too fast. He explained that the proper learning curve for a new man on the job was one which showed fairly rapid improvement for about a week and then a gradual slowing of progress, so that it would take several weeks to reach average output. He was making his output conform to this proper pattern, since, if he improved too fast, the foreman would know that the group were taking it fairly easy and would try to make them increase their output.

A Study of Restriction

While most of the phenomena which we have been discussing are fairly common knowledge to anyone with much factory experience, there have been few attempts to study them in detail. Probably the most careful study of restriction of output and its related factors is that made at the Hawthorne Works of the Western Electric Company. The following excerpts taken from the detailed report on the Bank Wiring Observation Room, which worked on a group piecework system, may serve to illustrate this discussion.[1]

In interviews with the operators in the department before the study began, the investigators encountered certain beliefs which the employees seemed to hold in common. Chief among these was the concept of a day's work. This idea kept cropping up in interview after interview. Of the thirty-two men interviewed in the department before the study began, a group which included the nine wiremen later selected for the study, twenty-two discussed rates of output. Of these twenty-two, twenty said that the wiring of two equipments constituted a day's work. The other two men said they were supposed to try to make the bogey, which they correctly stated as 914 connections per hour. . .

From comments such as these it was apparent that the operators were accustomed to thinking of two equipments a day as a day's work. This was verified by the observer, who found that the operators frequently stopped wiring when they had finished their quotas even though it was not officially stopping time. This concept of a day's work was of interest for two reasons. In the first place, it did not refer to the bogey or any other standard of performance officially imposed. . . . .

In the second place, the idea of a day's work was of interest because it was contrary to one of the basic notions of the incentive plan. Theoretically, the incentive plan was intended to obviate the problems attendant upon the determination of a day's work. . . .

As the study progressed, it became more and more apparent that the operator's concept of a day's work had a much wider significance than has thus far been implied. The interviewer, while inquiring further into this belief, found that it was related to other beliefs which the operators held quite generally. These other beliefs, which incidentally are quite common and more or less

---

[1] F. J. Roethlisberger and W. J. Dickson, *Management and the Worker* (Cambridge, Mass.: Harvard University Press, 1939), pp. 412, 414, 416–17, 419–20, 421, 422, 423, 428–29.

familiar to everyone, usually took the form: "If we exceed our day's work by any appreciable amount, something will happen. The 'rate' might be cut, the 'rate' might be raised, the 'bogey' might be raised, someone might be laid off, or the supervisor might 'bawl out' the slower men." Any or all of these consequences might follow. . . .

Statements like these indicate that many apprehensions and fears centered around the concept of a day's work. They suggested that the day's work might be something more than an output standard, that it might be a norm of conduct. The data obtained by the observer provided additional evidence in support of this interpretation. He found that men who persisted in exceeding the group standard of a day's work were looked upon with disfavor. This was manifested in subtle forms of sarcasm and ridicule. . . .

W6 and W2 were the first in output and it was toward them that most of the group pressure was directed. W6 was designated by such terms as "Shrimp," "Runt," and "Slave." Sometimes he was called "Speed King," a concession to his wiring ability. W2 was called "Phar Lap," the name of a race horse. W1 was nicknamed "4:15 Special," meaning that he worked until quitting time. W5 was also called "Slave" occasionally.

One of the most interesting devices by which the group attempted to control the behavior of individual members was the practice which they called "binging." This practice was noticed early in the study. The observer described it as follows:

"W7, W8, W9, and S4 were engaged in a game which they called 'binging.' One of them walked up to another man and hit him as hard as he could on the upper arm. The one hit made no protest, and it seems that it was his privilege to 'bing' the one who hit him. He was free to retaliate with one blow. One of the objects of the game is to see who can hit the hardest. But it is also used as a penalty. If one of them says something that another dislikes, the latter may walk up and say, 'I'm going to bing you for that.' The one who is getting binged may complain that he has been hurt and say, 'That one was too hard. I'm going to get you for that one.' . . ."

In addition to its use as a penalty and as a means of settling disputes, binging was used to regulate output of some of the faster workers. This was one of its significant applications and is well illustrated in the following entry:

W8 (to W6): "Why don't you quit work? Let's see, this is your thirty-fifth row today. What are you going to do with them all?"

W6: "What do you care? It's to your advantage if I work, isn't it?"

W8: "Yeah, but the way you're working you'll get stuck with them."

W6: "Don't worry about that. I'll take care of it. You're getting paid by the sets I turn out. That's all you should worry about."

W8: "If you don't quit work I'll bing you." W8 struck W6 and finally chased him around the room.

Obs (a few minutes later): "What's the matter, W6, won't he let you work?"

W6: "No. I'm all through though. I've got enough done." He then went over and helped another wireman. . . .

Another idea frequently expressed, directly or indirectly, by the employees in the interviews was that their weekly average hourly output should show little change from week to week. This does not mean that all of them should try to achieve identical average hourly outputs each week. It did mean that each of them should try to be fairly consistent week after week irrespective of differences in the absolute levels of their outputs. Their reasons for this were similar to those they advanced for not exceeding their day's work. They felt that if their output showed much change either from day to day or from week to week "something might happen." An unusually high output might thenceforward become the standard their supervisors would expect them to maintain. The men felt it would be a way of confessing that they were capable of doing better. On the other hand, they felt that a low output would afford their supervisors an opportunity to "bawl them out." If output were kept fairly constant, they thought, neither possibility could happen. . . .

The department permitted employees to claim daywork for unusual stoppages which were beyond their control. It did not, however, define what an unusual stoppage was or attempt to state which stoppages were and which were not beyond the employees' control. Such a definition would have been difficult to make because practically all delays were in some sense subject to employee control. Moreover, if the wage-incentive plan functioned as it was supposed to, there was no need for such a definition. It was assumed that the employees would resent any stoppage which interfered with their work and, as long as the opportunity to do piecework was present, that they would never either deliberately bring about a situation in which they could get only daywork or claim more daywork than they were entitled to. Yet that is exactly what happened. Some of them claimed more daywork allowances than they were entitled to or contrived to bring about occurrences which would justify their claims. The interesting thing about these claims is that they meant nothing to the operators in terms of payment. The operators were addressing themselves not to financial gains but to the security they felt came from uniform output curves. They said, of course, that the more daywork they were allowed, the less output they would have to produce in order to maintain a given output rate.

RATE CUTTING

Rate cutting is generally considered "unfair" by both management and workers, and it is clearly recognized that attempts to cut rates on high-earning jobs kills any incentive which the worker may have to try to increase his earnings. In order to convince the workers that management is trying to be fair and will give them the benefits of any increase in output and efficiency, it is often necessary to make a formal guaranty of the rates. This may be given merely as a statement of policy or may be incorporated into union contracts. In any event, management reserves the right to establish rates on any new job or on an old job in which there is a significant change of method. Thus, a change in method of drilling holes in a part, so that, instead of drilling each hole separately on a single-spindle drill press, they can all be drilled at one time on a multiple-spindle press, would call for a new piece rate. Thus, as a result of rapid technical development in tools and methods and of changes in design, piece rates are apt to be continually changing. Since these technical developments are originated by management or by its technical experts, the engineers, the shop often interprets the changes as a method by means of which the rates can be cut if earnings prove excessive. In many cases, not only workers, but foremen and other shop supervisors as well, actually claim that, whenever piecework earnings on a job go too high, the engineers will look it over as a good place to show savings by a change in methods. No doubt an engineer who is trying to make a showing by improved job methods will look for the spots where changes are likely to show the most results. A good chance for savings occurs at any spot where labor costs appear to be high. This does not mean that engineers devote their attention only to the jobs where piece-rate earnings are high, but in many cases it is undoubtedly a factor in their decisions as to what to work on.

Furthermore, it is usually true that, when a very fat job is re-engineered, it comes out much leaner. This all combines to convince the workers that the most they can expect from an incentive system, in the long run, is a moderate increase over what they would earn on straight daywork and that they will probably work much harder for it. As a result, the assurances of management that they want the workers to work hard and earn as much as possible seldom really convinces them that they gain anything by extending themselves to the utmost. The changing of rates with improvement in methods also tends to discourage the workers from trying openly to make improvements in the job. If they figure out some short cuts, develop better tools or fixtures, or improvise better ways of doing the job, they must keep the improvements hidden, or sooner or later a new rate will be set. As a result, they may work out improvements that will help them do the job better but keep them hidden from the eye of the foreman or the engineers.

On jobs which have run steadily over a period of years without change in methods or rates, it is often found that the earnings have increased gradually until they have reached a level very much above what is customarily thought of as high for that particular plant. In these cases the ceilings have apparently been moved upward over a period of years until quite a high level is accepted by management and considered "safe" by the workers. These high earnings on such jobs are often the result of a combination of factors, one of which is the acceptance of the fact that nothing will happen to the job because of the high earnings. Also, in many cases there may be gradual improvements in the quality of the parts or materials used, and conditions which formerly slowed down the job may no longer exist. Furthermore, over a period of years the workers develop a high degree of skill on the one job, learn all the tricks and short cuts, memorize the instructions, and generally improve their efficiency.

On completely new jobs, especially those which require considerable dexterity, it is often impossible to set rates until the workers have developed the necessary skills. In such cases the rate setters prefer to wait until the workers have reached what is assumed to be a normal level of output and are stabilized there, before timing the job. As a result, the workers often restrict their output and slow down the rate of learning the job, since they feel that if they level off at a comfortable working pace the rate will be set on that basis. They hope that this will give them a fat rate on which they can make fair earnings without much effort. This presents a problem to rate setters, of course, since they do not know whether the workers have actually reached a high degree of skill and are giving a reasonable output for the job or whether they have restricted their work at a low level in order to get excessively fat rates. At the same time, supervisors and workers may be demanding that the rates be set promptly on the new jobs so that they can have the advantage of piecework earnings as soon as possible.

This feeling that they must protect themselves from the rate setters is almost universal among workers, as pointed out earlier. If a rate setter just appears in a shop department, the whole tone of the place is likely to change. When he actually times a job, the worker tries to give the impression that he is working steadily at an even pace, so that he cannot be accused of stalling on the job. At the same time, he is very careful to follow every detail of job instruction, avoiding all short cuts, and putting in a few inconspicuous extras, if possible, to slow him down. Experienced rate men, however, are usually familiar with all these devices and are inclined to cut a bit off the actual timing when it comes to setting the rates. In one case, a group, who worked together in assembling a complicated and large-sized steel framework, had worked out a system to be used only when the rate setter was present. They found that, by tightening certain bolts first, the frame would be slightly sprung and all the other bolts would bind and be very difficult to tighten. When the rate setter was not present, they followed a different sequence; and the work went much faster. As a result, they never had any trouble in making high earnings on that job; but they were always careful not to go too high lest the engineers make a careful study and figure out their trick.

THE MERITS OF PIECEWORK

In view of this discussion, it might seem that piecework has no virtue whatever as an incentive. In spite of all the difficulties and the consistent restriction of output, however, experience has shown that a sound piecework system usually does increase efficiency and actually gets more output per man than a straight daywork system. In fact, some experts claim that the use of piecework will increase output as much as 50 per cent over daywork. This does not actually mean that the workers work 50 per cent harder, but only that output increases that much as a result of a lot of changes in the total work situation. When properly introduced, a sound piecework system does serve as some incentive to the workers; and they will make added efforts to increase their efficiency even while they are careful to restrict their output and earnings within certain limits.

Another factor in the improvement of output under piecework is that the work group generally gives more attention to keeping the job running smoothly. On daywork, if there is some time lost waiting for materials, or for setup men, or because of machine breakdowns, the operator may take it as a matter of course. If he is on piecework and this lost time threatens his earnings, he is likely to complain to the foreman and put pressure on him to prevent these losses.

Piecework earnings of groups or departments often serve, too, as one of the important records which top management uses as an index of shop performance. As one executive explained:

When I look at the records of a department and see that the piecework earnings are going along at what is felt to be a fair level and without much fluctuation from month to month, I know that they are getting the work out and there will probably be no serious delays in delivery of orders. Also, I know that the people will probably be pretty well satisfied, as any serious trouble would affect earnings and any sharp drop in earnings would cause dissatisfaction.

If I see a sharp drop in earnings, I know I can expect trouble with employees and probably trouble from other sources where people are affected by the drop in output in that department.

When looked at in this way, the piecework earnings reports are a potential threat to the foreman. He knows that, if he allows anything to slow down the job or otherwise cut down the earnings of his group, his superiors will be demanding explanations. This really keeps him on his toes in planning and organizing the work so that there will be few delays. It also stimulates him to put pressure on the employees to maintain their efficiency. On the whole, this can prove to be a very powerful pressure upon the foreman, and in some cases it seems to be the real source of improved performance under piecework. As one foreman put it, "Piecework isn't so much an incentive for the workers as a whip over the foremen."

This aspect of piecework was especially apparent in a plant where a number of new jobs were being put on group piecework. Before the groups, mostly new workers, had really developed their skill on the jobs, the rates were set at the level it was expected they would ultimately attain. In some cases this was far above the present level of output, and as a result the groups showed losses on the piecework earnings reports; that is, their piecework earnings did not equal the daywork rates which they were guaranteed. In many cases the difference between what they were actually producing and what they would have to produce to make any piecework earnings was so great that the workers all felt that they could never hope to make the rates and did not try very hard. The foremen, however, were under terrific pressure to get the earnings out of the red. In spite of the indifference of the workers, the foremen managed to get improved performance until the groups were just about breaking even. By this time, the workers were getting the feel of the jobs and began to see some prospects of piecework earnings. This served as a stimulus and gradually they came up to where they were earning a few per cent over their daywork rates. This was not enough for higher supervisors, however, who insisted that the job should earn between 15 per cent and 20 per cent; so the pressure was still on the foremen. They, in turn, kept the pressure on the workers and continued to try to improve the planning of the job and the flow of work so that there would be as little waste motion as possible. They gradually pushed the earnings up until they reached the desired 15 per cent. The pressure was then off, and the earnings stabilized there. If left to their own devices, the workers would have leveled off their output even below the daywork rates; they were forced to go higher only because of the insistence and assistance of the foremen.

13. THE TECHNIQUES OF ORGANIZA-TION

As we go from organization to organization, we find that each has its own special personality which gives it a special tone or atmosphere. Thus, status systems and status concerns appear in all except a few very small ones; yet, in some, status anxieties run rampant, and worry over one's relation with superiors overshadows everything. In others, this anxiety is comparatively slight, and other concerns hold the attention of the group.

These differences between organizations are not due to differences in the people but to differences in the way the whole is put together and to the forces acting on it. In order to understand these things better, let us examine some of the techniques of organization and their influence upon human relations.

SYSTEMATIC TECHNIQUES AND METHODS S.O.P.

It is quite apparent that the way an organization accomplishes its goals can range all the way from highly systematized techniques and procedures, to which the employee is supposed to adhere rigorously, to no techniques or procedures at all. Assembly-line factories represent one end of this scale, while "arty" organizations represent the other. In factories, everything is arranged in accordance with standard work practice and well-defined procedures. Deviations from these procedures cannot easily be countenanced. In many cases, an effort is made to control the work habits of the individual employee; he is told how to do the work and is not permitted any individual variations from the routines that have been set up. In organizations where predetermined work routines and procedures have not been established, the employee is permitted a great many more individual choices in how he performs his work. He is not asked to adhere rigorously to precisely defined work practices.

Since we know that large numbers of people react negatively to situations where it is difficult, if not impossible, to express their own individuality, it can be expected that morale will suffer in organiza-

223

Arty ← Procedural

tions which have a tight, systematic technology. This certainly has been borne out in studies and observations which the authors have made. Whenever employees are called upon to perform highly routinized, repetitive work in accordance with rigorously prescribed procedures, they begin to feel as though management is treating them like children. "It's like a kindergarten around here," they say.

A distinction should be made here between a highly rigorous technology which is based on scientific knowledge and a technology based entirely on arbitrary procedure. The reactions of employees appear to be partially determined by the extent to which the technology makes sense to them. A technology based on science is reasonable in the sense that the logic of nature confirms it. You can verify what you are doing, either in elaborate experiments or by objective observations in real life situations. An employee in a factory usually is able to make some sense out of what he is doing, particularly after he has acquired a knowledge of mechanics and some notions about time-motion economy and methods engineering. More than that, he can see something very real being accomplished.

A technology based on procedure can be, and often is, purely arbitrary. It is just one way of accomplishing the task; there may be other ways that are equally as effective. As often as not, a procedure is founded in historical precedence; it appears to be the best way of accomplishing a particular task simply because "we have always done it that way."

The purpose of any procedure is simply that of setting up a formal way of accomplishing a particular task in order to reduce to a minimum the need for constant decisions on matters of detail. In one sense, a procedure is to an organization what a habit is to an individual. If we had to think through all of the details involved in getting ourselves dressed in the morning, we would never get to work, so engrossed would we be with buttoning our shirts and tying our shoelaces. In the same way, a procedure in an organization eliminates the necessity for thought about minor matters. Just so long as you follow the procedure, you can be assured that the right people will be notified and the proper records kept. Everything will be conducted in a "businesslike" manner.

Overelaboration of Procedures

Carefully worked out procedures can have a practical value in the operation of a business. But there is a strong tendency for many organizations to develop procedures for handling practically every problem situation—to define everything to the point of eliminating all individual decision and initiative. In considering many modern industrial organizations, it would seem almost as though they were being slowly strangled by an overelaboration of procedures and policies. In some organizations, no one dares to breathe unless he first finds out what the procedure is. Everything has been defined. Nothing has been left to the imagination or individual decision. Rigid, unadaptive bureaucracy reigns supreme!

Another feature of procedures which creates poor morale among the employees who are subjected to an overabundance of them is their tendency to persist long after they have outworn their usefulness. Indeed, it appears as though a procedure, once established, seldom dies a natural death; it usually has to be murdered in cold blood if it is to be done away with at all. Probably one reason why procedures are taken for granted and allowed to continue *ad infinitum* is that they were originally set up to eliminate thought. As a consequence, and we are speaking seriously here, they are never thought of again until some inquisitive person happens to ask what this report is used for, or why this procedure is being followed. More important than this, perhaps, is the fact that procedures are generally determined by higher authority. Therefore, no one down the line dare make modifications.

Regardless, however, of the reasons for the persistence of procedures, employees are frequently aware of their purely arbitrary character and feel that they are unnecessary and restrictive. Particularly is this true when employees themselves play no part in determining the procedures. Under such circumstances, they develop the notion that management does not trust them to develop a systematic and intelligent way of handling things. Whenever you hear employees saying, "They do all your thinking for you around here," you can be sure that morale is low, or else on its way down.

Unnecessary Procedures

In many cases management prescribes procedures which are actually unnecessary for the accomplishment of the over-all task of the organization. Many such procedures are set up merely to insure good "business practice" among employees. Gate passes, passes to first aid, procedures for securing gloves or rags—passes and procedures for this, that, and the other thing—all fall into this category. Many of these practices are necessary for an orderly operated organization.

Nevertheless, when they become overelaborated, employees begin reacting against them. Frequently such procedures are set up as though most or all employees would not be businesslike or honest in their work if they were not closely controlled and watched in all situations. While it is true that a reasonable amount of supervision must be exercised, the fact remains that most employees will follow orderly business procedures, once an explanation of the reason for the procedure is given, and particularly if they are permitted to assist in setting up any formal procedure which may be decided upon. It is the implication that management considers them dishonest, irresponsible, or "like children" which creates injured feelings.

One case is so flagrant an example that it bears recording here. The manager of the organization involved was extremely suspicious of subordinate employees. He felt that most, if not all, employees, were essentially irresponsible and interested solely in keeping as far away from work as possible. His own work habits were good, at least as far as the routines were concerned. He came to work an hour early; he stayed late; he was always on the go. He consumed most of his energies during this period, however, wondering what his subordinates were doing and prying, in all sorts of petty ways, into the details of their work and of their personal lives. Since this was a factory organization, the manager had no difficulty finding members of his staff who tended to confirm his views. He enlisted the help of his auditor and a few others in setting up a system of oppressive rules and regulations which had his organization reeling in very short order. First, all the gates were locked, except at specific times, in order to be sure that no employee, once on the grounds, could get out. This was done because it was suspected that a few employees were slipping out for a cup of coffee at unauthorized times. Next, the cafeteria was closed during the morning hours because a small number of employees were using it for coffee during their rest period. Then the guards were instructed to take the name of any employee coming in after the whistle blew. This was done even though employees had to punch a regular time card in their own departments. It was felt that some employees were coming to work early, punching in, and then slipping out for coffee and staying out until after the starting whistle. The lunch periods were reduced in number from three to two in order to gain closer control over employees during this time. It was strongly suspected that employees were slipping downtown to do their shopping at lunch time. Employees began to ask the personnel department when management was going to mount machine guns at the gate. The final blow came when the cafeteria was closed without warning and the door was bolted and barred so that employees could not use the area even to eat the lunches they had brought with them. The ostensible reason for this action was that the company could not afford to clean up after them. The answer to this challenge was simple: the employees refused to go back to work until the cafeteria was unlocked. Actually, what management was expressing here in the establishment of these various procedures was a considerable hostility toward the employees, which the employees quite naturally felt. In such a situation, it is difficult to argue against control because it appears as though you are arguing against virtue and for sin. After all, why should employees slip out for a cup of coffee after the starting whistle? The point is, of course, that the great majority of them do not and that the offenders, and only the offenders, should be punished and controlled.

Reasons for Overelaboration of Controls

An overelaboration of procedural controls frequently develops whenever the economic situation becomes tight. Under such circumstances, management has the vague feeling that "we have to cut out all this tomfoolery; employees have to toe the mark or else. . . ." Some tightening down, of course, is necessary; but, for the most part, this kind of managerial action does far more harm than good to the organization. It would be more intelligent, and certainly more effective, to solicit the help of employees in reducing expenses and increasing output, rather than to lash out at them indiscriminately and arbitrarily in the hope that fear will drive them to greater productivity and increased interest in the welfare of the organization.

Unions, in many cases, tend to stimulate the proliferation of procedures where they did not exist before. Most union-management relations are characterized by a formal definition of rights and privileges. A "legal" situation is created with all that this implies. Management is required to set up formal procedures for handling various matters of mutual concern to management and the union in order to insure adherence to the provisions of the contract. This is particularly true in conflict situations where the union is suspicious of management and watching every move it makes. Another effect of unionization is the tendency to centralize the determination of procedure and policy. The interpretation of the contract is often thought of as a legalistic activity, which indeed it is. As a consequence, many organizations feel safer if this interpreting is done by experts and kept out of the hands of lower-level supervision. This is true, also, of union officials who want all handlings negotiated with their top representatives in order to prevent any concessions which might be granted by less-experienced stewards. There is, therefore, a definite trend toward the centralization of control, even with regard to minor details, on higher and higher levels. This trend tends to reduce still further the opportunities which the individual employee has of participating in decisions which affect him; although on major issues, such as the election of his representatives and the acceptance of the contract, he may have considerably greater opportunities than he had without the union. This is not an argument either for or against unions but is merely designed to show the effects of unionization in increasing the overelaboration of procedures in industry.

The size and complexity of an organization can have a good deal to do with the tendency of management to attempt to control all activities by prescribed procedures. In such cases, management is aware of its lack of control over the various things going on in the organization and attempts to reassure itself by setting up procedures for the handling of details. This is supposed to insure that the job gets done in the proper manner. Anyone familiar with large organizations knows that no amount of procedural administration will guarantee control to management over all parts of the organization.

Management tends to lean heavily on procedural controls whenever, for any reason, it fears that it lacks control over what is happening in the organization. Such fears are especially likely to occur as the size and complexity of the organization increase. Excessive development of procedural control may also result from management's desire for protection from legalistic or other reprisals by the union if certain policies are not carried out, or it may arise from suspicion of the worker and the conviction that he is not co-operating with his bosses in getting the work done. It may get its impetus from fear of economic failure in times of stress or from the fear and anxiety inherent in the personalities of management representatives. But, whatever the cause, an overelaboration of procedural controls is likely to create resentment and bad feeling among employees.

Routine Work and Obsessional Thinking

It is apparent from our studies and observations that a particular technology, or way of accomplishing the work of an organization, influences morale positively or negatively to the extent that it permits individual choice and decision by employees on the job. It is also apparent that employees are more likely to accept a work demand which ties in with actual production than a strictly procedural demand which may be arbitrary and even unnecessary. However, in either case, any work which is routine and repetitive is likely to be a morale liability. It is not that employees cannot stand repetitive work; as a matter of fact, some like the rhythm of the job, the steady hum of machinery, and the chomp-chomp-chomp of the presses. However, repetitive, routine work employs only the muscles and kinesthetic sense of the worker; his mind is free to wander. This, in itself, is not demoralizing to the worker; his reveries may be very useful to him in passing the time. But, with many people, this opportunity for uncontrolled projection of thought opens the way for preoccupation with events occurring in the organization, situations at home, and personal problems. He begins to brood over things that happen and to develop obsessions. The effect of obsessional thinking on the employee's productivity and personal well-being is described in considerable detail in Roethlisberger and Dickson's *Management and the Worker*. Here it is stated:

The important role repetitive work plays in creating an ideal setting for the development of discontent has been frequently overlooked. Work in modern industrial organizations consists not so much of hard manual labor as repetitive jobs which require a minimum of skilled attention and allow a great deal of time for preoccupation. It is apparent that for many workers engaged in repetitive or semirepetitive tasks the point of proficiency is soon reached; that is, the amount of attention that the job can carry for the worker is less than the amount of attention the operator is capable of giving. In such a situation, where it is no longer possible for the worker either to elaborate or change his job, he can either switch his attention to other things in the immediate surroundings or indulge in revery. In the absence of any real social situation in which to participate, his reveries frequently take the form of brooding futilely about his personal problems.[1]

The rather extensive development of counseling in industry is partly a result of the tendency of employees in repetitive and routine work to become preoccupied with personal problems. Getting the employee to talk about his problems and listening to him with an understanding ear often is sufficient in itself to relieve him of many of his symptoms. In this way, he becomes aware of his overthinking and

---

[1] F. J. Roethlisberger and W. J. Dickson, *Management and the Worker* (Cambridge, Mass.: Harvard University Press, 1939), p. 322.

preoccupations and is able to deal with his real-life problems more objectively and constructively.

Many employees prefer work which permits them to move around rather than tying them to the workplace. They say that the work is more interesting and less boring if they have an opportunity to move about. In one warehouse that was studied, it was found that employees who were tied to one place had higher turnover and lower morale than stockmen who had to move from place to place in carrying out their activities. This has been observed in other organizations as well. In fact, some organizations have made it an administrative policy to shift people around on routine, repetitive jobs in order to give them sufficient variety in their work to prevent boredom and unnecessary personal preoccupation. Apparently this has been done without loss in efficiency, for most employees are quite capable of learning diverse jobs of the same skill level without too much difficulty.

Pressure of Work

Another aspect of technology which can have an effect on the morale of employees is the pressure of the work. Some organizations, like restaurants and assembly-line factories, work under extreme pressure. Any slowing-up of effort at any point in the line can impede the work of the entire organization. As a consequence, employees and supervisors are almost frantic in their drive to get the work out. Pressure of this sort tends to aggravate personal antagonisms, stimulate outbursts of temper, and generally give employees the feeling of futility and frustration which comes with any continuous drive to accomplish the impossible.

It has been our experience that employees prefer a cycle of activity rather than either constant drive or constant inertia. Employees frequently do like a great deal of work. Beating a deadline or meeting a quota can be a stimulating experience. But when they are drawn through a knothole day after day, the situation begins to lose its novelty and, certainly, its stimulating effects.

WORK SIMPLIFICATION AND ITS EFFECTS

One of the basic principles of the industrial engineer is that increased productivity and decreased costs can be obtained by reducing jobs to simpler and simpler work elements. The extreme of this development is seen in the mass-production assembly lines, where the worker performs the same simple operation over and over, day after day. In other cases, the same results are obtained by changes in methods, improved tools, new design, etc., to the end that the level of skill is reduced and the worker does only the simplest operations. In any case, the result is that less-skilled people are needed, the learning period for new workers is lessened, and costs are generally reduced.

Along with the reduction of jobs to their simplest elements in the interests of mass production, there has been a tendency for the determination of work processes to become more and more a function of management staff departments—particularly the engineering and methods departments. The worker is not asked to think about improved methods of performing his job. This is a management function. He is asked only to do the job as he is told to do it, even to the extent, in some instances, of penalizing him if he tries to be ingenious. "After all, you cannot have just anybody messing around with expensive dies and equipment. Better leave that function, too, to somebody who knows something about it!"

Unquestionably, work simplification can be carried too far. Work can be deskilled to the point where it becomes meaningless and actually creates inefficiency and restriction of output. In one factory, where a group of girls were making raincoats, the work was broken down into its simplest possible elements so that each had one small specific task to perform. Management felt that each would develop an unusual proficiency in her own assignment and would, therefore, increase her efficiency and productivity. This particular work unit became, instead, a real trouble spot. Productivity and efficiency failed to come up to expectations, and morale sank. For want of something better to try, management decided to put the job back together again. Each employee was permitted to make a complete raincoat in her own way. The result—increased productivity and efficiency and improved morale.

Another real threat to efficient organization arising from an oversimplification of jobs is the administrative problems it creates. There is reason to believe that, when work tasks have been deskilled to the point of meaninglessness, employees no longer see the connection between their efforts and the end product. The man who does nothing but drill a hole in a piece part, the ultimate destiny of which he is ignorant, is hardly going to see the necessity for careful workmanship and enthusiastic work effort. Artificial stimuli and rigorous supervisory control are the only ways that he can be kept in line. The efficacy of some of these stimuli is discussed in the chapter on wages and restriction of output among employees (Chapter 12).

The fact remains that, from an administrative point of view, there is no substitute for a job situation that makes sense to the workers in it. The problem of maintaining a complex system of operations—functionally tied together, but each one by itself meaningless—can become an administrative undertaking of insuperable difficulty in a complex organization. In one medium-sized plant with which the authors are familiar, there are over 25,000 separate operations, each with its own rate. These operations are further broken down into the thousands of distinct elements that constitute them. An elaborate time-study department is working full time to keep up with the rating of jobs. An equally elaborate time-keeping department keeps track of the employees' time on various operations as he moves from job to job. Supervisors spend 75 per cent of their time seeing that the right men are assigned to the right jobs and are properly paid for their various activities, whether in doing a job or sitting in the corner on their thumbs. An expensive labor relations department is maintained to deal with the union, mostly over issues arising out of methods of pay, rates, and job classifications. The employees spend thousands of dollars to insure that they have the proper representation in these negotiations. The entire system is overelaborated, ponderous, and top-heavy. One wonders whether it does not create more problems than it solves.

THE FUNCTIONAL TYPE OF ORGANIZATION

Another notion of administration which has had wide acceptance in management circles is that increased efficiency and productivity can be achieved by lumping together in one department all closely related activities. Like the idea of breaking jobs down into their simplest possible elements, this notion seems to be confirmed by logical deduction and scientific fact. It seems apparent that, if you can bring together all employees performing a particular kind of work, their activities can be better co-ordinated, more closely supervised, and better distributed. The thinking involved here generally follows the pattern of observing, first, that certain departments have employees performing similar tasks and that these employees are not always busy. Next, the efficiency expert conceives the idea that, if all of these employees could be brought together in one department, not only could they be more closely supervised but the work could be systematically laid out so that all of them would be busy all of the time. Unquestionably, the reasoning goes, productivity would be increased because employees would be working continuously on the same jobs. Furthermore, efficiency would be likely to improve because employees would be supervised by a person highly trained in the particular activity of the department and would have an opportunity themselves to gain greater proficiency.

There are, however, certain definite liabilities to this kind of organization. For one thing, it takes employees away from the department which gave meaning to their work. In one organization where this administrative notion was applied, a group of record clerks who formerly maintained perpetual inventory records for individual buyers were physically and organizationally separated from the men for whom the records were maintained. Instead, they were lumped together in one department in order to achieve greater record-keeping efficiency and better utilization of time. In the old setup, the record keeper was an integral and significant part of a small buying unit. Her job made sense to her. She knew why she was keeping the records and what they were used for. Under the new arrangement, she merely maintained a set of meaningless figures day in and day out. Needless to say, the morale of this group was materially reduced.

Another difficulty inherent in this kind of administrative action where functionally related jobs are lumped together is that it considerably increases potential conflict in the organization. Whenever a group of functionally related activities are separated from their mother departments and brought together in a department of their own, the original line departments no longer have control over these activities. This means, of course, that the work of the new department cannot be planned entirely in accordance with the needs and demands of any one of the original line departments but must be accomplished in proper order in accordance with the requirements of all. As a consequence, stresses and strains develop between the original line departments, which are demanding special favors and consideration in order to get their work done, and the new service department, which must maintain some order and system in its work effort. The authors have seen conflict between line departments and service departments time and time again. The line makes special requests for handlings which are refused by the service department on

Destroy some of logic of line

the grounds that they cannot give any special considerations for fear their own work will suffer.

In factories, this functional type of organization is very common. For example, in one factory there may be a series of functional departments, such as punch presses, screw machines, drill presses, milling machines, plating, painting, assembly, etc. Parts in process may move back and forth between departments for every separate operation, making necessary a great deal of handling, checking, and record keeping. Also, each department has its own hierarchy, and in a large plant there may be elaborate management groups for every function.

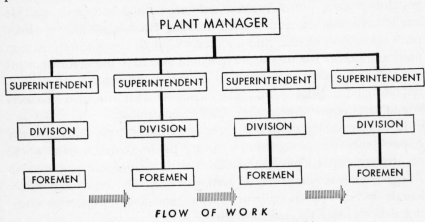

FIGURE 15.—Flow of Work between Divisions

In one large factory the functional development was carried so far that the workers were constantly working on parts that had no meaning, and they often had no idea where the parts were used or how their work affected the work of others. At the same time, there was an elaboration of inspection, with parts being inspected and counted after every operation. This meant that the work was not only constantly moving between functional departments but was also passing at every move through the hands of the inspectors.

This organization had developed a fairly elaborate hierarchy with four levels of supervision (Fig. 15). As the work moved through the plant, it moved from the jurisdiction of one chain of command to another. Any complaints about the work, such as assemblers complaining that the parts didn't fit well or workers protesting that inspection was unfairly rejecting too much of their output, had to be handled between separate chains of command. Gradually the conflicts between groups became so great that only minor complaints could be settled at lower levels. Anything of any importance would be carried up the line, and division chiefs and superintendents spent much of their time settling such disputes.

Finally, the conflicts and inefficiencies in the system forced the management to reorganize the plant on what was called a "product" basis. Selecting a limited type of product, they organized a shop to produce this one product, so that a single department would have full responsibility for the production of a single product. The department head might have charge of a machine section with a variety of different drill presses, punch presses, welders, milling machines, etc. He might have another section with finishing equipment, plating tanks, paint spray booths, etc. Still another would be the assembly section putting together the product. He would also have inspectors; but instead of their being responsible to an outside department, they were responsible for helping maintain quality so that the final products would pass inspection after they left the department.

In these product shops the chain of command was short, and the responsibility was pushed down toward the bottom. Also, the whole department could identify themselves with the product and develop a feeling of real teamwork in getting it out. The result was better morale and co-operation, better quality and lower inspection costs, and a much more efficient operation.

While such product shops have many advantages, both for the workers and for management, they constitute a significantly different world from that of the functional shops. This difference is especially pronounced in the machine sections.

In a functional machine department, such as a punch-press department, all the presses of every size and type are assembled in one location. The youngster starting work usually begins in some simple job such as a helper or trucker. After a time he is put on a light press; and after learning to operate it, he begins to help the setup men and to learn to set up the press. Then he moves on to bigger presses and more skilled jobs, until gradually he may become familiar with every machine and type of work. From there, he might advance to become a setup man and even on to become a foreman.

In such a system, the young man is thrown into contact with the older skilled men; he learns the lore of the job from them; and he becomes familiar with the more skilled jobs without the need of a special training program. Thus, he is placed in a system in which his daily activities, contacts, and observations help prepare him for advancement. He can see clearly the route to advancement and, at the same time, recognize the skills and abilities of the older men who have moved up the path ahead of him. It is such a system that develops the foremen who can boast that they know every job and every machine and can step in and handle them all. And in such a system the foremen are respected for that knowledge.

Now, in the product-type shop, the big functional groups are dispersed. A machine section rarely has a complete hierarchy of skills but exhibits only a collection of special skills. Here the young man may be put on one simple machine, but its mastery does not lead anywhere. No matter how skilled he becomes on a drill press, he does not graduate from it to a milling machine. Any shift may mean that he starts learning a new type of job and starts from scratch. The pathway to success is not clear; there is no simple logic of skills and advancement which everyone can see. So, the individual often feels trapped—doomed by forces he cannot control to live out his days on one job and in one status position.

This also creates a special problem for management in providing the necessary skilled mechanics. The skilled people cannot rise gradually to the top, through the normal processes of the work, but must be specifically trained. Under such a system, management must develop special training methods, often regular schools, in order to teach people much of the skills which they would spontaneously acquire in the other type of organization.

Another difference lies in the characteristics of the supervisors. In the product shop, the foreman must be a man who can organize the work and keep it moving. He cannot hope to master all the skills; so he must be able to use and direct the skills of others. Also, he cannot hope to hold the respect of the skilled mechanics through his superior knowledge in their specialty. He must retain leadership through skill in dealing with people rather than through mastery of machines. This means that the foreman will be a different kind of person, in terms of background and experience, and often will be selected from outside the work group.

Thus, the two types of shops are, in effect, two different worlds. In one, all skills are related and the workers and supervisors are integrated in terms of the particular skill; prestige is related to the job knowledge and experience; and progress is along the lines of the skill hierarchy. Often the work of one department is unrelated to the work of another, and there is no integration, or even need for much co-operation, in terms of the product.

In the other type of shop, everything focuses on the product and the integration of the jobs and skills in terms of producing the product. Thus, co-operation and teamwork can be developed around the goal of production, and the failures or poor performances of one of the group will directly affect the work of others. Furthermore, if the product shop is not too large, the individual has some understanding of the entire sequence of operations and sees how things fit together and how he fits in. In this way, there can be a goal which he can understand and a team of which he can be a part. These two types of organization may exist in every factory or business, or some firms may be almost completely organized on one plan or the other. Some small firms are entirely functional in their activities. For example, there are concerns which only manufacture screw machine products, and the whole shop is a functional organization operating a variety of screw machines. The shop may turn out thousands of different products on these machines—all parts to be used by other manufacturers. In some other small firms making a few special products, the whole factory may be a product shop with only general functional divisions into groups, such as the machine shop, assembly, office, etc.

However, except in very large organizations or in special types of organization, the variation between the two types is a matter of degree. Most organizations have some of the characteristics of both, depending on the types of processes, the kind of business, and management's ideas as to the best way to build an effective organization.

THE "TALL" VERSUS THE "FLAT" ORGANIZATION

In most treatises on organization, there is considerable emphasis on the "span of control." Out of experience in military organizations have evolved firm beliefs as to how many subordinates should report to a superior—that is, how many others one man can supervise. These beliefs have been given supposedly scientific backing by mathematical calculations which show that the possible combinations of interpersonal relations in any group of over a dozen people will run up into the thousands and will be too great for any supervisor to deal with. However, such reasoning, though mathematically correct, bears no relation to the realities of human relations.

In spite of this, there has been developed fairly general acceptance of the ideas that one supervisor for 12 to 15 workers is a reasonably correct ratio in most factory operations and that, at higher levels, an executive should not have over 4 to 7 people reporting to him.

Application of these concepts of the span of control, then, forces the development of a certain pattern of supervisory and executive structure. If a plant has 300 workers, it should have 20 foremen, 4 department heads, and a superintendent. If it increases to 1,500, then it needs 100 foremen, 20 department heads, 4 superintendents, and a manager to supervise the superintendents. If it goes to 7,500, it increases accordingly and will require 4 managers and a general manager to supervise them. Fortunately, business executives are never this rigid in their thinking about organization and usually fit the structure to the realities of what will work best rather than to a mathematical formula.

However, in these theories of the span of control are certain unstated assumptions concerning the supervisor's or executive's job. If it is assumed that the job of the department head is to know all about what is going on, to check on every action or decision of his foremen, to know how they stand on every job, and to be able to answer any question his superior might ask, then he can only handle a small department and four or five foremen. If he does this, he can be said to be in control of the situation, can prevent any mistakes, and can keep his superior completely informed.

Now, if this is his concept of his job, how does he work? First, he spends a lot of time on the job, watching the work and talking with his foremen. His presence makes it easy for the foremen to discuss things with him, to ask his advice, and to go to him with problems or information. Also, he keeps his eye on the details of the work so that he can ask them endless questions as to why they do this or that.

In addition, he may spend a lot of time going over records. He watches production reports, earning reports, and what not. From these he gleans further things to ask the foreman or information to pass on to his superior.

He also spends time with other departments, straightening out any difficulties, checking to see if they will have parts ready for him, etc. Finally he devotes time to his superior, partly just to keep him informed and partly to ask his advice and get his approval on decisions.

When functioning in this way, the smaller his department the more completely he can enter into every decision and can know about everything that happens. But, if he has a large department—say 10 foremen—then he is lost. He cannot be constantly available to give advice on instructions; he cannot keep track of every detail; and he cannot discuss everything with his superior. And he will feel that he has lost control, that things will go wrong, and that the foremen will make mistakes for which his boss will criticize him.

Now, observation shows that the span of command and the nature of the supervisory hierarchy vary a great deal from organization to organization. Furthermore, in the same type of business, some units function efficiently and profitably in one way and some in another. And we also see that, in practice, there are two types of structure. One we call the "tall" organization, which has a hierarchy with several levels, conforming roughly to the hierarchy which evolves from the theory of limited span of control. The other, which we can call the "flat" type of organization, has fewer levels and more people reporting to each superior.

In this flat organization, the steps from top to bottom are fewer, the chain of command is short, and the direct attention the superior can give to each subordinate is limited. You might say that supervision is spread thin and that each must handle his job without looking to his superior for detailed guidance. Such an organization can work well only if the supervisory groups know their jobs, are able and willing to stand on their own feet, do not hesitate to make decisions and accept responsibility for their mistakes, and can run their jobs as part of the whole system.

With persons who are poorly trained, whose judgment is poor, who are afraid to make decisions, or who want to do things their own way without regard for the rest of the organization, such a structure is hazardous. It does not provide the tightness of control necessary to prevent serious mistakes, to support the dependent or those with poor judgment, or to keep the unruly in line. In effect, such an organization depends on individual ability at all levels, with a minimum of control from above.

On the other hand, the tall structure depends on tight, and even autocratic, control. As James C. Worthy says:

Many businesses closely resemble the authoritarian state in the sense that all direction, all thinking, all authority tends to flow from the top down. While the top administrator may delegate certain parts of his responsibility and authority, the delegation is largely in terms of those at lower levels of the organization merely implementing and effectuating policies and directives which have already been set up. While the over-all directive may be broken down into a series of parts and parcelled out to different people, and while these people may be expected to show initiative, drive and judgment in executing their work, their activity is essentially that of merely carrying out an order.

To make such an organization work, management is forced to set up a rigorous system of controls to see that things get done and to insure that people do not make too many mistakes in carrying out their orders. In other words, a minimum of reliance is placed on the people in the organization, and the system depends primarily on the initiative and judgment of those at the top.

A corollary to this tendency is the elaboration of staff organizations, because if the exercise of judgment and skill is largely reserved to top administrators, they must be assisted by specialized advisory staffs. The result is a further extension of the system of controls through the efforts of the staff departments, as well as a considerable complication of the organization structure, thus leading to the necessity for more controls to hold the whole organization together and make it work. At the same time, because of the necessity for operating the controls and because people at each successive level must be closely supervised and directed in their work, the supervisory hierarchy becomes more and more extended.[2]

In these tall organizations, certain characteristics tend to develop to a greater degree than in flat ones. With the extended hierarchy and close supervision and control, worry and concern over what the boss thinks and expects increases. With the boss on hand all the time, the subordinates will naturally devote a great deal of attention to his personality and to his likes and dislikes, and, in general, to the problem of responding correctly to him at all times. Furthermore, this concern will exist even where the general morale is high and the attitudes toward the company and superiors are friendly. Thus, this anxiety and worry is accepted as normal and inevitable by people in such organizations, and members adapt to it without doing much to change it.

Another problem in tall organizations is that of communication. The more steps in the chain of command, the more the flow of information or ideas from the bottom up is censored and retarded. Also, with close control, all decisions and all initiation of action tends to be pushed up the line. Thus, if a foreman wants to make some change but feels he has to clear it with his boss, and his boss must discuss it with *his* boss, etc., it may take days to get it done. This tends to discourage the foreman from attempting to try new ideas, until finally he just sits back and follows instructions from above.

The tightly controlled organization is frequently the product of strong, autocratic leadership at the top. The president who wants

---

[2] James C. Worthy: "Democratic Principles in Business Management," *Advanced Management*, March, 1949.

things done his way, who is sure that he is right and doubts his subordinates, wants an organization which carries out his decisions to the minutest detail. Under this sort of pressure, every level acts in the same way: all are concerned with knowing the commands from above and trying to make a showing by obediently carrying them out. This forces more and more decisions up the line, stimulates the development of detailed systems of controls and of rules and regulations, and increases the subordinate's fear of acting on his own without the approval of his superiors. In such a system, nobody "sticks his neck out"; the rule is never to take a chance.

Not all these tightly controlled organizations are headed by autocratic leaders. Some develop this pattern because of acceptance of the theory that this is the most effective structure and that such close control is necessary or leads to greater efficiency. In such cases, you often hear expressed the theory that there is always one best way of doing anything—whether it is setting up an organization, answering a phone call, supervising a work group, or what not. Therefore, management, often with the help of experts, decides what that one best way is and then gets everyone to use it. Such "one-best-way" thinking leads inevitably to rigidity of form and methods, to elaborate rules and instructions, to controls, and to policing to see that the "best way" is followed.

Once the pattern of the organization is established, it tends to become stabilized and to maintain itself. New members take on the behavior typical of that organization and are rapidly trained in what is proper. If a young man, unaccustomed to worrying about what the boss will think, speaks up freely or attempts to go ahead without checking with the boss, he soon learns that that is not the way to act. When others say, "You stuck your neck out on that," or "You've sure got nerve to talk up the way you did," or "Better be careful," he soon becomes conscious of these things. Thus, he rapidly learns what the group thinks should or should not be done, even though his superior may not be critical at all. In fact, in an organization where such apprehensions are strong, a new executive will receive from his subordinates the same concern, the same deference, and the same expectations as his predecessor. And unless he is unusually alert to these things, he rapidly fits into the pattern of going into details, making minor decisions, and letting his subordinates depend on him.

Certain kinds of activity tend to develop in the tall organizations much more than others. In general, manufacturing lends itself readily to the concepts of the tall organization with tight controls. This is partly due to the need of proper timing and integration of activities so that the work flows smoothly. Thus, the greater the need of co-ordination and co-operation, the greater the tendency to try to achieve this through close supervisory control. In many cases, the growth of an elaborate hierarchy can be observed in new plants when under pressure to get the job started. For example, one case was observed of a large new factory opened just after World War II. The company was struggling to get the new plant into production promptly and staffed it with experienced supervisory personnel from their other plants. However, with new products, new equipment, and with new and, often, inexperienced workers, they had a lot of difficulties. When the foremen complained that they just couldn't keep on top of all the problems, the management gave them assistant foremen. When the department heads felt they were losing control of the job, management gave them assistants, and so on, until three levels had been added in the chain of command.

One episode showed clearly how this worked out. A machine broke down and tied up one small production line supplying parts to the main assembly. The assistant foreman called the foreman, who called a setup man. He found a broken part on the machine, and it was taken to the machine shop for repairs. As it was a rush job, the machine-shop boss put one of his best mechanics to work on it. Within a few minutes the assistant department head came by, saw the shutdown, and questioned the foreman, who explained the trouble and described what was being done. However, the assistant department head had to see for himself; so they both went to the machine shop, talked to the boss, and interrupted the mechanic to see how he was getting on. Shortly, the department head came by and went through the same routine, and following him was the superintendent and a couple of engineers. In short, everyone was maintaining control over the job by checking and rechecking. Yet not one of these executives did anything essential; in fact, they merely wasted the time of those actually getting the job done.

Now, some organizations meet such conditions without extending the chain of command. If a foreman is swamped, instead of subdividing the group under assistant foremen, management gives him help in another way. If too much of his time must be spent in training inexperienced workers, he is given a skilled worker to help him train others. This worker is not a supervisor but is there to help the others learn their jobs. If there are a lot of interruptions because of poor scheduling or missing materials or parts, management gives the foreman someone to help check on those things and to help keep them moving. By skillful delegation of such things, the foreman can keep on top of the job and really be a supervisor rather than a combination of errand boy, expeditor, mechanic, etc., with no time left to supervise.

In sales organizations or department stores, the flat organizations are more common. In these, the activity of an individual member of a sales department can go on independently of other salesmen or other departments. Thus, the high degree of co-ordination and supervision is not so necessary, and the tendency toward elaborate controls is not so great.

Mfg. Tool - Department stores Flat

1. Analyze the type of org. to see how to act when there.
2. Most are combinations of the two - so need to know the depts.

14. THE INDIVIDUAL IN THE STRUCTURE

WE HAVE seen that the individual is part of a larger community and society which determines to a great extent his basic sentiments and attitudes. He brings to the job his own personality, his unconscious needs, as well as his conscious goals. Also, he brings to the job many habits and expectations which have been taught him through his life experiences. As a result, he may have an underlying need to dominate others yet expresses it in ways which are common and acceptable to our culture. Thus, the personal satisfaction he attains in his work depends on the extent to which, through his work, he satisfies the complex patterns of unconscious drives and needs, as well as the extent to which he meets his requirements as a social being.

Work Adjustment and Personality

Each individual can be thought of as having a basic psychological personality which is expressed in his behavior, motivations, and desires. Thus, an aggressive, domineering person may be "bossy" in his relations with others, be outspoken with his ideas, and generally seek to be the center of activity and attention. Or the extremely insecure person may be afraid of any change which forces him into new situations or relationships.

This problem of personality as it relates to work behavior and adjustment is extremely complex—too complex to be covered here. It becomes especially complicated when we consider that the person who makes a good adjustment in one work situation may make a poor one elsewhere. For example, an effective salesman may have personality characteristics unsuited for a factory job. Or a man who does well under a strong-willed, decisive boss may do poorly under one who is less firm and clearcut in his orders. Similar differences may be seen in students, some wanting to know exactly what the professor expects of them, and others feeling quite at ease with vague assignments in which they have to figure out for themselves the details of what should be done.

245

The Meaning of Work

The work itself has great importance to the individual and has many meanings. First, it has social approval in our society. Work is a virtue; idleness is wrong, or even evil. Work is serious and dutiful as contrasted to play—and while play is approved within limits, "playboy" is a derogatory term. So we can assume that working at something is part of our way of life, and everyone in business and industry expects to work.

The work one does provides one of the important definitions of who you are. In the first place, it defines your general status, tells how important you are, and indicates much about your probable way of life. The lawyer is different from the factory worker in importance, in activity, in way of living, in types of friends.

The work implies a definite pattern of activities which differ from one occupation to another. Some jobs mean simple manipulations repeated over and over—the simple, routine factory or clerical jobs. The machine operator deals with objects, the mathematician with abstract symbols, the salesman with people. In fact, in a way, all jobs deal with either things, people or ideas, or usually with combinations of the three. Thus some jobs are largely dealing with things, others are interacting with people, and others are thinking—probably no jobs are exclusively one or the other.

Also, one's job may determine the amount of physical activity, the degree of novelty and change, the contacts with people. Each job provides a setting which offers both opportunities and limitations. At the same time, the organization within which the work takes place becomes the setting of the job and part of the opportunities and limitations.

Significance of the Industrial System to the Individual

To the individual employee, the industrial organization consists of machines, benches, tables, and desks, all of which are symbols of positions and jobs occupied by people. Furthermore, he is aware of a system of technical processes and interrelations between these various positions and functions, which determines (a) the tasks which employees must perform, (b) who shall interact with whom, and (c) under what conditions and circumstances this interaction shall take place.

However, he sees the industrial organization not only as a technical process and a set of relations between specific work tasks but as a social system where the various functions and positions of the system have social meaning and significance to him. To the rank-and-file employee, the boss not only is a functionary who co-ordinates work activity but also is a person in a position of authority who occupies a superior social rank. The social nature of this relationship has much to do with the adjustment which both the rank-and-file employee and the boss will make to the work situation.

In the same way, all of the positions and functions in an organization are socially interpreted and classified by employees and thus take on an aura of significance and meaning, which influences the individual who occupies the position, as well as those who must interact with him. A punch press is not merely a machine but a symbol of the role that the individual employee occupies in the social system of the factory. The employee, therefore, must adjust to the work demands which the machine imposes upon him, not only in a physical sense, but in a social and psychological sense as well. The work routines of the job, the people with whom he works, the boss from whom he receives his orders—all these determine what he can and cannot do and directly influence the conceptualization that he makes of his role in the social structure of the factory.

With these views in mind, the importance and significance of the day-by-day, routine experiences of the employee within the industrial system become apparent. The ordinary job activities of a factory or business are typically so commonplace that we often take them for granted and miss the significance they have for the individual. Yet, these common, everyday activities determine to a surprisingly large extent how the employee feels about his work environment. They set the dimensions within which the employee must adjust his own individual demands and his personal conception of himself. If his daily work experiences run contrary to his self-image, he will feel unhappy and disgruntled. On the other hand, if he is able to integrate his own social needs and demands into his day-by-day job activities, then he will feel satisfied and tend to support and accept the organization that gives him these personal satisfactions.

Because of this tendency among employees to identify and integrate their own personal demands and needs into the system of work activity, change in the organization and system of work may be interpreted by the individual employee as a personal attack on his own personality and ego. Thus, we can see that the job that he does and the daily tasks that he performs are much more to him than a set of routine, technical functions; they are part and parcel of his whole conception of himself and the role that he plays both inside and outside the factory.

Interpersonal Relations and Individual Adjustment

To the average person, some of the most important elements in the job and work situation are the interpersonal relations. The boss or bosses, the people he works with, all those he must contact—all may add or detract from his satisfactions at work. And in this area, the interplay of personalities becomes especially important.

As we have seen, everyone sees the boss as having certain rights to command and supervise. Nevertheless, the individual's reactions to the supervision may vary with his own personality. Some individuals are somewhat (or extremely) rebellious against authority and are disturbed by any signs of authoritarianism. In short, they have a hard time taking orders, and will overreact to direct order and will want an order disguised as a request. Those extremely hostile to authority often resent anyone in position to give them orders and are rebellious against company rules and regulations.

On the other extreme, we find people who are submissive to authority—who not only accept it but are most comfortable when being directed. These can accept even autocratic supervision as being right and expected, and they adjust easily to rules and directives.

The pattern of the individual's reaction to authority will be an important element in his adjustment at work and in his work satisfaction. If he overreacts to authority, a job with close supervision or a demanding autocratic boss may be intolerable. Often the same type of job, but with a different boss or less close supervision, may be completely satisfactory.

In many cases, a person's reaction to superiors is influenced by his feelings of his own importance or by his desire for greater status. For example, a highly skilled toolmaker may easily accept as his boss another skilled toolmaker, but may be extremely rebellious if an engineer is put in charge. In this, he feels that he can take orders from his own kind because they represent the skill he respects; but the engineer is different and has no understanding of his skill. In essence he says: "I can be a subordinate to one who represents the same knowledge and values which I hold, but I cannot tolerate anyone who does not."

An extreme type of case is that of a man who is given a woman supervisor. Regardless of the woman's ability, the man is likely to feel that he loses status by taking orders from a woman. By the definitions of our society, the man should be the superior, and any reversal of this role is disturbing to the man.

Thus we have both the individual's personal reaction to the boss, and to authority, and the social definition of whom he can accept as a boss. To the average person, it is usually easier to be "bossed around" by someone high in the particular hierarchy than by one low. Most people will accept direct orders from the president much more readily than from their immediate supervisor.

To many factory and office workers, the social environment created by the work group provides some of their major satisfactions. For example, a girl who worked on a routine job in a radio assembly line said: "I just love to come to work. All the girls are so friendly. I'd say they are my best friends. We talk and kid each other all day long. We talk about our boy-friends and our dates and all sorts of things. Sometimes the boss tells us not to talk so much, but he's good-natured and doesn't really mind so long as we keep up with our job." Here we have a girl who gets no particular pleasure from the work itself, but her job satisfaction derives from the friendly relations with the other girls.

What one seeks and expects in these situations varies a great deal. Many, as the above girl, seem to seek a warm, friendly group such as the cliques of close friends so common in adolescence—a group in which you find warm acceptance and interest.

In other cases, we find individuals who react competitively to their fellow workers. Some seek to dominate their fellows, try to "boss" them around, show superior knowledge, always try to win arguments, or become competitive in the work. These more aggressive individuals may become leaders and spokesmen in their group, and they become the ones to whom the others look for advice or direction. In other cases, their aggression generates hostility, and they become outcasts—or they are the constant target for jokes and kidding.

The individual's reactions to people are especially significant in jobs which are built around interpersonal relations. A salesman who dislikes meeting people has a hard time calling on customers. Or one who is submissive and unaggressive in presenting his views may have trouble in convincing customers, and will be too quick to accept a refusal. On the other hand, one who is too aggressive and domineering may irritate customers and drive them away. In the same way, an engineer who is ill at ease with shop people may have difficulty in getting their co-operation. Or a staff man who tries to dominate others may create resistance to his ideas.

In terms of personality, we find many people who have problems in relating themselves to others. They may be excessively hostile or competitive. They may be ill at ease and withdrawn. They may be more or less effective with men than with women. Often many of these are more at ease in dealing with objects or ideas. And as a result, they often develop interests or occupations which take them out of contact with people. They may become scientists or engineers, or prefer solitary occupations where they work with tools and are not bothered with people. In this·sense, a skilled toolmaker, a trucker, and a pharmacist have this in common: their jobs do not require frequent dealing with people or close working relationships.

PROBLEMS OF ADJUSTMENT

Since each person must adapt himself to his place in the organization, each movement within the structure means a fresh adjustment. Just as we recognize that there is a very extensive adjustment of behavior and attitudes expected of the young man who changes his role through marriage, so every change of place within the factory means readjustment. If an individual is moved from this punch press to that one, he makes only a small adaptation; yet to many workers, even this is so difficult that they prefer to stay on the same machine.

Other types of movement also create serious problems of adjustment. The salesman who becomes sales supervisor or manager must shift his concept of himself and his job. He must learn how to get other salesmen to call on customers and make the sales, and not try to do it himself. He must worry about selection, training, motivation, and supervision, rather than about how to handle a particular tough customer.

The engineer who becomes a shop foreman, the production superintendent who becomes a labor relations man, or the accountant who becomes a production man—all must adjust to new activities, different responsibilities, new problems, and to new concepts of themselves.

Experience and Expectations

While many movements require only slight changes in behavior or in physical activities, many other moves result in decided changes in ways of thinking, in attitudes, and even in the whole orientation of the individual. This is especially true of changes from one level to another in the supervisory hierarchy, such as from worker to foreman, or from department chief to division chief. If an individual moves upward in the structure, he must adjust himself to completely new activities, to new relations with others, and to new ways of thinking. A similar shift is found with changes from one type of organization to another, such as from engineering to manufacturing or to personnel administration. The individual who moves within the structure not only must face new work problems but must learn to think properly for his new position; he must learn to think like a foreman, or a division chief, or a personnel man. This, on the whole, is one of the least understood aspects of the adjustment of individuals to changes in position.

The individual is not an inert plastic being forced into a social mold; he does not automatically change in conformity with each new role. Instead he has been "conditioned" by his experiences in all his different roles in all the different structures; and he brings to his job a complex pattern of behavior, attitudes, and concepts which are a result of his whole life experience. Out of this background of experience, he has developed attitudes and expectations of the job and ideas as to what is expected of him and what he can expect of others. He may have developed habitual ways of acting which are so routine that he is no longer conscious of them; and to change his role and learn new behavior and attitudes may be a slow and painful process.

Furthermore, the individual may be thought of as bringing to his job his own personal set of "demands." He is seeking certain satisfactions; he expects the job to perform certain functions for him; and he judges it constantly in terms of these demands. These expectations are another product of his conditioning; they grow out of the society itself and out of his place and experience in it. Thus the son of a banker, with a college education, has different expectations and makes different demands of his job than the son of a day laborer with a grammar-school education. These differences in expectations and demands mean a difference in the way they each look at the job, a difference in the way they react, and a difference in the meanings they attach to everything that happens in the work situation.

Looking at it this way, we can describe the well-adjusted person as one who finds some balance between the satisfactions he is seeking, between his demands and expectations, and the satisfactions which the job provides. The poorly adjusted individual is the one whose demands are much greater than the satisfactions he receives. The individual who is seeking status and recognition in the community, for example, will be dissatisfied with a low-status job; and the person who is trying to maintain his position in a group of friends with high incomes will be dissatisfied with the pay of a semiskilled shop job. A single girl living at home, on the other hand, may feel that a friendly work group is more important to her than high pay. Neither high wages nor good environment, however, automatically produce satisfied and well-adjusted workers. The adjustment and satisfaction of the individual on the job is not just a simple matter of wages and physical working conditions but also an adjustment within a complex pattern.

Because the satisfactions which the individual is seeking are expressions of his past conditioning in the society and of his present positions in the social structures, there are certain uniformities in attitudes and expectations among people at work. People with similar positions, backgrounds, or experience are likely to have similar expectations of their jobs. Thus, we can make some predictions about the way an individual will react if we know something about his place in various sets of relationships. As pointed out, the son of a well-to-do professional family is not content to remain long on a low-status shop job; and when we see him in such a situation, we can expect his behavior to reflect his disturbance. This is so well known that most employment men hesitate to put such people on shop jobs except for limited periods, such as vacation employment of college students or as a training period.

The patterns of the society itself, the groupings into which people fall in their relations in the home and community, are the basis of many of their attitudes toward their jobs. Men and women, for example, have different roles in the society, and this is reflected in different attitudes toward their jobs. Patterns of behavior and attitudes vary with age, too, and with one's role in the family group, so that a boy does not have the same activities or expectations as an old man, or a young girl the same as a mother. People also fit into groups in the class system of the society on the basis of their status relationships with others, and the members of one class or status group act and think and hope differently from members of the other groups. His place in each of these groupings, and in others, has a part in determining a person's attitudes toward his job and the satisfactions he looks for in it.

Over a period of years, any one individual may be seen to change his attitudes and expectations from time to time. Many of these changes are the result of new experiences; they are expressions of changes in his pattern of relationships or his role in either the work group or the outside society. Some of the changes are so common to all of us that we can say that there are certain phases through which nearly everyone goes which create problems of adjustment.

Furthermore, the adjustment to change is influenced by the personality pattern. Many people show patterns of anxiety and insecurity so strong that they tend to cling to familiar situations. Any change is seen as threatening, and they dread the unfamiliar. In many cases, they will accept the established situation, even though unsatisfactory, rather than face the uncertainties of the unknown.

Sex Differences

Women generally think about their jobs quite differently from men and expect quite different satisfactions. The normal or expected role of the woman in our society is that of wife and mother, and this is supposed to be her primary center of interest. Men, on the other hand, are expected to be the breadwinners, whose lives are centered around their jobs and who are earning a living for their families. This difference is clearly reflected in the attitudes of the two groups, in the things they talk about, the decisions they make, and in their evaluation of jobs and of work situations. Among factory workers, for example, men are more concerned about opportunities for advancement than women. Men do not often refuse a transfer to a more important or better-paying job, while women frequently refuse such opportunities. This contrast is especially clear between young single girls and young single men who are just starting to work in industry. The girls usually look on their jobs as a temporary filler-in from the time they leave school until they marry. Even among groups who will probably spend most of their lives working, the girls think of marriage as a chance to stop work, keep house, and raise a family. Working after marriage, they think, will be only a temporary expedient to help pay for furniture, accumulate savings to help raise a family, or help out in emergencies. With those attitudes they judge their jobs in terms of whether they enjoy the work or the group, whether it provides opportunities for meeting potential husbands, whether or not it interferes with their dates and social activities. Their jobs are judged in terms of immediate satisfactions rather than in terms of future possibilities.

With the young men we see something quite different. As soon as they leave school and start to work, they begin to think of their roles as adult men. They often become concerned over their rate of advancement in both status and pay. They often wonder how long it will take them to be earning enough to get married and keep a family, and how they can get to be recognized as full-fledged adults. They grow impatient with "boys'" or beginners' jobs and with the processes of advancement, often slow in ordinary times. They show much less concern over whether the work group is friendly and worry less about making friends in a new group. When offered a transfer to another job, they want to know whether it is a better job, if it means more pay, if it has more opportunity for advancement.

School versus Factory

Both young men and young women who are just out of school and taking their first factory jobs, find a problem in adjusting to the work routines. In school, as in the factory, they come and go on a fixed schedule; but the school activities during the day are varied. They move from room to room, from subject to subject; they have "gym" and study periods; and there is continual opportunity for contacts with other students. In the factory, they are often put on simple repetitive jobs where they stay at one work position all day long doing the same job over and over, often with little contact beyond the people right around them. This may go on day after day, even after they have learned the job thoroughly and developed considerable skill. In school, not only were the day's activities varied, but they progressed from day to day. They did not work the same problem day after day, or read the same book; as they learned, they advanced to something new and more difficult. In the school, too, the promotions were frequent and the requirements were very clear. At work, however, the situation is quite different. Not only do they go on day after day doing simple routine jobs, but the channels of advancement are not clear; the how and when of getting ahead are not well defined. When they ask their boss how they can get ahead, he can say only that if they work hard, do a good job, behave themselves, and try to learn about the work, eventually they will be given a chance at better jobs. He cannot say that, if they do this and this and this, they will be promoted at the end of so many months as they do in school, because industry does not work that way.

While both boys and girls have been accustomed to the same school system, their adjustment to the job conditions is often quite different and seems to be directly related to the different meaning that work has for them. Most factory girls adjust quickly to the routines; and if the work group is friendly, they do not mind the simple repetitious jobs. They rarely express anxiety about getting ahead or complain about the monotony of the work. To them it is only a temporary interlude until they "get their man." The boys, as we have seen, react quite differently. They often have a hard time settling down to the work; they like to play around; they soon get tired of doing the same thing all day long, and their attention wanders. As soon as they learn one job, they become impatient to get on to something else; they begin to complain about monotony and wonder about getting ahead. In many cases, they have so much difficulty in making this adjustment that they do poor work and quit, and sometimes they are fired from several jobs before they settle down.

Age Differences

The attitudes and adjustment of both men and women vary with age, too. The attitudes and expectations of the older women are much different from those of young girls. Those who have not married finally begin to realize that they may never marry, and they begin to accept the idea that they will work all their lives. This change in attitude usually takes place around the age of thirty, depending on the customary age of marriage for girls from their place in society. In many cases this change involves a period of emotional disturbance and anxiety which disturbs their relationships both at work and outside. Once they have made the change, their expectations of the job become more like the attitudes of men. They become more interested in advancement and more concerned over status and security than the younger women.

Married working women have still a different pattern. Many of them work to help out in the home; they may be widowed or divorced and have children to support, or their husbands may be sick. In such cases the home is still the primary interest and the work is supplemental to it, although working is no longer thought of as a temporary thing. These women, like older unmarried women, often put considerable emphasis on stability and security; but they are less inclined to be ambitious and are less interested in their futures and their careers as workers. Older men, too, are concerned with stability and security. Most factory workers have reached their ceilings by the time they are forty, and after that they are not likely to advance to higher grades of work or learn new skills. They have usually adjusted to the work they are on and are interested in maintaining their position as it is.

Class Differences

When we examine the adjustment of people from various levels of society, we see that the evaluations of the job vary with social position, too. That is, the way a person thinks of jobs—his feelings that certain jobs are "good" or "bad"—depends in part upon his background. The good job to the son of a janitor will seem a poor job to the son of the president. As we have pointed out, the boy from a high-status family usually is dissatisfied with a low-status factory job; the daughter of a prosperous doctor or lawyer cannot bear to work in the shop but must have an office job. Suppose we consider the case of John S., a young college graduate who had difficulty in adjusting to factory work because of his middle-class background.

John S. was raised in an upper-middle-class suburban neighborhood composed of the families of successful doctors, lawyers, businessmen, and top executives. His father was the successful vice-president of a large manufacturing concern, who had worked himself up from the ranks. John, along with his clique of friends from the neighborhood, went off to college where he took a liberal arts degree. When he finished college, his father urged him to take a factory job and work his way up as he himself had done. Although he was not enthusiastic about factory work, John felt that, with his background, it would be just a temporary thing and that he would soon receive recognition and promotion.

At the same time, many of his friends were returning from college and making their choices of occupations. One, whose father was a doctor, studied medicine; and when he returned his father took him into his practice. Another studied law and was taken into a small law firm where he could gain experience and build up his own clientele. Another entered the family business in a minor executive position. Each of these other boys started in jobs which had status; they were doctors or lawyers or businessmen, all occupations comparable to the occupations of their fathers. Even though their earnings might be low at the start, they could all expect fairly rapid improvement; and in the meantime they were developing the skills that they would later use as lawyers, doctors, or businessmen.

In his contacts with his old group, John began to feel ill at ease. When they talked about their jobs, they could talk as professionals of the interesting cases, the problems they must deal with, the decisions they must make. But John could talk only about his difficulties in getting enough speed on the assembly job he was working on, or the way his foreman treated people, or the way the other workers acted. At first he could treat all this as a sort of initiation for future executives, something you had to go through to learn what the work was like and how workers feel, to learn the business from the ground up, but not as an opportunity to learn the skills that you would use later. At first he could hold his own with his group on this basis. He would explain that it was important to get this understanding of the work and that all the big companies preferred to promote people who had actual factory experience.

As months passed, however, he had less and less to talk about, since he was still doing the same job and the newness had worn off. The others were still finding something fresh to talk about—their medical or legal victories, their clever decisions. John began to feel more and more out of it. He often avoided the group or was glum and irritable when with them. His concern over the situation reflected itself in his work. He lost interest and was always willing to stop and talk with anyone who came along. He was indifferent to the others in the work group and did not get along well. He was apt to complain a good deal and frequently said that he was not given an opportunity to show his ability. The foreman thought that he was capable enough but that his attitude was wrong; and he felt that he could not recommend him for advancement unless he settled down to the work.

This case is typical of the problems of executives' sons when they start out in industry. Unless times are very good or they are very fortunate, they will probably have to start at the bottom, and the way up may be very slow. This is especially true of people at the intermediate levels, whose connections are limited to one company or even to one plant, so that they cannot give their sons the benefit of wider contacts at top-management levels, which would make it easier for them to gain recognition and wider opportunities. Thus, these boys cannot inherit their fathers' status; they cannot step into their fathers' shoes, but must start out on their own.

Problems of Getting Ahead in Business

Boys from working class families have different problems. Many of them have only modest expectations in terms of job status and level of earnings, and to them the jobs that John S. would scorn may be very satisfactory. These fellows soon adapt themselves to the routines of shopwork when they reach a level which they consider indicates satisfactory progress. Many of them look to such jobs as toolmakers, machinists, automatic screw machine operators, as being the height of their ambitions; and they try to get special training to prepare for such jobs. Moreover, when they have reached that level, they are generally considered successful in the eyes of their families and friends. On the other hand, many boys from the families of workers are not content to remain at that level but are driven by a desire to rise in status. This ambition, this urge to get ahead, is sometimes a very powerful drive, forcing them to struggle for more education and training and more recognition on the job. They often have many of the same symptoms as the higher-status boys, like John S., who are forced into shop jobs; and they are impatient with the slow progress, bored with the monotony of shopwork, and anxious to know how to get ahead. Thus, there are two groups with quite different backgrounds who react to their jobs in a very similar manner, but the meaning of this urge to get ahead is quite different for the two. To the higher-status person, the shop job is a threat to the position he has known all his life; it upsets his relationships at the level where he feels that he belongs; and all his efforts are directed toward returning to a comfortable equilibrium at that level. The ambition of the lower-status boy, however, is to rise about his former position; he must do better than his father and outstrip his boyhood friends. And, if he succeeds, he must establish an entirely new set of relationships, not only at work, but outside in the community as well.

When a person with this mobility drive does not receive satisfaction through recognition and advancement on the job, he often tries in a variety of other ways to receive satisfactory recognition. He may turn to hobbies or sports and put a great deal of effort into excelling in them. The story is told of one man, now a top executive in a large concern, who took up one thing after another, when he was just a young fellow in a low-status job, and put all his spare time and effort into each until he could excel in it. His need for success was so obvious that his associates interpreted his efforts to excel in such things as tennis or chess as part of his effort to gain the satisfactory recognition which was lacking on the job. In another concern, there was a large engineering staff with many young graduate engineers in the lowest-status engineering jobs. While these were good jobs and fairly well paid as compared to shop jobs, they were, nevertheless, at the bottom of the engineering hierarchy; and advancement was often slow. Among the employees of the company a very active camera club was developed in which many of these young engineers participated; there was a great deal of competition for recognition in photographic exhibits and for positions as officers of the club. Through this camera club they apparently received the recognition which they felt was lacking in their jobs. As soon as they began to advance in the supervisory hierarchy or otherwise gain status on the job, they began to lose interest in the club; they found they "did not have time" to compete in exhibits, and often would practically give up the hobby.

When a person is not able to gain recognition in these activities, he is likely to lose interest in them; and he may become very critical of the hobby club, its members, and the way it is run. In one instance a man who worked very hard at photography, but who had never received any mention at exhibits or at the camera club to which he belonged, was extremely critical of the judgment of others; he claimed that the judges did not know how to judge the work properly and that the other members in the club were prejudiced against him and would not listen to his good advice. In his work he showed a terrific desire to get ahead. He would work very hard at different things in addition to his regular work, thinking that this would show how superior he was to others in his department. He apparently lacked the ability to do an outstanding job, and everything he attempted was coolly received and left him feeling frustrated. Each time he would react with criticism of everyone in the department from his boss on down, and would talk in much the same way as he talked about the members of the camera club.

The mobile group, with their great desire to get ahead, generally have high expectations. They visualize themselves as achieving important positions in the company, as becoming part of management. With these feelings, they tend to have a strong identification with management rather than with the workers. This is especially true of the group from the higher-status background, of course, who have been brought up in the attitudes of the business and professional group and expect to return there. As long as these people feel that they are making satisfactory progress toward their goals, this attitude, this acceptance of management's point of view, is reinforced. When, however, they feel that their progress is blocked and that they cannot obtain the status they are seeking, they tend to turn against management. In these cases they express great dissatisfaction with the company; they become critical of all its policies and suspicious of all its motives. If they are shopworkers, they often turn to the union and become active in it, or perhaps are active in organizing a union. Sometimes through this union activity they find the recognition they have been seeking, just as others find it in other types of organizations. And sometimes the fellows who are effective in union affairs catch the eye of management and receive promotions, which would not have come their way if they had remained unnoticed as mere operators doing their jobs.

"Status Anxiety"

"Status anxiety" is a kind of individual disturbance found frequently at all levels in industry. In these cases an individual expresses concern over his position relative to others. He is disturbed if someone else gets more recognition from the boss than he does; he worries over status symbols; he is concerned if others do not recognize his proper status; and he is worried about advancement and especially about his rate of progress relative to others. This is a common development among those mobile people whose progress has been blocked. Their anxieties may become so extreme that they develop into severe neuroses, accompanied by feelings of persecution, insomnia, inability to concentrate, and other nervous disorders. One striking example of this was the case of an engineer who started in with a large concern soon after he finished college.

Herbert R. was very ambitious, and the first few years he progressed satisfactorily, although not spectacularly. Then the depression reduced the force; and although he was kept on, his progress was stopped for several years. He was moved around to various jobs and was finally put on one which required considerable contact with outside suppliers. He stayed on this for several years with only a little increase in wages or other recognition. He wanted to get onto some other job which would give him more opportunity, but nothing was done about it.

As time went on, he became more and more disturbed about his situation. He became active from time to time in outside organizations but never seemed to get satisfaction out of them. Then the people in his department began to notice erratic behavior. He began to try to attract attention to himself in various ways. He went to department parties, and, after one or two drinks, he would get up on a table and put on acts or make speeches and generally try to dominate the group and hold their attention. Finally, outside suppliers began to comment on his erratic behavior, which seemed to be his way of getting attention and impressing them with his importance. As a result of this, his superiors "bawled him out"; and shortly afterward he had a "nervous breakdown" and spent several weeks in a sanitarium. His peculiar behavior reappeared, however, soon after he returned, and he was moved to another job. Although there was no cut in pay, the job was with a lower-status department and required daily contacts in the shops.

At this point he was extremely disturbed again, could hardly work at all, and could sleep only with the use of sedatives. In fact, he took several times a normal dose of phenobarbital, was still not able to sleep except for brief periods, and would be too dull to work the next day. He believed that his boss was persecuting him, that he had refused to give him opportunity or recognition, and that he had talked against him to other supervisors. He felt that the boss had his favorites who got all the "breaks" and were getting ahead while he was being held back. Now he felt demoted to a really poor job, and he could see no hope of ever getting ahead. He was extremely excited whenever he talked about the way he felt about this job. He told how he hated to have the people with whom he had formerly worked see him at his new job down in a shop location. On one occasion he had gone out in the shop to get some parts to be tested, and as he was coming back with a box under his arm he saw an old friend coming. He was so ashamed to be seen carrying a box of parts that he turned and hid until the friend had left. Formerly he had driven home from work with some engineers from the old department, but now he rode the streetcar because he couldn't bear to go near them. At the same time, he was embarrassed if anyone whom he knew saw him on the streetcar, because he felt it was such a loss of status to be seen with all the shopworkers. In fact, every little thing which could be associated with loss of status was magnified in his thinking and he would brood over each one by the hour.

This case also illustrates the adjustment problem of the mobile individual who has reached what, at least for the time being, is his ceiling. In many of these cases, especially if the ceiling is fairly low in terms of ambitions and expectations, the individuals go through a period of intense disturbance and maladjustment, often lasting several years, until they accept the realities of their limitations.

Another case of this type was that of Albert N., about forty-five, who was a well-paid expert in a special technical field.

Albert N. worked in a small department consisting of about a dozen experts at his level and a miscellaneous group of technical assistants, secretaries, and clerical helpers. He himself had risen from the ranks of the technical assistants with the aid of evening-school study. For a number of years an elderly man approaching retirement age had been the head of the department, and he was very friendly to Albert. For the last two years before his retirement, this department head had been ill a great deal, and in his absence he had delegated more and more responsibility to Albert and generally made him his right-hand man. In this role, Albert was in constant touch with what was going on in the department. He sat in on decisions about the work; he sometimes had to supervise others; and he handled much of the correspondence. During this period he felt that when the chief retired he would be made head of the department, and probably his chief thought so, too.

When the chief did finally retire, however, his superior officers decided against Albert, and brought in a man who had handled similar work in another organization but who had had a better education and broader experience in other phases of the work. This man had been in the department some years before, and Albert had known him then; but he probably did not understand the distinction Albert had attained more recently as informal assistant to the department chief. At any rate, when he took charge, he treated Albert just as he did all the others at his level. Albert was no longer "in the know" on all problems of the department; he no longer was brought into discussions of policy and practices; he did not handle any correspondence for the chief nor take charge of things when he was away. He began to worry about the situation, about his relations with the new chief, and about his own future; and he developed severe anxieties and worried over many little things which he felt indicated loss of status. Whereas formerly he had been the first to see any memos or letters which were circulated to the group, now the new chief had a rubber stamp with the names of the men at Albert's level arranged in alphabetical order; and any correspondence was sent around in that order. Albert was at the bottom of the list and was the last to get the material, so that, instead of being the first to know about any new developments, he was often the last unless he was told by others. Also, instead of discussing all the work problems with Albert, the new chief took up only those pertaining to Albert's own work and never discussed the problems of others with him. Where Albert had previously spent more time with the chief than had any of the others, he no longer felt free to drop in to see the chief; and he actually began to avoid him. Thus, he had lost his former informal status and all the little symbols which went with it, and he had become just one of the group again.

For a couple of years, things went along this way; and although Albert was disturbed by the situation, he was able to handle his work to the satisfaction of his new chief. Gradually, however, he grew more and more discouraged. He complained to his chief about the work, wanted to know what was wrong, and generally showed dissatisfaction. The chief began to feel uncomfortable in his contacts with Albert and began to avoid him. He began to spend more time with the others, drawing them into his confidence and leaving Albert out. Noticing this, Albert began to feel that his superior "had it in for him"; and he spent hours worrying over the cause, which he finally attributed to an incident which occurred when he had been just a young fellow in the department and the present chief had seemed annoyed at a joking remark he had made. He soon reached a stage of feeling quite persecuted. If his chief failed to talk over his work with him, he felt that he was being ignored deliberately; but if the chief did comment on his work, he thought he was being criticized. If he saw the chief talking or laughing with one of the others, he saw in it fresh evidence that he was not liked or wanted. In fact, practically anything the chief did was interpreted in terms of these feelings of persecution.

Along with this, he began to develop insomnia and stomach trouble, and to worry about his health. So when he was not lying awake at night worrying about his status and his relations with his boss, he was lying awake worrying about his health. He felt tired all the time; he would get home at night feeling exhausted; then he would work in the garden so that he would be tired enough to sleep; but he would end up taking a sedative after all. After this, he worried about the possible ill effects of taking so much sedative. He withdrew from his former social activities, refused to play bridge or golf, and would sit around the house in the evening, not wanting to go anywhere or see anyone.

Finally he reached the point where he could hardly do any work at all. He would sit by the hour gazing out of the window or just staring at papers on his desk without seeing them. The boss sent him to the doctor who diagnosed his case as "neurasthenia" and recommended a few weeks' rest in a sanitarium. After a few weeks away from the job, his condition improved; he returned to work; but soon he was as bad as ever again. This recurred several times; each time he would improve after a period away from the work, and then he would have a relapse within a few weeks of his return. He was finally put under special treatment, but it required about a year before he had made a readjustment, before he could accept his situation and carry on his work and personal life in a normal manner.

This adjustment of the individual to his ceiling of attainment is not usually accompanied by such severe symptoms. In the case of Albert, of course, his reactions were accentuated by the fact that the next step had seemed to be so clearly within his grasp and had then been snatched away by forces beyond his control. In other cases, the approach to the ceiling is much more gradual and the individual adjusts his expectations almost without realizing it. Also, it is probable that in most cases the individual has reached a level which gives him a satisfactory status, so that, although he might like to rise higher, he feels no great frustration at his actual level of attainment.

Possibilities for Advancement

All these problems of adjustment are related to the whole problem of upward mobility in the industrial structure. In the first place, we have seen that the structure forms a pyramid with fewer and fewer people at each higher level. This means that it is impossible for everyone at one level to rise to the next. This is especially true for the non-supervisory or worker level, where there are at least ten workers for every foreman or supervisor and there may be fifty or more in some types of work; here only a relatively small portion of the lower group can ever rise into the supervisory ranks. And it also means that only a few from the foreman level can ever move up to higher supervision.

This limitation on movement from the ranks to supervision does not mean, however, that there can be no hope for progress for the mass of the workers. As we have seen, there are highly developed status systems within the work level through which the individual can advance. There are the gradations of jobs into varying degrees of skill and prestige, and the individual may progress from the low-status beginners' jobs to the higher-status and better-paid jobs requiring greater skill and experience. There may also be a wage structure which provides for wage advancement on the basis of merit or service even though the individual remains on the same job. Then there is the possibility of moving from low-status organizations to those of higher status, or from shopwork to office work. In fact, whenever there are status differences in jobs, there is a possibility of some degree of status advancement.

Unfortunately, there is no clearly marked pathway to advancement in most factories; there is no clear-cut plan of action and no timetable by which the beginner can plan his progress. He cannot say, "I will do this and this, and by next year I will have reached that place." While we like to tell the youngster that if he works hard and shows ability he will progress, we must admit that, for the average run of people, chance also plays a major role in his progress. We must not only be ready and able to move on to the next step, but the opportunity must be there.

Within the hierarchy of jobs we do find many cases in which there are certain steps necessary for progress from one level to another. For example, in many of the crafts there is provision for the training of young people through an apprenticeship which they must pass before they can be accepted as a full-fledged mechanic. In such cases there are usually only two or three steps in the system: apprentice and mechanic; or apprentice, class B mechanic, and class A mechanic. When a youngster starts on such a course, he knows pretty clearly what his ceiling will be and about how long it will take him to get there. If he wishes to go farther, he must move out of that particular system entirely. Even in such a system, of course, there are decided limits, since the group usually limits the number of apprentices to the apparent demand for the mechanics (often in depression years no one will be admitted to apprenticeship).

With the vast majority of factory jobs there is no similar road to advancement; the beginner just comes in, takes any job he is put on, and then wonders where he goes from there. In many cases the experience and skill he develops on one job may lead almost directly to a better job of the same type. In such cases the beginner feels that the sooner he learns the job and develops his skill, the sooner he will be able to move to the next level. Unfortunately, any such move also depends upon there being need for additional workers at the next level; and until there is an opening, no matter how good the newcomer may be, he will not be able to advance. Here again the needs of the structure must govern, rather than the desires of the individuals.

In every large plant there are many blind-alley jobs which have but limited possibilities in themselves and do not lead to anything better. Many of these require the development of special abilities or skills which are of no particular value on other jobs. In fact, in many companies there are some jobs which are so specialized that they are unknown outside the one company and thus have no value anywhere else. Sometimes these jobs are fairly well paid, and they may require months or even years to develop a high degree of skill and to rise to the top wage level. An individual on such a job, who is not satisfied to have risen to its top level, often finds himself in a difficult position. In order to advance further he must go to another kind of job where he will have to start all over again at a lower level and learn new skills. Suppose, for example, a man, who has risen to the top level of a specialized job at which he earns $2.00 an hour, is not satisfied and wants to get into toolmaking, which has much greater possibilities. But to do this he will have to start at the bottom as an apprentice in the toolroom at $1.50 an hour. This may seem an unusual case, but it is surprising how many jobs in modern large plants are so specialized that their skills are not transferable to other work. Indeed, the same situation can occur in a retail store, where a topnotch salesman does so well in promoting his own line of merchandise that he cannot afford to accept a lower-paying, but higher-status, supervisory position —even though this offers him greater opportunity for advancement. As a result, many employees find themselves in the position that, no matter how hard they work or how well they learn their jobs, they are not preparing themselves for a step upward.

Problems of Selection

For the ambitious individual, it is unfortunate that all transfers, promotions, or upgradings are directed in accordance with the needs of the organization rather than with the desires or needs of the individuals. When a foreman has a job to be filled, he has to think in terms of who can best handle the job rather than who wants it most. In many cases the one who works hardest or is the best at the lower level is not the one who can do best at the next level. This is especially true where there is no particular relation between the skill at one level and the next. A youngster, for example, who did very well on a routine assembly job, but who did not get along well with other workers might be a very poor choice for a job where he had to keep other workers supplied with parts and materials. Or a file clerk may not make a good secretary. In such cases the boss's selections may seem very unfair to some of the group.

This problem of selection is especially acute in the movements into the supervisory level. The best mechanic or the most efficient operator does not always make the best foreman; the ability to handle a group does not develop naturally out of the ability to handle machines. As a result, the expert machinist or the extremely efficient worker may find that he is being passed over in favor of others with much less skill or knowledge of the work. The highly skilled worker finds that he must take orders from someone who, he feels, does not really understand the job. In addition, management is putting more stress upon getting a different type of foreman from the old-timer who was selected because of his technical skill. Foremen who have more education, who understand management's logic, and who are skilled in dealing with people rather than machines are in demand now. All this makes it harder for the ambitious man to rise by virtue of hard work and skill with his hands.

When selecting a person to fill any position, there are two things which should be considered. The first is the ability to do the job, and the second is the effect of the selection upon the group. The first is rather obvious: if you want a typist, you select someone who can type, and this is, in fact, usually given first consideration. The second is not always so obvious a consideration and is often overlooked, especially when moving people within a work group. Suppose we take a few typical cases:

1. A new and improved press was brought into a printing department. None of the pressmen, mostly long-service men, had had experience with this type of press, and it was decided to train one of them for it. One of the few short-service pressmen, a very alert and capable man, was selected for the new job. The group looked on the job as being a real opportunity in terms of both security and status, since the new press required more skill and might eventually displace some of the older ones. The selection of a short-service man upset all the older men, who felt that, because of their service and experience, they should have been given the first chance at the job.

2. In a shop department the inspector's job was at the top of the informal job hierarchy. When a vacancy occurred, the foreman selected an operator who was a hard worker but who was very unpopular with the group because of his unfriendly attitude and his unwillingness to help the others. The group thought the choice unfair and did everything they could to make the work difficult for this new inspector.

3. A machine department had a large group of old and highly skilled operators. They had group chiefs whose principal duties were of a minor supervisory nature—distributing work, checking upon individual jobs, keeping records, and seeing that raw materials were on hand. When one of these positions was open, a man was transferred in from another department instead of one being promoted from the ranks. The more ambitious men felt that they were being ignored and that one of them should have had the job. The skilled operators were annoyed at having someone over them who was unfamiliar with the work and who did not understand their problems and difficulties.

Sometimes selections are made because the foreman becomes interested in or sympathetic toward one person and thinks only of satisfying that person's needs without considering the effect upon the group. Some one worker talks to him about how much he wants to get ahead, and the foreman feels sympathetic; and the first time there is an opening on a better job, he puts that man in it. He forgets that there may be others in the group who feel just the same way; and because they have not talked to him, they have not caught his attention and interest. Or, again, one fellow may complain that he has not had a raise in some time, that the cost of living has gone up, or that he has more family responsibilities; and if he has been doing a reasonably good job, the foreman is likely to be sympathetic and give him a raise, or extra overtime, or a chance at a better job. Whenever he does this, there are always others who feel they deserve as much consideration and are being ignored. It is out of such incidents that the almost universal belief arises that "it is the squeaking axle that gets the grease."

Because they feel that the supply of foremen and executives cannot be left to chance, many large companies have programs for recruiting and training executive personnel. This usually means that they recruit people just out of college and put them through a special training which is not generally available. In many cases, part of this training consists of a tour of duty in the shops, during which, in theory, they go into the shops and work at various jobs just as any other beginner would. They are not, however, left to their own devices in climbing from there, but are moved around through various jobs and departments in order to give them a wide experience. Then when supervisory or executive jobs are open, they will be filled from this group. They are the privileged group, the "fair-haired boys," who will be the future executives. And the more management relies on such a group to fill their supervisory and executive positions, the less will be the opportunity for others to rise out of the ranks. All such plans for recruiting and training future executives indicate the significance of college training for the higher positions. Most, if not all, of such programs recruit almost entirely from college graduates. And certainly for those ambitious to rise above the rank of foreman, college training, whether in day or night school, is an important asset.

For successful adjustment as a shopworker, on the other hand, a college education seems to be of no help. In fact, the person who has obtained a college education usually has ambitions far beyond a factory job, either because the college training itself stimulates such ambition or because the training is a result of the ambition. Thus the boy from a working family, who makes the effort to get an education, usually does so as a means of rising above his background. He wants to do better than his father, or his family is urging him on. And the boy whose family gives him an education as a matter of course already takes the higher status for granted. As a result, both of these college graduates feel continually frustrated in shop jobs, are always explaining or justifying their position, and generally have difficulty in making adjustment. This condition is so well understood in industry that experienced employment interviewers usually differentiate people as shop types and office types, and they put all those with more than high-school education, unless it is some form of trade or skill training, into the office group. Even when conditions are such that college graduates are willing to take shop jobs, the companies prefer not to have them, because sooner or later they become dissatisfied and, unless there is the possibility of promoting them fairly rapidly, they will become serious problems.

Adjustment to Promotion

The ambitious, mobile people who manage to rise through the structure must, of course, face problems of adjustment somewhat different from those of more stable people who settle down at about one level. For example, when a man is promoted to the supervisory level, he must make much more extensive adjustments than the man who moves from a semiskilled to a skilled job. In the first place, his whole view of the work changes when he becomes a supervisor. He no longer thinks only of his own job, but every job in his group becomes his job and his responsibility, in a sense. Also, he must think of the other workers, not just as his fellows, but as people whom he must direct and supervise, encourage, and discipline. If he is in charge of the group of which he was once a part, he finds that all his relationships with them change. If he continues to be intimate with his old friends, then the others accuse him of playing favorites; if he drops them, they say he is "high-hat." All his social contacts are colored by the fact that he is now the boss, and the others act and talk with him differently because of it. He himself soon develops relationships with other supervisors; they may lunch with him or invite him to their parties, and he is gradually drawn into new circles of social activities.

This sort of adjustment goes on with every major change of rank or status and, to some extent, with every change of organization. This means that the mobile fellow who rises steadily or who is shifted around to gain experience in various organizations is continually adjusting to new concepts and points of view and to new sets of relationships with people. This even extends itself to his relationships in the community outside the plant. While he is a shopworker, he usually lives in a working-class neighborhood and associates with other workers. As he rises through the ranks, he moves to better neighborhoods and associates with different people.

Adjustment at Lower Levels

Fortunately, everyone in industry does not have a strong mobility drive. Many people make good adjustment at even the bottom levels and are able to get satisfaction out of their jobs. This does not mean that they would not want better jobs, or that they will admit to a lack of ambition; but, actually, many are sufficiently well adjusted that they will not make the effort or take the chances necessary for going on to something better. This, however, is counter to the beliefs of many people, especially those who do have strong ambitions, who feel that everyone should be motivated just as they are. Thus, many top executives, who have reached their positions because of their efforts and determination, believe that everyone feels as they do, and that everyone should respond to the same incentives to which they responded. As a result, they believe that by holding out promises of opportunities for advancement they can motivate their people to work the way they have worked. They also tend to view with horror anything like a system of seniority rights which may stand in the way of the rapid advancement of ambitious youngsters; and they think that the bulk of the workers do, or should, feel the same way.

To be well adjusted in the lower-status positions, or even the lowest-status position in a work group, does not mean that the individual is insensitive to status differences. In fact, we continually meet with disturbances due to minor shifts in status relationships and with cases of anxiety over relative status. For example, to give a raise to one individual in a group causes reactions among the entire group, usually accompanied by demands for similar raises and by criticism of that individual and of the foreman. In one such case the men said that they were perfectly content with their wages and would have had no complaint if the foreman had not given one of the group a raise. We see the other side of this when an individual is demoted from supervision to the ranks, is moved to a lower-status job, or has his pay cut. He almost always has a severe reaction, feels ashamed and embarrassed among his group, and may withdraw from contacts with them as much as possible. Sometimes an individual will quit his job entirely, even if it means taking an even worse job elsewhere, rather than face a loss of status within the same work group.

Stability versus Mobility

If we consider the people in industry in the light of what they are striving for, what satisfactions they are seeking, we can see two different tendencies. One, which is especially strong in the mobile individuals, is the desire to move from the position they are in to some other and higher status position in the structure. The other is the tendency to stay put, to retain their present position and protect it against changes; and this is found in those who have made a comfortable adjustment to their present place. Thus, we might describe one group as trying to maintain their established pattern of activities and relationships, and the other as trying to take on a new pattern. Most people, however, are not completely one way or the other, but only predominantly so; and people sometimes change their goals. During his life cycle an individual may pass from one phase to another. He starts out anxious to rise out of the youngster group in terms of job, pay, and status; he moves up a bit in the structure, reaches a level which satisfies his needs and to which he can adjust comfortably, and then stops pushing and settles down. In the first period he will be upset over lack of progress in too stable a situation and will complain about the boredom and monotony when he feels that he is not progressing adequately. After he has settled down, he will prefer stable relations, will not be bothered by routines and monotony, and will be reluctant to make changes. This cycle is often expressed in comments to the effect that young men want opportunity and older men want security.

SYMPTOMS OF DISTURBANCE

Closely allied with the whole problem of the adjustment of the individual is the significance of complaints and grievances. In general, we can say that most complaints are expressions of some disturbance in the individual's relationships either at work or elsewhere. In an exhaustive study of the complaints expressed in interviews with 20,000 employees, Roethlisberger and Dickson found three classes of complaints.[1] The first referred to objects or conditions which could be clearly seen and agreed upon, as, for example, a broken tool or a burned-out light bulb. The second were those referring to experiences or conditions which could not be clearly seen and agreed upon, such as, "The room is too hot," "The light is poor," or "The work is too heavy." The third class were complaints which did not refer to verifiable external conditions but were expressions of the sentiments of the person, such as complaints about wages, supervision, or advancement. They also found that a large portion of the complaints, in fact, the things about which people seemed most disturbed, were in the third group—things that could not be seen and agreed upon and which could not be dealt with directly as you deal with a burned-out lamp. They found, further, that, with any of the complaints, the things complained about were not always the actual causes of the disturbances; they were the symptoms, the outward expressions of some underlying problem or disturbance. Thus, to understand any complaint, it is necessary to understand the latent content of the complaint; it is necessary to know what the complainant is really talking about, what is really "eating on him." This presents a problem in understanding and diagnosis which is a major problem in dealing with these complaints. If a worker complains about his machine when his real trouble is that his foreman is pressing him to turn out more work, it does not do any good to "prove" to him that there is nothing wrong with the machine.

One of the interesting features of complaints about wages is that a surprisingly large number of them are merely symptoms of some underlying conditions, and many of them are not cured by wage increases. We are so prone to take for granted the idea that everyone wants more money that we often fail to look below the surface on

---

[1] F. J. Roethlisberger and W. J. Dickson, *Management and the Worker* (Cambridge, Mass.: Harvard University Press, 1939), pp. 255–69.

such complaints. We forget to ask ourselves, "What is he really griping about?" Yet time and again we meet with cases in which Jim wants more money because Joe got a raise, or because he feels that his foreman does not give the proper recognition for his years of service, or because in some other way the raise would symbolize status or other satisfaction he is seeking, and not because of any real need for the money. If we try to cure such complaints merely by manipulating wages, we find that we are only treating the symptoms and are not curing the disease.

Often the complaints about the most obvious of external conditions may be indicative of some disturbance of the individual. The individual who is satisfied with his job and his life, in general, tends to accept things which to another may seem intolerable. He may take for granted dirty surroundings, poor tools, or other conditions as long as they do not symbolize inadequacies or frustrations in his adjustment either at work or outside. But the frustrated worker may complain about these same conditions which the other takes for granted as part of the work situation. For this reason, it is important to treat complaints as symptoms; and even though the thing complained about can be and is corrected, it should not be assumed that the complainant will be satisfied.

Since complaints usually represent some disturbance in the equilibrium of the individual, they appear most often when a person is worried or anxious. Status anxieties, for example, are usually accompanied by all kinds of complaints about the work and the work situation as well as about relations with other workers and superiors. And though some complaints may be merely expressions of momentary or superficial annoyances, many are expressions of serious maladjustment and are part of a complex pattern of disturbances.

While a complaint in itself is often unimportant, the conditions of which it is a symptom are of serious import to the individual as a worker. Investigation has clearly proved that anxiety from any cause tends to reduce efficiency of the worker, no matter how satisfactory the job and the work situation may be. Actually, such findings agree with the experiences which most of us have had from time to time. Almost everyone can remember an occasion when anxiety over some home conditions, a quarrel with family or superiors, or worry about some difficult decision has prevented him from putting his full attention on his job and may even have reduced him temporarily to a state where he just could not work at all. Thus, any serious disturbance may produce a state of what Roethlisberger and Dickson refer to as "morbid preoccupation," in which the individual is so preoccupied or wrapped up in his worries about some personal situation that he cannot do his work.[2] You might say that his mind withdraws from consideration of the work and goes round and round on this other problem; and in a severe case he may develop other symptoms, such as nervousness, inability to sit still, inability to concentrate enough to read, trembling hands, avoidance of others, loss of appetite, and insomnia.

Such morbid preoccupations are not limited to any level in the organization and are not affected by status and education of the individual. It is often asserted that such behavior is an expression of low intelligence or lack of education and that it is not found, therefore, among college graduates, engineers, and others that have been trained to think. In general, such assertions come from successful executives who have reached a very satisfactory level of attainment and adjustment and are no longer subject to these kinds of disturbances. Actually, such conditions are found to exist at every level and often seem to interefere more with the work of those who work with ideas than those who work with their hands, for many shop jobs are so much a matter of manual routines that they require very little conscious attention.

Since the anxieties and preoccupations are part of a pattern of personal disequilibrium, they may appear whenever an individual must make a new adjustment either at work or outside. And since most work situations are constantly undergoing changes of some sort, they appear to be very productive of anxieties and the accompanying complaints. This is so clear that, knowing what changes will occur, it is possible to predict the areas of disturbance even down to the particular individuals and their probable reactions. Thus, a proposed change in organization, in which a certain department will be removed from one division chief's authority and given to another, will probably make the first one feel that he has lost status and make him wonder if his superior thinks he is not capable of handling such a big job. At the same time, the department chief who is being moved will probably have some anxieties about the new boss and will wonder what he will expect of the department. While in many cases the disturbances are only momentary and adjustment takes place rapidly, nevertheless there is almost always some touch of anxiety or uncer-

---

[2] *Ibid.*, p. 292.

tainty created by the change. Often the actual emotional adjustment is made before the change itself takes place; that is, the individual is able to adjust his attitudes and expectations toward the new conditions between the time that an anticipated change is announced and the time when it actually takes place. In other cases the adjustment may be very gradual and sometimes it extends over a period of months during which there are continual complaints and anxieties.

Not only are the complaints symptomatic of the anxieties accompanying such changes, but they often seem to play an important role in the adjustment of the individual. Apparently the free statement of the fears and anxieties provides some relief to the individual, and the more effectively he can voice his feelings, the more easily he makes the necessary adjustment. Furthermore, when the change is one affecting the entire group, the "griping" seems to give the individual a feeling of support from his fellows, a feeling that they are all in it together and all feel the same way about it. Then, as the adjustment begins to take place, the complaints begin to dwindle away and the individual gradually fits into the new pattern. There is, in fact, a rough cycle of adjustment which all individuals and groups seem to go through. First, there is the period of disturbance, characterized by a lot of anxiety and complaining. Next, the complaints dwindle, and the individuals begin to talk more constructively about the meaning of the change and to think about the actions they may take in meeting the change. Finally, there is the period of adjustment and settling down to the new equilibrium. In any change, therefore, the complaints should be viewed as part of the normal process and should not be repressed. Instead, they should be brought out into the open where they can be watched for evidence of more serious disturbances than have been anticipated.

15. MINORITY GROUPS IN INDUSTRY

THE GENERAL PICTURE

AN IMPORTANT element in the pattern of American industry is the continual process of introducing and assimilating new groups into the structure. For many years there was a constant flow of European immigrants into American industry, as one nationality group after another followed the promise of the New World. As each group arrived, it began to move into the industrial pattern as a new and strange minority seeking to make its way in an industrial structure dominated by the older groups. And in time each of these became an older group into which still newer groups were intruding.

In the industrial areas, each of these newcomers followed a similar pattern. Each new group tended to move in at the bottom of the community structure. The latest comers always had the lowest status; they moved into the poorest districts; they were looked down upon by all the older groups and were considered the poorest, dirtiest, least intelligent, and least desirable group in the community. Each new group formed its own neighborhood, speaking its own language and living its own culture, and generally formed a little island separated from the groups around it. The passage of time, however, gradually reduced this separation and its barriers. The children learned new ways and moved to new neighborhoods. And, as each group began to adjust itself to the new life and move upward in the occupational structure, there were still newer groups pushing in beneath them—people, again different in language and culture, starting at the bottom of the heap. On these new groups, in turn, were directed all the criticisms which the others had faced.

In spite of some increase in immigration since the end of the war, the major flow of European immigrants has been halted. As a consequence, many of the sharp differences between groups have disappeared, at least as far as industry is concerned; so that it is no longer necessary to pick foremen with an eye to their nationality background or their command of foreign languages, or to consider the ethnic composition of a group when hiring new workers. At the same time, with the shutting-off of European immigration, there is no longer the continual stream of new foreign groups to move in beneath the old, to take the heavy, dirty, unskilled jobs, and to be a new bottom layer whom everyone can scorn as ignorant, incompetent, "dumb laborers." These low-status, low-paid jobs must then be filled by members of the older groups or by their children and grandchildren. But the urge for improvement, the stimulus of better education and greater assimilation in the American life, with its traditions of getting ahead, has made these young people unwilling to accept these low-status jobs. Thus, we see forces operating to reduce the supply of workers who will freely accept the lowest jobs, and at the same time we have an increasingly large portion of the old group who are acutely dissatisfied when restricted to this occupational level. From management we hear complaints that the younger generation is not what it ought to be or what its parents were. Formerly, executives spoke disparagingly of the "dumb polaks" or "bohunks" who were good for nothing except the lowest sort of jobs and who were content to spend their lives in them. Today these same executives speak with nostalgia of these same workers and recount their virtues, their faithful plodding service, their willingness to accept whatever job was offered, their interest in a steady job and modest income. In contrast, they point to the restlessness of the next generation, their unwillingness to take the hard and dirty jobs, their grasping for the symbols of mobility, and their spendthrift ways.

This occupational impasse has to some extent been averted, and at the same time been complicated, by recent migrations within this country. The need for workers in different parts of the country, especially during the war and in recent years, has stimulated an internal movement of people from rural areas to industrial centers, much of which has been from the rural South. The movement of southern whites and Negroes has been so extensive that they may, in fact, be considered the latest immigrants into industrial areas. Simultaneously, women have been moving into industry in increasingly large numbers and are now employed in many industries and occupations previously closed to them. Each of these new groups has faced problems similar to those of new nationality groups. Each has had to come in at the bottom of the industrial structure starting as common labor in unskilled jobs, and each has spread upward through the structure only slowly. Each has had to accept a subordinate role; each has been ridiculed and criticized by the superior groups and has had its work scorned: "That is only woman's work," "That job is only fit for niggers." As these minority groups begin to press toward the better jobs and higher status, they find barriers raised against them—barriers of tradition, of beliefs concerning their incompetence, of reluctance to accept them into other groups. And like the other groups when they were new, they are the ones who have the least security in the system and the ones who will fill the ranks of the unemployed during times of depression.

NEGROES: NEW INDUSTRIAL IMMIGRANTS

The movement of southern Negroes to northern and western industrial centers is similar to the migrations of Europeans in some respects. They are culturally and racially different and set apart; they come in at the bottom of the social and occupational structures; they are looked down upon and unwanted either as neighbors or fellow workers; they are considered dirty, dangerous, untrustworthy, ignorant, stupid, and so on. Unlike the European immigrants, however, Negroes are not likely to become assimilated in a generation or two, for the white society maintains a strict caste system with effective controls for keeping Negroes separate and subordinate. Furthermore, the Negro is conspicuous. Whereas the European immigrant could gradually lose his identity and blend with the general population, the Negro is branded by his skin color, so that he cannot lose himself in the mass. This fact is one of the most important reasons why his adjustment in the industrial population is a slower and more difficult process than that of any other group.

The Caste System[1]

The position of Negroes in our society and the generally accepted attitudes toward them produce serious problems in their introduction into a plant or work group. In the first place, there are very common,

[1] Space does not permit a detailed description of this system here. The reader may find a comprehensive discussion of Negro-white relations, the American caste system, and its codes and controls in the following studies of southern communities:

a) Allison Davis, Burleigh B. Gardner and Mary R. Gardner, *Deep South—A Social Anthropological Study of Caste and Class* (Chicago: University of Chicago Press, 1941).

b) John Dollard, *Caste and Class in a Southern Town* (New Haven: Yale University Press, 1937).

c) Gunner Myrdal, *An American Dilemma* (New York: Harper & Bros., 1944).

and very strong, beliefs in the uncleanliness and tendency to disease of the Negro, which are a part of the whole caste system in which he is kept separate and subordinate. Accompanying these attitudes is the reluctance, and even refusal, on the part of white workers to share washrooms, locker rooms, and eating facilities with Negroes. In many cases, open clashes and work stoppages have resulted from trying to bring Negroes into white locker rooms or washrooms or into company restaurants. The whites always explain their attitude and resentment in terms of the uncleanliness of Negroes and fear of disease. Actually, these attitudes are expressions of the social processes by means of which Negroes are kept at a distance and "in their place." No matter how strong the feeling may be, there is never any objection to a Negro acting as janitor or washroom attendant or as cook or dishwasher in the restaurant. It is only when he sits down to eat beside a white, when he washes at the same basin in front of a white, when he undresses at an adjacent locker, it is only when he does these things as a fellow worker and an equal that the whites begin to worry about being contaminated by contacts with him.

Segregation and Discrimination

While these attitudes toward Negroes may be considered irrational, they are so strong that management must take them into account in dealing with the problem. In the past the simplest procedure was to provide separate facilities for Negroes. This avoided the problem and also served to maintain the segregation of Negroes within the plant. In many cases, they were even restricted to certain departments and worked in separate groups. They were also generally limited to the dirty, disagreeable, and low-status jobs, such as laborers, material handlers, janitors, and porters. In this way the problem was solved by perpetuating the caste system within the plant.

From the point of view of management, this worked very well during the prewar period, but during the war the problem became more difficult to solve. In 1940 the federal government began to take steps to prevent discrimination in essential industries. This movement culminated in the Executive Order 8802 and the establishment of a Committee on Fair Employment Practices. This immediately led to actions to prevent any form of discrimination in defense industry because of "race, creed, color, or natural origin." At the same time, the growing labor shortage in industrial areas impressed management with the need to make the fullest possible use of all available workers and not to allow any prejudice against Negroes to prevent their use. Thus, not only was there pressure from the federal government to prevent segregation of Negroes or their restriction to the lowest types of jobs, but also the manpower shortage made it desirable to use them on any jobs for which they could be trained. At the same time, the attitudes toward Negroes still persisted among white workers, supervisors, and management, so that, regardless of the need to use Negroes, the problem of how to use them still remained.

In plants where Negroes were already established in the low-status jobs and with separate facilities, there was the problem of breaking down this established pattern before Negroes could be mixed in with the whites and moved to better jobs. On the whole, this has been more difficult than the problem of introducing them where they had never worked before. Where they are completely new to a plant, there was no need to change established customs but only to overcome the initial resistance and suspicion and fit the Negroes into the patterns customary for any new employee.

Introducing Negroes as Equals

In some cases, management, having decided to hire Negroes and put them on the same jobs as whites, merely issued orders to this effect and expected to have Negroes moved in immediately in large numbers. On the whole, such methods did not work very smoothly; open friction was frequent and the whites often refused to accept the Negroes. The sudden appearance of Negroes in the work groups, especially if they were brought in in considerable numbers, always aroused antagonism and fears as to what was happening to the job and whether Negroes would supplant the whites. The sudden movement of Negroes into positions of equality and close association was always interpreted as a threat to the superior status of the whites, and they reacted accordingly.

Many concerns, on the other hand, went about the change in a more cautious manner. The most generally successful procedure was one in which management first paved the way for the change by having discussions with various levels of supervision and sometimes with union officials. In such discussions, management found it best to take a firm stand to the effect that they had no alternative but to employ Negroes and that they could not segregate nor discriminate against them. Management could then ask the subordinates what they thought the difficulties would be and how they could be worked out. The group was assured, at the same time, that only the "best type" of Negroes would be picked and that careful examinations would be given to be sure that they were free of disease. After these discussions the plants would hire a few carefully selected Negroes and spread them around through the shops, and in some cases a few were put in the personnel organization in clerical or stenographic jobs. Then, as the Negroes began to be taken as a matter of course, more could be brought in gradually without difficulty.

By having these discussions beforehand, the supervisors were prepared for the Negroes and given a feeling that they were being taken into the confidence of management and given a chance to express their ideas. At the same time, management was able to reassure them as to the purpose of the move and the reasons for it. Thus, before the Negroes actually appeared, the supervisors and even the workers were already becoming accustomed to the idea, and the actual appearance of Negroes on the job was not a sudden shock threatening their security. The careful selection of educated, "nice-looking" Negroes, who were quite different from the average concept of the Negro, created a favorable impression which was strengthened when the whites became acquainted and saw that the Negroes could do the work and were pleasant people to work with. This further broke down their ideas as to what Negroes were like; and white workers and supervisors began to see them as individuals to be judged as individuals and not merely as members of an inferior group.

The movement of Negroes into more skilled jobs has, of course, been hampered by their lack of training and experience. Since they had generally been kept in unskilled jobs which gave them no opportunity to learn to operate machines or to become familiar with more skilled work, they were not prepared to move up in the job hierarchy. This meant that, unless they were given special training, they would still be limited for the most part to the simpler jobs and that few of them could be moved to the higher levels.

Negro Class Differences[2]

The Negro population as a whole has a much lower average level of education than the white population; their living conditions are

---

[2] Further discussion of Negro class behavior may be found in the following studies:

a) Allison Davis and John Dollard, *Children of Bondage—The Personality Development of Negro Youth in the Urban South* (Washington, D.C.: American Council on Education, 1940).

b) W. Lloyd Warner, Buford H. Junker, and Walter A. Adams, *Color and Human Nature* (Washington, D.C.: American Council on Education, 1941).

poorer, their incomes are less, and their work experience more limited. As a group they have lived in severe poverty in slum areas without education or opportunity to better their conditions. Furthermore, those Negroes who have managed to maintain themselves above this level, who have received more education and training in spite of the general restrictions, have generally not been able to obtain the skilled or white-collar jobs in business and industry. As a result, when industry first started to hire Negroes, they were able to select men and women from the higher-status group, who came from middle-class homes with high-school and even college training. Many of these high-caliber Negroes were eager to break into industry at something above the janitor level and gladly took the ordinary shop jobs. Thus, there were a group of high-status Negroes moving into shop jobs beside the lower-class white workers. The whites recognized this status difference and in general were favorably impressed, in many cases commenting on the intelligence and quality of the Negroes.

As the employment of Negroes spread, however, this group was rapidly exhausted and industry began to bring in lower-class Negroes who more nearly fitted the picture of what Negroes were expected to be like. In this group there was the usual lower-class belligerence and aggression, a tendency to settle arguments by fighting, an inclination to carry knives as weapons, and so on. At the same time, these Negroes had, for the most part, never associated with whites in any position of equality. They had worked *under* whites, never with them. In schools they had been in all-Negro or predominantly Negro schools and had little or no contact with whites either in the schoolroom or on the playgrounds. With this limited interracial experience, they came into a working world which was largely white, and they moved into positions of relative equality with whites. They had had little opportunity to learn, even among themselves, the patterns of co-operation and co-ordination necessary for comfortable and effective group work; and most of them were not accustomed to the steady, routine grind of factory work.

Such a situation is pretty obviously "dynamite." And it is no wonder that there have been many cases of friction between Negro and white workers under these conditions. As already pointed out, the many pressures of the daily work situation often give rise to irritation and friction between individual workers without the added complication of racial differences; and the irritation of the white workers seems to be increased by the Negroes' lack of training and general unfamiliarity with factory work. When white workers expressed their irritation, the Negroes often reacted in typical lower-class fashion, meeting aggression with aggression, profanity with profanity, and threats with threats. In such cases, the whites almost invariably felt that this behavior justified all their beliefs about Negroes. The Negroes, in turn, united against the whites; and the resulting situation was ripe for serious racial conflict and even riot. Generally, tension of this sort can be traced to irritations and difficulties which grow out of the work situation itself; and though they may be accentuated and exaggerated by the racial factor, they are not specifically due to having Negroes on the job. In other words, job pressures, crowded locker rooms, inexperienced workers, and long hours all give rise to irritations and open conflict; and as long as only white workers are involved there are no racial implications. But the moment the difficulty involves both whites and Negroes, the whites conclude that the Negroes are really vicious and dangerous, as they have suspected all along, and should be put back in their place; and the Negroes conclude that the whites do, indeed, have it in for them and that they must stand together against white aggression and domination.

Among the better-educated and higher-status Negroes, who were a valuable addition to the work groups and made an easy adjustment at first, certain problems of a different nature developed later. In the first place, they took the factory jobs with the idea that this was the first step toward an equality in industry both for themselves personally and for Negroes generally. In many cases, they were individuals of considerable education, technical training, or general ability, and they expected that their ability would receive recognition. Like all college-trained men in the shops, they soon became impatient with the normal rate of progress, and their advancement to higher-status jobs was further slowed down by the fact that they were Negroes. This problem became acute when Negroes of lower status and less education were brought in at the same job level as these superior groups. After a period of time, when their excellent performance and high morale brought them no recognition or advancement, these exceptional Negroes became discouraged and restless; and they began to feel that there was no real opportunity for their race in industry, free from discrimination. As this feeling developed, their work deteriorated; and they began looking for other jobs, or turned to union activities for recognition and satisfaction and as a means of fighting against the color restrictions.

WOMEN WORKERS

During the war period, too, there was a rapid and extensive increase in the employment of women. They moved into plants which formerly had been completely closed to them and into almost all levels of skilled jobs. Special training programs prepared them for jobs as welders, machinists, inspectors, and many other jobs which had been considered strictly men's work. In thousands of cases the jobs were re-engineered to require less skill or strength so that women could do such work, and often the tools and equipment were especially designed to make the work more suitable for women. All this meant not merely an increase in the number of women in industry, but, more important, their spread beyond the accepted categories of women's jobs, and the breaking down of many former beliefs concerning women's lack of mechanical ability and other limitations.

This influx of women into industry was different from the introduction of Negroes or other groups, since it was not accompanied by a wave of migration. Women were not a strange new group but were drawn from the general population. The extensive employment of women in industry did not mean the introduction of a new element in the social organization but meant a change in the role and activity of a group which was already part of the established system. The problem, then, was not one of assimilating a new group which was trying to make a place for itself; it was one of readjusting both industry and the society so that women could function in a new role. To some extent, of course, women had always worked in industry. Certainly at the working-class level of society a large proportion of the women had worked as a matter of course, and many had had to work to support dependents. Nevertheless, the war produced such a rapid increase in their numbers that the readjustment created a considerable problem.

Although women were neither a new group in the society nor wholly new to industry, certain elements in their assimilation were similar to those of Negroes and other new groups. Like the Negroes, they had not as a group been trained for the higher-skilled jobs until recently, and they had not had opportunity to develop their mechanical knowledge and ability. In the past they had been relegated to jobs which had become established as woman's work, and no effort had been made to prepare them for other kinds of work. This is in contrast to the average man going into industry, who is expected to be able to move to higher jobs, who seeks out opportunity to learn these jobs, and who may be assisted in his advancement by older workers or by a system of training or apprenticeship. Like the European immigrants, the women have been considered inferior workers, ignorant and incompetent; and like the Negroes, they have had little chance for advancement.

The Woman's Role

Woman's role in our society has an important effect upon her position in the industrial world. At all levels of society the accepted function of a woman has been that of wife and mother, whose first interest is in the family and the home, and whose most important duties are those of caring for the home and rearing the children. In contrast to this, the accepted function of a man, as a successful father, is that of providing home and sustenance. Thus, while the successful wife and mother is expected to spend her life in the home, the successful husband generally spends his life working outside in order to support the home and family. This difference is sharply illustrated in the different attitudes which young men and young women express toward their jobs. As pointed out earlier (Chapter 14), the average girl taking her first full-time factory job looks upon it as a temporary thing to fill in the time before she gets married and settles down to rearing a family. She is not usually much concerned over advancement or future opportunities in the work but is interested in whether it provides opportunity for meeting single men, whether it will interfere with her social life, and whether it is a pleasant job with a friendly group. A young man, on the other hand, is constantly concerned with the opportunities of the job. How fast can he get ahead, and how long will it take him to reach a level of income where he can afford to marry? In other words, a girl is filling in time while she finds a husband and begins her *real* career, while a boy is establishing himself in his lifework and is wondering if it will soon bring him to his adult role as husband and provider.

"Woman's Work"

Since this is the usual and generally accepted pattern, the woman who does not marry, who instead seeks a career in business or industry, is looked upon as unfortunate, as failing to perform her proper womanly function, and sometimes as a "misfit." At the same time, because younger women starting in industry have been considered only temporary, management has hesitated to develop them for supervisory or executive positions or even to train them for skilled work. As a result, factories have developed a group of jobs which require little skill and training, into which women can come and go without disrupting the work; and these jobs have become accepted as "women's work."

Furthermore, in all things having to do with factory work or machines, women were considered to be less able than men. It was natural, therefore, that women's jobs should be paid less than men. This was reasonable as long as women were restricted to separate and lower-skilled jobs, since the pay differentials could be rationalized on the basis of the difference in the work. In many cases, however, men's jobs which were of no greater skill than the women's jobs were paid at a higher rate; and for jobs which were held by either men or women, the women were usually paid less. This pay differential for equivalent types of work was usually rationalized on the basis that women were poorer workers, that they were lighter and weaker than men and could not work so hard, that they had to be assisted with heavy work, that they did not turn out as much work, and that the quality of their work was poorer. With this precedent, when women began moving into men's jobs, many companies managed to maintain the women in the accepted inferior role by means of a systematic pay differential.

Women in Men's Jobs

These two factors—the inferior status of women's work and the lower rate of pay—give rise to certain difficulties when introducing women into men's jobs. When a woman first comes into what has been considered a man's job, the men on the job almost always react unfavorably. They express doubts as to whether she can do the work; they often ignore her and give her no help in learning the job; they do not try to protect her while she is adjusting to the new work, but stand by and criticize her; they point to every mistake as showing that a woman cannot really handle such difficult work. At the same time, they are often worried by her presence and wonder if women will displace men on the job. If the company pays her the same rate as the men, they feel that they have lost status, since they are worth no more than a woman; and the other men workers may kid them about doing women's work. If the company pays her less for the same job, they worry for fear the company may eventually cut the rate for all of them or replace all the men with the cheaper women. In this very unfriendly atmosphere, with no assistance from the group, the woman worker often fails in her job or gives up.

Women as Supervisors

The advancement of women to supervisory jobs has always been a problem. In the first place, there is the general belief that women make poor supervisors, that they are too emotional and "take things personally," that they cannot command the loyalty and respect of their subordinates nor the co-operation of their equals. In the face of such beliefs, which appear among executives as well as workers, women are rarely given a chance at supervisory positions. And when occasionally one is given such an opportunity, her superiors are always doubtful, as if to say, "We know women don't usually make good supervisors, so we really don't expect you to succeed." At the same time, especially if she is the only woman foreman or supervisor among a group of men, the other supervisors treat her much as the new woman worker is treated by the men on the job. Instead of accepting her as one of them and helping her adjust to the new job, they stand aloof and watch her critically, expecting her to fail. In this atmosphere of distrust and expectation of failure, every move she makes is watched critically. If she asks for help, it shows that she does not know the job; if she does not ask for help, she is acting as if she knew everything; if the strain begins to get her down so that she is irritable and acts annoyed, then she is acting "just like a woman"; and it all goes to prove that women do not make good supervisors. Under such conditions the probability of failure is high.

The fact that women in our society are generally considered inferior and are expected to be subordinate to men also creates problems when placing women in supervisory positions. Most men dislike the idea of working under a woman; and, no matter how competent she may be, they feel a loss of status in taking orders from a woman. Even if the individual man accepts the idea of having a woman for a boss, his friends are sure to make it hard for him, commenting on it and kidding him about it. Among older men, especially those accustomed to ruling their wives and families with an iron hand, subordination to a woman boss is unthinkable. Because of these attitudes management is always reluctant to place a woman over a group of men and usually tries to use them only for groups of women.

Even when placed in charge of other women, however, the woman supervisor has difficulties. For the most part, women themselves prefer to be supervised by men, and few express a preference for a woman as their boss. They usually complain that the woman supervisor is likely to be unfriendly, or too critical, or too concerned with petty details, or too strict a disciplinarian. Sometimes these attitudes and criticisms seem to be expressions of jealousy and competition, but in many cases they are based on real weaknesses in the performance of women supervisors. For one thing, women are often put in supervisory positions without sufficient training, and they do not know how to act as a boss or how to manage those under them. Newly promoted men, too, often have this same handicap; their failures are taken as evidence of individual weaknesses, but the failure of a woman brands all women as poor supervisors. Actually, much of the behavior of women supervisors is typical of new supervisors generally. Any new supervisor who feels unsure of himself, who feels that his boss is watching him critically, is likely to demand perfect behavior and performance from his people, to be critical of minor mistakes, and to try too hard to please his boss. A woman supervisor, responding to the insecurity and uncertainty of her position as a woman, knowing that she is being watched both critically and doubtfully, feels obliged to try even harder. And for doing this she is said to be "acting just like a woman."

In spite of the difficulties, however, it has been found possible in many instances to move women into new kinds of jobs and into higher-status positions. The supposed limitations of women in industry have, in fact, been found to be myths based merely on their inexperience and not on any real evidence or experiment. In the war years the frantic grasping at any straw to relieve the manpower shortage clearly showed that there was not, on the whole, a great difference between the work that men could do and the work that women could do. This was especially true of jobs requiring skill and mechanical knowledge rather than strength and endurance, since it has been clearly shown that, with proper training, women can do even the most skilled work. It has become evident that women succeed or fail in industrial jobs, generally, not so much because of their physical or mental ability but because of the social situations in which they work. Quite simply, women usually succeed in their jobs when they are expected to succeed and helped to succeed and when their supervisors have faith and their work groups are friendly; and they generally fail when they are surrounded by doubt and hostility. Finding or creating the proper social environment should be the first consideration of management when placing women on any new jobs, for women can generally be expected to succeed when the setting is conducive to success.

16. THE PROBLEMS OF CHANGE

EQUILIBRIUM IN THE ORGANIZATION

IT HAS been pointed out in an earlier chapter that all organizations which have persisted for any length of time tend to achieve a certain equilibrium or balance. All that this means is that people in the organization develop a particular set of relations with the various elements in their environment. They reach a point where they know how to deal with the environment and have made the necessary adjustments to it. While they may not be completely satisfied with the relations which have developed, at least they have the security of knowing what to expect and, in general, how to handle things. Thus, the employee gets up in the morning, dresses, has his breakfast, catches the streetcar at the corner, passes through the gate at work, goes to his workplace, finds things as he expects them, has dealings with the foreman whose moods and attitudes he knows well, gets busy when the big boss comes around, slows down when the time-study man puts in an appearance, jokes with the fellows at lunch, and so on. He develops a certain sense of security, simply because things happens as he expects them to. His environment has been categorized, labeled, routinized, and mapped out to the best of his ability; and he has made a more or less successful adjustment to it. At least, it does not threaten him in any important ways.

Now when change is introduced into a man's environment, it is apparent that he must make adjustments to it. If his department is moved from one end of the building to the other, he may have to reorganize a considerable part of his work life. Instead of entering at Gate A, he will now have to go in at Gate Z. He can no longer grab his lunch in the little hamburger stand across the street from Gate A. Instead, he has to bring his own lunch; and he loses the conviviality and good fellowship that was a source of satisfaction to him over at Joe's Slop Kitchen. A drinking fountain used to be located right in the department near his machine, when they were situated over near

289

Gate A. Now, however, he must walk down to the second floor. All these things are petty, little details that do not amount to much; but it is, nevertheless, amazing how many changes occur in a man's life when his department is moved. The adjustments involved for the average employee are sufficient, in fact, to cause some surprising drops in morale unless employees are properly oriented before the change occurs.

In order to understand why morale does drop when changes of various kinds occur in an organization, we have to know something about the psychology of learning. Learning, whether it takes place among rats or men, follows pretty much the same pattern. We tend to repeat those responses which bring us rewarding satisfactions. We inhibit responses which bring us pain and punishment. This process continues throughout our lives, although basic responses and sets are learned very early in life. Whenever we go into a new situation, we learn what responses to avoid and which ones to accept and develop. Those which tend to bring us the most satisfaction or the least dissatisfaction are reinforced and become part of our life pattern. Now, just suppose that, after we have learned a set of responses and a way of behaving which have proved satisfactory to us in a particular work situation, the situation is in some way changed. Suppose that former patterns of behavior and reactions which once brought us satisfactions of various kinds can no longer be followed. Worse still, suppose that responses which once brought us satisfaction and reward now bring us only punishment and pain. It is easy to see that, unless an adjustment to the new situation can be made, we can become frustrated and, in extreme cases, demoralized.

This is exactly what happens in many work situations. Employees are called upon to accept and adjust to changes which are sometimes hard to take. They receive little or no help from management, to whom they look for guidance in assisting them to adjust to the changes; and, as a result, it sometimes takes years for complete readjustment to occur under such circumstances. One situation where such a long, drawn-out adjustment period can occur is with a change of management—one of the most important of the changes which can affect the average employee's work life. Particularly is this true of employees in the middle-management brackets. However, reactions to top management change can run far down the line into the rank and file itself. The pattern of symptoms involved in poor morale resulting from management change is so clear-cut that it can almost be described as a distinct organizational disease. Usually the disease runs a course somewhat as follows: The new manager comes into the organization, all fired up to make a showing for himself. The employees soon get the definite impression that he is not satisfied with them, that their old ways of doing things are no longer adequate. For a time, however, they make some effort to adjust. This initial effort to adjust soon gives way to personal insecurity and anxiety as the employees find that the new manager is not too well satisfied, no matter what they do. There is a growing feeling among individual employees that they, personally, are not measuring up to standard. They think they see the better jobs going to outsiders. They see unfair treatment in every decision involving an old-timer. Then they make the important discovery that a number of other old-timers feel as they do. When this happens, a resistance group develops, which sets itself against the new manager and becomes actively involved in blocking his efforts to get a job done. This group may even go so far as to try to get rid of him by appealing to higher authority in the organization. Usually this pattern of reactions takes from one to two years, or more, to complete its cycle, depending upon the new management's skill and awareness of the problems which are affecting employees in the organization.

Whenever employees in an organization are unable to make the necessary adjustments to changes which occur, the organization can be said to be in a state of disequilibrium, or unbalance. It is very important, therefore, for management to develop the skills needed to maintain the stability of the organization through the variety of changes which can affect employees. This is particularly difficult, since our modern industrial world is characterized by change.

Most industrial and business organizations present a picture of constant changes of one sort or another. There are technological changes of machines and processes, changes in products, changes in organization, changes in personnel, and changes in relationships among individuals. This means that the individual employees are frequently making new adjustments, which vary from that involved in learning a new skill to that of assuming a new position in the status system. As we have seen, every major change in his situation may mean a serious problem of adjustment for the individual; and the ease and speed of readjustment depends largely upon the meaning of the change for the individual and his attitude toward it. Thus, changes which involve loss of status usually result in severe emotional reactions; and adjustment may be slow and painful. Furthermore, many changes which appear to be minor on the surface may be interpreted by the individual as a threat to his status or security; and he may react to them accordingly. Bringing a new, improved machine into a department, for example, may not directly affect the work of the operators of the old machines, but they may look on it as a threat to their positions and skill. Such situations present some delicate problems to either personnel men or supervisors in helping the individuals to adjust.

CHANGES WHICH AFFECT THE EQUILIBRIUM OF THE ORGANIZATION

Any change will affect an employee. However, there are some to which it is easy to adapt. The most important changes affecting employees in modern industrial life are those involving economic fluctuations, social movements and trends, changes in management and key personnel, changes in company policy (particularly with reference to rules and regulations affecting work routines), technological change, and change in departmental location.

Economic Changes

Of these various changes, economic fluctuations can have the broadest and most significant effect upon employees. There is nothing more demoralizing than the loss of a job when the prospect of securing another is remote. It is true that certain groups of employees—particularly those in the lowest working class in our society—are not nearly so concerned with the loss of jobs as higher level groups, at least from a psychological standpoint. Nevertheless, for the average workingman, cutting off his income is a hard economic and psychological blow. For middle-class employees, it frequently happens that loss of job during a depression is taken personally; they feel that some failure on their part must have caused the layoff. With such employees, the psychological effects may be far-reaching. Many men, such as these, never recovered personally from the effects of the Great Depression. This was true also of older men for whom loss of employment meant the end of their work career and dependency in old age.

Almost as important as a loss of job which results from wide swings in the economic activity of the nation is seasonal employment. In industries where the seasonal peaks and slumps are erratic, employees do not know from one month to the next how long they will work. They can make few, if any, plans for the future, and they are forced to lead a more or less hand-to-mouth economic existence. Savings are eaten up rapidly during even short periods of unemployment. Bills acquired during times of good employment become burdensome and threatening when the money is no longer coming in. Some employees practically never get out of the hands of creditors; they pay exorbitant sums to loan agencies in interest for money borrowed to satisfy other creditors who are pressing them for payment of bills. Any personnel manager knows what the average employee goes through from an economic point of view during such periods of unemployment. What he does not see, however, is the loss in prestige at home which the man of the family suffers when he is no longer working. The psychological cost to the unemployed worker is incalculable.

The amount of effort expended by management in attempting to reduce the psychological and economic effects of a layoff are very frequently at a minimum. Many companies announce a layoff no more than twenty-four hours in advance. In unorganized plants, layoffs may be announced on the day on which they are to occur, with no warning at all to the worker. The attitude in many companies is that the problem of layoffs is purely a management consideration. The only role in the situation which employees are asked to play is the passive one of coming to work when asked and going home when no longer needed. It is not commonly felt that employees should be taken into the confidence of management and told when layoffs are impending or likely to occur.

Under these circumstances, it is easy to understand why unions are so much concerned with an orderly procedure for effecting layoffs. With seniority clauses in the contract, employees know at least who is likely to be laid off if a cutback occurs. Furthermore, with plant-wide seniority, the older employees know that they will be kept on, even if they are forced off their regular jobs due to a departmental cutback. In most contracts, also, there are usually protective clauses which guarantee that the employee will receive at least some notice prior to a cutback. The trend is for the length of time of notification to be extended. More than this, there is a definite trend toward guaranteed annual incomes which provide the employee even more security against economic fluctuations.

It is quite apparent that the solution to the problem of layoff and unemployment does not lie in the hands of the management of individual companies. This is part and parcel of our entire economy. Nevertheless, much can be done locally to smooth out production and eliminate seasonal fluctuations. In one small company, during one of the best years of that company's existence, when thousands of dollars in profits were made, employment fluctuated from a low of 875 to a high of 1,200. When you consider that approximately 250 of these employees were a relatively stable group of office and supervisory workers, this meant a fluctuation in factory employment of over 50 per cent during a prosperous year. This is inexcusable from a purely humanistic standpoint; from an economic and morale point of view, it is very costly.

Changes in Company Policy

The importance and significance of economic changes to the stability of an organization are obvious. Less apparent, however, are changes in the rules and regulations of an organization. Changes such as these, when they are not reasonable and where employees are not given proper consideration and notice prior to their effective date, can be very demoralizing. Here, again, the management of many companies does not see the significance of change and its effect on the attitudes of employees. Since the creation of rules, regulations, and policies is primarily a management responsibility and prerogative, employees, often as not, are not permitted to participate in establishing them. The attitude, again, is that employees are merely supposed to follow the rules and that it is part of their job to do so. In fact, any infraction of the rules is regarded as a direct challenge to management's authority. As a result, management in many organizations goes blithely along, setting up new rules and changing old ones with little or no awareness of what this purely arbitrary action is costing in good will among employees. As a matter of fact, the very thing executives are attempting to accomplish among employees, namely, improved discipline and work habits, is being subverted and impeded by this frankly unilateral establishment of work rules and regulations.

The problem of rules and regulations is tied up closely with the problem of work discipline. In every organization, there have to be some rules if it is to operate in a relatively businesslike manner. Employees must come to work at specific times, take their rest periods in an orderly manner, eat at the proper times, smoke only in certain areas, and so on. Without regular procedures of this sort, employees themselves would be confused and the organization would be a chaos of individual wishes and desires. Most employees like to know what they can and cannot do and are more than happy to adhere to rules and regulations, provided that these are fair and reasonable. A few employees are unwilling to comply with any regulation. These constitute a small group of "goldbrickers" and "boondogglers." Furthermore, relatively conscientious employees sometimes indulge in poor work practices for purely social reasons: coffee clubs, smoking groups, and bridge clubs extending beyond the lunch period fall into this classification. In general, however, such employees can be easily brought into line merely by pointing out the effect of such behavior on the work effort. Moreover, some of these practices can be overlooked without too much concern because they can serve as a relatively inexpensive means of keeping employees tied to the workplace.

In some cases, however, management feels that practically all employees are out to take advantage, if they can possibly get away with it. As a result of this highly shortsighted view, rules and regulations are set up as a system of close and rigorous control. Employees begin to feel that they are working either in a kindergarten or a prison. They strongly suspect that management regards them as irresponsible children, requiring definite instructions on practically everything they do. Resentment grows when employees see representatives of management taking advantage of the very rules and regulations which they themselves have set up. Indeed, there is no better formula for wrecking the morale of an organization than setting up a group of arbitrary rules and regulations designed for the sole purpose of keeping employees in line.

Technological Change

Technological change is undoubtedly one of the most important of the changes affecting employees in industry. On the broad historical level, the industrial revolution represents a basic technological change which has required adjustments of major proportions throughout our whole social system. From a rural, agricultural society, we have become an urban, industrial nation within a few generations. This has meant changes in our entire way of life—the kinds of families we have, the way we bring up our children, our work habits, the jobs and skills we have, where we live and under what conditions. There is, in fact, no part of our lives which has not been touched by the massive changes in technology which have occurred during the past hundred years.

On a less epochal level, however, technological change can still be very important in the lives of employees. In his research in Yankee City, Professor W. Lloyd Warner made particular note of the effects of the deskilling of jobs in the shoe industry in Yankee City, resulting from the introduction of complex machinery to take the place of the skills of the craftsman. This decline in skilled jobs, according to Professor Warner, had the effect of reducing the worker's opportunity for upward mobility in the community. The consequent frustration of losing his status in the community with no chance for improvement made the Yankee City worker an easy bet for union organization and mobilization against management. Indeed, Professor Warner sees in this gradual elimination of skill hierarchies through technological change the development, at least in part, of the strong and powerful industrial union organization in this country during the last twenty years.[1]

Within each industrial and business organization itself, minor technological changes are continuously taking place which have a direct and immediate effect on the employee. A simple change in method has an effect similar to the change of procedure which was described previously. The employee who has acquired skill in doing his job one way tends to resist new ways of doing the job. As a matter of fact, he may resist so much that the new way, although actually an improvement in method, may not work out as planned. In some cases, instead of production improving, it actually drops off and declines.

Changes in technology may seriously affect the status of employees in an organization. In one clerical department in a large organization, management introduced a business-machine system for accomplishing the same operation formerly performed by the clerical employees. These employees strongly resented the introduction of the machines —but not because of the threat to their job security, for there were job openings for all that wanted them elsewhere in the organization. What they resented was their loss of status, because they now considered themselves "machine operators" and something below regular office workers.

There is a threat of loss of status in every new change which is introduced. Older employees who are used to a particular way of

---

[1] W. Lloyd Warner and J. O. Low, *The Social System of the Modern Factory* (New Haven: Yale University Press, 1947).

doing things find themselves unable to keep up with new methods. They are, therefore, critical of innovations. "They don't make things the way they used to," said one old-timer. "Why, twenty years ago this stuff really had quality; it was built to last. But now they just throw it together." Actually, this old-timer was simply expressing the rigidity of old age and lack of willingness to adjust. The truth of the matter was that the product to which he was referring was far superior in every respect to the product of twenty years ago. It was not only better designed but better made. The old-timer, however, feared a loss in his own status and the threat to his own, no longer useful, skills.

Technological changes give rise to other adjustment problems. In many companies the engineers are originating a continual stream of changes in products, machines, and processes. These changes are designed to improve the product or reduce the costs, and they generally mean a simplification of processes or the introduction of more automatic machinery. Such changes may affect the individual in a number of ways. They may eliminate his job entirely and force him to learn a new job; they may reduce the number of workers needed and force him out of a job; or they may result in extensive transfers of people, substitution of women for men, or low-skilled jobs for high-skilled jobs. The following example was observed by the authors:

One factory used a large volume of nickel-plated parts, which required many skilled polishers to polish the parts before and after plating. A change in design, which changed the finish on most of the parts to a black enamel instead of nickel plate, eliminated most of the polishers and substituted a few sprayers. This meant that a large group of skilled polishers, some of whom had spent fifteen or twenty years in the work, had to be absorbed into other types of work in other departments. Since most of them were not experienced in other work, they had to be transferred to less-skilled jobs with a cut in rates. As a result, the skill they had spent years in acquiring and in which they took considerable pride was no longer of value. Also, the group in which they had spent years was broken up.

Thus, they had to learn new skills; they had to adjust to lower earnings; and they had to adjust to the change from a work group of which they had been a part for a long time, and in which they had high status because of their skill and experience, to groups in which they were new, inexperienced, and of low status.

Even where technological change does not substitute lower skilled people for the highly skilled, it often substitutes one skill for another.

For example, if, in the manufacturing of an intricate part, die-casting is substituted for machining, skilled die-cast operators may replace equally skilled machine operators. This means that for that particular job the machine operators are displaced even though there might be no actual reduction in the number of skilled workers needed. In some cases, there may actually be a substitution of more highly skilled people for those displaced, although this is rare and usually means a sharp reduction in total numbers needed. In general, we can say that, for a given quantity of goods produced, the technological improvements tend to reduce the average level of skill required and the number of people required.

Personnel Changes

Any change in personnel among employees can create repercussions (even those not involving supervisory personnel). Let us consider, for example, the impact simply of introducing a new employee into a work group. Most modern companies have a procedure for inducting the new employee, acquainting him with company policies and the conditions of employment, and introducing him to his supervisor and fellow employees. However, few of them recognize the problems of adjustment which the older employees must face every time a new face is brought into the work group. Usually, of course, this adjustment process is relatively simple and uneventful, if the newcomer knows his way around and is willing to accept the patterns of social behavior already established. However, if he should get out of line in any important respect, a small-sized volcanic eruption can occur. In retail stores, for example, the introduction of a so-called "hot-shot" salesman can often have dire effects. Most selling departments in retail stores have a fairly well-organized status system which determines, to a great extent, the amount of sales which each employee can or will make. It is apparent that the ability to get sales is very much dependent, not only on sales ability and personal confidence, but also on who is allowed to approach the customers and who is permitted to sell the higher cost items. Higher-status salespersons naturally have all the advantages in this regard. They can compel lower-status employees to defer to them in the choice of customers and in the selection of the better selling areas of the department. If a new employee comes into the department and refuses to recognize this status system, the department will organize to squeeze him out. Even the supervisors will join in attempting to control the newcomer who threatens to wreck the morale of the entire department. Older salesmen will bracket the "hot shot" on the selling floor so that he cannot easily approach a customer coming into the department. The supervisor will give him stock work to do which will keep him off the selling floor. He will be reprimanded for "unethical tactics" if he does not follow the accepted practices in approaching a customer and attempts to beat out others in the department who may already have spotted the prospect. These kinds of social pressures generally are sufficient for the person with average aggressiveness. However, even under these conditions, a few still do not respond and fall into line. Under these circumstances, friction and poor feeling can persist in the department for long periods of time. In many such cases, the "hot shot" finally has to be taken out of the department, in spite of his excellent sales record.

The same kind of adjustment problem occurs in factories when a "rate-buster" is introduced into the department. Here, the technique of control may not be so subtle. The newcomer is simply told by the others what is the accepted "fair day's work" in the organization, and he either responds or lays himself wide open for a variety of social pressures, ranging from joking ridicule to open threats.

The problem of adjusting to a change of personnel on your own, or a lower, level, however, is not nearly so difficult as adjusting to a change in supervision, particularly higher-level supervision in a position to alter established work practices and procedures. Any such alteration is a threat to the established social system of the organization; and anyone who has a stake in that system will be likely to face a new manager or supervisor with considerable anxiety and trepidation. The reaction, however, to a change in management will vary, depending to some extent on the attitudes which employees had toward the former supervisor whose place the newcomer is taking. If there was a good deal of cordial feeling toward the previous boss, the newcomer will be regarded as a usurper; he will be watched closely for shortcomings and weaknesses. If the feeling about the former boss was negative and unfavorable, the newcomer may be received with welcome relief. In a retail store with which we are familiar, a change of management of this order had occurred, with the following results:

The previous manager was thoroughly disliked for very personal reasons. However, the attitudes of employees toward the company in general had remained quite favorable; the feeling was that eventually the disliked manager would be removed and transferred elsewhere. This actually happened; and when the new manager came in to take over, he called all employees together, and said, among other things, "Work can be fun!" Then he spent his first few days in the store simply walking around, shaking hands with everybody. The effect of this procedure was electric, as far as employees were concerned. It keynoted their own feelings; they began quoting the new manager's words as though they were their own, "You know, work can be fun!" Needless to say, the problem of integrating into the store was simple for the new manager.

In another store, however, the reverse situation occurred:

The old manager had been well liked by a large segment of the store. The new manager, who had just come back from a long stint in the army, called employees together and told them that he had been a colonel in the army and, as far as he was concerned, he would continue as such in his new assignment in the store. These may not have been his exact words, but that was the way that employees interpreted them. In any event, he thereupon disappeared into his office and left his anxious and somewhat perturbed people to shift for themselves. Morale swung lower over a period of time. A year later there was a strong resistance group among a number of employees who were actively working against management.

It is apparent from these few comments about change in personnel that the principal problems of adjustment are: (1) the integration of the newcomer's attitudes and behavior with the demands of the work group into which he is moving, and (2) the group's adjustment to the demands of the newcomer if this is necessary, as it is in case of change of supervisor. The adjustment of the group is always more difficult because it involves shaking up, and even destroying, an established status system in which employees have an important personal stake.

Organizational Changes

Another problem of individual adjustment results from the changes in organization or structure which management originates. Management is always interested in changing its organization so that it will work better, or so that it will meet changing conditions of one sort or another. Many of these are changes in formal organization at a level which affects the supervisory structure and may involve the shifting of departments from one division to another without changing the actual work. Changes which have much more direct impact on the work level are those involving reorganization of the work or regrouping of the jobs, change of physical location, and so on. At whatever level such changes take place, it must be remembered that the people, even though they be top executives, must make an adjustment to the new state of affairs.

At the supervisory and executive level, these organizational changes are often interpreted as affecting the status relationships of those involved, and this may result in serious reactions and anxieties. To take a department away from one division chief and place it with another, for example, may be interpreted as loss of prestige for one and a gain for the other; and the one who has lost status may show anxiety over the reasons for the move and about his standing with top management. Even when such moves are obviously logical from the organizational point of view, there will probably be some such reactions unless the superiors give great reassurance. And even if he has been reassured about the meaning of the move, the division chief who has lost a department knows that everyone at his level and below will comment on the change and wonder if it means that he is "slipping."

Reorganization at the higher level often means little to the workers, since such changes can be accomplished without changing the work or the work location. But when the changes mean that the work units are shifted around, they become directly significant to the workers. For example:

One company made a change in its accounting organization which broke up large accounting units in a central location into small units in shop location. This removed the members of the organization from the preferred office location and put them in the lower-status shop environment. It also separated them into small groups isolated from each other, and broke up many of their cliques and social activities which they had carried on as one large group. Furthermore, they were in much less frequent contact with their superiors and felt that they were isolated and ignored. The adjustment to this change required several months, during which time there were continual complaints about the change, about the poor working conditions, the noise and dirt in the new location, the isolation from higher supervisors, anxieties about being lost in the shop, and many similar expressions of disturbance.

The adjustment to all these changes presents a very difficult problem from the point of view of management. In every case where there is serious disturbance, the effectiveness of the individual or even the entire organization is reduced for a time and, in some cases, permanently. Nevertheless, such changes are often unavoidable, and the problem is how to handle them so that there will be a minimum of disturbance and the quickest possible adjustment. Often, by failing to anticipate the disturbance, by thinking of people as though they were inanimate objects which would not react to such changes, management fails to take the reaction into its calculations and does things in such a way as to increase disturbances. In many cases, proper attention to the individuals will reduce anxieties and pave the way for rapid adjustment. In other cases, modification of the proposed changes will remove the features which give rise to the most serious reactions. In general, to announce an important change without preparing those involved beforehand increases disturbances; but if it has been discussed in advance and the subordinates have been able to express their ideas and have had some hand in the planning, then they become adjusted to the idea and accept it more readily. In any case, the superiors should anticipate the way their subordinates will react and give increased attention to them during the change and the period of adjustment. In no case should it be assumed that by giving a simple logical reason for the change the disturbance can be avoided. Explanations play a useful role in the adjustment, but they should be accompanied by increased sympathetic attention from the superiors. Unfortunately, in many cases the intermediate levels, such as department and division chiefs, are just as disturbed as the foremen or workers, and because of their own feelings are unable to give attention to their subordinates and to reassure them.

Change in Departmental Location

Change in departmental location hardly seems like the most important of the changes which can occur in the work life of an employee, and it is not; but the reactions to it can sometimes be so vehement and emotional that some discussion of it seems appropriate. Life, when you think about it, is made up of a set of very elemental, simple routines. None of these routines, in itself, is very important. But picture for yourself the adjustments which you would have to make if, instead of arising at 6:30 A.M., you were compelled to arise at 5:30 A.M. Not much of a change, but your wife has to get up at the same time, or else you get your own breakfast. More important, you have to go to bed before 10:00 P.M. if you want a decent night's rest. And you are hungry as a horse at 11:00 A.M., but you still have to wait until noon to have lunch. Moreover, because you are more tired when you arrive home at night and are, therefore, more irritable, the children wonder whether Daddy really has finally "cracked," as Mamma often said he would. And so it goes, with the change working its way into the very fabric of your life.

In the same way, a change of departmental location requires that employees make a whole series of minor adjustments. Things are never quite the same. The worst part of a change in location, however, is that very often employees are not informed of the change until it is about to happen. Seldom are they taken into management's confidence in planning the change. Indeed, it seems unnecessary to do so. What difference does it make where employees do their work? Space is space, no matter where it is! But the implication of the change is apparent to employees. They think that management does not have the interests of employees at heart; that management does not care whether they have to use the small rear elevator, which is always so "jam-packed" in the morning, instead of the group of larger elevators at the main entrance where the traffic is much lighter; that management does not concern itself with the fact that the new location does not have the window space that the old location had; that the lighting is poorer; and that employees now have to walk half a block to the washroom, and so on.

Very often a change in departmental location has status implications. In this event, the reactions of employees can be very severe, as shown below:

In one organization studied, a small group of employees in a statistical department were moved away from the mother department and top supervision to a location in a separate building. They had built up a good deal of camaraderie in the new location and felt considerable relief in being away from the watchful eyes of the department manager. However, one day, without explanation, they were moved back to the old location. Immediately the question arose, "Why?" Rumor had it that they were being punished for their behavior in the new quarters. Gone was the old camaraderie and good spirit. What's more, employees in the old location avoided them like the plague. Until they were sure of the reasons for the shift, they were not going to put their own security on the block by associating with them. The tension in this department when it was studied was very great.

If the new location is clearly undesirable, employees definitely feel a loss of status. The implication is that their department as a whole does not rate in the organization. Departmental status can, of course, be very important to employee morale. If they feel that they are a part of a going department, one which is accepted and respected in the company, they generally have greater pride and satisfaction in their work. Moving to a poorer location is one sure way to inform employees that their department does not rate and that their supervisor has not enough strength in the organization to protect his people from all kinds of indignities. While this may not be true, of course, it is, nonetheless, a disheartening experience.

Change in Job or Office Location

A change in the place in which you do your job within a department is closely related to a change in the location of the entire department. Here, however, the status implications can be very clear-cut. Particularly is this true in offices where some of the important symbols of status are the type of desk, location of desk, size of office, and location of office. Simply moving an employee from a desk to a table may have serious status implications for him. In some offices, moving an employee from a double-pedestal desk to a single-pedestal desk would constitute a demotion to him as real as though you cut his salary ten dollars a week. Locating a man with a group of women in an office has also created anxiety on many occasions. The following example of the effects of change in office were observed in one large office with which the authors have considerable familiarity:

Every year or so there is a General Moving Day. This shifting about of office personnel is necessitated by the fact, that, because of promotions each year and transfers of key personnel, offices with a good deal of status significance are left vacant. The office that you eventually get constitutes a clear definition of your status. There is always considerable anxiety when a change of this sort is about to take place. Employees on the same general status level talk about those on higher levels, but, of course, they do not talk about themselves. There is considerable effort to relieve tension throughout the entire procedure by joking about it. When it is all over, employee reactions depend on how closely their new office location actually measures up to their own conception of their status in the organization. Sometimes, there are hard feelings, but generally not, because management in this organization is very much aware of the status significance of various office locations and plans the changes carefully.

SUMMARY

The changes which we have been discussing are some of the more common ones which can occur in the typical business and industrial organization. However, it is apparent that any change can affect the feelings of employees. When you consider that our industrial world is characterized by change—indeed, reveres change as a fundamental part of the American system—it is easy to understand that the problem of helping employees to adjust to change in the work environment should be one of the principal concerns of management. However, it has been equally characteristic of business management that adjustment to change is regarded as a problem of the individual employee, something which he must work out for himself. As a matter of fact, employees do make considerable adjustment to change on their own; after all, even the most rigid humans are unusually flexible and adaptive. But the cost in employee feelings of anxiety and insecurity and the loss of productive energies and efficiency, engendered by changes affecting the well-being and status of employees, are significant items of human and economic expense. This is especially true when it is so easy to relieve much of the anxiety caused by change and do an intelligent job of management in this important area.[2]

---

[2] See Chapter 17, "The Industrial Relations Organization," Chapter 18, "Personnel Counseling," and Chapter 20, "Human Relations and Management," for ways in which problems of change can be handled effectively by management.

17. THE INDUSTRIAL RELATIONS ORGANIZATION

THE industrial relations or personnel organization has a peculiar function which often makes its role a difficult one. Fundamentally its function is similar to that of all other staff organizations; that is, it exists in order to make the total system work better; and it is expected that the factory will be a better running, more effective organization because of it. The real difficulties arise out of its particular area of endeavor, the things which are expected of it, and the limitations of its tools.

To go back to the purpose of the factory organization, we see that it is a complicated mechanism, set up to produce goods. In this system, every element is co-ordinated to those productive ends. The line, the staff, and the control organizations are all concerned one way or another with the problem of getting the work out. In such a system the individual may be seen as part of the productive effort, another type of tool, and he is judged in terms of his effectiveness in the system. Furthermore, the things of importance to the individual, the satisfactions he is seeking, all tend to play second fiddle to the needs of the organization. Thus the normal working of the factory organization tends to create problems of individual frustration, dissatisfaction, and maladjustment, which, in turn, interfere with the effectiveness of the productive system. This interference may come about through excessive internal friction, high turnover, constant complaints, strikes, or work stoppages. Once management becomes aware of such difficulties, it begins to think about ways of improving work morale and co-operation; and out of this a personnel organization often develops.

DIFFERING CONCEPTS OF THE PERSONNEL FUNCTION

Means of Counteracting Individual Dissatisfactions

An industrial relations organization and its activities are generally expected to counteract and deal with the human dissatisfactions and disturbances which interfere with the work. In some cases, manage-

307

ment holds a somewhat oversimplified concept of the sources of dissatisfactions and of their cure, and may limit the treatment accordingly. In some cases, for example, management believes that economic insecurity is the main source of disturbances, and it provides employee sick benefits and pensions as an antidote. In other cases, managers feel that they can improve morale and co-operation through economic motivations; so they provide wage incentives, bonuses, or profit-sharing plans. In still other cases, they may think that the only problem lies in selecting the proper kind of employees, and so they pin their hopes on better employment methods. In none of these instances do they have an industrial relations organization as it is usually thought of, but only an employment office or a few individuals handling details of a benefit or incentive plan.

Since a personnel organization is primarily concerned with developing good employee relations, it is concerned with the individual and with directing attention to his attitudes and needs. Thus, its point of view is quite different from that of the other organizations, which are primarily interested in getting the work done and, therefore, subordinate the needs of the individual to the needs of the job. Personnel people are bothered when foremen fail to consider the feelings of individual workers or when they expect workers to adjust to the job and to accept their decisions without complaint or dissatisfaction. They have a feeling that management and all levels of supervision fail to make use of the point of view and understanding of the personnel organization, that they have a blind spot when it comes to employee relations. This same feeling exists to some extent, of course, in all organizations and especially in all staff organizations, but it seems to be especially strong among personnel people. This is probably due to the fact that they are the only group which is more concerned with people than with production and which, therefore, looks at the whole system from a unique angle.

Antidote to Unions

Personnel departments are often thought of by management as an antidote to unions and as a means to avoid, or make unnecessary, a union organization. This is not, of course, a recent concept but one which usually increases in periods of unsettled labor conditions. In such companies the problem of employee morale is approached by trying to give the workers the same sort of concessions, in things like wages or working conditions, as they might expect to gain through a union. Companies with this idea may plan elaborate benefit programs, pay liberal wages, and improve working conditions; and, along with this, their industrial relations organizations may be expected to impress the workers with the fairness and munificence of management. They may be expected to show how favorably the wages compare with those of other companies, how liberal the benefits, or how pleasant the working conditions are. They may be expected to "sell" management and its point of view to the workers, and to "interpret" policies and practices, which means presenting management's logics in such a way that the workers will accept them. In these cases, too, there is the feeling that the workers just do not understand. Therefore, one of the duties of the industrial relations organization is to figure out ways of presenting the company's point of view through bulletins, pamphlets, employee magazines, lectures, and so on. All this is done in the firm belief that, if the workers are presented with the concepts, if the workers are properly educated, they will sympathize and agree with management.

When this kind of thing is expected of them, the personnel people find themselves in a difficult position. If they feel strongly identified with management and accept and agree with its reasoning, they find that they are looked on as management's stooges, who do nothing but give the workers a lot of empty talk. They often feel that they are pushing constantly against an inert mass of worker attitudes, and they become convinced that the workers are a stupid lot who will not listen to reason. And the more indifference they meet on the part of the workers, the more management criticizes them for being ineffective. Thus, they find themselves caught between pressure and criticism from management and the dislike and resistance of the workers. This is a situation which is sure to produce severe feelings of frustration and anxiety among personnel people.

Representative of the Workers

More frequently, however, management does not think of "selling" the company to the workers as the principal duty of its personnel organization. Often it really believes that the workers have legitimate reasons for complaints and dissatisfactions and that something should be done about them. Such companies consider that the personnel organization's function is to find the sources of dissatisfaction and either to correct them directly or bring them to the attention of management. If the company is opposed to unions, it hopes to reduce the employees' feeling of need for a union by constant attention to these complaints; and, in effect, it tries to take over the functions of a union. With this approach the personnel people are inevitably identified with the attitudes of the workers, and their sympathies are with the individual. They are able to maintain better relations with the workers, who may recognize their sympathetic interest and good intentions. At the same time, the personnel people find themselves in the difficult position of being critical of management and the supervisors. In effect, they see things through the workers' eyes and evaluate everything in terms of its impact upon the workers. They are critical of the foreman who, in trying to get the work out, fails to consider the feelings of the workers, makes excessive demands on them, or is irritable with them. They are critical of the company if its policies and practices seem to run counter to the sentiments of the workers. They are continually upset about poor supervision and about the inadequate communication of workers' problems up the line.

These critical attitudes often lead to friction and suspicion between foremen and personnel people. The foremen feel that the personnel people are prone to accept as fact every complaint from a worker and that they judge things without seeing the entire picture and, especially, without seeing the foreman's problems. This feeling increases when the lower ranks of the personnel organization are filled with college people who have little or no shop experience. At the same time, the personnel organization is frequently a channel of communication through which criticisms of the foreman may go up the line. Thus, he feels that they are a group who see only the workers' side of any question and who are critical of him to his superiors without giving him a fair chance to defend himself. As a result, there is often a great deal of antagonism in the relations between foremen and personnel people, even though it is usually kept veiled behind a polite and friendly exterior.

Substitute for a Union

Even though management thinks of it as a channel for the communication and adjustment of employee complaints and grievances, the personnel organization has difficulty in functioning in a way that is satisfactory to the employees. Certainly it can never actually replace a union in handling complaints. In the first place, since it is actually an agent of management and a part of the structure which is devised by management, it is not primarily an agent of the workers which is sanctioned by the workers. As a result, it can exert only as much influence or pressure in settling problems as management will accept. If it is too militant in its defense of the workers' point of view, management may get annoyed and "cut its throat." If management wants to delay decisions, the personnel organization cannot insist on a hearing; if management refuses to settle a grievance to the satisfaction of the group, there is nothing the organization can do about it. In short, when it comes to a showdown, the personnel people have no effective ways of putting the pressure on management; they can quit or be fired, but they cannot call a strike. For this reason they often do not know how far they dare go in pressing an issue, for fear of ruining their relations with their superiors; and they are frequently in a state of anxiety over the way management will judge them and their work. Consequently, the workers may think of them as sympathetic friends who will try to settle their grievances; but they do not think of them as the fellows who will carry their complaints right on up the line, the ones who can really go to bat for them.

There have been experiments from time to time in which management has tried to set up a personnel organization which could actually substitute for a union in handling employee complaints. In one such experiment the main element of the personnel organization was a staff of people called "counselors," who were assigned to keep in close touch with all employees, to take up any complaints, and see that they were settled satisfactorily. They were instructed to think of themselves as shop stewards who were representing the workers and not management. During a period of about two years these counselors found themselves constantly in a position of criticizing the foremen and carrying their criticisms up to the top of the structure. They were also frequently criticizing top management for the effects of its policies. There was a constant turnover in the personnel organization; morale was low; and there was a general anxiety over the situation. At the end of two years the plan was virtually discarded; there was a drastic reorganization among supervisors and staff, and practically the whole personnel force was eliminated.

As a rule, personnel organizations are not expected to take such extreme positions in the problem of dealing with employee complaints. Those whose activities are primarily administration of benefit plans or employee services often have duties sufficiently clear-cut that they can do their jobs without becoming involved in conflicts with the line or with other parts of the structure. This is especially true of employment people, whose sole duty is the selection and hiring of employees and who have no further contact with them. People in such positions can frequently live in relative isolation from the turmoil of the factory.

Relation of Personnel Function to the Problems of Employees

Since the personnel organization is primarily concerned with the problems of individual workers, most of their attention is directed to those phases of the work situation which frequently cause disturbance. Roughly, the problems of workers and, therefore, the functions of the personnel organization can be divided into four types: those involved in (1) the induction of new employees, (2) advancement through the structure, (3) adjustment to change, and (4) serious personal crises. Although this may seem an oversimplified classification of workers' problems, it does define the principal areas in which personnel organizations can and often do function effectively.

PROBLEMS OF THE NEW EMPLOYEE

In a factory, as in any other social organization, there is a problem of whom to accept as members of the group; and there are usually highly formalized procedures by means of which the new individuals are selected and inducted into the organization. In college fraternities there is a cycle of induction beginning with "rush week." The newcomers are looked over by the different organizations; then each club votes on the various prospects and "bids" the ones they have selected. With the acceptance of the "bids" there are various social activities and ceremonies designed to bring the newcomer into the group. Next comes a period of trial or apprenticeship; and finally there are elaborate initiation ceremonies which make the newcomer a full-fledged member of the organization. The normal procedures of employment in industry have some of the same features of initiation as fraternities. The newcomer appears at the employment office, where he is put through certain routines (or we might call them "stages") in the selection ritual, in which he talks to various people, fills out papers, takes tests, and so on—all to the end of deciding whether the organization wants him as a member. Once he is chosen, he may go through an induction process which involves talking with personnel people about the company and its rules and regulations; or he may go directly to his new supervisor, who talks with him about the job; or he may merely be put to work without any talk or explanation. Then he goes through a period of learning the work and the people with whom he is working. They may put him through their own initiation, "kidding" him, telling him tall tales, and playing practical jokes on him; or they may take him in very readily and accept him as a part of the group after only a very brief period of getting acquainted; or they may ignore him and hold him off at a distance until he gradually breaks down the barriers and becomes one of them.

Selection of Workers

A factory, however, is different from a fraternity in that it is organized for the production of goods and not merely for the satisfaction of its members. In keeping with this general objective, the selection and induction procedures in a factory are methods of obtaining people who will best contribute to the productive aims of the organization. Furthermore, these procedures are set up and sanctioned by management, and they are expected to operate according to the concepts of management. Thus the selection is directed toward satisfying management's ideas of what is a good worker, rather than toward satisfying the workers' ideas of whom they want to work with.

The concepts underlying the average methods of selection are similar in some respects to the concepts involved in selecting a machine. They think of the individual in terms of his ability to do the work, his dexterity, skill, experience, knowledge of the work, health, and so on. They give him tests designed to measure his basic abilities or his learned skills. They interview him to find out what jobs he has done in the past. They give him physical examinations to see if he is in good health and physically able to do the work. They check with former employers to learn if he has actually had the experience which he claims and to see if he was a stable and satisfactory worker. And, finally, they sometimes give consideration to the question of whether he will be acceptable to the group and make adequate adjustment to the job as a social situation.

It is rare to find selection procedures set up to examine the individual's real ability to adjust to the social system of the factory. Some testing programs are built around the assumption that an adequate adjustment of the individual depends upon his being placed on work which is fitted to his basic abilities, and that by proper testing and placement the problems of employee morale and adjustment will be solved automatically. There does not seem to be any significant relationship between such factors as mechanical aptitude, dexterity, or intelligence and the satisfactions the individual is seeking and what he expects from the job. Thus, the individual who is in ability better fitted to be a machine operator than an executive does not automatically make adjustment when put on a machine. This is well shown in the cases of children from professional or executive families whose whole background gives them expectations which prevent effective adjustment to shop jobs regardless of their particular abilities. Furthermore, ability to do the work well does not mean that an individual will achieve a comfortable acceptance into the group, and without this he is likely to be dissatisfied. In other words, the "square peg in the round hole" theory of individual maladjustment, which is propounded by many experts in testing, is certainly inadequate if the only measures of "squareness" are the commonly used aptitude tests.

Initiation of Workers

In comparing the employment routines of the average company with the initiation processes of a fraternity, we see certain things lacking which are of considerable importance to the individual. When he is hired, he is put through all those elaborate processes for determining his fitness to belong; but it is often done with about as much real interest in him as the purchasing department has in a new machine which it inspects and tests. Furthermore, when he is finally accepted, he may be dropped into the job without further ado; often nothing is done to make him feel that he is really a welcome member of the group or of the company; and he is quite apt to be ignored. Now, compare this to what happens when he joins a club. Once he is accepted, he is well received and made to feel that he is a member of the group. He may go through certain initiations, but they serve to make him aware of the group and of his place in it. He is introduced to everyone; they tell him how glad they are to have him, what a wonderful group it is, and how much he will like it. The old-timers want to get acquainted and make an effort to see that he feels at home. In fact, the whole organization acts so as to make him feel that he "belongs." But after his first day at work in a factory, he often feels that it is a cold and unfriendly place, that he is just an unimportant atom in a big indifferent machine.

The Personnel Department and Formal Induction Procedures

In some companies, attention has been given to this problem, and there are regular induction procedures for the new employees. Booklets or other material for new employees are usually prepared, which are designed to stimulate interest and answer questions. This may be coupled with a tour of the plant, lectures on safety, company rules, or other matters; and there may be other efforts to make him feel that he belongs. Such activities are usually carried out by the personnel organization, either through the employment office or through some other department working in conjunction with it; and, in general, such efforts are well received. These initial efforts may be followed by personal interviews a few days or a week or so after the new employee starts on his job.

There are, however, certain limitations to what the personnel organization can do in the induction of the new employee. It is a staff organization which sits off to one side and with which the employee may have only periodic contact, once he has been inducted; it is not, therefore, a significant part of his daily social environment. The group into which he must fit is the group with which he works—the supervisors and the fellow workers—and it is into this group that he must be integrated. Thus, no matter how carefully the personnel people may prepare him and try to make him feel welcome, he will still be in an unfriendly world if the other workers receive him coldly. And no matter how the personnel people may build up the company and paint a picture of idyllic conditions and friendly management, he will probably believe that it is an awful place to work if the other workers tell him so. But if the workers and supervisors are friendly and try to make him feel welcome, if they help him with his difficulties from the moment he starts on the job, and if they think it is a good place to work, he will go home with a feeling that he really belongs, certain that he will like his job and get along well on it. For that reason, no formalized efforts on the part of personnel people can be nearly so effective in the integration of a new employee as the influence of his work group.

Most formal efforts for the induction of new employees are too concerned either with informing the individual or with "selling" him the company. They supply him with pamphlets to read; they explain this and that; and zealous personnel people give him "pep talks" about the wonders of the company and the importance of their work. He is all too often flooded with information which he can neither remember nor digest. This approach overlooks the fact that the new employee is likely to be overwhelmed by the strangeness and newness of the scene. He is often so concerned over what the job will be like, and whether he can handle it, that he does not remember much of what he hears. When this is understood, there is no reason to be surprised or annoyed if a week or so later the new employee has forgotten all the things so carefully explained to him the first day.

Induction of the New Employee within the Department

Since the new employee is likely to feel lonely and uncertain during his first few days on the job, it is important that he be encouraged and reassured. The foreman is in an excellent position to provide the reassurance. However, frequently he is too busy to take the time, and he leaves the new employee to his fate, without instruction or help. Sometimes employees complain that their foreman does not see them for a day or two after they start, which leaves them feeling neglected and anxious about the work. If the employee is working as part of a close group, the other workers may give him the necessary advice and reassurance. In any case, there should be someone responsible for seeing that he gets acquainted with others and has some confidence in his own work. The foreman is the ideal person to do this, since he is the one to whom the employee looks for encouragement or criticism.

The importance of the foreman in the induction and initiation of new employees into the work group has been widely recognized in industry since the end of the war. A number of companies have developed regular induction procedures in which the foreman picks up where the personnel department leaves off. In this way, the new employee moves smoothly and easily from the employment office into the work group with a minimum of anxiety and concern. Here again, however, formal induction procedures are no substitute for the supervisor's real interest in the new employee as an individual and his genuine understanding of the problems that the new employee faces in learning new work routines, getting acquainted with fellow employees, and adjusting to unfamiliar demands and expectations.

Some companies have become increasingly aware of the fact that employees are, to a considerable extent, inducted into the work group by fellow workers. The most elaborate induction procedure in the world can be counteracted by the unfavorable attitudes of associates in the workplace. By the same token, if older employees already in the workplace are favorably disposed toward the company, the new employee will usually develop like attitudes. For this reason, some companies have set up a sponsor system for inducting new employees in which an older employee is given the responsibility for seeing that the new employee is shown his way around, introduced to fellow workers, and in other ways sponsored and guided during the first few days or weeks of adjustment to the new work environment. This program has the advantage of enlisting the assistance of older employees in the department and giving them a degree of responsibility in integrating the newcomers.

PROBLEMS OF GETTING AHEAD

The problem of getting ahead is of considerable concern to many workers, as pointed out in our earlier discussion of individual problems. This is especially true of the younger men who start at the bottom of the wage system and are eager to earn enough to support a wife and family. While among the older workers there are more who have reached a satisfactory level of attainment, there are still many who feel blocked and frustrated. Also, even among the ones who have settled down at one level, the opportunities and methods of advancement are still of interest; and a policy of promotion which seems unfair can seriously hurt the morale of the group. For that reason, some large companies have tried to formalize the system of promotion so that each person can know the channels through which he may rise. In some cases, elaborate charts are prepared showing just where each job stands in relation to others and the lines along which promotions are made. With such a system under the control of the personnel organization, it is apparently quite simple to fill a vacancy by selecting a man from the appropriate spot in the line of promotions. In the ideal operation of such a plan, one promotion near the top of the job hierarchy would result in a chain of promotions until finally a new man would be hired for the bottom job.

These promotional plans, which are usually set up and administered by the industrial relations organization, give the impression of a very orderly system in which the individual knows just where he stands and how he can get ahead. They are generally thought of as being very useful as an incentive, since a personnel man or supervisor can show a worker just how, by hard work and faithful application, he can move up the ladder. Where they are emphasized, however, the people in any one position come to feel that they have a vested right to the job above them in the promotional system; and, if such a vacancy is filled from some other source, there is a serious reaction. This makes it difficult to take care of surplus people through lateral transfers, to shift the versatile workers around, or to continue to promote the exceptional individuals who have reached a ceiling in a limited field but who have potentialities for some other type of work. When adhered to rigidly, such a system becomes a strait jacket which prevents easy adjustment to fluctuations of activity or to exceptional circumstances.

The other extreme, having no promotional system but just leaving it up to the foremen and department chiefs to handle each case on its merits, becomes a sort of free-for-all in which each man must look out for himself. With this system, or lack of system, those who are outstanding in performance or who make a good impression on their superiors can move very rapidly; and for the very mobile people, those who are very anxious to get ahead, it may offer much more incentive than a more rigid and formalized system. However, indiscriminate promotions of this kind, which usually mean promotion of the younger, short-service people, often make the older people feel that they are pushed aside and forgotten and give rise to complaints of favoritism and discrimination on the part of the supervisors. Such complaints always disturb the personnel people, who see in them other instances of the foreman's lack of understanding and of the way he abuses his power and creates unnecessary problems. And since they are charged with improving employee relations, they feel that there should be a system whereby they can control the foremen and prevent such unfair occurrences.

The real problem, especially for large organizations, is how to have a promotional system or policy which will work reasonably well, both from the point of view of management and supervision and from the point of view of the workers. Management is usually opposed to a rigid system and prefers one which is sufficiently flexible that it can be readily adjusted to changes in conditions. The workers want a system which will fit their ideas of fairness; and they generally prefer a flexible system as long as it meets this requirement. If they distrust management or the supervisors, however, they may feel that they can expect fair treatment only through a rigid system or fixed rules. This often leads to demands for seniority rules covering promotions, which assures the old-timers of being given their chance and not being side-tracked for some youngster who is the favorite of the foreman.

PROBLEMS OF PLACEMENT

In any large plant which produces a wide variety of products, there are fluctuations in activities in various departments which, from time to time, produce a surplus of workers in some while there is a shortage in others. In other cases, technological changes may require some shifting of workers. In a small plant this can be watched and controlled very easily on an informal basis. But in a large plant with many departments, one may not even know that there is a surplus of people in another; and without some system of control there is apt to be a situation in which one department is laying off people while another is hiring new people from outside. To avoid this, a placement organization is often set up within the personnel department to organize the shifting of people from one job to another, keep records of any surplus or shortage of people, and try to fill openings with people from within the plant. In some cases the placement department has the responsibility of actually finding places for surplus people, explaining transfers and new jobs to the individuals, and handling the entire process. In a system of this sort, when a foreman needs more people, he notifies the placement organization; and if there are any workers available, they are brought over for him to interview.

The work of the placement organization is often extended to handling cases of individuals who are dissatisfied with their jobs and want a change. They may also administer a promotional system; when openings occur, they see that selection is made from the proper group; and they even participate in the selection. In such a case, they become the group in personnel to which the individual may turn when he is dissatisfied, when he wants to escape from an unpleasant job or an unfriendly foreman, or when he wants a better-paying job or more opportunity.

Function and Importance of the Placement Organization

A competent placement organization is often quite important from the point of view of both management and the workers. Through the proper handling of surplus help and the handling of individual dissatisfactions, they can often reduce turnover considerably. This is especially true in normal times when there is no difficulty in hiring people to fill any needs, so that an individual foreman, without a placement organization, would have no hesitancy in laying off extra help, even though other departments might be hiring.

The general plan of placement work seems simple. The main function is to keep track of the jobs which need people and the people who need jobs and to fill one with the other. It must, however, be realized that people cannot be moved around according to some master plan the way a planning engineer moves machines. People are affected by the way the move takes place, by the meaning it has for them, and by their attitudes toward both the old job and the new; and their success or failure in the new job depends upon all these factors. Every move means the adjustment of an individual to a new job and a new human environment. From the point of view of the workers, the effectiveness of placement work depends upon the consideration given to these human factors and upon the aid given during the process of adjustment. It is not enough to tell a worker that he is no longer needed on his present job and is to be placed on some other work, if we expect good morale and rapid readjustment.

Limitations of the Placement Organization

Unfortunately, the placement organization is usually quite limited in what it can do with regard to these factors. In many cases, most of its work is a result of fluctuations in shop activity, so that it is continually dealing with difficult problems and anxious individuals in disturbing situations. Every time a department has considerable surplus of help, the workers are likely to be worried about who will be transferred to what jobs. Usually, all a placement man can hope to do is to place the people on jobs where they have no loss in earnings. He usually feels, too, that so long as there is no loss in earnings, an individual should willingly accept the change and should have no great problem of readjustment. Generally he finds, however, that he has to "sell" the new job to the worker, that he has to try to convince him that the new job is just as desirable as the old because he will earn the same amount. Since he is really dealing with anxieties about the change, with feelings of insecurity and loss of status, the placement man frequently finds that his arguments, his perfectly logical explanations, fall on deaf ears. As a result, he is likely either to feel that the workers are a stupid and illogical lot or else to be disturbed by his own helplessness in the situation. And if he identifies himself with the workers' sentiments, he really "takes a beating" in times of severe layoffs, when he must be continually making decisions either to discharge people or place them on poorer jobs.

The ordinary placement organization can do little to facilitate the adjustment of workers to new jobs. Since it is an outside staff organization, it does not form a part of the normal daily work situation to which adjustment must be made; and no matter how well placement counselors explain the new job and try to prepare the worker, he must still make his own adjustment. Hence, about all the placement people can do for the individual is to try to alleviate some of his anxieties and permit him to express his feelings about the change. They can then consult with him later to see how the new job is working out and give him a chance to talk about his difficulties.

The Role of the Work Group

The work group plays an important part in the adjustment of the individual to a new work situation, as already pointed out. On his first day, the transferred worker usually feels strange and lonely. He is not sure what is expected of him, and he does not know the other workers and how they feel about him. If the group is friendly and takes him in, if the boss is reassuring and stops by occasionally to see how he is getting along, if the workers ask him to eat lunch with them, then he will feel that he is wanted and that it will be a good group to work with. When he gets this sort of start, he usually makes a rapid adjustment to the group itself, and that, in turn, makes it easier for him to learn the job. In many cases the friendly group which takes the newcomer in and makes him feel at home makes his adjustment to even a serious loss of status much easier. On the other hand, he may find himself in a group which is indifferent or even opposed to newcomers, one which has nothing to say to him or criticizes him and makes derogatory remarks, and perhaps with a foreman who ignores him. Then he ends up his first day feeling that everything about the job, the work group, and the boss is unpleasant. This increases his feelings of anxiety over his change, makes it harder for him to learn the new work, and sometimes causes him to quit.

In all major changes which affect the individual, the group plays an important part in his adjustment. Such changes are major crises to the individual in which he feels that he is faced with unbearable problems and decisions. If he is a member of a well-knit group which can understand his problems and express interest in him and appreciation of the way he feels, this helps to sustain him in his trials. This is similar to what happens in a small town or a well-integrated neighborhood when someone is sick or in trouble. The friends and neighbors rally around to express sympathy and offer help, and serve a real need in helping the individual to face his troubles. But the individual who is not part of a well-integrated group, who has no one to rally around when he needs aid, is forced to face his problems alone; and he seems to have much more difficulty in meeting situations and adapting to changes.

The daily routines of the work, the constant interaction with other people, the minor changes in the situation, and the small difficulties which arise, all may be sources of disturbance to some individuals, even under the most stable conditions. Apparently, the need for constant interaction and co-ordination of effort with other people gives rise to irritations which can lead to friction and conflict. When an individual has been working in a stable situation for a long time, he gradually adjusts to these daily conditions and accepts the minor difficulties without much reaction. When he is new to the situation, and especially if he feels the group is unfriendly, his reaction is stronger and may cause him to do or say things which irritate the others. In the same way, if he has status anxieties, is worried over family situations, feels frustrated in his desire to advance, or has other disturbances, he is likely to react more to the work difficulties or the actions of other workers.

The irritability of one individual may affect the entire group. If one worker is upset and begins to fuss at the others and complain about the way they do things, the whole group may respond in kind. This, in turn, generates more friction; and the tension may build up until there is serious conflict. This condition may be looked on as a form of unstable equilibrium in the group; and when it exists, small things may start a series of reactions which will disrupt the entire group. In other cases, we see groups which do not react so seriously when one member is irritable; they say, "Joe has a grouch today," and let it go at that, perhaps avoiding him temporarily. Such groups may be said to have a stable equilibrium in which the minor individual disturbances do not upset the relationships of the group.

The conditions necessary for the development of this stable equilibrium in a group are not very well understood. In fact, it is sometimes hard to see just what does make the difference between a stable and unstable group, for they often occur side by side in a plant under what, on the surface at least, appear to be uniform working conditions. It does seem clear, however, that in many cases excessive pressure from the foreman has a disrupting effect on the group which stimulates internal friction. Constant criticism from the foreman, praising one at the expense of the others, hanging over them while they work, watching every detail and demanding that everything be done his way—all these things seem to irritate the group; and they are likely to vent their irritation on each other.

To the individual, the difference in groups is important. If he is in a stable group, he finds a friendlier atmosphere, of course; his daily contacts are pleasant; he receives welcome co-operation when he needs it; and in times of personal disturbance he receives sympathy and help. In unstable groups, there is a general feeling of tension and apprehension and frequent friction over the work and minor difficulties; they may be split into antagonistic cliques, and friendships are of short duration. Because of these differences many workers refuse a transfer out of a stable group or demand a transfer from an unstable one, and this all adds to the problems of the placement man.

PROBLEMS OF PERSONAL CRISES

Response of the Group

Every individual at times must face serious personal crises, such as sickness, injury, unemployment, death, or illness in the family. Most of these are universal problems which appear among all kinds of people all over the world, but the consequences for the individual vary with the response of his group. In a well-integrated primitive group, for example, the serious illness of one individual becomes a crisis for the entire group. They rally around him; they may crowd into his hut and participate in the treatment given by the local medicine man or witch doctor; and they may have magic songs or dances to drive out the evil spirits. Thus, the group comes together to assert their solidarity against the powers of evil which are threatening their member. In case of death, the group again gathers round; they join in the mourning and in all the ceremonies attending death. Primitive groups, furthermore, have established methods for looking after their members, so that illness or death of a husband does not mean poverty for his family.

Compared to this, a modern industrial city is very poorly integrated. To begin with, it is not just one group but a conglomerate of innumerable groups of all kinds. An individual city dweller does not automatically belong to any group and is often relatively isolated. Among the groups, furthermore, the degree of integration varies tremendously. Some groups have many characteristics of a primitive group and rally around their members in times of crisis; others are poorly integrated and seem indifferent to their members. But, because of workers' dependence upon their earnings and because of the heavy expenses incurred in illness or death, these crises are a severe threat to the whole way of life of the worker and his family. And the informal organization of the group is not able to sustain the individual in these crises as the primitive group does.

In spite of their limitations, however, some factory groups do react to individual crises in much the same fashion as a primitive group. If a member is ill, they call on him, send him flowers or gifts, and even take up a collection to help with his expenses. In case of the death of a fellow worker or member of his family, they send flowers and attend the funeral. Sometimes they give financial aid to the family, but this is rather limited at best. Gathering around, expressing sympathy, and the ceremony of sending flowers are felt to be very important; it is the proper thing to do, and anyone who fails is thought to have failed in his duty. This is true of supervisors, too; and many foremen make a special point of attending funerals and calling on workers who are ill for any length of time.

The degree of stability and integration of the work group is reflected in their response during such crises. The very friendly groups, and especially those which have been together for years, are, of course, more concerned over the death or illness of members and more sympathetic with them in any crisis than the newly formed groups or those in which there is considerable friction. This does not mean that these latter groups actually ignore these crises but only that they do not feel them so deeply. It means that the individual does not receive the same sort of support as he receives in more stable groups.

Employee Benefits

Most personnel organizations, in considering these crises, direct their attention first to the financial problems; and certainly this is the aspect in which the individual receives the least support from his group. The interest of personnel people and management in these problems has given rise to a large number of benefit plans which provide sick benefits, insurance, pensions, termination allowances in case of layoffs, employee loan funds, and so on, in various combinations. In some cases these are a gift from the company, and in others the employees contribute a share of the costs. Either way, the expense is justified on the grounds that such benefits will improve employee morale, will attract a better class of employees, and will create favorable attitudes toward management. Actually, management has no way of knowing that such benefits do produce these results, but it carries them on as an act of faith. Such benefits really do serve an important function to the individual, however, and they may indicate to him a sympathetic interest on the part of the management.

The reaction of employees to such benefits often seems to be determined by the way they are administered. If they are considered as a gift for which the employee should be eternally grateful, or if they are hedged around with red tape and annoying rules and regulations, then the employee cannot be expected to feel that management is really concerned about him. Apparently, to be well received by the employees, the plan should provide the sympathetic consideration of which he feels the need in times of crisis. In one well-run employee benefit plan, for example, the benefits were quite liberal; and the benefit department had at its disposal, besides, special funds for meeting unusual situations which required more aid than was provided by the regular plan. In case of the death of an employee, a representative of the department called on the family at once, offered their services in making funeral arrangements and handling other details, and, if necessary, advanced the family money to take care of current needs. This was done not in any spirit of paternalism or condescension, not with a feeling of looking after the poor, but rather with the attitude of a good neighbor standing by in a crisis.

PROBLEMS OF CHANGE

One of the most important factors, creating problems of adjustment among employees, is change within the organization itself. Industrial and business organizations are characterized by continuous change in methods, procedures, personnel, division of labor, etc. Any of these changes can have an impact on established patterns of relations among employees within an organization and, because of this, cause serious personal disturbances. As we pointed out in Chapter 14, the industrial environment—with its various positions, functions, and processes —has a social, as well as a technical, significance to employees. As a result, when changes occur in these formal activities of the organization, they may affect the personal satisfactions which an individual employee or a whole group of employees is securing in the workplace.

Because of the significance of change to the equilibrium of an organization, Chapter 16 was devoted to an examination of the typical changes that can occur in industry and a discussion of the effects of these changes on employees. In this chapter, we should like to focus more directly on the role which the personnel department should play in insuring that economic, technical, and procedural changes in the organization do not create serious disturbance in the work force. The most useful function which the personnel department can perform in this regard is constantly to emphasize to management and supervision the effects of contemplated changes on the thinking and attitudes of employees. There are many instances of changes being made just for the sake of change itself. The personnel department should be in a position to scrutinize such changes carefully in order to be sure that they are actually necessary, in terms of the productivity and efficiency of the organization, and that the dislocations among employees that they would cause would not outweigh the advantages to be gained by their introduction.

If the contemplated changes are necessary—and many of them are —the personnel department should be able to point out to management which groups of employees will be affected and the reactions they are likely to have. The personnel department should know the organization well enough to be able to assist and guide management in the introduction of any changes, so that they will be accepted by employees as smoothly and easily as possible. This is important from the standpoint, not only of the personal well-being of employees, but also of the successful introduction of the change itself. Employees are in a position to "sabotage" any change, no matter how necessary, if they are unwilling to accept it. This has been known to happen time and again.

Once a change has been introduced, the personnel department should be alert to personal disturbances among employees. In some cases, direct action might be necessary to handle real problems of dislocation among employees. However, in most situations, the problems will be more attitudinal than real. The problem of handling individual disturbances of this kind will be discussed in some detail in the next chapter, on "Personnel Counseling."

THE LABOR RELATIONS FUNCTION

Another role which frequently falls to the lot of the personnel or industrial relations organization is that of formalized dealings with the union. This means dealing with the vast array of problems which come within the scope of collective bargaining, whether it be handling grievances, interpreting the contract, or what not. And in sizable plants with aggressive unions, these activities often require the full-time attention of one or more personnel people. In fact, in many organizations it has become a highly specialized field, is set apart as a "labor relations" department, and functions to a considerable extent independently of the rest of the personnel activities—independently, that is, unless the other activities attract the attention of the union, either in the form of grievances or in demands during contract negotiations.

In many cases these dealings with the union are approached in formalized and legalistic manner. On any grievance the first question is often one of procedure: Has it been brought up in the proper manner, passing through the necessary stages of handling, with the correct records, etc.? Next, the question is: What does the contract provide in such a case? This question also involves elaborate interpretations of meaning and intent. Where the grievance is not precisely and clearly covered by the contract, the question is one of precedent: What has been the custom in such cases? What has been the settlement in similar cases? Finally, if the grievance is not settled at one stage, the union can appeal to higher authority until the final authority of an arbitrator is reached. Such a system provides an orderly method for handling grievances. It has this shortcoming: that it primarily works to adjudicate between the parties in terms of their contractual rights, but it is not focused on the problem of interpreting grievances and telling both sides how to solve the basic problem. It is set up to tell management or supervisors what they can or cannot do in terms of the contract; and it does not tell them how to avoid difficulties. Since, however, many grievances are symptoms of other underlying disturbances, the legalistic settlement of a grievance does not relieve the basic condition.

The contract negotiations themselves become complex affairs in which the union is attempting to accomplish a number of things. For instance, it is trying to set up a contract which will correct conditions to which the workers object. It is trying to give concrete results in the form of better wages, better working conditions, or other benefits. In addition, the union is trying to show the workers that their union leaders are fighting for their interests. It may be trying to further some of the broader goals of the top union organization, or it may be trying to vent its hostility toward management. Any or all of these may enter into the negotiations out of which a contract will develop. On the other hand, management, while usually willing to do what it considers right and fair, still sees things through the eyes of its own position. Also, it wants to keep everything flexible, so that it can meet changes and handle problems as it sees fit. It wants to feel that it is still "running the business." And as normal human beings, managers tend to meet aggression and hostility with equal aggression and hostility. No wonder contract negotiations are often such a trial to both sides!

However, out of this develops a set of rules and procedures by which certain kinds of complaints can be dealt with. And it is the job of the labor relations people to help the organization make it work. For that reason, it is important that they do not content themselves with the legalistic interpretations; they should also help supervisors to handle the situations in such ways that grievances do not develop. As a rule, the extent of such efforts is merely to try to keep the supervisors informed as to the do's and don'ts of labor relations and as to the provisions of new contracts and working agreements. The real need of the supervisor is for the kind of help which can assist him in analyzing his human relations problems, so that he can avoid developing the conditions which breed grievances.

THE ROLE OF PERSONNEL ADMINISTRATION

In conclusion, we may say that the role of the members of personnel or industrial relations departments should be thought of as that of specialists in the field of people, of human relations, and of organization. They are there, not to spread sweetness and light, not to play Lady Bountiful to the workers, but to help develop an effective organization. Certainly, they will have the bias of their own special fields; but they, above all other specialists, should understand their bias and not let it interfere with their judgment and actions.

Their role is a complex one, and they must strive to be many things to many people. First, to top management they should give help in:

  a) Sound evaluation of the state of morale in the organization and anticipation of the effects of anything which might change it *b*) Accurate diagnosis of problem situations and development of plans for correcting them

c) Analysis of the personalities of individuals to fill positions of responsibility

d) Analysis of the structure of the organization and in development of more effective patterns

To supervisors, they should be a source of counsel and help on:

a) What to do about problem situations
b) What to do about problem individuals
c) How to become better supervisors

To the workers, they should be a source of sympathetic interest and thoughtful guidance, to whom they can turn for help on many personal problems.

On top of all this, they will be saddled with the regular problems of procurement and selection, and of operating benefit plans, training programs, counseling programs, and what not. The sad part of the personnel field is that too many of its members get lost in the operating of plans and systems and never get around to their more significant duties. In fact, many cannot see beyond the systems and never learn to do anything else. However, the need is great, and gradually there may develop professionals who are truly experts in the field of human behavior.

18. PERSONNEL COUNSELING

GENERAL PLAN AND PURPOSE

Most of the adjustments which an individual must face involve an emotional adjustment, as well as a change in behavior. The ease with which he adjusts to a lower status, or learns a new job, or accepts the daily routine of his work, all depend to a large extent upon his attitudes and his emotional state. If he is filled with anxieties or with feelings of frustration and if he develops morbid preoccupations over the change, then his adjustment is painful, difficult, and slow. If the situation is satisfying, if the change is felt to bring status and opportunities, if he looks forward to it, then the adjustment is rapid and easy. Thus, one of the big problems is that of aiding the emotional adjustment and relieving anxieties so that the proper adjustment of other behavior can take place.

The significance of this emotional disturbance is well recognized. Everyone in personnel work is continually impressed with the importance of feelings of anxiety or insecurity in the acceptance or adjustment to any change. Foremen have all witnessed instances of excessive anxieties growing out of some seemingly insignificant event. The trouble is that, although they recognize these things, they still do not know what to do about them. They have no effective tools for dealing with such problems. This gives rise to feelings of irritation with the people who present such problems and a wish that they would keep their feelings to themselves and not worry others with them. One common result of this is the tendency to avoid the person who is disturbed, to treat the anxiety as if it did not exist in the hope that it will eventually disappear of its own accord. Unfortunately, such treatment by avoidance often makes the upset worker feel that his boss or the personnel people either are unsympathetic or do not like him; and this, in turn, is likely to increase his feelings of insecurity, anxiety, or hostility.

331

USUAL APPROACH TO COUNSELING

Counselor's Duties

Within the past several years, there has been a widespread use of what are called "personnel counselors" or "women's counselors." These counselors are concerned with all the individual worker's problems, his anxieties and preoccupations, and they attempt to help him solve his problems. The place of these counselors in the structure varies with different companies, but they are generally part of the personnel organization, rather than the line. In order to maintain contacts, they must be convenient to the workers, and so they are usually located in the shop or spend most of their time there. While their duties also vary considerably from plant to plant, most of them have some or all of the following types of functions:

1. To help workers with personal problems arising outside the work situation
2. To help them adjust to the work situation, and to handle complaints and disturbances in the work situation
3. To communicate matters of company policies and practices to the employees
4. To communicate the attitudes of employees to management

The usual approach to the first two kinds of problems is one of direct action in the form of advice or assistance. If an employee is having difficulty with his family relations, for example, the counselor may give him advice, point out his mistakes, try to reassure him, or suggest that he get in touch with some social agency which handles problems of family adjustment. In case of health problems, a counselor may recommend a specialist, get in touch with the company doctor, arrange for hospital care, and so on. In case of friction in the work situation, the counselor may give advice, talk to the foreman or the other workers, call them together to discuss the difficulty, explain to the employee that he is wrong in his attitude, or reassure him about his relations with others. With a new employee, he may explain the company policies and rules, answer his questions, introduce him to the group, or otherwise help him to feel at ease. Sometimes counselors are expected to explain the company's rules and policies to all the workers, to answer questions for them all, and to see generally that the people have the right understanding of management and its efforts. At the same time, they are expected to keep management informed concerning the attitudes and morale of the workers, to keep an eye on the administration of the various personnel policies, to make suggestions for improvements, and generally to provide an additional channel for communication to management of matters concerning human relations in the work situation.

Many of these duties are, in effect, a fairly direct service to employees; and some companies have, in fact, set up counseling on that basis. Some counseling organizations help new workers with housing problems, arrange transportation, arrange for loans, plan recreation, provide for the care of children, give help during times of illness, and generally aid with the many problems which the worker and his family face from time to time.

While the simple, direct employee services play a useful role, they rarely get at the basic problems involved in the adjustment of the individual. It is one thing to help a new employee to find living quarters convenient to the plant, but quite another sort of problem to help him with the difficulties which arise because he has to live with his wife's family, and still another problem to deal with complaints of discrimination by the foreman. Yet it is just these last types of problems which are so crucial in the adjustment of the individual.

Direct Action and Advice as a Counseling Technique

In examining the way many of these counselors operate and the way they think about their jobs, we see that they generally think in terms of direct action, of "doing something" for or about the people and their problems, of making decisions for the employees and then seeing that the decisions are carried out. Thus, they may be labeled as "fixer-uppers" who busily go about fixing up everyone else's affairs, who are never at a loss for a word of advice or cheerful encouragement. They are always making decisions as to how the disturbed employee should act, how he should feel, or how he should think, and then doing everything possible to get him to act, feel, or think in that way. We see them deciding whether the disgruntled worker has been unfairly treated; and if they feel that he has, then they tell him so and spring to his defense. But if not, they must show him where he is wrong in feeling that way; they must convince him by arguments and explanations, or change his mind by clever suggestion. And we see them constantly dealing with the superficial aspects, the symptoms, of the underlying problems, since it is always easier to do something about the manifest symptoms than it is to diagnose and act on the basic difficulties out of which they arise. Thus, it is always simpler to help the dissatisfied worker to transfer to another job than it is to get at the underlying causes of his dissatisfaction.

When we consider the problems with which these counselors are dealing, it would seem that they have a very important function in the organization. The real question, however, is not whether the problems are important but whether the techniques they use are effective in dealing with the problems. For that reason, it might be well to consider the techniques, the problems involved in their use, and their general effectiveness.

Ordinarily, personnel people, especially those in the counseling role, give little thought to the problems involved in the use of their most common tool, advice. If a worker has a home problem, they advise; if a foreman has trouble with his people, they advise; if a policy is wrong, they advise; whatever the problem, they pour out advice. In fact, most of them take it for granted that advice is an effective tool, that it will aid the individual in solving his problems and assist him in his adjustment. Yet if we are really to judge such a tool, we must answer two questions: first, "Is the advice any good; does it point to the proper action which should be taken?" and second, "Can the individual make use of it?"

In one type of questions which may be brought to the counselor, the correct answer requires only a simple type of knowledge; and the answers can be readily given and readily used. These usually deal with external situations or objects and require information more than anything else. For example, if the employee wants to know where to buy safety shoes, it is quite simple to give him the information. Or if he wants financial or legal advice, he can be referred to the proper experts. In such cases, the counselor merely has to have the knowledge himself or know where to obtain the information; in other words, he becomes a sort of information bureau. Actually, these questions do not present any real problem to the average employee, for if the counselor cannot give him the advice or information, someone else can. The really important problems, however, are the ones in which he is seeking help on matters which are of emotional importance to him. He is trying to decide whether he should get a divorce; he feels that his boss is unfair and wants to know what to do about it; he has been offered another job and cannot decide about it; or he thinks the company is not giving proper attention to the old-timers. In such problems the counselor faces the difficulty of understanding the underlying problem in all its complexities and knowing the individual so thoroughly that he can decide what is the proper advice for that person. Actually, most counselors rarely have the detailed and intimate knowledge necessary for such decisions, and they either make superficial judgments or else accept the decisions of the individuals. If a person wants a divorce, they may either accept that and tell him how to go about it; or they may listen to his story and on the basis of very inadequate facts decide that he is justified; or else they may try to show him that he is wrong in wanting a divorce. When we see the limited facts that the counselors have at their disposal and the extent to which they make decisions based on their own emotional reaction to situations, it becomes evident that a large portion of the advice showered upon the workers is inadequate or just no good.

In view of the deficiencies of the advice, it is probably fortunate that most of it is never taken. Time and again, personnel people are confronted with the sad realization that for all their good intentions workers rarely take their advice. No matter how often they tell workers to "cheer up" or not "be so sensitive," they rarely change their attitudes and go on being just as depressed and sensitive as ever. And if they tell a worker to talk it over with his boss, he is still reluctant to do so. In fact, examination of a great deal of evidence suggests that the only time direct advice is effective is when it is in accord with a decision which the individual has already been considering and about which he needs only a little reassurance to enable him to carry it out. Certainly, it is a matter of serious doubt whether the extensive use of advice as a tool for aiding the individual actually makes any serious change in his attitudes or behavior.

Reassurance as a Counseling Technique

Going hand in hand with advice, we see attempts at reassurance. The counselor tries to strike a cheery note and find some argument to show that "everything is going to be all right." Yet he continually finds that the individual does not feel reassured, although he may agree with the counselor at the moment for politeness' sake. We also find the counselor struggling to reassure the worker concerning the good will and intentions of the foreman or management; and, in spite of his efforts, the reassurance has only a momentary effect at best. In many cases, his efforts are interpreted by the workers as a defense of management; they place the counselor on the side of management and therefore not to be trusted. It has been found, too, that constant reassurance from the counselor tends to prevent the worker from talking freely about the way he feels or from expressing his own doubts. With either of the two reactions, the effect is to shut the worker up, so that the counselor can never get a clear picture of his feelings.

While much of this counseling work is quite new in the industrial field, work with similar problems has been going on for years in the fields of social work, child guidance, student counseling, and psychiatry. From this work, considerable knowledge has developed concerning the problems and the methods available for dealing with them. With regard to the value of such techniques as advising and reassuring, one authority says:

A third approach has been the use of suggestion, in the sense of reassurance and encouragement. To this approach belong such procedures as that of Coué and his notions of autosuggestion. Here also should be included the many techniques of reassurance used by counselors and clinicians the world over. The client is told in a variety of ways, "You're getting better," "You're doing well," "You're improving," all in the hope that it will strengthen his motivation in these directions. Shaffer has well pointed out that such suggestion is essentially repressive. It denies the problem which exists, and it denies the feeling which the individual has about the problem. It is not unusual for the clinician or counselor to make so many statements of approval and reassurance that the subject does not feel free to bring his less acceptable impulses to the clinical situation. While this approach is still used by many counselors, there is no doubt that faith in it has steadily declined.[1]

The same authority goes on to say further about the use of advice:

One commonly used type of psychotherapy is advice and persuasion. Possibly it might be called intervention. In this type of approach the counselor selects the goal to be achieved and intervenes in the client's life to make sure that he moves in that direction. We find extreme examples of it in certain radio "experts" who, after listening to a complex human problem for three or four minutes, advise the individual as to exactly what he should do. While every trained counselor is well aware of the viciousness of such an approach, it is nevertheless surprising how frequently this technique is used in actual practice. Often the counselor is unaware of how much advice he gives or the extent to which he does intervene in the life of the client. In any complete record of counseling, such phrases as "If I were you . . . ," "I would suggest . . . ," "I think that you should . . . ," occur very frequently.[2]

---

[1] Carl R. Rogers, *Counseling and Psychotherapy* (Boston: Houghton Mifflin Company, 1942), p. 21.
[2] *Ibid.*, p. 22.

In view of the limited effectiveness of these two techniques, it is interesting to consider why personnel counselors in industry continue to lean so heavily upon them. It might seem that when they were tried and found wanting, the counselors would discard them for something more effective. At least, we ordinarily assume that that is what happens, on the theory that man learns from his mistakes. Actually, there seem to be several difficulties which prevent the ready discard of these tools, one of the most important of which is that more effective tools are few and hard to come by. They are not acquired through reading a book nor do they often develop through trial and error; they must be learned through long and patient work under proper direction.

Advising and reassuring, furthermore, provide something very simple and tangible for the counselor to take hold of. Some one asks what to do and you tell him; he is depressed and you reassure him—all very simple and straightforward. At the same time, once you have offered the advice or reassurance you have done your duty; he now knows what to do and should feel encouraged; and the rest is up to him. If he does not follow the advice, or if he does not feel cheered up, the fault is his and not yours. Besides this, the role of advice-giver is quite a superior role. It sets the counselor above the weak mortals who come to him for answers; it is a great "builder-upper" for his sense of importance. Thus, it provides a very comfortable position for the counselor.

From the point of view of management, this presents a serious situation. If the counselor is expected to aid the worker in his emotional adjustment, if he is to relieve anxieties and disturbances in the work situation, it is not enough for him to follow methods which do not work. And if he does not learn by his mistakes but continues to cling to his ineffective methods because they provide him with personal satisfaction, it might be expected that management would rapidly lose confidence in the counselor's ability to perform his function and even in the effectiveness of the whole plan of counseling.

Communicating Company Policies

The communication of company policies and practices to employees presents a different sort of problem. In the past, many companies have relied upon the foremen to handle this sort of thing, with the idea that the foremen is closest to the workers and can easily answer their questions and make the necessary explanations. But with the growth of organizations and the increasing need for communicating company policies to employees, management has turned to other avenues for keeping employees informed. Management often expects the personnel organization to take the responsibility for such communication, to see that announcements of changes in rules or policies are posted on bulletin boards or distributed to the workers, or to answer questions directly. Under such conditions, if the worker has any questions concerning the policy on leaves of absence, on sickness pay, on merit rating, or any such matter, he may expect the personnel organization, and especially the personnel counselors, to give him the answers. Sometimes, when this is the case, the supervisors do not even attempt to give the answers but send the workers directly to the counselors for information.

Usually it is not enough for the counselor to supply information but he is also expected to justify the policies, to make the worker understand why they are—and convince him that they are—right and fair. If he attempts this, the counselor finds that he is continually defending management to the workers; he is trying to convince them of the fairness of management and the correctness of its judgment. As a result the workers feel that there is no use in going to him with their complaints, since he is really only concerned with defending management. It is very difficult for the counselor to explain and defend management and still retain the trust and confidence of the workers; and it becomes still more difficult when, as often happens, he does not himself agree with many of the rules and policies.

Communicating Worker Attitudes

The communication to management of the attitudes and problems of workers is even more difficult than communication to the workers; yet management is often very insistent upon it. Management often feels the need of some system of communication which will keep it in touch with the attitudes of workers; and it would, in fact, like to have a system which would bring weekly or monthly reports showing the morale of workers, comparable to reports on costs. Since the counselor is in constant contact with the workers and presumably has a relationship which enables him to know how they feel, he is picked to make such reports. Management also wants to know, via the counselors, just how its policies are being carried out and how the intermediate levels, especially the foremen, are functioning. Thus, the counselor is expected to function as a special channel of communication for information concerning human relations at the work level and a channel which can operate independently of the shop supervisory structure.

If the workers look on the counselor as someone to whom they can turn with their complaints and problems, and especially if they think of him as being on their side even against the foreman, the counselor will hear a lot of complaints involving supervisors or other workers. Each worker may come to him with complaints of unfair treatment, of friction in the group, of favoritism on the part of foremen, of lack of consideration for their problems and feelings, and so on. He may face a barrage of complaints, many of which are directed against the foreman and place him in an unfavorable light. As a rule, the counselor is sympathetic with these attitudes on the part of the workers; and he, in turn, is critical of the foremen. Then, when he reports back to management, he is likely to report the mistakes of the foremen, the things they do to upset the workers, and their inadequacies in handling human problems. This, of course, puts the foremen "on the spot" and creates anxieties on their part concerning the activities of the counselor. They may then develop defense tactics, take care in what they say to the counselor, try to discourage the workers from talking with him, and in talking to their superiors accuse the counselor of stirring up trouble, of encouraging the workers to complain, and of weakening the authority of the supervisors.

The counselor sees not only how the workers react to the supervisors but also their reaction to the company policies or practices determined by top management. If he sees adverse reactions, he is prone to be sympathetic with the workers' criticisms. He often feels that management does not take the workers' point of view into account, that it has a blind spot with regard to the things that matter to people. As a result he often attempts to communicate these criticisms to management and to suggest changes. If management does not respond to his suggestions, he feels frustrated and tends to be more critical of management. Such critical attitudes are not well received by management, of course, and the counselor, in turn, is likely to be rebuffed.

In attempting to communicate these human problems to management, the counselors are likely to fall into the same difficulties as the other specialists who emphasize their own point of view to the exclusion of others. Furthermore, their relation to the workers is usually such that they get the full impact of all disturbances and, to some extent, reflect the worker complaints. If, for example, a woman worker wants a leave of absence because her husband is taking a vacation and she wants to be with him, the counselor thinks of the request in terms of what it means to the woman, while the foreman or management think of all the job complications of letting the woman off or of the effect on the group if one is given a leave and the others refused. Or else the counselor may see the effects of a foreman's decisions without seeing all the factors which force him to make these decisions or the pressures which force him to act hastily and without enough forethought. As a result, the foreman frequently feels that the counselor sees only one side of the picture and fails to consider supervisory problems which the foreman must solve.

It is apparent that the personnel counselor is in a very difficult position. He is expected to be effective in aiding the adjustment of the workers; yet the tools with which he works are inadequate. He is expected to explain and justify the actions of management to the workers; yet he often feels that management does not understand the workers. He tries to communicate the problems of workers to management, and meets with suspicion on the part of supervisors. Decisions concerning policies and practices are made without him, and he feels that his knowledge is of no use. Thus, he often feels blocked and frustrated and ineffective in dealing with either management, supervisors, or workers. At the same time, he has considerable anxiety concerning the way he is being judged by his superiors; he worries about what management expects of him, and about how he can make a showing.

COUNSELING AT THE WESTERN ELECTRIC COMPANY

The Scope of the Work

Of all the work done in personnel counseling, that developed at the Hawthorne Plant of the Western Electric Company is by far the best known. Its whole history has been reported in great detail by those most active in its development and need not be described here.[3] This program and its techniques were developed as a result of research into problems of employee attitudes and work behavior in which the Western Electric Company and the Harvard Graduate School of Business Administration collaborated. This personnel counseling pro-

---

[3] Roethlisberger and Dickson, *Management and the Worker* (Cambridge, Mass.: Harvard University Press, 1939).

gram has been operating since 1936 and has gradually been extended to other plants of the Western Electric Company.

The whole industrial relations program of the company is well developed, with a high degree of specialization. At the same time the company has a wide variety of employee services and benefits; it provides for innumerable employee recreational and educational activities, and generally attempts to cover all aspects of employee relations. Thus, its personnel counseling is one element in an extremely well-developed industrial relations program and is not thought of as a substitute for proper selection, training, placement or wage policies.

As a result of extensive research, it was found that, in spite of the development of the customary tools of good personnel administration, there was still need for some methods whereby the individual could be assisted with the problems arising out of his relations with others and could be aided in either adjusting to his social environment or in taking effective action to modify it. This is, in effect, what many other counselors and personnel people are attempting to do through the use of advice and encouragement. Fortunately, however, this was seen as a very complicated problem involving the emotional adjustment of the individual and one which would not readily succumb to such direct approach. Instead, they developed as their major tool an interviewing technique which they found to be very effective in aiding the emotional adjustment of the individual and in helping him to deal effectively with his problems.

As we have seen, the individual brings with him to the work situation certain patterns of behavior, certain attitudes, hopes, and expectations. In adjusting to the work situation he must adjust to the needs of the job and the limitations it sets. In many cases, the adjustment requires considerable modification of his attitudes and expectations and often involves severe emotional disturbances. Even after this adjustment takes place, however, there are constant changes and stresses which may also give rise to disturbances. There may be changes in the individual's personal situation, in his relations with his family, friends, or neighbors. There may be stresses due to the ordinary pressures in the work situation. There may be changes in formal organization which affect the position of the individual, or technological changes which upset the work situation. Whatever the cause, all these things mean fresh adjustments on the part of the individual and more problems for him to solve.

While in many cases the adjustment required may be a relatively minor one amounting to little more than a change in attitude toward the situation, the experience at Western Electric Company has shown that during the process of adjustment the individual develops anxieties and preoccupations which lessen his work effectiveness, disturb his relations with others, and lower his morale. Furthermore, this seems to be true of all people regardless of job, status position, education, level of intelligence, or other factors, although undoubtedly some people react more strongly to those problems than others. This disturbed behavior is extremely annoying to others, especially the individual's superiors, since they feel that he should not be upset over what seem trifles to them. However, it is to these problems that the personnel counselor addresses himself, and he is not concerned over whether the individual *should* be disturbed, but is interested in helping him make the necessary adjustment.

The Interviewing Technique

In this work the counselor uses a technique in which the individual is allowed and encouraged to talk freely about those things which worry him. The counselor does not have a set of questions to which he wants answers; he does not try to get the individual to see things in a different light; he does not try to persuade or to encourage him. The counselor uses his skill to get the person to talk as freely as possible about the things which matter to him, and the counselor is intent on understanding what he has to say and the way he feels and thinks. Experience has shown that, if the individual can talk freely about his problems and disturbances, and especially if he can get below the surface aspects to the underlying factors, he becomes less disturbed and can act more effectively.

In order to enable the individual to talk so freely about things which may be very personal, or about which he feels some embarrassment in telling another person, or about feelings which are often considered "wrong," it is necessary for the counselor to conduct the interview very carefully. Unless properly handled, it may make the individual feel uncomfortable, or make him think that he is expected to give certain information or tell certain things to the counselor; and in such cases the interview is not usually very effective. The counselors must, therefore, be thoroughly trained in the interviewing technique before they can function properly. To aid this training, the organization has developed the following set of rules for interviewing:[4]

1. The interviewer should listen to the speaker in a patient and friendly, but intelligently critical, manner. This means that he is listening to what the other has to say with complete interest and attention. He is not listening with half an ear, with his thoughts on something else; he is intensely interested in every word and will not interrupt or cut the interview short. An "intelligently critical" manner does not mean that the interviewer is trying to see what is wrong but only that he wants the other to make things perfectly clear so that he is sure that he (the interviewer) understands what he is saying.

2. The interviewer should not display any kind of authority. He should not be in a position of authority, so that he is making decisions about the speaker; he must not have to do things to him, for him, or about him. If he has authority and must make decisions, then the individual talking to him will feel that he must say the right things and make the right impression, which will inhibit his talking freely and without anxiety.

3. The interviewer should not give advice or moral admonition. He should not attempt to advise or direct the other or to make decisions for him. Neither should he pass judgment on him. He should not point out what is right or wrong; he should never be shocked or critical, because such attitudes prevent the individual from talking freely.

4. The interviewer should not argue with the speaker. Any argument is in some way an attempt to direct his actions or his thinking or implies that he is wrong; and almost invariably it interferes with an effective interview. Furthermore, it often forces the individual to defend himself rather than to examine his attitudes and behavior. If allowed to talk things out he may often change, but argument seems only to reinforce the emotional attitudes and prevent change.

5. The interviewer should talk or ask questions only under certain conditions. He is there to listen to the other person and not to express

---

[4] A more detailed discussion of the interviewing method may be found in Roethlisberger and Dickson, *op. cit.*, chap. xiii, "The Interviewing Method."

Another discussion of the use of the interviewing method in dealing with problems of individual adjustment may be found in Rogers, *op. cit.*

It is significant that Rogers in his work in clinical psychology and Roethlisberger and Dickson in their work in industry independently developed identical interviewing techniques.

his own ideas, and everything he says or does should be to the end of making it possible for the other to talk freely. He may have to start the interview with a little social conversation to put the interviewee at ease. He may want to ask a few questions about the interviewee's job, or his family, or some other comfortable topic. He may have to explain his function as an interviewer, give assurance about the confidential nature of the interview, explain that he has no authority, or do whatever is necessary to relieve the interviewee of anxiety concerning the interview. He may want to express his interest in what is being said or his appreciation of the other's efforts in trying to make his meaning clear. He may need to ask questions to clarify some statement which he fails to understand. But whatever he says, it should be directed toward helping the other to talk more freely.

One of the important conditions of this type of personnel counseling is that the interviews be strictly confidential. The interviewee must be sure that the things he says will not be used against him in any way, that they will not be carried to his foreman nor to anyone else who will act upon them. Unless he is sure of this, he will always have his doubts about talking; there will be things which he dare not talk about, criticisms he dare not express. And if the counselor does fail to keep things confidential, sooner or later the workers begin to think of him as a "stool pigeon," a spy; and from then on they talk only in a superficial manner.

To the worker, the counselor stands in a unique relation. He is the one person to whom the worker can turn who is wholeheartedly interested in him and what he has to say, who is always friendly and sympathetic and never critical, who never tries to judge or direct but only tries to understand the way he feels. The counselor is the one person to whom it is safe to talk, to whom you can criticize your boss or your wife without worrying about it getting back to them, and to whom you can express your secret fears and weaknesses.

Effects of Interviewing

When we examine the effects of this upon the individual, we see several results of such interviewing. The first, and in many ways the most striking, effect is what is technically referred to as emotional release or catharsis, or, in the language of the shop, "blowing off steam" or "getting it off your chest." Often at the beginning of the interview a person may be emotionally disturbed, angry, in tears, extremely tense, or so upset that he can hardly talk coherently. He may dwell continually on some immediate disturbance, repeating over and over some story of mistreatment or worry about his relations with his superior or his family. As the interview proceeds, the nervous tension usually begins to disappear; he becomes more relaxed in posture and gestures; his speech becomes more coherent and less explosive, and his statements more rational and less emotional, until by the end of the interview he appears quite calm again. Such a change does not mean that the problem is solved or that adjustment has taken place, but it does indicate that the emotional tension has been relieved.

Another effect is that it helps to clarify the individual's thinking. When under severe emotional stress, the individual usually has difficulty in thinking through his problems; he jumps to conclusions, makes irrational interpretations, and rushes into actions which prove ineffective or even harmful. Thus, under the stress of the emotional disturbance he may interpret every act of his superior as indicating dislike or criticism and may magnify minor incidents until they seem to him to be major calamities. Or he may rush into drastic actions, such as going over his boss's head to accuse him of being unfair or prejudiced, demanding a transfer, or even quitting—actions which do not really solve his problems and may even make them worse. If through the interview the emotional stress is even temporarily relieved, the individual is able to see his problem more clearly and to think about it more rationally. Thus, as the interview progresses, the individual begins to re-examine his problem; the molehills of minor incidents no longer appear to be insurmountable mountains; he sees new angles and makes new interpretations. He may immediately make decisions as to what to do; or he may decide that no immediate action is necessary and that he should think things over some more, get further information, or await other developments. Sometimes his decision is not difficult to arrive at; it may even have been one which he has considered before but which he is able to accept and act on only after his emotional stress has been relieved.

This "problem-solving" effect may occur during the interview, or it may take place later. Often the interview seems to start the individual thinking through his problem; and though he may not arrive at any conclusion at the moment, he continues to consider it more clearly until finally he comes to some conclusion. In such cases the individual may tell the interviewer the next day that after thinking over the problem he has decided what to do. In many cases this problem-solving effect operates even where there is no particular emotional disturbance. In these cases, too, the free discussion of the problem helps to clarify the individual's thinking and leads to more effective decisions. Part of this effect seems to be due to the effort to make the problem clear, to explain it to another person, since by the time he has made it clear to someone else he sees it more clearly himself. This is often recognized by both workers and supervisors who will seek out the counselor to present some problem on which they are working, even though the counselor does not make suggestions nor try to direct their thinking.

In many cases it is surprising to note the speed with which the behavior of an individual is altered. Foremen often say to the counselor, "What do you do to them in these interviews? Why, Jack has been a changed man since you had him out this morning." Many times a person who, before the interview, has been noticeably worried or depressed, or a girl who had been crying and unable to work, is relieved and cheerful afterward and returns to the job with renewed vigor. Sometimes it is observed that output actually increases after an interview. In general, such obvious results are seen in those cases where the emotional tension is great and the change follows the relief from this tension. In some cases the operators themselves have commented that their efficiency decreases when under an emotional strain and improves again after an interview.

Another type of result is what may be called the "readjustment" or "reorientation" of the individual. This involves more than the momentary emotional relief or the solving of some immediate problem. It involves a general readjustment of the individual when he has been incapable of either achieving his own satisfactions or of adapting to the demands made upon him. Thus, the individual who has reached his ceiling but who is still seeking higher status and more recognition may be in such an agony of frustration that he is ineffective in his work or in his relations with others. In some cases the only possible solution may be an acceptance of his own limitations and the limitations of the job and an adjustment of all his hopes and expectations. In other cases the individual may be escaping from the realities of his situation by excessive drinking or by withdrawing from contacts with others. The readjustment of these individuals is, at best, a slow and difficult process. In still other cases, they are people who have been chronic problems for years, often growing progressively worse until their behavior can no longer be tolerated. To achieve adequate readjustment, such that they can continue as acceptable and normal workers, may require months or even years. Generally, however, a few weeks of repeated interviews will enable them to make sufficient improvement so that they can stay on the job. The heavy drinker will reduce his drinking temporarily; the anxiety cases will be somewhat relieved and able to put their minds on the job; insomnia disappears, and so on. This relief, even though temporary, allows time for the slow process of reorientation to begin.

Counselors and the Work Group

This discussion of the interviewing method might give the impression that the counselor is concerned only with the individual who is disturbed or maladjusted. Actually, he is constantly working with the entire group and takes care that he does not limit himself to problem cases. In fact, he is assigned to a particular territory which may comprise certain organizations or certain shop locations; and his job is to develop friendly relationships with every individual in that territory, to have frequent contact with each, and to have formal off-the-job interviews whenever possible. In this way he is constantly around and available whenever any of the group want to talk with him; and at the same time he is building up the kind of relationships which will enable them to talk freely to him. By giving attention to everyone, he is able to dispel the idea that only people in difficulties are interviewed, which in itself would prevent many people from going to him. Under these conditions, it is found that even the best-adjusted people from time to time face problems which are disturbing, or get involved in frictions within the group; and they benefit from the opportunity to have someone with whom they can talk.

When there is friction and disturbance within the work group, counseling can often ease the situation. In the first place, interviews with an individual tend to affect his relationships with others in the group. An improvement in the emotional equilibrium of the individual generally improves his relations with those around him and thus affects the entire situation. At the same time, the counselor is working with all the members of the group, relieving the emotional tensions, giving each of them a chance to talk about their difficulties with the others, voice their annoyances, and generally "blow off steam." When they talk to the counselor of these things, the talk does not aggravate the situation, as it may if they talk to one another, because the counselor does not repeat the talk nor become involved in the difficulties.

Counselor and the Foreman

Another important result of counseling at the Western Electric Company has been to improve the relationships between workers and supervisors. When he is active in the group, the counselor stimulates the supervisor to consider the effects of his own actions upon the workers. At the same time, the counselor keeps in touch with the foreman, encourages him to discuss his problems in dealing with the workers, and even interviews him. Also, in his interviews with the workers, he relieves emotional tension, so that the workers are better able to present their own problems to the supervisor and make themselves clear if they have complaints. As a result, the workers begin to feel that the foreman is actually concerned about them as individuals, and the foreman, in turn, gains a better understanding of his workers.

In order to gain the most benefits from counseling, the supervisor must make use of the counselor personally. Counseling is not something just for the workers but should be used by everyone in the situation. Experience demonstrated that when a supervisor discusses his problems and expresses his own emotional attitudes, when he talks about the way he feels and the way his people feel, he not only gains better understanding of his own problems but he sharpens his perceptions about the way his workers feel. When the counselor is able to work closely with the foreman as well as the workers, there is invariably an improvement in the whole situation.

APPLICATIONS OF THE INTERVIEWING TECHNIQUE

Although the interviewing technique has been applied at the Western Electric Company primarily as a tool for the personnel counselors, it has also proved to be of considerable value for other personnel people and for foremen and supervisors. There and elsewhere, attempts have been made to train others in the basic concepts and techniques of these interviewing methods, and it has been found a very useful tool for anyone who deals with people. It is safe to say, in fact, that whenever a person tries consistently to apply this point of view in dealing with other people, he finds that his relationships improve and that he is able to act more effectively. For that reason, all personnel people, whatever their duties, should try to understand the method and develop skill in its use; and they should not make the mistake of dismissing it because their particular role does not provide the most satisfactory conditions for its use.

Probably one of the most important ideas which most people obtain from training in this method is the realization that they must understand other people to be effective in dealing with them and that they can get this understanding only by listening to what they have to say. Closely allied with this is the realization that arbitrary orders, logical arguments, or exhortations do not change a person's attitudes nor convince him that he is wrong. Unfortunately, we see supervisors, engineers, personnel people, and others continually trying to win arguments, gain co-operation, or change attitudes through these devices. Once they stop trying to sell their ideas and point of view and try instead to understand the other person, they find that the attitudes of the other toward them changes and they obtain much better co-operation.

With the training comes, too, the realization that one has to get below the surface of complaints, antagonisms, lack of co-operation, and similar difficulties in order to know what to do about them. Those in positions of authority are accustomed to taking complaints at their face value and dealing with them at that level. If a subordinate complains that he needs more money, or that the work is too hard, or his machine is no good, his superior usually accepts that as an accurate statement of what is thought to be wrong, and he either corrects the condition, tries to prove that his subordinate is mistaken, or decides there is nothing he can do about it. If the subordinate refuses to accept such actions, he is labeled as a "griper" who cannot be satisfied and must therefore be ignored. Once the supervisor realizes that there may be other things behind the manifest complaints, and that by interviewing he may get to the real root of the problem, then he is encouraged to try to deal with these difficulties instead of avoiding them. Not only do these efforts enable him to handle complaints more effectively, but his increased interest in trying to understand his subordinates improves his relations with them and reduces the frictions and disturbances growing out of the supervisor-subordinate relation.

19. EXECUTIVE PERSONALITY AND ORGANIZATION

RELATION OF EXECUTIVE PERSONALITY TO ORGANIZATION

WHEN examined as a structure, any organization has a pattern which is independent of the individuals in it. Furthermore, this pattern is one to which the individual must adapt himself. In spite of this, management is continually facing the problem of the effect of individual personality upon the organization; and, in many cases, adjustments in the organization must be made to adapt it to the personalities of key individuals.

This interrelation between personality and organization is especially important in the top positions, where the actions and thinking influence the whole organization. In fact, in many cases it can be said that "the organization is the lengthened shadow of a man." This is especially true of the business that has been developed through the energy and initiative of one man—an organization that is inevitably an expression of himself, his likes and dislikes, and his judgment. For example:

One small manufacturing company was founded by a very able man who built it up into an extremely profitable business. He was the kind of man who lived the business; when it started, he knew every detail and made every decision; and, as it grew, he still made the decisions—he ran it, and everyone knew it. At the same time, he liked people; he was very tolerant of their weaknesses, and took a very paternal attitude toward his organization. Out of this grew the kind of organization in which he, himself, made all significant decisions, planned for the future, and felt it was his responsibility to take care of the others. He had under him only people of average ability, who would sit back and let him do the thinking. They were quite content to carry out his orders, but rarely came up with any real ideas themselves. Furthermore, if an employee or supervisor had been with the company long, he was "part of the family" and must be taken care of—which meant also that he had to be very inefficient to get fired. Thus, he had a loyal organization but one without much drive and, in the supervisory and management levels, people of only mediocre ability.

This case is fairly typical of many small and medium-sized firms. They are essentially "one-man shows" in which the dynamic individual who built them maintains tight control and develops a dependent organization. In fact, in many cases he is so essential that, when he dies or retires, there is no one able to carry on the business and, unless new management is imported, it will fail. In many cases, this weakness in management explains the failure of firms that have been successful for years and then seem suddenly to decline.

Another such case was the following, that of an independent creamery company in a medium-sized city:

The owner had built up and maintained a very profitable business in spite of strong competition from the big corporations. Then, one day he went to the president of one of these large companies and offered to sell out and stay on as their manager. When asked why he wanted to give up his profitable business, he explained that he had a bad heart and might soon be forced to retire. With this in mind, he had examined his organization and found that, while he had some able men who could carry out his plans, he did all the thinking and planning. Without him, he knew that the organization could not hold its own against the alert competition of rival companies.

INTEGRATING KEY EXECUTIVES INTO A WORK TEAM

The problem of any management, then, is one of building an executive group which will be an effective team and which will not be dependent upon the leader. The effective team is not usually one in which the individuals are all alike in personality or ability. In some cases, a combination of the cautious and conservative with the expansive and enthusiastic makes a more effective team than an executive group with all one type or the other.

For example, in retail stores, particularly in large chain operations, there is a general type of organization (see Fig. 16). The merchandise manager is primarily concerned with selling. He plans sales events, develops promotional ideas, watches sales figures, etc. He is generally enthusiastic and full of ideas and is often impatient with details, especially those of budgets, cost control, etc. On the other hand, the operating superintendent is concerned with the control of store property. He sees that the store is kept clean, that lights are turned on, that repairs are taken care of, that the necessary personnel is available when needed. He must understand accounting and office methods and

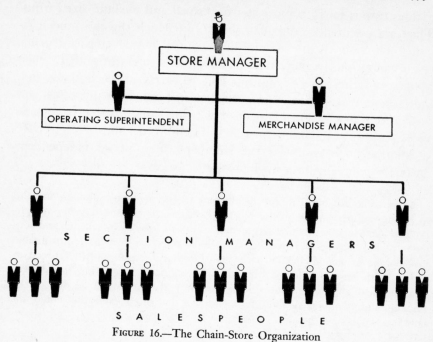

FIGURE 16.—The Chain-Store Organization

routines. He tends to have a sharp eye for routine details and, especially, for costs.

Now, the store manager is, in effect, the over-all co-ordinator between the two activities. He must be imaginative in selling, yet concerned with costs; he must be able to use good judgment on both sides. If his background is strictly the sales and merchandising side of the business, he is likely to be, both by temperament and experience, a merchandiser. He will tend to be a "loose" operator, who will be impatient with the details of running the store or keeping within the budget. In such a case, he should have a strong, experienced operating superintendent who will not be afraid to insist on his point of view. However, he can manage with a weak or inexperienced merchandise manager, since he will devote much of his own time to that side of business.

On the other hand, if the store manager came up as an operating superintendent, he may run the store beautifully in terms of housekeeping, costs, records, etc.; but he is likely to be weak on merchandising. He probably will have a smoothly operated store, but one which isn't selling merchandise. This type of man should have a strong merchandise manager, one who could stand up and argue for his side and who could fight to get an adequate advertising budget, special sales promotions, etc.

PERSONALITY OF SUCCESSFUL EXECUTIVES

Now, this matter of the effective organization team goes beyond the question of experience or technical ability. Also to be considered is the personality structure of the executive, which affects the way he will function in a given position or in relation to other individuals. For one thing, there are certain personalities that find it very hard to adjust to subordinate roles; and there are others that have difficulty in functioning independently. This area of executive personality and the problems involved have been well presented by Dr. William E. Henry of the University of Chicago in a speech before the American Management Association.[1] He said:

The man who runs a machine has a comparatively simple task in front of him. While his job may require advanced degrees of skill or may demand extremes of physical endurance, it is still a simple job. It is simple in that the skills and preciseness which it may require of him take only a small part of his attention and utilize only a segment of his total potential skills and abilities. Those skills which the machine job does utilize tend to be manual in nature and to stress adeptness in physical movement. But the job leaves untouched and unused the abilities that lie in the areas of *ideas*, in the area of *dealing with people*, and in the area of *complex planning for future action*.

Further, the man on the machine job requires and can generally be taught, several fairly specific manual skills. These skills he can practice and he can finally become adept at them. Once he has learned these skills to a high degree of competence, he is a success in his job. As long as he stays in this particular job, these skills will be his mainstay—he will use them in the same way from day to day, varying them only for some emergency or mechanical irregularity in his machine.

But once he leaves that job and that machine, he must start again to learn new skills and new techniques of dealing with his new job and new machine.

The man who holds an executive job is in a quite different position. The skills which make him a success tend not to be specific to that given job nor to be readily learned on the job. They tend rather to be generalized abilities that have been a long time developing. They tend, further, to be the kind of abilities that frequently are useful in both professional and social situations. These abilities are generally adaptable to executive positions in a wide variety of business and industrial fields.

In contrast to the man at the machine, the executive underplays specific skills and stresses generalized knowledge. His greatest abilities lie in the areas

---

[1] Dr. William E. Henry, "Executive Personality and Job Success," American Management Association, Personnel Series No. 120.

of *ideas*, of *dealing with people*, and in *complex planning for future action*. These complex skills of the executive take a great part of his potential energy and abilities—they call heavily upon all his adjustment possibilities, both during and after office hours.

It is for these reasons that the proper study of executive ability and job performance is not centered about specific job skills, but about the total functioning executive, the executive as a professional and social individual, the executive as an individual personality.

In our research efforts to discover the attributes of the successful executive, and hence to assist us in the selection of better executives, we have investigated the personality of some 300 executives in various types of business and industrial firms. These studies have to date shown us several things:

First, there is a personality configuration, a personality type, that makes the best executive.

Second, where failure has occurred, it can be traced directly to certain personality characteristics.

Third, the presence of certain personality characteristics is of as vital importance as the presence of certain intellectual characteristics.

Fourth, the role of the executive in modern business has both its own rewards and its own punishments. One of the greatest hazards of the executive's job is not possible failure, but the chance that success will double back on the executive and make him pay personally for his own success.

Fifth, this personality configuration is a matter of long-time development. Parts of it have been in progress since childhood and in fact may depend upon what happened to them during their early years.

Sixth, the successful utilization of this personality type depends to a large extent upon the nature of the social situation in which the executive finds himself. The interpersonal relations on the job may help or hinder the individual executive and will alter the importance of certain of the personality attributes.

EXECUTIVE CHARACTERISTICS

Let me discuss some of the characteristics of the executive as we found them. These, in a sense, comprise the personality pattern of an executive. They are the characteristics that seem to us the most important in the executive personality configuration, which seem to have contributed most to success in the executive role, which are present most frequently in the personalities of those individuals whom we would call successful in this area.

We are all familiar with the generally accepted social stereotype of the executive. He is first of all the man who always wears the pin-stripe suit. Second, he is the man who always arrives at quick, trigger decisions every morning. There are several other aspects to this stereotype, one of them being ulcers at a later age.

Desire for Achievement. The first characteristics which we struck upon was what might be called strong achievement desire. By this I mean that most of these executives had internally built feelings that they must accomplish something, they must do something—and not only must they do something but they must do something more and they must do it faster than anybody else. This I would distinguish from the sort of pseudo achievement drive which is found in many not-too-successful executives, shown by a feeling of delight in the final accomplishment.

The successful executives are not those who are most proud of the final accomplishment; they were far prouder of the fact that they are doing it, and that they are going to be doing something tomorrow. The real executive achievement desire is a matter of the constant day-to-day feeling that one must accomplish, one must achieve, and that at any moment there will be something else to be done. While this feeling motivates toward accomplishment, I think we can also say that it presents hazards for the executive.

(2) *The Mobility Drive.* The characteristic which is closely related to the achievement desire is a strong mobility drive. That is, each of these men strongly feels the need, not only to do something, but to move upward. They are not too sure what upward means or where they are going when they move upward, but they must move upward in some sort of hierarchy. This is one reason why titles have become so important in the executive area, I think.

If one can become a second vice president in charge of something instead of a third vice president, this is good because it is better than something else. The need for some concrete demonstration of successful mobility within a hierarchy of some sort is involved here, in my opinion.

(3) *The Social Mobility Drive.* Another area of mobility drive which I would distinguish somewhat from that shown in the executive job hierarchy is what you might call the social mobility drive. Among many individuals who show some interest in mobility outside the job situation—and particularly among vice presidents, we found—are men who seem to be largely motivated to social status, often by their wives. Their notion of mobility involves not becoming vice president instead of second assistant, but having a bigger house in a better community, being seen at a better club and in a better car. This type of mobility drive can often be disastrous if it is isolated—i.e., if it occurs without the other type of achievement and hierarchy mobility drive.

I might mention as an example one executive who worked in a large corporation, who was asked to take the tests. He did, and the tests revealed that he was smart, that he had all the necessary skills and the techniques for his position, that he had years of experience and training. However, he had not been promoted for about five years, and the general manager of the concern wanted to know why. He himself did not know why he had not been promoted. Yet he had come up for consideration every two or three months for a promotion.

Everybody would agree that he was swell—"a good guy, a great guy, knows his job, has years of experience in his field. Let's promote him." They never quite knew how, but when they got to the end of each meeting and were reading the minutes afterward, it would turn out that this fellow had gotten a $200 increase but no promotion. Every so often they would give him a token raise, but no one was really willing to commit himself to promote the man.

The reason for it was revealed in his test results. Here was a man whose primary preoccupation was the social symbols of success. It was far more important to him to have a title than to do the work. It was also far more important for him to leave the office at five o'clock because his wife had managed to invite the president of another organization for cocktails and it didn't make too much difference whether the work got done but it was important that he get home at five-thirty for the cocktail party.

There was a whole series of strong indications of these particular special interests in social mobility. For example, he was the kind of person who never admitted that he worked for anybody else. He assumed himself to be the top of the hierarchy and he was always looking down. Once I casually remarked to the manager that when this fellow came into his office it must be something like going to a social tea rather than to a conference of business men. This seemed to strike home with the general manager, who said, "Every time this man has come into my office, I have felt that I have been visiting him."

Attitude toward Authority Figures. Another attitude which was conspicuously characteristic of the executive was the feeling toward authority—the tendency to regard authority as a controlling and helpful force. By authority, I mean everything from the chairman of the board to the individual's father, the policeman on the block, and other general socially stereotyped symbols of authority. The individual among those studied who looked toward these authority figures as people who are out to get him or people who are really occupying jobs which he himself should have, seemed usually to run into difficulty at these points.

Most of the successful executives we studied look toward authority figures as helpful, controlling figures. Authority figures might be people who were perhaps more erudite, more experienced, but they were still essentially people who guide others, who form them, who are interested in assisting their subordinates. Those who felt that the authoritative figures around them were prohibiting and destructive forces constantly got into difficulty in the job situation, either by overt resistance or in some more obscure fashion.

The "Self-Made" Man. One other special example concerns a man whom we used to call "the self-made man"—the individual who looks to himself as the ultimate authority, who cannot look up the line to others of greater power, but who conceives of himself as the top of the hierarchy. This particular individual is a good example of the relationship of personality configuration to the social setting in which he finds himself.

The man I am thinking of was put up for consideration as the head of a plant. The job was a good one. It paid something like $20,000 a year. The candidate was tested and one thing emerged clearly in the test results. He had absolutely no concept of authority above him. This is fine if you are working in an organization where you are the top; but it is bad if you are working in an organization which places great emphasis upon teamwork and cooperative endeavor. It was with considerable difficulty that the organization decided against taking this man on our recommendation. They decided against him largely on faith and then proceeded to investigate.

Everyone said, "Wonderful man, great guy." Everyone thought he was swell. Then the vice president in charge of personnel visited the people who had written the letters of recommendation. The conversations—about four of them—went something like this:

"I've come to ask you about John Smith."

"Oh, yes. A great guy. I hear he's working for you. He's a good man. You'll like him."

"Well, what is the matter with him?"

"Oh, nothing—nothing. Great guy."

"Then why isn't he working for you?"

"Well, he is a great boy, but no one will work with him."

Which was the essence of the diagnosis! He is a great guy—he is informed, he is competent. But no one will put up with him. It was a matter of either having him run the whole organization and firing all the other vice presidents or getting rid of him. The company chose the latter procedure. The difficulty was, unless this man was the one who had the original idea and unless his original idea was carried out as he planned it, he was not interested. The notion of other people's ideas and cooperation with others related to another area of authority was foreign to him.

I should mention the real finish of this case. It seemed obvious to us that in any kind of cooperative organization this man would be a failure. Upon our recommendation to him, he went into business for himself, where he, of course, was top dog and was doing all the directing. In the past three years, he reports, he has made a quarter of a million dollars.

Failure, then, is a purely relative concept, and depends upon the system of values within which it is defined.

 Decisiveness. Another interesting aspect of the executive's personality, one which I consider a double-barreled characteristic, is a general notion of decisiveness, the ability to arrive at a decision. This is almost a popular stereotype, but it appears to be a true stereotype. It may be that the decision is "I don't know, but I'll find out." But the general ability to arrive at this kind of decision is a most important means of spotting the successful executive. He is able to come to some sort of decision, even though it may be the decision that he needs more information.

Once this particular characteristic of the executive breaks down, his superiors become very queasy about him. He can do almost anything else, but once he gets to the point where he becomes indecisive or doesn't quite know what he is going to do—the point where he isn't sure what is going to happen tomorrow or isn't sure what his facts mean—his superior feels, "We have got to get rid of him. We're not sure about him—he may collapse at any moment. We've just got to get rid of him."

Useless Decisiveness. An interesting point about the factor of decisiveness is that the constant ability to arrive at a decision does not stop when there is no decision to arrive at or a decision cannot be arrived at on the basis of what the executive knows about the situation. A company president may have been so in the habit of arriving at decisions, for instance, that he keeps right on arriving at them, although he may be using a technique outmoded for 20 years or may be arriving at decisions which would have been appropriate to a growing organization but are useless in an established organization. The ability to arrive at a decision persists and the man continues to arrive at decisions even when his judgment is bad or when his information may be outdated. This appears to be one of the difficulties reported by executives handling conferences with some vice presidents. Many of them comment, "There is no real point in a conference with this vice president because no matter what the problem and no matter what the facts, the solution he presents is going to be the same." This negative aspect of the ability to arrive at a decision, if unmodified, if it cannot constantly be re-adapted to new situations, begins to get in the executive's way and everybody else's way.

(6) *Blocks to Mobility.* The individual whose mobility in the job situation is blocked, either because mobility is not readily afforded by the organization or because the techniques used by the individual or the presence of certain disabilities prevent him from being promoted, is in a situation of considerable frustration in which difficulties arise. These difficulties may be physical or psychological. Men in such situations are the ones who most readily develop ulcers, who most readily develop all sorts of physical symptoms which are in constant need of treatment. These are the situations in which disruptions of procedure take place most easily, which most readily develop quarrels, where the executive is most likely to find himself in the position of forcing decisions down the throats of other people simply to prove that he can do it.

(7) *Assertiveness.* One other characteristic of the successful executive is a strong feeling of assertiveness. By this I do not mean that such men are always shouting around (although many of them do), but they do reveal a general emotional orientation toward activity, toward asserting their own points of view, toward making known what they feel. In general they make overt and act out their own feelings and their own convictions. It is another reflection of the feeling that they must be moving, they must be doing, they must be on their way, they must be active in every situation—at least emotionally active, not necessarily physically active.

As a matter of fact, I might say that most of the executives having this characteristic get to the point where they are also physically active, pacing the floor or engaging in some other physical movement like the constant twirling of some object or constant motion of the feet. Those executives who do not act out this motivation drive are usually the ones who act out internally, which means abdominal disorders and many similar psychosomatic symptoms. This characteristic, like the ability to make a decision, is also a drive that cannot be turned off. It becomes most obvious during what executives call "vacations."

Not long ago I was visiting a director of personnel. I asked if we could arrange another meeting. Well, no, we couldn't have a meeting next week because he was going on a vacation. He was all excited about that vacation. What was he going to do? Well, he had it in his desk drawer—a great long list: "Now, at 3:03 on Tuesday I arrive in Miami. At 3:25 on Tuesday I am ensconced in the Hotel Dah-dee-dah. At 3:45 I have hired a fishing boat, and at 3:47 the captain is ready and we are off. At 5:02 I have caught a tuna and am back at a cocktail party at 5:56. . . ." And so forth. This man was simply transferring his complete personality orientation and being an executive about fish. Also he will be most disappointed if the fish are not cooperative.

This is only one example of the hazards I mentioned—one of the built-in punishments of the individual in the executive type of role that he cannot avoid unless early in life (and by early, I mean 20) he starts a systematic technique toward not being an executive in those situations where there is no point in being an executive.

The Fear of Failure. Another factor, closely related to the factor of assertiveness, is a general one which I would call apprehension, or fear of failure. I should say that this fear runs through the personality organization of the executive in varying degrees. It is a constant apprehension that all will not be the same tomorrow. In any situation in which doing more, doing better, getting more, getting places, getting there faster, is important, this personality factor is important. This constant fear runs through the personalities of even the successful executives. This feeling of the perpetually unattained plagues the executive and motivates him further toward success and at the same time toward increased apprehension.

The Reality Orientation. Another characteristic of most of the executives we studied I will simply call strong reality orientation. This is what we usually term "practicality" in the business situation. I would like to remark on one aspect of this characteristic, again to emphasize the fact that most of these characteristics have polar expressions: One of the hazards in the executive situation is being too practical, in the sense that no one was ever a man of vision who couldn't get his nose off the ground and see what might be over the next hill. An individual with a strong reality orientation, with a tendency to look always at the facts, has great difficulty in imagining what the facts *might* be. This again is one of the viewpoints that seem to characterize most of our executives—a feeling not so much of what the facts will be as an emphasis upon what the facts are and have been.

Carry-Over of Childhood Ties. An attitude which I think quite intriguing is the executive's feeling about his own childhood. I might say here that most of the characteristics of development of this personality configuration of the general executive type are by no means characteristics he has acquired since he became an executive. Many of these characteristics are found in many other people, in different configurations, and are subject to quite a long period of development.

For example, the executive's general attitude toward his own parents has come out in our test situations. In a sense the successful executive is a man who has left home. He is a man who has broken the binding emotional ties to the parental relationship. In general, these men are first of all men who have broken the binding emotional ties to their mothers. Every man in the executive situation who has felt that his mother was still the center of the universe (a feeling that everybody has initially but which is presumably discarded by the age of 20 or so, though frequently not) has been a failure in the executive role.

On the other hand, we find that the feelings of the man who does not break, but maintains, a positive identification with his father or with the general notion of a father seem to warrant success in the executive role. This identification seems to characterize positively those individuals who maintain themselves in executive spots. This does not mean that the executive in question may not be living with his mother-in-law or his mother. But it does mean that *he* runs the house and not she.

THE SPECIFIC-QUESTION TYPE OF TEST

The techniques which were used in our survey can best be described by contrast. We have all had the experience of making out an application for a job or an application to get our child in a nursery school or some similar experience. You come into an office. You sit down. You meet Mr. So-and-so, the director of personnel, or Miss So-and-so, the head of the nursery school, who hands you a little piece of paper and says, "Sit down and fill this out." So you sit down.

Then you look at the form. There are many questions: "What is your name?" "What is your address?" and a few other seemingly innocent questions. Then you see a question like "Do you feel dizzy when you stand at the top of a high building and look off?" Well, being alive and inclined to stay that way, you say to yourself, sure I do. You had better mark that one "Yes."

Another question: "Do you like to be alone or mingle in groups?" You think a moment. You say to yourself, yes, you like to be alone. But that is bad. That makes you a recluse. You have to be careful. On the other hand, if you say no, you prefer to be in groups, this makes you incurably gregarious, so you had better watch yourself there.

There are other questions, like "Do you love your mother better than your father?" Now being a product of middle class society, you know very well you are supposed to love them both equally, all the time. And if you do not, you are thrown to the psychoanalyst.

The particular techniques involving specific questions, the answers to which are reasonably automatic and evaluated in advance, give the individual respondent practically no leeway. That is, he can say "Yes," or "No." In some he can say "Maybe," but in general this is all the freedom of response he has. You are asked to decide on an already determined issue, the answer to which is already evaluated, which means in a sense that you are already determined by the examiner. This is a somewhat arbitrary, perhaps unfair, caricature of the specific-question type of test which I am using to describe the kind of tests we have been using in our investigation of the executive.

PROJECTIVE TECHNIQUES

The instruments we used are precisely the reverse. The response on the part of the subject is natural. He decides what the issue is, he decides what to think about it, he decides what is involved, he decides what the solution might be. The techniques used in this kind of test are called projective techniques of personality study and are exemplified by two specific instruments, the Rorschach, or ink-blot test, where the individual looks at a series of ink blurs and tells you what each one looks like to him; and the Thematic Apperception Test, or T.A.T.

The T.A.T. is a comparatively simple instrument. It is simply a series of pictures. The first picture, actually, is that of a boy seated at a desk. In front of him lies a violin. The violin is lying on something that might be a sheet of paper, it might be a tablecloth, it might be a sheet of music. It is not clear what it is. The individual taking the test is asked to tell a story about this picture, a story he makes up himself. He paints an entire drama about the picture himself.

There are from 10 to 20 pictures in this particular series, depending upon the examiner using it. Each of these pictures represents some different aspect of social and personal life. Most of the pictures are quite reasonable, representing events in an individual's life which he may well have encountered or which are at least familiar in type.

Anyone with a half-hour's instruction could administer this test. The trick, unfortunately, is in its interpretation, for it is through the interpretation of the spontaneous remarks made about these pictures that we have derived our pictures of the successful executives. It is these pictures which we are constantly using in the effort first, to describe the personality configuration of the individual and then, given this personality configuration, to say in what particular job area he would find himself most adaptable—in what kind of social situation he would find success the easiest.

I may remark in this context that the more we know about the informal aspects of the social situation into which a man will be put, the better our diagnosis, and the better our predictions as to the potential area of success and the potential area of failure for the particular individual.

The techniques used in the T.A.T., I think, are going to turn out to be the most useful ones in the area of gauging a man's potential. They are techniques, unfortunately, which take considerable experience to work with. They are also techniques which look like so much nonsense as you initially perceive them. But the only thing that is going to demonstrate that they are increasingly worthwhile techniques is their constant use in situations where we can check repeatedly on our diagnoses, where we can follow an individual through his job career, constantly referring back to the various kinds of observations—the anecdotes, the descriptions, and the various other procedures—we have made of his actual job performance.

Conclusion

In general, it is becoming increasingly apparent from our studies based on the technique I have described that many of the characteristics which are features of the successful executive are personality characteristics—personality characteristics which are descriptive of the total personality of the individual executive. They have developed during a comparatively long period of his life span. They are not techniques which are learned easily from a job situation.

I do not mean to imply by this conclusion that the individual executive cannot be trained. I do not mean he cannot learn or that he cannot become a better executive by constant experience on the job. I mean only that unless this general configuration of personality characteristics is apparent, he will always have difficulty in the executive situation.

EFFECTIVE USE OF PERSONALITY TYPES
IN ORGANIZATION

The whole problem is not solved merely by determining the personality patterns of successful executives. While successful executives do show certain traits, the real problem is determining how these traits relate to the effective functioning of the individual in his work situation—that is to say, successful executives will not all be equally effective in any work situation; and some who are highly effective in certain jobs may fail in other jobs or may succeed only at excessive cost to themselves.

Thus, it is a matter of common observation that many very successful research directors would fail as sales managers. Furthermore the star salesman often does not make a good sales manager. Also, the good production manager, accustomed to direct action in getting the work out, is often weak as an industrial relations director where he cannot use authority to accomplish his ends but must, through hours of discussion, attempt to influence others.

His attitudes toward authority are an extremely important element in the executive. There are some brilliant and able people who are constantly rebellious toward higher authority. They have difficulty in taking orders or accepting guidance and must always do things their own way. For such men, the average large company presents a very confining structure; there are too many people over them, too many do's and don'ts; and they often waste their energy in reacting against the organization. On the other hand, they are often very effective as heads of small organizations, or as professional men or consultants, where they can stand or fall on their own performance without hindrance by a boss.

At the other extreme are those completely submissive to authority. They expect to be controlled; they never doubt the right of their superior to direct them. They are the "good soldiers," who never question authority or orders. These can work comfortably in large organizations, under strong authority and tight control. But just put them on their own, where they must be self-directing; and they are likely to be anxious and indecisive and ineffective.

Between these two extremes lies the usual executive. He can accept authority and see superiors as people who are helpful and friendly and not hostile. He will not be completely docile in accepting their decisions but will judge for himself. He feels that he can make decisions and should be allowed to do so. Thus, he can accept the leadership of able superiors and be a loyal and eager supporter. But he will reject autocratic or incompetent superiors and seek to go his own way.

Another significant characteristic is found in one's feelings toward people. Some individuals are not at ease in dealing with people and prefer to deal with objects or records. Many research men and engineers are of this type; they are more interested in machines or processes than in people, and they feel better able to deal with nonhuman problems. As a result, they tend to ignore the human problem or feel harassed by them. They also try to work out some formula, such as incentive systems or detailed procedures, with which to eliminate or control the workers. Where this tendency is strong, the individual is unsuited for major supervisory jobs and should stick to technical problems.

As an example of this type of individual:

A young engineer was brought into a small manufacturing company. He started out in charge of a small department on very technical work. Here he worked with a small group of men, all technicians or highly skilled mechanics who knew their jobs and worked with a minimum of supervision. In this spot he did an excellent job in solving difficult problems. The actual supervisory work was minimal; and, as long as the men knew their jobs, he left them alone.

He was then promoted to head a regular production department with a lot of low-skilled workers, both men and women. Within a few months, management noticed that the department was in trouble: turnover was increasing; there were lots of complaints; production was down. When questioned, he blamed it on the poor quality of workers, complaining that they had to be driven or they wouldn't work, etc.

The personnel manager began to observe the department. He heard complaints from other foremen that this engineer couldn't get along with anyone and didn't know how to handle his people. He visited the department and found the head of it spending a lot of time at his own desk or out of the department. On one occasion a group of girls were having a hot argument in one end of the department, and practically all had stopped working. Instead of being there trying to get things straightened out, the department head was at the other end of the room, helping a mechanic set up a new machine. He gradually withdrew more and more from contacts with the workers and finally quit the job.

In an effort to find out why he was failing, the company arranged for him to be tested. The report showed that he was of high intelligence, well-suited for work on purely technical problems. He was, however, ill at ease with people, very critical of them, and would have great difficulty in his interpersonal relations. He would work comfortably with others only if he could deal with them almost entirely in terms of technical problems and did not have to give attention to them as human beings.

We cannot attempt to cover all the intricacies of personality as they relate to executive and supervisory effectiveness. However, management is constantly dealing with the problems of personality among key personnel, whether it understands them or not. Since the organization is built of people, the personality differences among people must constantly be considered. Thus, we find thoughtful management giving careful attention to such problems whenever considering shifts in executive personnel or changes in organization. Such management will try to anticipate the problems of personality as they affect the organization and will make many adjustments with those problems in mind.

1. Desire for achievement
2. Social drive
3.

20. HUMAN RELATIONS AND MANAGEMENT

IN THIS part of the book, we shall outline our observations concerning the problem of managerial leadership. We shall be concerned, however, not so much with techniques and tools of management, but rather with the over-all behavior and attitudes that constitute leadership in industrial organizations. As a matter of fact, there are no specific rules that can be passed along to management which, if followed, will invariably result in improved morale among employees. Managerial leadership is essentially an art based on a certain attitude of mind about human relations. Like any art, it cannot be taught as a mathematical formula or a mechanical process. It must be inculcated and infused into the very spirit of management so that all or most managerial behavior reflects the underlying attitudes and point of view on which it is based.

INTERNAL AND EXTERNAL PROBLEMS OF ORGANIZATION

We have seen that a business or industry can be viewed as an integrated whole, or as a social organism in which there is a continuity of activity and a constant process of adaptation to change. This process of adaptation is both external and internal. Any business exists within the larger framework of the total social and economic environment of which it is a part. It functions within the given economic system and must survive as a functioning economic unit. It must constantly adjust itself to the impact of economic changes, of technological developments, of governmental and legal controls, of the forces of public attitudes and opinions, and of all the forces operating within the society.

However, to meet these demands of the external social and economic world, a business or industry must maintain a well-integrated internal organization. No economic enterprise can survive for long if its internal structure is shaky and inefficient. When problems of industrial strife and conflict begin to absorb most of the energies of employees on all levels in an organization, it no longer is in a position to meet and solve the problems of the broader environment of which it is a part.

In this connection, the problem of the internal integration of an organization is very similar to the problem of personality integration. An individual personality can be regarded as well integrated when it can deal with the problems of reality without being impeded and hampered by internal emotional conflicts. The neurotic person is one who is so bound up with emotional difficulties and conflicts that he is unable to make adequate adjustments to the demands of the external world. Many industrial organizations can be regarded in this sense as "socially neurotic." They are so bound up with internal conflicts and administrative difficulties that they are no longer able to make adequate adjustments to the demands of the external social and economic worlds. The energies of the organization become almost completely absorbed in industrial strife and personal antagonisms; there are not sufficient resources left in the organization to deal intelligently with the larger problems which it must solve if it is to survive and grow.

It is apparent from these observations that one of the most important problems management faces is that of building sufficient co-operation and teamwork throughout the organization so that the energies and personal resources of executive, supervisory, and rank-and-file employees are not wasted in conflict but, instead, are released for the constructive task of getting the job done. The truth of this statement is evidenced by the strong conviction among a number of top executives that the strength of an organization lies in its people, not in its systems, technologies, procedures, or capital resources. A company which can weld able people into a loyal and co-operative team can hold its own, competitively, and can withstand the buffetings of social and economic change. General Robert E. Wood recognized the significance of this when he said: "While systems are important, our main reliance must always be put on men rather than on systems. If we devise too elaborate a system of checks and balances, it will only be a matter of time before the self-reliance and initiative of our managers will be destroyed and our organization will be gradually converted into a huge bureaucracy."[1]

---

[1] Boris Emmet and J. E. Jeuck, *Catalogues and Counters: A History of Sears, Roebuck & Company* (Chicago: University of Chicago Press, 1950), p. 371.

MANAGEMENT'S DILEMMA IN DETERMINING POLICY OF EMPLOYEE RELATIONS

Although most representatives of management cannot help but agree that a co-operating, well-integrated work force is of crucial importance to the success of a business enterprise, they face a serious dilemma in attempting to achieve these ends. The dilemma revolves around the question: Should the demands and needs of the organization be adapted to meet the personal interests and demands of employees, or should employees be expected in all cases to subordinate their own interests to the over-all requirements and goals of the organization? The direction which management will take in its administrative policies and practices will depend, in the final analysis, on the answer it gives to this important question.

Management's answer to this dilemma is frequently influenced by its strong economic interests and over-all view of the organization. Many managers sincerely feel that the demands and functions of business are based almost entirely on economic and business considerations which cannot be modified. For this reason, they are convinced that employees must bear the entire burden of adjusting to the demands and requirements of the organization. After all, they say, business is set up to achieve certain economic ends. Whether employees like what they are required to do or not, they must co-operate; otherwise the entire organization will fail. Uncompromising as this view appears to be, actually it is not very far from the truth. Any business organization must meet the demands of a competitive, economic world. Failure to subordinate individual and personal interests to these demands may cause serious difficulties. This bleak, economic view of administration, however, merely points up the importance of gaining employee co-operation. It does not in any way dismiss or eliminate the problem, nor does it relieve management of its essential responsibilities.

Most representatives of management are aware that an uncompromising, economic view of administration is not adequate to meet the problems of present-day industrial relations. Some of the more forthright, accordingly, have forgotten their pride, and proceeded up what has subsequently proven to be the blind alley of conciliation. Instead of placing the entire burden of adjustment on employees, they have decided to build the functions and goals of the organization entirely around the needs and interests of employees. It is not difficult to see what is likely to happen if this policy is carried to an extreme; the organization will simply cease to have any purpose beyond the purely political one of satisfying special interest groups and selfish, individual demands. This actually has happened to a greater or lesser extent in a number of organizations.

Usually, this program of conciliation has taken the form of attempting to buy employee favors by giving them various material benefits, such as bonuses, recreation programs, improved working conditions, and, sometimes, houses, recreation parks, retail buying facilities, and what have you. Recently, in a national magazine, we observed that one manager had given new cars to all his employees with more than one year's service. While this approach is laudable from the standpoint of management's apparent interest in employee welfare, it generally has not achieved the ends for which it was designed. Employees just do not sell their loyalty—a fact which management has learned to its dismay on too many occasions. Indeed, if we can judge from the experiences which many companies have had, paternalism has tended to create more resentment than good will among employees. In the minds of employees, it apparently has been regarded as an unwarranted intrusion into their personal lives.

There have been other, less materialistic, efforts on the part of management to win employee loyalty by anticipating and meeting their every personal need. Welfare programs of all types fall into this category. The fact remains that, whenever management takes upon itself the burden of handling employees' problems for them, it only succeeds in creating a class of dependent persons who are unable to meet and solve their own problems. This is the danger which many people recognize in their criticism of benefit plans, social security programs, and the welfare state generally. While they agree that the end results gained by these programs are good, they are afraid that they will encourage widespread dependency among people and foster the attitude that "the world owes me a living."

So far it sounds as though management is "damned if it does and damned if it doesn't." The answer, however, to the dilemma regarding who shall bear the brunt of adjusting to the industrial environment lies in a broader evaluation of the problem. All of our observations lead us to the conclusion that management's real responsibility with reference to employee interest in the work situation is to build and maintain the kind of organization in which employees themselves can satisfy their own personal needs and ambitions. It is not necessary for management to satisfy their needs for them but, rather, to provide the kind of organization and environment in which they can do the job themselves. It begins to look as though management does not have to subvert the goals and functions of the organization to meet the whims and caprice of employee demands. Instead, it appears that it can stimulate and integrate the energies of employees in such a way that the organization actually is able to achieve and maintain itself on new and higher levels.

ORGANIZATIONAL PATTERNS MOST CONDUCIVE TO HIGH MORALE

Examples from Research Involving Small Work Groups

It remains to describe the kind of organization that so neatly accomplishes these ends. To do this, we shall draw from several isolated studies of work situations before attempting to reach any general conclusions. Beginning with the Western Electric studies, we find that a small group of employees there, who were set apart from their fellows and who were subjected to a series of experimental changes in working conditions, showed, over a long period of time, greatly increased productivity and much improved morale.[2] Why? The cautious conclusion of the researchers was that the experimental situation itself changed the relation of employees to the work environment, engendering closer co-operation among them, better feelings toward supervision, higher productivity, and improved morale. In short, it appeared that the latent energies of employees were released when the job atmosphere was changed from the usual restrictive and drab one of the typical factory to the meaningful, permissive climate of the test-room situation.

Some twenty years later, French and Zander reported another interesting experiment involving the introduction of technological changes among several groups of employees in a garment factory. In this experiment, the changes which were to be made were introduced to employees in three ways. With the first group, employees were simply told about the changes that were taking place. They were allowed to ask questions but nothing more. With the second group, a committee of employees met with management, discussed

---

[2] F. J. Roethlisberger and W. J. Dickson, *Management and the Worker* (Cambridge, Mass.: Harvard University Press, 1939), especially Part I, pp. 3–179.

the changes which were to be made, and together arrived at decisions about important matters concerning work design and rates for the jobs. With the third group, all employees met with management and, in this total discussion, made the necessary decisions regarding the changes to be made. The results were not unexpected. All three groups showed a sharp drop in production after the changes were introduced; but the nonparticipating group never did get back to previous production standards during the period of the study; moreover, morale was low. The second group of employees, where representatives were allowed to meet with management, recovered previous production levels in two weeks; here morale was higher. The third group, with total participation in the introduction of the changes, not only recovered previous levels of production within a few days but actually improved their output by 15 per cent. Furthermore, morale was highest in this group.[3] Again, we ask the question, "Why?" And here, again, it appears that the latent energies of employees were released by a change in the relation of employees to the job situation.

Example from Research Involving a Large, Complex Organization

These two studies, however, involved small work groups. What about larger business organizations? In an article appearing recently in the *Harvard Business Review*, James C. Worthy, a member of the personnel department of a large merchandising organization, reported the results of extensive human relations research conducted over a period of twelve years. In this article, he reached a number of very pertinent conclusions which we should like simply to list here in our words without comment:

1. Employee morale appears to result from a complex of interdependent factors. No single factors, such as high wages or good employee benefits can, in and of themselves, create high morale and enthusiasm among employees.

2. Because of this, material rewards and employee benefits are significant to morale only in so far as they are evidence of management's attitude toward employees. If all other indications are that management is not concerned with the welfare of employees, high wages or liberal benefits will not engender positive morale among them.

3. First-line supervision, while definitely related to employee morale, usually

---

[3] French and Zander, "The Group Dynamics Approach," *Psychology of Labor-Management Relations*, Arthur Kornhauser (ed.), Industrial Relations Research Association, Publication No. 3, pp. 73–74.

reflects the broad administrative patterns set by top management in the organization.

4. Employees want an opportunity to develop and exercise their skills and abilities. Furthermore, they want to feel part of an organization in which their particular talents and efforts are appreciated.

5. Morale tends to be higher in smaller organizations, where there is an opportunity for greater personal contact between management and rank-and-file employees and where individual employees better understand the part they play in the total efforts of the organization. Larger organizations create administrative difficulties and problems of communication, which set upward limits on the level of morale that can be achieved in the organization and also impair operating efficiency.

6. Large organizations can achieve the benefits in efficiency and morale of smaller, well-integrated work teams through an administrative program of decentralization. By decentralization is meant "the placing of authority and responsibility as close as possible to the scene of action and permitting a wide range of discretion to those at each level in the system." As such, decentralization refers to the dispersion of decision making as far down the line as possible, not to the formal breaking-up of a company into highly centralized, but relatively autonomous, units.

7. The structure or design of an organization can implement or impede this process of decentralization. "Broad" or "flat" organizations with a few layers of supervision force the delegation of authority downward. "Tall" or "obeliscal" organizations by their very nature militate against the dispersion of authority and responsibility.

8. Decentralization of authority can also be strengthened and promoted in larger organizations by discouraging overspecialization. "This policy recognizes the definite advantages of the flexible, versatile 'general practitioner' (particularly at the executive level) in contrast to the narrower and less adaptive specialist."

9. Overspecialization can also involve whole departments in an organization, as well as individual employees. Many organizations are set up in such a way that the jobs of entire departments are so specialized and so minute a part of the total task of the organization that administrative difficulties are enhanced and morale impaired.[4]

Worthy's observations are something of a landmark in top management thinking. Many of his views, which are based on elaborate research and study, run directly counter to accepted administrative practice. Yet, in spite of their unorthodoxy, they appear to work quite successfully in his own company. Something of the implications of his observations can be obtained from a summary which he provides at the end of his article:

---

[4] James C. Worthy, "Factors Influencing Employee Morale," *Harvard Business Review*, Vol. XXVIII, No. 1 (January, 1950).

Our studies suggest that factors such as these are in many ways the root cause of poor employee morale in broad sections of American business and that, until they are corrected, no substantial improvement in either employee relations or productive efficiency is likely to be possible. This is true because of the repercussions these factors are likely to have on the executive staff and, through them, on employees at all levels in the system.

In the more elaborate and complex organizations, the individual supervisor or executive is subject to constant control and direction and has little opportunity to develop the qualities of initiative and self-reliance. In systems characterized by extensive management decentralization (and therefore by a relatively simple organizational structure), primary reliance is placed on the personal initiative and capacity of the people in the organization. There is a conspicuous lack of detailed supervision and formal controls, permitting executives and supervisors (and to a large extent rank-and-file employees) to enjoy considerable freedom in the way they accomplish their jobs.

They are judged primarily on their results, not on the details of the way they get those results. This concentration of higher management on end-results, together with alertness to recognize and reward good results, develops initiative and self-reliance and generates a far more powerful driving force than could ever be imposed from the top down. This pattern of administration not only gets today's job done better but permits the individual to grow and develop far more readily than under the alternative system. Furthermore, it contributes strongly to morale and esprit de corps because employees work in an atmosphere of relative freedom from oppressive supervision and have a sense of individual importance and personal responsibility which the other type of arrangement often denies them.[5]

The Key to High Morale and Productivity among Employees

It is apparent from these three sets of observations—two dealing with small work groups and one encompassing a large, sprawling business empire—that a thread of commonality runs through all of them. Each reflects a basic underlying factor which appears to be the key to the kind of business and industrial organization which is able to achieve a high level of adjustment to the external social and economic world and, at the same time, attain greater morale and a consequent release of productive energies among employees on all levels. The common underlying factor is found in the basic attitudes and sentiments which employees themselves bring with them to the workplace. In Chapter 2, "The Dynamics of Human Behavior," we discussed a number of these sentiments and beliefs. There we found from observation and study that employees generally make definite and clear-cut demands on the work environment—for opportunity

[5] *Ibid.*, pp. 71–72.

for self-expression, freedom on the job, freedom from arbitrary authority, and opportunity for self-development and recognition. These demands all express the more general belief that people should stand on their own two feet and have an opportunity to behave and be regarded as intelligent human beings. This view strongly suggests that most American workers (there are exceptions, but they are a minority) are motivated and stimulated by meaningful job activities, where there is an opportunity for them to use their own God-given judgment, where they can work together with others in the achievement of common tasks, and where they can develop their own skills and abilities and receive recognition for them at the same time. In short, American workers want "social and psychic space" in which to breathe and expand.

Going back now to the three studies previously reported, we find that all of them describe situations in which the morale and productive efforts of employees have improved because they have been given an opportunity to "breathe and expand" as adult human beings. In the test-room situation at Western Electric, employees were bodily removed from the restrictive atmosphere of the usual factory environment. They were placed in a location by themselves and marked off for special treatment. Instead of the usual driving supervision, the researchers attempted to gain their co-operation and willing participation in the experiments to be conducted. Top management showed an interest in them. The entire atmosphere of the work situation was changed. Small wonder, then, that employees in their willingness to co-operate dramatically increased production. They had gained self-esteem, a feeling of dignity and worth, and a keen sense of responsibility for the success of the experiments.

The study of the introduction of technological changes in the garment factory illustrates a pattern similar to that found at Western Electric. Although this study was much less elaborate than that conducted at Western Electric, it is, nevertheless, of special interest because it was conducted in a totally different industry and city some fifteen or twenty years later. The garment workers' study shows that the positive energies of employees were constricted and inhibited when they were not permitted to participate as responsible adults in making decisions about job changes affecting them. On the other hand, when they were allowed to participate, they were able and willing to make the changes easily and successfully.

In the study of the factors contributing to morale among employees in a large organization, again we find that morale is higher, and energy output greater, when the patterns of administration and organization are such that the basic drives of employees for self-expression, self-development, recognition, and status are stimulated and satisfied.

We could go on applying this principal to any number of studies and observations which have been made by industrial researchers and administrators, but the point is already sufficiently clear. Employees behave like adults when they are treated like adults; they behave as though they have a sense of responsibility when they are treated as though they are responsible; they are willing to co-operate when supervision and management gives them an opportunity to co-operate. Organizations are stronger, more adaptive, and able to meet the problems of economic change to the extent that they are able to release the productive and creative energies of employees on all levels in this way.

ADMINISTRATIVE PATTERNS MOST CONDUCIVE TO HIGH MORALE

Management is the key to the kind of organization which is most conducive to high morale and productivity. Decisions made by management regarding patterns of administration and organization are of crucial importance to the employee attitudes and behavior which develop in the organization. The manager who decides to operate his organization like a machine, by that decision alone, determines the pattern of supervision, division of labor, flow of work, and executive behavior that will characterize the organization. The manager who relies on people, rather than on system, infuses a totally different spirit into his organization and thereby initiates a different pattern of relations among employees on all levels. It is apparent that an organization is built from the top down. It starts with the thinking, ideas, and behavior of the manager; it spreads out to include his key staff; it is translated into a variety of specific actions and patterns of behavior throughout the organization. If the original ideas of management are wrong, the trends in thinking and action which permeate the organization are well-nigh irreversible—as infusive and irreversible in fact as garlic in a chef's salad. If, on the other hand, management's basic thinking is sound, this, too, will be reflected throughout the organization.

Because of the importance of the problem of managerial leadership, we have been continuously asking ourselves during the past several years in all of our studies of organization: Just what kind of leadership functions best? What managerial attitudes and actions seem to achieve the most effective results in building morale among employees and meeting the external problems of the organization? We think we have at least the beginnings of an answer to this question.

ADMINISTRATIVE LEADERSHIP

The problem of leadership in a business or industrial organization is basically that of enlisting the help and assistance of persons with varying backgrounds and interests in the accomplishment of a common task in which each person's contribution is just a part of the whole. The preceding pages of this book should be sufficient evidence that this is not an easy undertaking. Most business and industrial organizations are complex, even from the technical and formal point of view. When you add to that the myriad of informal relations which make up the social structure of organization, the problem may seem overwhelming. The manager who is capable of encompassing both the technical and social areas of knowledge necessary to running a business and using them intelligently may be rare, indeed. He has to be at once a person of action and of thought. He has to be able to reach prompt decisions. He has to be mobile and personally ambitious enough to want to assume positions of power and, yet, aware and self-conscious enough to know himself, know his personal idiosyncracies, and understand the role he plays in the social structure of the organization of which he is a part. Rare though these qualities may be, we have seen them often enough to know that they can happen.

The kind of leadership which has appeared to be most effective in the industrial and business setting is a type which, for want of a better name, we choose to call "administrative leadership." We call it "administrative" because it is concerned with getting people to perform co-ordinated tasks in the accomplishment of goals. Administrative leadership at its best is based on conscious planning. It is not a hit-or-miss proposition where the leader has simply guessed what to do on the basis of intuition. Instead, he knows what to do on the basis of understanding the internal problems of his organization and the external problems it faces. It is the kind of leadership that is fostered and promoted by self-conscious, intelligently aware individuals, who know what the goals of their organizations are, understand the implications of these goals to the total society, and realize in what important ways their decisions affect the entire economic and social fabric of the nation. More than this, it is the kind of leadership that is concerned with the internal affairs of the organization and recognizes the importance of developing individual satisfaction, self-esteem, and personal responsibility among employees on all levels within the organization.

Significance of Administrative Leadership

The significance of administrative leadership can be best illustrated from research conducted under the direction of Elton Mayo, during the war, of turnover and absenteeism in the aircraft industry.[6] The purpose of the research was to determine the reason for high turnover and absenteeism. The studies revealed that turnover and absenteeism were not spread evenly throughout the organization but were concentrated among those work groups which were not integrated and where morale and *esprit de corps* generally were low. It was found that, where employee integration and morale was high, turnover and absenteeism were low; employees had a sense of responsibility which brought them to work and kept them on the job. Apparently this sense of responsibility was tied in directly with the closeness of the relations the employee had with his fellow workers on the job. Mayo went on, then, to distinguish between three types of integrated work groups. One he called a "natural" group; this consisted of employees who, because of their personalities and the situation in which they found themselves were able to achieve a high degree of integration, co-operation, and sociability with each other. The second he called the "family" group; this consisted of a hard core of closely integrated old-timers—an original "natural" group—that was able to induct and train newcomers who came into the group. (The newcomers just did not stay long if they did not fit.) A third group which Mayo was able to distinguish was the so-called "administrative" group; here the integration was achieved by conscious effort on the part of the supervisor, who was aware of what he was doing and made an effort to provide the goals and kinds of satisfaction in the situation which make for enthusiasm and team spirit among employees.

---

[6] Elton Mayo and George F. F. Lombard, *Teamwork and Labor Turnover in the Aircraft Industry of Southern California*, Business Research Studies No. 32 (Boston: Harvard Business School, 1944).

Most important in Mayo's studies of group integration was the fact that, whereas a "natural" and "family" group necessarily had to be small and compact, an "administrative" group could be much larger. In other words, where natural, chance conditions are depended on, to integrate a group of employees, integration occurs in our complex society rather infrequently and certainly only among small numbers of people. However, with a conscious, deliberate effort, the same kind of integration can be achieved with a much larger group of employees.

Our own observations and studies have tended to confirm Mayo's research. We have been able to observe two types of supervision which appear to achieve high morale among employees. One we can call "personality" leadership. In this type of leadership, the supervisor was able to secure good group spirit and integration in his organization by the personal tie he was able to make with all or most of his employees. The other kind of supervision which was observed can be called "administrative" leadership. Here the supervisor obtained high morale and group collaboration by means of a conscious effort on his part to set positive goals for his organization to which most or all of his employees could subscribe. Moreover, he made an equally conscious effort to help employees in various ways to achieve those goals. He did not depend on his own effervescent personality to carry the load for him.

It was our further observation that high morale through personality leadership could be achieved only with small groups of employees—roughly fifty people or less. Administrative leadership was capable of functioning over a much wider area, however. In our opinion, there were no upward limits to the size of organization which could be integrated and infused with high morale when conscious, deliberate effort was made by management to achieve these ends.

THE ELEMENTS OF ADMINISTRATIVE LEADERSHIP

Setting Meaningful Goals

With these two studies in mind, we can now proceed to spell out some of the essential elements of administrative leadership. To begin with, this kind of management is generally keenly aware of the significance of setting meaningful goals for the organization at which everyone can shoot. The most elemental sociology tells us that you cannot integrate a group of people unless they have a common goal or set of goals around which to organize their efforts. Yet, many business and industrial organizations have no such common purpose. Indeed, in a number of situations which we have observed, management has unthinkingly determined upon goals which are completely inimical to employee interests and unconsciously designed to create cleavage and division in the organization rather than co-operation and collaboration.

Importance of Meaningful Activities in the Workplace.—In order to illustrate the significance of positive, meaningful goals in creating morale and co-operation among employees, we should like to draw from a study made of a group of warehouses in a large merchandising organization. These warehouses were attached to retail stores in various parts of the country and performed certain services, such as storing heavy merchandise, preparing merchandise for delivery to the customer, repairing merchandise that had been damaged or worn out, etc. In general, morale was thought to be low in these operations. However, our studies showed that a number of them had relatively high morale. Because of these differences, a more detailed study was made, comparing the warehouse with lowest morale with the one showing the best feelings among employees:

The warehouse with lowest morale exhibited an obvious group of symptoms. Employees were apathetic and uninterested in their work. They did what they were told, and that was that. They were listless and unaggressive, unwilling to do anything to help themselves or the organization. One older employee reflected the attitude of the entire warehouse when he said in an interview: "I need tools to assemble this equipment. I asked management for some, and they said they'd fix me up. Let's see, now—that was a year ago. I haven't said anything since—except, once in a while when they come around, I say, 'Sure would be nice if I had some tools.'" This sort of unaggressive, dependent behavior characterized the organization.

We proceeded, then, to examine at length the attitudes of employees toward company benefits and policies, conditions of employment, supervision, and management. Frankly, we found very little to explain the apathetic feelings of employees. Attitudes toward the company and its policies were good; employees were satisfied with first-line supervision; there was some concern with wages, but this was not sufficient to account for the general lack of spirit and drive in the organization. Finally, we turned to the last important factor in the work environment, namely, management itself. Here again, our research at first appeared fruitless—management was well liked. The manager and his operating superintendent were personally accepted as "nice guys." When we began to examine the mode of administration, which had been adopted by local management, however, the missing pieces of the puzzle began to fall together. Management felt that its main job was to operate an efficient, cost-conscious organization. The warehouse simply performed a storage and delivery service for the retail stores at the cheapest possible cost. This "cost-conscious, efficiency" attitude of local management was reinforced by the attitudes of top management, which rated warehouses in terms of their costs and efficiency. Local management, therefore, was very much concerned with its relative standing on the regular monthly comparison reports sent out by the central office. If it rated low in comparison with other managements, it was very unhappy and felt driven to get costs down. As a result of these pressures, management of the particular warehouse with which we are concerned here operated a cheap, cost-conscious organization. Wages were low; the number of employees hired was kept to a minimum; working conditions were relatively poor and needed improvement. But these things were not nearly so important as the fact that no positive goals were provided employees. Management was, in a sense, asking employees to co-operate in keeping wages low, working conditions poor, and the amount of work exhausting. Management was saying in so many words: "We want to build here a cheaply operated, cost-conscious, efficient organization. We want employees to get behind us and really give their all to this noteworthy purpose. Of course, there won't be any rewards for any employees; there can't be because they would cost too much. So let's get in there and really sweat for good, old ABC Company!" The response of employees pretty well fit the "inspiring" program which management offered them.

The attitudes of employees in the warehouse with high morale contrasted sharply with the organization just described. Employees were far more aggressive and enthusiastic. They knew what the job of the organization was and how their work contributed to the whole. Moreover, they were certain that management would reward them for the contributions that they made. In general, their attitudes were positive and action-oriented rather than negative and passive. Management somehow had been able to achieve the kind of internal integration of employees on all levels which is so necessary to the success of the organization in meeting and solving its external problems.

The difference between these two warehouses did not lie in differences between the working force in each organization, as might first be suspected. This factor was examined carefully, but there was no evidence of any essential differences. Furthermore, the difference did not lie in the personalities of the two managers. As a matter of fact, the manager of the warehouse with lowest morale was more personable in some respects than the manager of the high-morale operation. The main difference, to make a long story short, lay in the different kinds of administration involved in each organization. In the warehouse with high morale, management thought of its job as that of providing service to the customer. It did not consider its function to be simply that of giving retail outlets a cheap warehousing and delivery service. It felt that the warehouse had an important and significant job of its own to do. There was a keen awareness that sales could be made or broken in the kind of service that is provided the customer, and that the sale was not completed until the merchandise was finally delivered intact and at the right time to the waiting customer. Coupled with this positive attitude toward the service function of the warehouse, management followed through by recognizing and rewarding those employees who contributed to this over-all function of the organization and by punishing those who contributed little or nothing. As a consequence, employees worked in a purposeful environment, where they knew what they were shooting at and how they themselves could gain personal recognition in the attainment of those goals.

Naturally, the reader is wondering which of the two warehouses actually did achieve the lowest cost operation. After all, costs are important. As a matter of fact, both organizations achieved approximately the same cost picture. Both were at the top of the heap when compared with other warehouse operations in the company. However, the organization with low morale achieved it by keeping wages low, refusing to spend money on improved working conditions, and maintaining a close, rigorous control over all expenditures. The organization with high morale achieved the same economic picture as a by-product of high morale and enthusiasm among a group of employees who knew what they had to do and were rewarded handsomely and deservedly for doing it.

This study illustrates the importance of management's setting goals for the organization which are integrative and meaningful to large segments of the work force. It is, as a matter of fact, the first step in building the kind of organization in which employees themselves can satisfy the needs and demands which they bring with them to the workplace. It is apparent that employees cannot begin to fulfill their desires for recognition and self-esteem until they know what it is they have to do to gain rewards and personal satisfactions.

Determination of Meaningful Goals.—Our warehouse illustration shows the importance of meaningful goals in developing a well-integrated organization; but there are a number of questions which it does not directly answer. First of all, when is an organizational goal meaningful to employees? This question is not an easy one to answer, because it depends ultimately on the attitudes of employees. What may be meaningful to one group of employees may not make any sense to another. For example, top management may consider purely economic goals to be very meaningful. Lower-level employees, however, may derive no inspiration at all from these aims. There has been a trend recently to secure greater acceptance of the American economic system among employees by giving them "lessons" in elemental economics through the medium of movies, lectures, and conferences. These programs generally take the form of showing employees where the company sales dollar goes, then relating this by some devious route with the American way of life, and finally wheeling in Ben Franklin to talk to the boys about what he had in mind when he set up these United States. Employees are supposed to leave these sessions starry-eyed and filled to the brim with pure inspiration. From that point on, they are expected to be able to make the connection between operating a punch press and the meaning behind the Statue of Liberty. In general, although employees are not averse to these programs of economic education, they get very little out of them which they can associate with their day-by-day experiences in the workplace.

A goal, to be effective as a means of drawing people together in common, co-operative endeavor, obviously must have something to do with their daily work. Furthermore, it must have something to do with the work and activity of all employees, from top to bottom. To the extent that anyone is left out, he is not a significant and meaningful part of the organization. Wide coverage, therefore, is one of the very important attributes of any goal which is supposed to integrate employees in a business or industrial organization. With this in mind, contrast the probable effects on employees of a management which sets its sights solely on profits and dividends with a management which is out to build the best quality "whazzit" at the lowest possible cost to the customer. Contrast the probable effects of a management which is primarily concerned with improving job methods and efficiency in the organization with one which is determined to develop a topnotch organization in its field. Contrast any goal which employees can interpret as a threat against their own interests with one which is concerned with building the organization or making it more secure for its members. It is apparent that those goals and aims which make sense, in terms of the security and survival of the organization and of the people in it, will be very effective. Furthermore, it is evident that any goals which tend to build the status and significance of an organization and of the people in it will be equally, or even more, effective. Thus, the management which says to employees in so many words, "We're going to build the best 'whazzit' factory in the business, and here are the ways we can do it," is going to get response and co-operation from employees. The management which says, "Our jobs are threatened; here's what we have to do to protect the organization," will also find employees ready and willing. But the management, which is not able to translate the problems of doing business into broad, organizational goals which employees can understand, will find employees resistant and obstructive, for they will see the actions of management as threats against their own personal well-being.

Use and Function of Meaningful Goals in Retailing.—Nowhere in industry or business has the use of meaningful goals as a means of creating enthusiasm and co-operation among employees been so highly developed as in retailing. The authors have had an opportunity to observe a number of retail situations and have been very much impressed with the ability of retail management in many of these situations to create zeal and enthusiasm among employees. There are a number of reasons for this, which will be discussed in some detail in this section.

The function of any merchandising organization is to sell. Any such organization which does not keep this well in mind does not last long in the competitive retail market. In general, this fact is foremost in the thinking of management. Efficiency in operation is generally thought of as secondary to the achievement of sales. This does not mean that efficiency, as such, is not important. But efficiency in operation is usually thought of as the means by which profits are made after sales have been achieved. In other words, you have to make the sale first; then, after that, you either make a profit or lose your shirt, depending on how efficiently you can operate. As a consequence, in most retail stores, you have a merchandising organization consisting of buyers and sales promoters; just beside it you have an operating organization which is concerned with the cost of space, displays, personnel, store property, and what have you, and which is constantly reminding the sales organization that it costs money to make sales. These two important functions of the retail store tend to balance one another, swinging back and forth as general economic conditions fluctuate. However, in no case is the operating function given priority over the sales activity. There is no money made in retailing until the sale has been achieved.

The attitude in retailing can be contrasted with that in the typical factory organization. It is just as apparent that the principle purpose of the factory organization is to produce. However, unlike retail, there is a limitation on how much you can produce; it does not matter at all how many sales you achieve in retail—the sky's the limit; but it does matter in manufacturing how much you produce; at some point or other, increased production becomes economically unsound. As a consequence, management in industrial organizations is primarily concerned with holding production well within the bounds of good reason, avoiding overproduction, and achieving efficiency and profit in all operations. This point of view permeates the thinking of factory management and limits the possibilities of setting positive goals which employees can understand and accept.

It can be seen that quite the contrary is true for a large segment of the retail organization, at least. The positive, constructive goal of sales can be set in retail and be accepted by a great majority of employees with wholehearted enthusiasm. The achievement of sales in retail not only means success for the organization as a whole but for each individual employee. For sales not only mean profits; they mean commissions and high earnings as well. Moreover, unlike factories, there is no clear-cut limitation as to how far you can go. Management is not so prone to worry about high earnings of commission salesmen. The attitude generally is: "If he's making sales, he's earning his money!"

It should be pointed out that we are not suggesting here that retail-store management is of a higher caliber than factory management and that invariably morale is higher in retail than in factory organizations. What we are saying, however, is that retailers are in a far better position than manufacturers to provide positive goals which mean something to employees and provide some basis for their enthusiastic support of management.

Retail management has gone a long way toward the development of techniques for promoting the goal of sales. This is to be expected; after all, most store managers are, first, last, and always, merchants; they can sell the idea of selling just as well as they can sell anything else. The various techniques and devices which are used and have been observed by the authors are of interest in themselves from the point of view of their application elsewhere in the business and industrial world. One device which is continuously used is group meetings, or "rallies." Retail stores are the "meetingest" places on earth. These meetings frequently involve *all* employees, not just a committee or the top brass. Those who lead the meetings are generally experts; they know how to make speeches, how to move people, how to flavor what they have to say with enough humor, enough sentiment, and enough fact, to swing a group. Around these meetings, ceremonials of various kinds have been developed. There are sales for each season of the year—midwinter sales, white sales, Easter sales, vacation-days sales, August fur sales, back-to-school sales, fall sales, Thanksgiving sales, and Christmas sales. Interspersed between these are sales events built around some personality in the store or company —"King for a Day" sales, "John Smith Day," and what have you. Each sales event, depending upon its importance, is promoted in various meetings with employees. These meetings may involve singing, skits, humor which is pointed to the particular event, dinners and banquets, and simple and direct exhortation. Testimonials from various key figures in the store highlight the event. Devices, such as raffling, lotteries, drawings, etc., are used to create interest in the meetings. Anyone who has ever witnessed a typical "jumpin' sales" event knows that the old-time revival meeting is not dead in America but has merely been transferred to the retail store.

With every sales event, there is follow-through all along the line. For one thing, the displays are a constant reminder to employees of the immediate purpose and goal of the store. This is true, of course, not only of window displays, but of interior decorations as well. If it is Christmas, it looks like Christmas and it sounds like Christmas. There are carols and Christmas trees and bells and snow and Santa Claus. You are in the thick of things, literally and figuratively, and you are in tune with the times. You are playing a part in an important seasonal event. Any employee who does not know what he is doing in a situation like this is either feeble-minded or demented. You do not have to educate employees regarding their role in the total efforts of the organization. They know. It is right there in front of them.

Providing Rewards and Punishments

Not only must management set positive goals for its organization in order to build employees into an effective working team; it also must set up a system of rewards and punishments in order to reinforce the desire of employees to accomplish the over-all goals of the organization. People want to do those things which are rewarding to them and inhibit those things which bring punishment in their wake. Furthermore, people feel pleasure in the anticipation of reward, and they feel anxiety and insecurity in the anticipation of punishment. It is amazing to what extent these facts are forgotten in the administrative practices of many business managers. Most work situations are devoid of rewards of any kind. Many are actually punishing. Small wonder that employees in such situations develop feelings of anxiety and insecurity which directly influence their work efforts!

In some ways, the complete lack of both reward and punishment in a work situation is worse, from the point of view of work effort, than continued punishment. Punishment at least has some effect of stimulation on the worker. Unfortunately, a number of industrial supervisors have discovered this and have found that increased work effort can be obtained by setting up a punishing, highly disciplined administration. However, in spite of the initial stimulating effect of this kind of supervision, the organization which is administered in this way will suffer. First of all, grievances and complaints will increase. As a consequence, administrative woes increase proportionately. More than this, turnover and absenteeism tend to increase. The cost of maintaining an adequate work force is, therefore, greater. Finally, the incalculable effects of poor morale take their toll, influencing employee, community, and customer attitudes toward the company.

The effect of a complete dearth of reward and punishment, however, is boredom. This, frankly, is the situation very common in business today. In organization after organization, you can find employees who are simply "bored to death." These are employees who come to work, start their machines, run them for eight hours, and go home without having once during the day found themselves more than mildly interested in what was going on around them. It is not that the situation is punishing; it is just that it is nothing at all. Work becomes a drudgery; a task which must be performed like washing the supper dishes; you do it because you have to, not because you are interested. As many an employee has put it, "I just work here; there's nothing in this for me."

Good administrative leadership utilizes the stimulating effects of both reward and punishment to achieve a co-operating, enthusiastic work team. The proper use of reward and punishment involves, however, a clear-cut knowledge on the part of management of what the over-all goals of the organization are. If these goals have not been properly conceptualized, then any rewards and punishments which are dealt out will be arbitrary and capricious; but, if the goals are clear-cut and understandable, the number and variety of opportunities to provide employees with recognition for a job well done is amazing.

Translating Meaningful Activity down the Line

In addition to meaningful goals for the organization as a whole, management must also consider the more difficult problem of setting up an organization in which the various subfunctions and activities make sense to employees. We have already shown in previous chapters that the trend toward overspecialization of jobs and functions in industry has reduced a great majority of work activities to a level that a robot would find uninspiring. This trend continues, in spite of the serious effects it is having on employee morale. It is fostered out of the mistaken belief that any specialization will invariably result in greater skill and productivity on the part of employees. There is good reason to doubt at least some of these assumptions. Certainly, in light of the effect that overspecialization has been having on employee morale, its validity should be tested carefully.

Results of Overspecialization of Jobs.—The important thing about overspecialization is not the fact that it reduces employees to routine, repetitive tasks; there are many persons who actually enjoy, or at least do not actively dislike, routine jobs. The important thing is that employees, by the nature of their work, become aware of management's lack of respect for them. They cannot help but realize that their work effort is unimportant to the company and that they are hired, not because they wanted and accepted as a whole man, but because they have two hands and a foot that can be used to operate a punch press. Actually, the attitudes and feelings that develop are very subtle and difficult to trace. But, if you consider the work history of the average factory employee, you can more easily visualize the problem. The typical factory worker is brought in, given a routine job to do, is told to do it only in a certain way, is sent home when the machine breaks down, is not asked for his opinion on anything, and is expected simply to perform certain operations when those operations are needed. It is not long before he begins to realize that his relation to the organization and its management is a purely economic one. We recently had occasion to document the development of this attitude in an office worker. She said: "I used to feel very much a part of this organization and put everything I had into my job. Then, they started clamping down and treating us like irresponsible children. From that point on, I figured that my relationship to the department was strictly an economic one. If that was the way they wanted it, that was the way they were going to get it. Now, I do all the superficial, obvious things, but I don't throw myself into my work the way I used to." In situations such as this one, management is simply getting back what it has handed out; it's an old story.

Lack of Career Opportunities.—One very important aspect of this whole problem is the lack of career opportunities which highly specialized business organizations provide the average employee. Most employees cannot see any future in the work they do. They acquire all the skill they need to do the work in a few short weeks or months;

there is no opportunity for them to develop increasing skill and, over a period of time, carve themselves out a niche in the organization which will give them recognition and status. We are not implying here that opportunity in America is dead; highly competent, unusual people can still move from the bottom to the top in a lifetime. But the average man has fewer chances to gain recognition and self-esteem, as his job is broken down into more and more elemental components. Moreover, as his opportunities for gaining a personal stake in the organization decrease, he becomes increasingly less likely to identify himself with the company and its demands. Management can perform no more useful service to its organization as a whole than identifying and, if necessary, creating career opportunities for lower-level employees who are unable or unwilling to move up the supervisory hierarchy to higher-level positions. The career ladder does not have to be very long for most people. It may amount simply to moving into a higher-status department or onto a machine requiring a modicum of individual judgment. Furthermore, it is not necessary that everyone move. The important thing is that some move and that the same opportunity is open to others who want to put forth the effort. Intelligent and careful planning on the part of management can do a great deal to give employees the feeling that there is a chance for them to carve out a niche for themselves as they develop greater skills and proficiency.

Closely related to this problem of career hierarchies and over-specialization is the underlying and more basic notion that employees want a whole job to perform, not a piece of one. They want to perform some activity which is an integral part of the organization and for which they personally are responsible. This is the key to developing the kind of organizational structure, division of labor, and job breakdowns, generally, which will engender high morale and productivity among employees. A man will feel part of an organization to the extent that he can see that his particular work activity is an integral part of the activity of his department and to the extent, also, that the work of his department is an integral part of the entire organization. He will identify himself with the problems of the organization to the extent that he feels that his work is important to the success or failure of the organization. This kind of feeling can only be engendered in an employee or a group of employees who have been given a whole job to do. So long as they feel that they are working merely on minor and unimportant assignments, employees cannot possibly develop a sense of responsibility for, and identification with, either their own work or the work of the organization as a whole.

Building Co-operative Work Effort in the Organization

Integrating Employees into the Organization.—Thus far, in our discussion of the elements of administrative leadership, we have been describing the importance of setting meaningful goals for the organization and of providing meaningful tasks for employees on all levels. Now we should like to discuss some of our observations regarding the role which management and supervision should play in their day-by-day relations with subordinate employees. In our experience, the essential elements characterizing the behavior of good administrative leadership are two: first, good administrative leadership is "integrative" in the sense that it is concerned with involving as many employees in the affairs of the organization as possible; second, it is "team-minded" in the sense that it is concerned primarily with building co-operative work teams in the organization. We shall discuss the notion of integrative behavior first.

Exclusive or Inclusive Management.—The role which management will play in an organization depends partly on its notions of who constitutes the organization. Some business establishments are little more than the stage for a "one-man show." In such organizations, the curtain rises at 8:00 A.M. with the "one-man show" sitting at his desk. There are a number of scenes after that, but always the same act—namely, the "one-man show" acting out all of his own personal ambitions and drives. Those vague, shadowy figures that you see rather infrequently in the background are employees who are brought in once in a while to carry out the "man's" bidding or to stimulate his soliloquizing with an occasion "Yes, sir!" Though this description is somewhat overdrawn, there are, nevertheless, people in management positions who play a role very similar to this. They conceive of their organizations as extensions of themselves, are uncomfortable if anything happens—good or bad—which they did not have a hand in doing, and are suspicious of employees in whom they do not see a direct reflection of themselves. Usually, an executive of this type demands the utmost loyalty from his people, which he sometimes gets from dependent subordinates who do not mind at all sitting around and watching him make all the decisions. Very frequently, however, he engenders antagonisms and hostilities in his organization with which he finds it increasingly more difficult to cope.

Although the "one-man show" is not an infrequent phenomenon in industry, the usual picture is one where the organization is thought of as consisting of the executive force and, perhaps, the supervisors. Most, or all, other employees are regarded as extraneous. Now, as a matter of fact, we all know that management does not typically go around the organization, beating itself on its collective chest and proclaiming to all within earshot: "We're the organization around here. You guys just work for us." Nevertheless, by implication, something of the same effects are achieved. When management does all the thinking and allows no one outside of the chosen few to exercise independent judgment, it is literally excluding large groups of employees from participation in the organization. When management provides itself with unusual special privileges without regard for the effects of this action on lower-level employees, again it is announcing that the organization is set up for the satisfaction and benefit of a small group of the elite. Indeed, whenever management behaves as though the boundaries of the organization end with the front office, employees will very quickly realize that they stand on the other side of the fence and should involve themselves as little as possible in the affairs of the organization except as specifically directed. We recently had an opportunity to observe the effects of such acts of exclusion in the following situation in a factory which was attempting to promote greater economy and efficiency into its operations.

Management was "beating its brains out" trying to think up ways to cut costs. Rank-and-file employees, however, were excluded from these considerations; they were expected merely to respond to management's bidding whenever it came up with a new idea. The results were that employees resisted management's efficiency and economy drive, step by step. One astute employee summarized the situation with this cogent statement: "A helluva lot of good it's going to do to have all that efficiency in the management group if we don't have it among the men down here." Management finally did achieve the economy it was hoping for at a later date. No employees were late; they took no time off for smoking; they no longer used an excessive number of wiping rags or paper towels; the machines were kept in good order. Neither was there any production, for the employees were on strike!

The management which we have observed to be most effective in getting things done in an organization and in building enthusiasm and high morale among employees is the one which is integrative in its thoughts and action with reference to the organization. This is the kind of management which conceives of the organization as including everyone who works in it. It feels successful to the extent that it can involve as many employees as possible in the problems of the organization. Usually it regards itself as a functional part of the organization, not as the organization itself. It conceives of its job as that of helping, training, and stimulating others to do the work. It enjoys setting the wheels in motion and seeing them go around *under their own power*.

Importance of Participation.—One of the important managerial practices fostered by "administrative" leadership in integrating employees into an efficient working team is that of permitting them to participate in making decisions about things which affect their jobs and work environment. Participation is one of the best ways of involving employees in their work and the problems of the organization. From a psychological standpoint, it is difficult to be critical of, and unresponsive to, anything which you personally have played a part in creating. You want it to be successful because it involves you and your own personal self-esteem. The truth of this is confirmed in any number of studies. The case of the garment workers, described previously in this chapter, is an excellent example. Our own observations in the following instance also provide good confirming evidence.

Recently, in the shoe division of a department store, a group of the salesmen went to management, demanding a higher commission rate on their sales. They claimed that they were not being properly compensated for their work effort. Examination of the situation, however, showed that they were primarily concerned with the distribution of stock work. In any shoe department, the problem of putting shoes back in stock in their proper order is a laborious task. The proverbial lady customer who comes in and tries on everything in the division before making her choice is not too far from the reality of the situation. Although stock work is an important part of every shoe salesman's job, he does not like it because it keeps him off the sales floor where money is to be made. In this case, since the salesmen felt that the stock work had been unfairly distributed and that they were being asked to do more than their fair share, naturally they wanted extra compensation to make up for sales lost. The division manager was questioned regarding his method of distributing the stock work among the salesmen, since this appeared to be the crucial problem affecting them. He said that he had done everything possible to handle the distribution fairly but that his employees were never satisfied. Since store management was interested only in the fact that the stock work was accomplished and not in the details of doing the job, it advised the division manager to permit the salesmen themselves to work out what they felt was a fair and equitable distribution of the work. This was done, and the complaints among employees promptly ceased.

The notion of participation involves the broader idea of delegation of authority and responsibility. The trend in business and industrial organizations has, of course, been toward greater and greater centralization of authority. This fact has served to concentrate the thinking and understanding portions of doing business into fewer and fewer hands. It has created a large group of nonparticipants in industry who, literally, stand around waiting for the next job. They actually do not know what to do unless they are told. Indeed, some organizations are so highly centralized that nobody except the top brass knows what the "score" is.

Significance of Overspecialization.—This trend is part and parcel of the trend toward overspecialization. As men are replaced by systems and the systems become more and more complex and devious, it is necessary to have these systems administered and controlled by "experts." For example, the typical factory organization is set up with an industrial engineering department, the primary responsibilities of which are to devise improved methods for accomplishing each job, determine tool and labor routings, set up work standards, determine the piece rates on each job, and generally attempt to cut the costs of materials and processes utilized in manufacturing operations. The industrial engineering department does the job for management of "experting" each job through the plant. It is essentially a department of highly trained engineers who are concerned with the details of getting the job done. When the industrial engineer finishes laying out a job, nothing is left to the imagination. He specifies the way the job is to be done, the tools to use, the setup of the machines, the materials to use, the standard work practices, and the rate the employee is to receive for doing the work. All the foreman and employees must do —that is, if everything goes right—is to follow instructions.

There is good reason to believe that the gain in productivity achieved by overspecialization and its twin brother, overcentralization of authority, has been lost in the debilitating and ennervating effects that they have had on employee morale and willingness to cooperate. One large company in the merchandising field which has fostered a decentralized mode of administration throughout its organization, has enjoyed unusual expansion and profit during the past several decades. This organization, on the whole, is characterized by very high morale among its employees, particularly on the executive level.[7] Other companies, too, have promoted a number of these ideas with apparently excellent success.[8] The pattern of decentralization exhibited by these companies is characterized by management's greater concern with over-all results rather with than the details of getting the job done. It is characterized also by a greater reliance on men rather than on systems and control. It derives its original spark from an essential and fundamental faith and confidence in people.

We can think of no better way of ending this section than by reporting the views of a supervisor of a small service unit of about one hundred men. He didn't look like an executive when he discussed these ideas with us, but he exhibited a native executive talent when he said: "Frankly, I'm more interested in total results than in the details of every individual job. When we have a new job to do, I talk it over with the employee and get his ideas. If I can improve on them, I make my suggestions. However, if the employee feels that his way is the best, I let him try it. Sure, he might make a mistake. But, so what! A man won't learn anything unless you give him his lead once in a while. What's more, the chances are he won't make a mistake anyway because, when he takes his own lead, brother, from there on, it's his baby—win or lose!"

Developing Teamwork in the Organization

Previously we said that good administrative leadership is teamminded in the sense that it is concerned with building co-operative work teams in the organization. By this we mean a kind of management which is primarily concerned with maintaining well-integrated and collaborative behavior among employees on all levels in the organization. Chester I. Barnard has said:

The primary efforts of leaders need to be directed to the maintenance and guidance of organizations as whole systems of activities. I believe this to be the most distinctive and characteristic sector of leadership behavior, but it is the least obvious and least understood. Since most of the acts which constitute organization have a specific function which superficially is independent of the maintenance of organization—for example, the accomplishment of specific tasks of the organization—it may not be observed that such acts at the same time also constitute organization, and that this, not the technical and instrumental, is the primary aspect of such acts from the viewpoint of leadership. Probably most leaders are not ordinarily conscious of this, though intuitively

---

[7] See James C. Worthy, op. cit.
[8] See Robert W. Johnson, Or Forfeit Freedom (New York: Doubleday, 1947).

they are governed by it. For any act done in such a way as to disrupt co-operation destroys the capacity of the organization. Thus the leader has to guide all in such a way as to preserve organization as the instrumentality of action.[9]

Barnard, with his years of experience as a top-flight business administrator, has been impressed with the significance of co-operation in an organization. He is keenly aware of the fact that co-operation is basic to any organized effort—so basic, in fact, that he regards its preservation in any organization as the primary concern of management.

This is one of those concepts about which most management representatives will say, "Yea, verily!" Yet, we have a good deal of evidence that it is a notion which is only vaguely understood. Very frequently, when management thinks of co-operative work relations, it is thinking primarily of the workers' willing acceptance and adjustment to the formal demands of the organization. This view, while perfectly legitimate, is not what Barnard means, however. What he is saying, if we interpret him correctly, is that the first requirement of any organization is people working together. For, if they are working together, then you can be sure that they are doing the best job possible within the limits that the formal demands of the organization place upon them. In brief, then, management must become alert to the work relations between people, for, if these are right, all other things will be right, too.

Importance of Teamwork among Key Executives.—With these views in mind, we can complete our construct of the proper functions of management in industrial organizations. It is apparent that the top man in any organization does not have direct and continuous contact with the great bulk of his employees. He works primarily with his key staff. The relations that he develops with these men are of crucial importance to his entire organization. For, if there is discord among them, it will be translated right down the line to the lowest levels; the organization, from the start, will be unable to solve the demands which are being made upon it. In our extensive surveys of organizations, we very quickly learned that an evaluation of the relations of top-level personnel was a necessary first step in understanding the relations existing in the rest of the organization. If there was a well-integrated work team among top executives in the organi-

---

[9] Chester I. Barnard, "The Nature of Leadership," *Human Factors in Management,* Schuyler Dean Hoslett (ed.) (Parkville, Mo.: Park College Press, 1946), p. 20.

zation we usually found that whatever problems did exist in the organization were localized in nature. However, when difficulties were occurring at the very top of the organization, the problems throughout the rest of the organization were generalized, widespread, and serious.

The development of co-operation and *esprit de corps* in the key staff depends upon a number of factors. Among the most important of these is the personal relation that exists between the top man and the members of the executive group. The whole purpose of this relation, as far as the manager is concerned, is to promote collaborative effort among his key people. To this end, he makes an effort, first, to choose and select a group of men whose personalities are not too conflicting and who can get along on a purely personal level. He tolerates no one on the team who is constitutionally unable to work with the others. Next, he indicates by all of his own behavior that he expects his key subordinates to solve mutual problems without running to him. He deliberately avoids placing himself in the position of having to choose between alternative decisions, particularly where it means deciding in favor of one staff member as opposed to another. He makes adroit use of temporary committees to solve problems of common interest. For example, if the organization faces a problem which primarily involves the production and personnel departments, the manager will assign it to the heads of both departments and ask them for a joint report on how to deal with it. All along the line, he will encourage the mutual solution of problems through spontaneous co-operative endeavor. He will reward employees, as a group, for their ability to work together and will judge their success individually in terms of their ability to promote their own special functions in collaborative relations with others. Finally, he will guard against any changes which will destroy or hamper this team relation among key employees, once it has been established. Through the relation which he himself develops with his key people, the manager provides his staff with the best possible training for handling their own subordinates. In this way, team work as a mode of administration is proliferated throughout the organization, even to the bottom levels.

Teamwork among Lower-Level Employees.—With this kind of administration, it can be seen that one of management's primary responsibilities is seeing that a high degree of integration and team spirit exists on all levels in the organization. To accomplish this task, top management must know what is going on in all parts of the organization. By knowing what is going on, we do not mean wallowing around in the morass of details that typically comprise the day-by-day activities of most businesses. These are supposed to be handled by lower-level supervision. We mean, rather, setting up a system of communication from the bottom to the top by means of which dislocations and breakdowns in team relations can be identified. There are a number of indirect means of communication that can be used for this purpose. Mayo was able to identify work groups where integration had broken down—if, indeed, it had ever existed—by studying absentee and turnover records. Some companies have identified problems by studying the number and nature of grievances emerging from various departments. In other organizations, the use of periodic employee reviews and departmental committees has provided a more direct approach to the problem of communication. Still other organizations have gone "all out" and developed morale survey programs through which the attitudes and feelings of employees have been tapped directly. However, whatever technique of communication is applied, the important thing is that management is able to use the information, once it has been obtained. Management must keep in mind that such information generally tells it only that a problem exists but does not tell it why. The task of determining the reasons for breakdown in team relations is something else again.

Diagnosis of Causes of Breakdown in Team Relations.—In previous chapters, we have reviewed in detail a number of the more important factors which affect the attitudes and morale of employees. These factors roughly fall into three groups: (1)) the purely formal factors of organization, which include such things as job and technical demands, division of labor, flow of work, hierarchy of control and authority, and systems of formal relations between departments and jobs; (2) social and status factors, which include all of the sentiments which employees develop as a result of the social and status roles that they play, both within the organization and outside the organization in the broader community; and (3) historical factors, which include the events and changes which have occurred in the organization and have created problems of adjustment among employees. In this and the preceding chapter, we have added a fourth group, namely, management and supervision factors, which have to do with the influence on employee morale of various patterns of administration and personality found among executives and supervisory groups. It is apparent that all of these factors play a part in determining the degree of integration that is likely to obtain in any work group or larger organization. If, for example, the formal and technical system of the organization is faulty (innumerable examples have been provided in previous chapters of this book), then unusual and excessive demands will be made on employees, and the potential for dissatisfaction is immeasurably increased. Furthermore, if changes occur which disturb established patterns of relations among employees, demoralization is likely to result.

Elimination of Frictions Developing Out of Formal Job Demands. —This framework of analysis provides management with an extremely useful approach, not only in diagnosing problems which occur within the organization, but also in building and maintaining stable work relations among employees on all levels. For example, a great deal can be accomplished in improving the morale of an organization by the proper and intelligent manipulation of its formal, technical structure. Too often, management regards the technical and formal side of doing business as an independent variable which is to be adjusted and changed only in terms of "good" engineering, administrative, and business practice without reference to its human implications. Although it is true that many formal business demands cannot be manipulated by management without seriously threatening the efficiency of the organization, nevertheless the latitude in which changes actually can be made to meet human demands is far greater than what is generally accepted. For this reason, management should scrutinize its organization carefully from the standpoint of the effects of job demands on employees. Among the formal elements in the situation, which should be examined more especially, are the relations which develop between departments and among employees, growing out of the division of labor of the organization. Oftentimes, this division of labor militates against the development of teamwork and actually enhances problems of friction and discord in the organization. Many of these points of friction can be minimized and even eliminated by changing and improving the pattern of formal relations that exists among employees.

Handling Changes Affecting the Organization.—Management can do a great deal to stabilize employee relations in the workplace by improving its administrative practices in handling changes in the organization. It is apparent that co-operation and teamwork cannot develop amid unstable and changing conditions. Co-operative effort and teamwork depend upon the development of regular work patterns and interpersonal relations over a period of time. Frequent changes in personnel, policies, procedures, methods, and job demands are all discouraging to the growth of stability in an organization. In such chaotic situations, the employees in the group feel isolated, unsure of themselves, preoccupied with their own personal problems, and highly individualistic in their attitudes. If they do develop co-operation among themselves, it will be in the form of a resistance group against management.

In work groups that are already stable and well integrated, change can disturb established patterns of relations among employees and thereby create problems of morale. Time and again we see serious disturbances on the part of individuals and even loss of morale for entire groups as a result of some act or executive decision which disregarded the status system of a work unit and upset status relationships. As pointed out earlier, these status distinctions are not a simple matter of wage differences or seniority but are subtle expressions of the way individuals think about themselves, one another, and their jobs. And since status is so subtle, it is very easy for the busy executive to overlook it in dealing with distant parts of the organization. Often he makes oversimplified assumptions about it; he feels that two jobs are of equal status because they have the same rate of pay, or that a transfer without cut in pay will not be felt to be a loss of status. When he acts on such assumptions, he is often surprised at the reactions he encounters; and he usually ends up by being extremely annoyed at the people involved and feels that they are being "childish."

Because disturbances arising out of problems of status are so prevalent and because status anxieties are so destructive to morale and efficiency, executives should understand these problems and give them careful attention. In order to do this, every executive should study the status systems within his organization, recognize their many ramifications, and become familiar with status symbols and the sentiments about them. Even with all this knowledge and understanding, executives cannot hope to eliminate status problems completely; but they can certainly avoid those thoughtless acts which cause so many unnecessary disturbances; and they can anticipate and prepare for problems which cannot be avoided.

Any change in the organization not only has far-reaching repercussions, but it also almost invariably results in feelings of insecurity and status anxiety for some individuals. This is especially true, of course, when the change in organization means a shift in functions and relative status for some people. Even when the change is an obvious improvement, however, and even when it will ultimately result in greater effectiveness and improved morale, the individuals involved usually go through a period of uncertainty and anxiety at the time of change. This occurs even when they see the ultimate value of the change; for each one is immediately concerned with its effect upon himself. The immediate superior and higher executives can help this condition and relieve anxieties by reassuring the group in various ways. They can discuss in advance the problems and the reasons for the change with the group immediately involved; they can keep them informed on the progress of the change; and, after the change has been made, they can discuss its effects with the group. At the same time, the superiors can watch the reactions and attitudes of the group and let them know that their ideas are being taken into account. In fact, during any period of uncertainty when there is apt to be anxiety over impending events, it is well for the superiors to increase their contacts and interaction with the group. The availability and interest of the boss during times of trouble is in itself very reassuring.

Two Ways of Handling Changes.—With regard to how change in organization should be handled, there seem to be two schools of thought. One has it that the change should be decided completely in advance and the lower levels informed only when it is finally put into effect. The change then comes formally from the top down, and even though it may have originated at some intermediate level, it is cleared through to the top before lower levels are informed. This plan has the approval of many executives because it gives them the opportunity to consider every proposed change, many of which are squashed or drastically revised before they are put into effect. Further weight is lent to this practice by the fact that news of an impending change usually gives rise to extensive rumors and disturbances, especially in the supervisory structure. Unfortunately, however, it is often impossible to keep the grapevine from picking up rumors of an impending major change, even though it is meant to come as a surprise, so that in any case the organization goes through a period of rumor and speculation which reduces its efficiency. Furthermore, the reaction to a last-minute announcement of a major change is often terrific. To call in a group and announce that, beginning immediately, their organization will be shifted around and their jobs changed, produces a more violent reaction and has a more lasting and devastating effect upon morale than does a change which has been anticipated. The group usually feels that the change has been completely arbitrary, that no consideration has been given them; and in many cases they do everything possible to resist the change.

The opposite method of handling changes (by informing the affected groups in advance, by discussing the change with them and considering their ideas in planning it) has much to recommend it. This method has the advantage of permitting all those involved to feel that they are being considered and that they even have a part in planning the change. It is true that this method is accompanied by a lot of rumor and speculation, talk and disturbance *before* the change goes into effect; but by the time the change actually takes place, emotional reaction and anxieties over it have largely disappeared so that adjustment to the change proceeds smoothly. On the whole, it seems that the more those involved can participate in planning an important change, the better the change will be received, and the more nearly it will achieve its objectives.

Stability and Adjustability.—An organization, and especially one with high morale, has a stability or equilibrium which involves everything from the concept of a fair day's work to the kinds of relationships and patterns of interaction between people at all levels. This stability also means an ability to resist rapid change, to protect itself from disturbing innovations. The top executive, unfortunately, is often in a position of trying to bring about these innovations. From where he sits, the relationships of his firm to the whole economic and social system of the society are of prime importance; and he is concerned with having the company make more and more effective adaptation to this social environment. As a result, he is constantly introducing new ideas, initiating changes, and demanding improvements in the way the organization functions. In other words, he tends to be concerned with making it more effective in achieving the objectives which he sets for it rather than with maintaining its internal stability. Almost inevitably, then, many of his demands and ideas smash headlong against the invisible wall of resistance by which the organization maintains its equilibrium. He often feels as if he were pounding a rubber ball which gives slightly under pressure but always returns to its former shape when the pressure is removed. Frustrated and irritated by this resistance, he may go on using his position and authority to put more and more pressure on the organization and even try to force drastic changes in organization and personnel.

In the interests of morale, it is important to maintain a high degree of internal stability; and in the interests of the business as a successful, going concern, it is important that the organization be adaptable to a changing outside world. To do both is a large order; but that is the top executive's job, and it has been done successfully in many cases. By developing an atmosphere in which changes and improvements can be generated from within the organization rather than imposed from above, the skilled executive can eliminate much of the organization's resistance to change without forfeiting any of its stability. Such processes are slow, of course, since they depend on the development of new ways of thinking and acting on the part of a lot of people. But they will produce better results in total performance, in stability, adaptability, and morale than the impatient demands of an irate top executive.

Personal Disturbances Affecting Team Relations.—There is one final factor which can create discord and unstable conditions in a work group and which, therefore, is of special concern to management. An employee who is personally disturbed himself can sometimes upset the morale and teamwork of an organization. The person who is worried about himself, the one who is overambitious, the one who feels inadequate to do the work, the one who needs constant reassurance and approval, the one who feels that he is losing status—all of these can become so intent on their own problems that they have difficulty co-operating effectively with others. Sometimes you find a whole group of employees (such as minority groups) who, for special reasons, are so preoccupied with their own situations that they cannot easily integrate into the team.

Personal disturbances of this kind not only affect rank-and-file employees but higher-level personnel as well. They are, as a matter of fact, much more important on the executive and supervisory levels, because they can have a wider and, therefore, more devastating effect on the morale of employees. The supervisor who, because of personal preoccupations, cannot deal effectively with his people can have an adverse influence on a large segment of the organization. The manager who is so affected can wreck the whole works. A number of the personality considerations involved in management were discussed in the preceding chapter.

Although many personality problems are untreatable, at least in so far as ordinary company facilities are concerned, many personal disturbances are amenable to correction. One of the best techniques available for industrial use is discussed in the chapter on "Personnel

Counseling." For higher-level personnel, many companies could well avail themselves of the services of psychiatrists. The expense that might be involved in psychiatric treatment would be saved a hundredfold if one disturbed top-level executive were prevented from acting out his personal feelings and emotions on his subordinates. Furthermore, such action would easily pay for itself if the useful life of a highly experienced, and previously capable, man were thereby extended and preserved. A number of companies in the larger cities have, in this way, made good use of psychiatric services.

SUMMARY

We could go on with a further elaboration of the problems involved in building and maintaining work teams in industrial organizations. However, it is not our purpose here to document completely the elements of administrative leadership. Frankly, we have intended only to profile and delineate the basic problems of management and to direct attention to the kinds of thinking and behavior which management must practice if it is to develop organizations capable of dealing effectively with present-day economic and social problems. The reader, however, cannot help but be impressed, throughout this discussion, with the extent to which administrative practices in industrial organizations depend upon the attitudes and personal orientation of top management. Good human relations begin with the ideas that management has about people. If these ideas reflect confidence and faith in the American worker and the American way of life, then all's well in the industrial world. But, if they mirror distrust, suspicion, and exclusion, the waves of industrial strife will spread out, grow larger, and finally rock the ship of state itself. As one employee said: "They say you gotta co-operate. You don't gotta do anything except die."

STUDY GUIDE

LEARNING about human relations in industry presents a number of problems to the student. Of greatest importance is the fact that there are no set principles of human relations and no simple techniques of diagnosis which the student can readily assimilate from his reading. The reason for this becomes apparent when we realize that evaluating and dealing with human relations problems requires judgment and insight that can come only with experience. There is an obvious difference between considering human relations in abstract, logical terms and looking at people in terms of their actual behavior and attitudes. Elton Mayo has pointed out: "The very fact that erudition (logic and systematic knowledge) can be so easily transmitted to others tends to prejudice university instruction in the social sciences heavily in its favor. Physics, chemistry, physiology have learned that far more than this must be given a student. They have therefore developed laboratories in which students may acquire manipulative skill and be judged in terms of actual performance."[1]

With these problems in mind, the authors have attempted to develop a study guide which not only will help students to acquire the basic concepts, ideas, and facts about human relations in industry but also will give them an opportunity to test their judgment and skills in analyzing actual case material. Practically all of the cases recommended in this study guide are drawn from Glover and Hower, *The Administrator: Cases on Human Relations in Business.*[2]

Throughout the study guide a number of field studies have also been suggested as an aid for students in developing their judgment about human relations problems. These studies have been set up, for the most part, so that they can be conducted both by full-time students in universities and by those already working in industry.

The recommended bibliography includes most of the works which the authors themselves have found very useful in giving students insight into human relations problems in industry. It is by no means an inclusive listing of books in the field; rather, it represents a consistent approach to human relations, based on experience and study in the field.

---

[1] Elton Mayo, *The Social Problems of an Industrial Civilization* (Boston: Harvard University, Graduate School of Business Administration, 1945), p. 16.

[2] Glover and Hower, *The Administrator: Cases on Human Relations in Business* (rev. ed.; Homewood, Ill.: Richard D. Irwin, Inc., 1952).

CHAPTER 1. THE DYNAMICS OF BUSINESS

Questions

1. Discuss the concept of business "strategy."
2. Analyze the strategic development of the typical business organization.
3. What are some of the important aspects of division of labor as applied in modern industry?
4. Discuss other common patterns of organization and administration in business.

Case Study

None.

Field Study

Describe the basic strategies of an organization with which you are familiar. This might be a business organization, fraternity, or any other ongoing concern.

CHAPTER 2. THE DYNAMICS OF HUMAN BEHAVIOR

Questions

1. What is meant by the "language of feelings"? Discuss and illustrate.
2. Why are feelings difficult to observe?
3. How can you sharpen up your observation of the feelings of others?
4. Discuss the social aspects of human behavior.
5. Indicate ways in which the typical industrial organization reflects the social aspects of human behavior.

Case Study

None.

Field Study

Describe an interpersonal situation in which you have been involved. Analyze your own feelings in this situation. Then analyze the feelings of the other person or persons involved. What were some of the social factors determining feelings in this situation?

CHAPTER 3. DIVISION OF LABOR

Questions

1. How is division of labor related to the over-all goals, functions, and technology of the organization?
2. What is the relation of division of labor to human relations in industry?
3. Why is the problem of management more difficult in a factory than in a retail store?

4. What is the effect of size of organization on its division of labor?
5. Define what is meant by "line" organization. What is the typical orientation of employees in a line department?
6. Discuss the relations that can develop between line organizations.
7. Discuss the potential for co-operation among employees within the line. Show how complication of the logic of the line can destroy this potential.
8. What kinds of relations are likely to develop between advisory and staff departments and the line?
9. Why do staff organizations often ask for more authority?
10. What relations are likely to develop between the personnel department and the line?

Case Studies

1. Read the "Haig Chemical Company (A)" in Glover and Hower, *The Administrator*, page 629.
   Analyze the functions and responsibilities of each of the engineering groups and the research department.
   How do you account for the reaction of the chemical engineers to the change in organization?
   What steps did Ryan take to insure co-ordination between the engineering groups after the consolidation of all groups into one department?
   What, in your opinion, is the best solution to the problem of the responsibilities of the research department versus the engineering department with reference to the development of new products and new manufacturing processes?
2. Read the "Haig Chemical Company (B)" in Glover and Hower, *op. cit.*, page 651.
   Analyze the duties and functions of the new product development department.
   Do you think that this department will succeed in accomplishing these functions? Why?

Field Study

Analyze the organization chart of an industry or business. Pick out the probable points of friction growing out of the nature of the duties and responsibilities of each major position or department in the organization.

CHAPTER 4. DIVISION OF LABOR (Continued)

Questions

1. How do service departments differ from advisory departments?
2. Why do problems arise between service departments and the line? Illustrate.
3. What is the principal function of control organizations? Why does friction develop between control departments and the line?

4. Evaluate control and cost reports and budget systems from the standpoint of their usefulness to management.
5. What are the functions of inspection, and how do they affect the relations of this activity with the line organization?

Case Studies

1. Read "Delmar Forge Company (A) and (B)" in Glover and Hower, op. cit., page 487.
   Why was it difficult for Carter to get White to act on various problems in the shop? Discuss.
   Why did White respond to the approach which Carter finally made to him?
2. Read "Westwood Paper Board Company" in Glover and Hower, op. cit., page 593.
   What do you suppose lay behind McGuire's reluctance to work in the inspection department?
   How do you feel about the way Blake introduced inspection into the plant?

Field Study

None.

CHAPTER 5. AUTHORITY SYSTEM AND CHAIN OF COMMAND

Questions

1. Describe the limitations of communication up and down the line of authority.
2. Why do distortions occur in communication up and down the line in industrial organizations?

Case Study

Read the case of the "Universal American Corporation" in Glover and Hower, op. cit., page 195.
Do you feel that Hodgson and Bowles really obtained a "clear picture of the frame of mind and problems of the men working in the field"? Give your reasons and illustrate.

Field Study

Describe communication up and down the authority hierarchy in any organization with which you are familiar. Show the nature of this communication system and how it operates.

CHAPTER 6. STATUS AND STATUS HIERARCHIES

Questions

1. What is meant by a "status system"?
2. Discuss the relations that develop among employees on various levels in the industrial organization.

3. Describe status distinctions between the shop and office.
4. What is the relation between status and wages? Status and seniority? Status and skill? Men and women?
5. Discuss the ways in which people in an organization "place" one another.
6. What effects can the status system of an organization have on the behavior of employees?

Case Study

Read the case of "John Edwards" in Glover and Hower, *op. cit.*, page 69.
Why did the three associates of John Edwards protest when he was promoted to a position of authority over them?

Field Study

Describe the status symbols in any office with which you are familiar.

CHAPTER 7. SYSTEMS OF COMMUNICATION

Questions

1. Discuss formal versus informal communication.
2. Describe the communication functions of control departments like accounting.
3. What are some of the advantages and disadvantages of communication which "short-circuits" the line?
4. What are some of the other channels of communication existing in the organization?

Case Study

None.

Field Study

Analyze the communication system operating in an organization with which you are familiar outside the regular authority hierarchy or chain of command. Discuss specifically the informal communication system that exists.

CHAPTER 8. THE FUNCTIONS AND PROBLEMS AT EACH LEVEL

Questions

1. Describe the duties and orientation of the foreman.
2. What happens when the foreman identifies with his subordinates? His superiors? Neither?
3. In what respects is the foreman a "forgotten man"?
4. What is the relation between the foreman and employee morale?
5. Describe the duties, orientation, and relations of the department chief.

6. What is meant by "visible" versus "invisible" authority? What is the effect of "social distance" on attitudes and sentiments?
7. Describe the duties, orientation, and relations of the top management group (i.e., the division chief through the big boss).

Case Study

Read "The Corelli Case" in Glover and Hower, *op. cit.*, page 605. What can you say about the problems of first-line supervision from what Corelli reports?
If you were the personnel manager, how would you evaluate Corelli's personality? What do you think of his story?

Field Study

None.

CHAPTER 9. THE UNION: ITS FUNCTIONS AND PLACE IN THE STRUCTURE

Questions

1. Describe the internal structure of a local union organization.
2. What are the functions of the local union organization?
3. Discuss union organization as a technique of communication.
4. What effect does the union have on the foreman?
5. Discuss top management's attitudes toward the union and its position in the organization. Why do you suppose management feels as it does about unions?
6. What is the relation between the union official and the worker?
7. What are some of the problems of union stewards?

Case Study

None.

Field Study

None.

CHAPTER 10. UNIONS AND THEIR STRUCTURE

Questions

1. What are some of the principal differences in orientation between union leadership and management leadership?
2. How do these differences sometimes lead to misunderstandings and difficulties in union-management relations?
3. Discuss craft versus industrial unions. Why do skilled workers in an industrial union sometimes rebel against the union?
4. Are all union officials elected?
5. Describe the hierarchy of authority in the typical international union. Discuss the functions and orientation of each level.

6. Why does a great deal of decision making have to be passed down the line in the typical union?
7. How does union leadership maintain control in the organization?
8. What kind of people rise to positions of union leadership and why?

Case Study

None.

Field Study

Analyze the structure and organization of a large international union from its constitution and bylaws. Try to determine the points of friction and possible conflict arising out of the way the organization is set up.

CHAPTER 11. WAGES AND WAGE SYSTEMS

Questions

1. How does management sometimes look at labor and wages?
2. Discuss the problems involved in determining wage rates.
3. What is the relation of wage differentials to the status hierarchy of the organization? Discuss the relation of methods of pay to status distinctions. What problems can occur if pay gets out of line with the status system of the organization?
4. What are some of the standards by which the worker determines what is a fair and adequate wage? How are these standards related to the worker's status position inside and outside the organization?
5. What are the assumptions of management in setting up a merit increase system? A piecework system?
6. What are some of the limitations of the merit-raise system? What are some of the problems involved in evaluating employees?
7. Why do unions frequently oppose merit-raise systems?
8. Why do piecework systems seem fairer than merit-raise systems?
9. What are some of the problems in setting piece rates?
10. What are the functions of the rate setter, and how do they affect his relations in the shop? Discuss the logics of rate setters.

Case Study

Read the case of the "Field Publishing Company" in Glover and Hower, *op. cit.*, page 455.

How do you suppose the men in the paper-storage room felt about the time-study men? Why do you suppose the time-study engineers reported that the attitude of employees to the time study was "very nice"?

Why did Herrick like the group plan of incentive pay that was set up in the pressroom?

What do you think of the incentive plan finally set up by Forsyte?

What was the basic purpose of this plan? How was it received by employees?

How, in your opinion, should Forsyte have handled the introduction of the new incentive plan and methods changes?

Field Study

None.

CHAPTER 12. WAGE INCENTIVES AND RESTRICTION OF OUTPUT

Questions

1. Why is restriction of output common in industry even under a piecework system?
2. How are ceilings on work effort established?
3. How does the group enforce its standards of work effort and production?
4. Discuss restriction of output in the Bank Wiring Observation Room at Western Electric.
5. What are some of the problems involved in cutting rates?
6. What are some of the advantages and values of the piecework system?

Case Study

Read the case of the "Lincoln Electric Company" and "Observations on the Lincoln Electric Company," starting page 533, in Glover and Hower, *op. cit.*

There does not appear to be a great deal of restriction of output at the Lincoln Electric Company. How do you account for the success of the company? Do you think that Lincoln feels that employees are motivated primarily by money and financial incentives? Show evidence.

What are the principal ways in which Lincoln creates incentive among employees?

Field Study

None.

CHAPTER 13. TECHNIQUES OF ORGANIZATION

Questions

1. Discuss the effect of systematic technologies on problems of human relations.
2. What is the difference between a technology based on science and one based solely on procedure?
3. Discuss procedures and the circumstances under which they can adversely affect employee morale.
4. What are some of the factors contributing to formalized procedures and controls in an organization?
5. Discuss "obsessional thinking."

6. How does the pressure of the work create poor morale among employees?
7. In what ways does work simplification cause lowered morale among employees? Can work simplification be carried too far?
8. Discuss the effects of the functional type of organization.
9. What are the characteristics of a "tall" versus a "flat" organization?

Case Studies

1. Read "Gibbons Finance Company (A)" in Glover and Hower, *op. cit.*, page 105.
   What was the effect of tightening-up on the company's collection policy?
   How did the outside collectors react to the new policy? Why?
   If you were a member of the company's board of directors, what would you do about the situation?
2. Read the case of "The Calhoun Company" in Glover and Hower, *op. cit.*, page 129. Answer questions Nos. 2, 3, 4, and 8 on page 134.

Field Study
None.

CHAPTER 14. THE INDIVIDUAL IN THE STRUCTURE

Questions

1. How can the common, everyday work experiences in the typical industrial or business organization affect the emotional satisfactions of employees?
2. Discuss social background and its relation to the adjustment of the individual employee in the work environment.
3. Discuss the differences in social robes and demands arising out of sex differences and age differences among employees.
4. What is "status anxiety"?
5. What are the three classes of complaints found by Roethlisberger and Dickson? Give examples of each.

Case Studies

1. Read the case of "Jim McFee (A)" in Glover and Hower, *op. cit.*, page 59.
   Answer briefly all questions listed on pages 63 and 64.
2. Read the case of the "Lamson Company" in Glover and Hower, *op. cit.*, page 45.
   What was the nature of the complaints of the twelve original crewmen? Why did they feel as they did?

Field Study

Describe a case of "status anxiety" with which you are familiar. Give as accurate a picture as possible of how the individual involved actually behaved in various situations.

CHAPTER 15. MINORITY GROUPS

Questions

1. In what ways has the assimilation of Negroes and southern whites into industry been similar to the assimilation of new immigrant groups in the past?
2. What procedures have appeared to work best in introducing Negroes into a new work situation?
3. Discuss the "caste system" with reference to Negroes.
4. Discuss "class" differences among Negroes and their effect on job adjustment.
5. In what ways has the assimilation of women into industry been similar to the assimilation of any minority group? In what ways different?
6. What is the usual conception of the "women's role"?
7. What are some of the considerations regarding women as supervisors?

Case Study

1. The ABC company had employed Negroes for several months. They constituted about 15 per cent of the work force, occupying most of the lower-level jobs in the organization. Only one Negro, Jim Lafitte, had achieved the status of a work head or first-line supervisor during this time. He was a hard-working man who had gained the respect of his superiors because of his diligence and effort.

   Jim Lafitte, interestingly enough, claimed not to be a Negro at all, although he looked like one. He was raised in a Louisiana parish, had a Catholic education, and spoke French as well as English. He said that he was a Creole. However, most supervisors and representatives of management regarded him as a Negro.

   A number of other Negroes were brought into the company and assigned to Jim's small work group. From the beginning, there seemed to be a great deal of difficulty in the department. However, this was attributed to the fact that the work was heavy.

   Things went along in this fashion until one of the younger men in the department became angry at Jim, ostensibly because of his methods of supervision. In a fit of rage, he struck Jim with a shovel and broke his arm.

   The young Negro was discharged, but he was interviewed by a personnel representative before he left in order to determine the reasons for his sudden anger. He seemed unwilling to offer any explanation except to say that he did not like the "driving" supervision of the department.

   Subsequent interviews with Jim, however, did not seem to bear out these accusations.

What do you think may have been behind the young employee's hatred of Jim? Discuss.

2. Read the case of the "Livingston Company" in Glover and Hower, *op. cit.*, page 167.
   What was the immediate source of friction among the employees in the company?
   What were some of the underlying and contributing causes?
   How did Margaret Bickers handle the problem? What do you think of her handling?

Field Study

None.

CHAPTER 16. THE PROBLEMS OF CHANGE

Questions

1. What is meant by organizational "equilibrium"?
2. What effect does change have on the equilibrium of an organization and the personal adjustment of the individual employee?
3. Describe briefly the problems of employee adjustment arising from:
   a) Economic changes
   b) Changes in company policy
   c) Technological changes
   d) Personnel changes
   e) Change in departmental location
   f) Change in job or office location

Case Studies

1. Read the case of the "Superior Slate Quarry" in Glover and Hower, *op. cit.*, page 93.
   Analyze the reasons for the reactions of the men.
2. Read the case of the "Stubton Company" in Glover and Hower, *op. cit.*, page 15.
   Why did Kay react as she did?
3. Read the case of "The Gordon Company" in Glover and Hower, *op. cit.*, page 183. Also read the commentary on students' reports on the case.
   Evaluate the students' reports in terms of your own thinking.
4. Read the case of the "Sussex Oil Company" in Glover and Hower, *op. cit.*, page 253.
   How can you explain the reactions of the office staff?

Field Study

None.

CHAPTER 17. THE INDUSTRIAL RELATIONS ORGANIZATION

Questions

1. What are some of the different concepts regarding the functions of the industrial relations department?
2. Discuss some of the problems of selection and induction of new employees from the human relations standpoint.
3. Review the problem of transfer and placement.
4. What are some of the problems involved in getting ahead in an organization?
5. What are some of the ways that the personnel department can deal with problems of change?
6. Discuss problems arising out of personal crises in the employee's life. What part does the work group play in helping the employee to adjust?
7. What is the role of the personnel department in labor relations?

Case Study

Read the case of the "Beacon Publishing Company" in Glover and Hower, *op. cit.*, page 261.

If you were the personnel manager in this company, what would you advise Kennedy and Clark to do? Give your reasons.

Field Study

Take any group situation (fraternity, work group, etc.) where a new member has been introduced. Describe in what ways the new member was inducted into the group. Cover both the formal and informal aspects of the induction procedure.

CHAPTER 18. PERSONNEL COUNSELING

Questions

1. How does the typical counselor in industry try to help employees with their problems?
2. Discuss the limitations of aid to employees through direct action, advice, and reassurance.
3. How effective can the counselor be in communicating company policies to employees? Employee problems and attitudes to management?
4. Discuss the rules of nondirective interviewing and tell why you think these rules are followed.
5. Discuss the role of the counselor in industry and his relations with employees, foremen, and management.

Case Study

Read the case of the "Brookmay Machinery Company" in Glover and Hower, *op. cit.*, page 243.

Answer the questions on pages 250 and 251.

Field Study

Get into conversation with a classmate, roommate, or employee, and, using the nondirective technique of interviewing, see how far he will go in a discussion of his problems, if any. Write up your results; but be sure to delete names, places, and other information which might serve to identify the person.

CHAPTER 19. EXECUTIVE PERSONALITY AND ORGANIZATION

Questions

1. Describe the relation between executive personality and the organization.
2. List and discuss the characteristics of the successful executive as described by Dr. William Henry.
3. List and discuss the characteristics of the unsuccessful executive.

Case Studies

1. Read the case of the "Peale Manufacturing Company" in Glover and Hower, *op. cit.*, page 515.
   What observations can you make about Gates's personality from his actions with reference to the two office girls?
2. Read "Zebra National Bank" in Glover and Hower, *op. cit.*, page 689.
   What is the relation between executive personality and the organization in this case?
   What should Barnett do about the situation?

Field Study

Describe, as accurately as possible, the behavior of some person whom you know well. See what you can deduce about his personality from his actual behavior in various situations.

CHAPTER 20. HUMAN RELATIONS AND MANAGEMENT

Questions

1. What are the relations between the "internal" and "external" problems of organization?
2. What kind of organizational pattern is likely to achieve maximum morale and work effort among employees? Illustrate from the human relations studies cited in the text.
3. What is meant by "administrative leadership"?
4. Why is it important for management to set meaningful goals for employees? Discuss also the problem of meaningful job and departmental activities from the standpoint of the individual employee.
5. Discuss the significance of reward and punishment in the work situation.

6. What is meant by "inclusive" versus "exclusive" management? Discuss.
7. Why is building teamwork one of the most important functions of management? How should management go about accomplishing this end?
8. Discuss the problem of diagnosing reasons for breakdowns in team relations among employees. What are some of the things that management can do about these breakdowns?
9. How should management handle changes affecting the organization?
10. What are some of the effects of personal disturbances on the organization? How can they be handled?

Case Studies

1. Read the case of the "Colebrook Box Company" in Glover and Hower, *op. cit.*, page 293.
   What recommendations should Graham and Green make to management in order to reduce absenteeism and turnover in the organization and improve the efficiency and morale of employees?
2. Read all of the nine cases on the "Marshall Company" in Glover and Hower, *op. cit.*, beginning p. 341.
   What are the strong points of the organization? What are the weak points?
   What do you think is the future of the company? What should the vice-president do in order to maintain the organization after his retirement?

Field Study

Describe the strengths and weaknesses of some organization of which you are or have been a member. Discuss what you would do if you were responsible for the effective functioning of the organization.

SELECTED BIBLIOGRAPHY

Texts and Collections of General Reading in Human Relations

Cabot, Hugh, and Joseph A. Kohl. *Human Relations*, Vol. I. Cambridge, Mass.: Harvard University Press, 1953.

Dubin, Robert. *Human Relations in Administration.* New York: Prentice-Hall, Inc., 1951.

Hoselett, Schuyler Dean. *Human Factors in Management.* New York: Harper & Bros., 1951. (Also 1946 edition.)

Miller, Delbert C., and William H. Form. *Industrial Sociology.* New York: Harper & Bros., 1951.

Moore, Wilbert E. *Industrial Relations and the Social Order.* New York: Macmillan Co., 1947.

Roethlisberger, F. J. *Management and Morale.* Cambridge, Mass.: Harvard University Press, 1943.

Management Funtions and Industrial Organization

Argyris, Chris. *Executive Leadership: An Appraisal of a Manager in Action.* New York: Harper & Bros., 1953.

Barnard, Chester I. *The Functions of the Executive.* Cambridge, Mass.: Harvard University Press, 1948.

Barnard, Chester I. *Organization and Management.* Cambridge, Mass.: Harvard University Press, 1948.

Brownrigg, William. *The Human Enterprise Process.* Birmingham: University of Alabama Press, 1954.

Chamberlain, Neil W. *Management in Motion: The Corporate Decision-Making Process as Applied to the Transfer of Employees.* New Haven: Labor and Management Center, Yale University, 1950.

Dimock, Marshall E. *The Executive in Action.* New York: Harper & Bros., 1945.

Drucker, Peter. *Concept of the Corporation.* New York: John Day Co., Inc., 1946.

Follet, Mary Parker. (Henry C. Metcalf and L. Urwick [eds.].) *Dynamic Administration: The Collected Papers of Mary Parker Follet.* New York: Harper & Bros., 1942.

Gordon, Robert A. *Business Leadership in the Large Corporation.* Washington: Brookings Institution, 1945.

Lepawsky, Albert. *Administration: The Art and Science of Organization and Management.* New York: Alfred A. Knopf, Inc., 1949.

Newman, William H. *Administrative Action.* New York: Prentice-Hall, Inc., 1951.

Selznick, David. *TVA and the Grass Roots: A Study in the Sociology of Formal Organization.* Berkeley: University of California Press, 1949.

Simon, H. A. *Administrative Behavior: A Study of Decision-Making Processes in Administrative Organization.* New York: Macmillan Co., 1947.

Industry and the Community

Davis, Allison; Burleigh B. Gardner; and Mary R. Gardner. *Deep South.* Chicago: University of Chicago Press, 1941.

Hughes, Everett C. *French Canada in Transition.* Chicago: University of Chicago Press, 1943.

Hughes, Everett C., and Helen MacGill Hughes. *Where Peoples Meet: Racial and Ethnic Frontiers.* Glencoe, Ill.: The Free Press, 1952.

Jones, Alfred Winslow. *Life, Liberty and Property.* Philadelphia: J. B. Lippincott Co., 1941.

Reisman, David. *The Lonely Crowd.* New Haven: Yale University Press, 1950.

Walker, Charles R. *Steeltown.* New York: Harper & Bros., 1950.

Warner, W. Lloyd, and J. O. Low. *The Social System of the Modern Factory.* "Yankee City Series," Vol. IV. New Haven: Yale University Press, 1946.

Warner, W. Lloyd, and Paul S. Lunt. *The Social Life of a Modern Community.* "Yankee City Series," Vol. I. New Haven: Yale University Press, 1941.

Warner, W. Lloyd, and Leo Srole. *The Social Systems of American Ethnic Groups.* "Yankee City Series," Vol. III. New Haven: Yale University Press, 1945.

Warner, W. Lloyd, et al. *Democracy in Jonesville.* New York: Harper & Bros., 1949.

Whyte, William F. *Street Corner Society.* Chicago: University of Chicago Press, 1943.

Human Behavior and Adjustment in Industry

Armans, George. *The Human Group.* New York: Harcourt, Brace & Co., 1952.

Bakke, E. Wight. *Bonds of Organization.* New York: Harper & Bros., 1950.

Ellsworth, John S. *Factory Folkways.* New Haven: Yale University Press, 1952.

Freedman, Eugene A., and R. J. Havighurst (eds.). *The Meaning of Work and Retirement.* Chicago: University of Chicago Press, 1954.

Gouldner, Alvin W. *Patterns of Industrial Democracy.* Glencoe, Ill.: The Free Press, 1954.

Jacques, Elliott. *The Changing Culture of a Factory.* London: Tavistock Publishing, Ltd., 1950.

Katz, Daniel; Nathan Maccroy; and Nancy Morse. *Productivity, Supervision and Morale in an Office Situation.* Ann Arbor: Survey Research Center, Institute for Social Research, University of Michigan, 1951.

Katz, Daniel; Nathan Maccroy; and Nancy Morse. *Productivity, Supervision and Morale among Railroad Workers.* Ann Arbor: Survey Research Center, Institute for Social Research, University of Michigan, 1951.

Mayo, Elton. *The Human Problems of an Industrial Civilization.* Boston: Harvard University, Graduate School of Business Administration, 1946.

Mayo, Elton. *The Social Problems of an Industrial Civilization.* Boston: Harvard University, Graduate School of Business Administration, 1945.

Purcell, Theodore, V.S.J. *The Worker Speaks His Mind on Company and Union.* Cambridge, Mass.: Harvard University Press, 1953.

Richardson, F. L. W., Jr., and Charles R. Walker. *Human Relations in an Expanding Company.* New Haven: Labor and Management Center, Yale University, 1948.

Roethlisberger, F. J., and W. J. Dickam. *Management and the Worker.* Cambridge, Mass.: Harvard University Press, 1939.

Walker, Charles R., and R. H. Guest. *The Man on the Assembly Line.* Cambridge, Mass.: Harvard University Press, 1952.

Whyte, William F. *Human Relations in the Restaurant Industry.* New York: McGraw-Hill Book Co., Inc., 1948.

Unions and Union-Management Relations

Bakke, E. Wight. *Mutual Survival.* New Haven: Yale University Press, 1946.

Bakke, E. Wight, and Clark Kerr. *Unions, Management and the Public.* New York: Harcourt, Brace & Co., 1948.

Chamberlain, Neil W. *The Union Challenge to Management Control.* New York: Harper & Bros., 1948.

Derber, Milton, *et al. Labor-Management Relations in Illini City.* The Case Studies, Vol. I. Champaign, Ill.: Institute of Labor and Industrial Relations, University of Illinois, 1953.

Golden, Clinton, and Harold Ruttenberg. *Dynamics of Industrial Democracy.* New York: Harper & Bros., 1942.

Gouldner, Alvin W. *Wildcat Strike.* Yellow Springs, Ohio: Antioch Press, 1954.

Harbison, Frederick H., and John R. Coleman. *Goals and Strategy in Collective Bargaining.* New York: Harper & Bros., 1951.

Harbison, Frederick H., and Robert Dubin. *Patterns of Union-Management Relations.* Chicago: Science Research Associates, 1947.

Sayles, Leonard, and George Strauss. *The Local Union: Its Place in the Industrial Plant.* New York: Harper & Bros., 1953.

Seidman, Joel. *Union Rights and Union Duties.* New York: Harcourt, Brace & Co., 1943.

Selskman, Benjamin M. *Labor Relations and Human Relations.* New York: McGraw-Hill Book Co., Inc., 1947.

Shultz, George P., and John R. Coleman. *Labor Problems: Cases and Readings.* New York: McGraw-Hill Book Co., Inc., 1953.

Whyte, William F. *Pattern for Industrial Peace.* New York: Harper & Bros., 1951.

Other Related Books

Cartwright, Dorwin, and Alvin Zander (eds.). *Group Dynamics: Research and Theory.* Evanston, Ill.: Row, Peterson & Co., 1953.

Guetzkow, Harold (ed.). *Groups, Leadership and Men.* Pittsburgh: Carnegie Press, 1951.

Rogers, C. R. *Counseling and Psychotherapy.* Boston: Houghton Mifflin Co., 1942.

INDEX

This book has been set on the Linotype in 11, 10, and 9 point Janson, leaded 2 points. Chapter numbers and titles are in 18 point Spartan Medium. The size of the type page is 27 by 45 picas.

30609